THE YEAR THAT BROKE AMERICA

THE YEAR THAT BROKE AMERICA

An Immigration Crisis,
a Terrorist Conspiracy,
the Summer of *Survivor*,
a Ridiculous Fake Billionaire,
a Fight for Florida,
and the
537 Votes That
Changed Everything

ANDREW RICE

HARPER
An Imprint of HarperCollins*Publishers*

HarperCollins books may be purchased for educational, business, or sales promotional use. For information, please email the Special Markets Department at SPsales @harpercollins.com.

FIRST EDITION

Library of Congress Cataloging-in-Publication Data has been applied for.

ISBN 978-0-06-297982-7

22 23 24 25 26   LSC   10 9 8 7 6 5 4 3 2 1

To Jennifer, my partner in crime and gardening,
and Eddie, who wishes this book had more stuff about baseball

CONTENTS

Inauguration Day

It had all happened before; it might happen again. But no one alive had ever seen an election like this one: so improbably dramatic, so narrowly determined, so bitterly fought to the end and beyond the end. It was strange to watch, like an event from some other country or an episode from the nation's uncivil early history. It made America once more a house divided, ripping up its rotting floorboards to reveal the creaky democratic machinery in the basement. It put cracks in the foundations. No one saw the constitutional crisis coming, and when the resolution came, it was messy. None of the nation's institutions, or its statesmen, cloaked themselves in glory.

But now the unsettling conflict is blessedly in the past. It is Inauguration Day.

Here they come, their fine shoes click-clacking through the marble hallways of the U.S. Capitol, the players in our national theater, ready to raise the curtain on another term. They pass in dignified succession, walking down a stairway and out the double doors to the platform erected on the building's West Front, facing the flag-bedecked National Mall.

First up: former president George Bush, basking in the freshening glow of American forgetfulness. Next comes Hillary Clinton, wearing a gleaming black leather coat and a satisfied smile, displaying her vindication to her many enemies. Next, the leaders of

Congress and nine justices of the Supreme Court, their black robes scarcely concealing their naked partisanship.

Out on the Mall, the atmosphere is intense. Half the country thinks the other half has stolen the presidency. Half the country thinks the other half tried to steal it and failed. Thousands of angry citizens have come to decry the injustice done to their man, the largest inauguration protest in decades. The day is frigid and sleety; the security is oppressive. The sound of circling helicopters beats down ominously through the fog shrouding the Washington Monument.

"The underlying vibe," a *Washington Post* reporter will write the next day, "was unrest." There are violent clashes taking place in the streets. Protesters chant, *Hail to the thief!*

Up above on the dais, though, the nation's leaders appear convivial. The fight has been conceded to the winner. It is time to perform the constitutional ritual. At the stroke of noon on January 20, 2001, a new president of the United States will be sworn in: George W. Bush of Texas. There is a reassuring familiarity to the transition. It is a new millennium, but the same old America.

Here's the departing tandem, in matching dark overcoats, coming down a hall flanked by marines standing at attention with bayonets. A military band plays ruffles and flourishes.

"Ladies and gentlemen," an announcer says, "the president of the United States, the Honorable William Jefferson Clinton, and the vice president of the United States, the Honorable Albert Gore Jr." They descend the stairs. Clinton is buoyant, shaking hands, squeezing every last drop of joy out of his office. Gore wears a dutiful rictus, knowing everyone is watching for a flinch.

"We can only wonder what Al Gore must be thinking," anchorman Tom Brokaw says on NBC.

It was a close thing, the 2000 election. Unimaginably close.

More than 100 million Americans voted, and it all came down to Florida, as if history were drawn there by some invisible gravitational force. Florida, the unlikely crucible, Flori-*duh*, the state that couldn't get it right. Florida, the nation's exotic misfit, a place of loose morals, louche wealth, fake bodies, and tropical conspiracy. Florida, with its redneck north and its polyethnic south. Florida, that land of booms and busts, strip malls and strip joints; habitat of the "Florida Man," the fantastically stupid criminal; and of the Florida celebrity, who was famous for some crass reason. Florida, the state that already was what the rest of America was becoming, was the one that swung it, by 537 votes.

Yes, it is safe to assume that Al Gore may be thinking about Florida.

Gore is the first candidate since 1888 to be denied the presidency while winning a majority of the national popular vote. And he lost it despite running as the candidate of the incumbent party in a time of boundless prosperity. The world was at peace, enjoying the placid interlude that began with perestroika. The U.S. economy was experiencing an unprecedented expansion driven by globalization and the creative force of new technology. The budget deficit? It was gone! There was now a national surplus, which was projected to amount to almost $5 trillion over the next ten years. Crime? It had miraculously abated, and as a consequence, big cities were thriving. As the sole remaining superpower, America's global influence and cultural power reigned unchallenged. It had been almost a decade since the U.S. military had gone to war.

Even so, events conspired to make Gore the loser. He blames the guy next to him. He and Clinton once had a warm partnership, but they hardly talk anymore. Their tortured relationship makes for delicious psychodrama, which is far more interesting to the Washington press corps than whatever seemingly minor policy differences exist between Gore and Bush.

The younger George Bush, known as "Dubya" after his distinguishing middle initial, ran as an easygoing centrist. He calls himself a "compassionate conservative." Bill Clinton, the cleverest political animal of his generation, knew Gore was in trouble as soon as he heard the phrase. Bush has presented himself as a candidate of continuity, with only modest plans for the country. He has promised that he will do just a few things as president and do them well. The universal consensus is that the 2000 election was a bit of a snooze, a campaign of small differences—at least until the votes were cast. Then, down in Florida, everything went crazy.

Time to set that aside—here come the winners. First, Dick Cheney, wearing that sidelong smirk. He's considered a steadying presence, a man of deep experience. He descends the stairs, turns to the right, and takes his place, standing in front of a leather wingback chair, behind bulletproof glass.

In a moment, there's Bush, chin upturned, eyes narrowed. He joins his running mate and his waiting family members: his wife, Laura, resplendent in blue; his beaming college-age twin daughters; his brother Jeb, the governor of Florida—*that* was awkward—who is taking pictures with a disposable camera. At the center is his dad, proud Poppy, who has taken to calling his boy "Quincy," after the last son to follow his father as president. Dubya has been reading up on him: John Quincy Adams, a one-termer, elected in dubious circumstances, dislodged by a bloodthirsty populist.

"Today we honor the past in commemorating two centuries of inaugurations in Washington," Senator Mitch McConnell, the Republican master of ceremonies, says in his sober opening remarks. "Witnessed by the Congress, Supreme Court, governors, and presidents past, the current president will stand by as the new president peacefully takes office. This is a triumph of our democratic republic, a ceremony befitting a great nation."

At the appointed time, Bush takes the oath administered by the chief justice of the United States, which only weeks before put an end to the electoral dispute, by a single vote, in the case of *Bush v. Gore*. The television cameras, focusing tight on the new president, capture a tear rolling down his craggy face. He is a God-fearing man, and he believes the Creator has put him in this place, at this moment, according to His unknowable design. Bush will not be remembered as a great orator, but on this day, he gives an address that even one of his most skeptical critics will describe as "shockingly good," replete with biblical references and calls for national healing.

"My fellow citizens, the peaceful transfer of authority is rare in history, yet common in our country. With a simple oath, we affirm old traditions and make new beginnings," Bush begins.

"Sometimes our differences run so deep, it seems we share a continent, but not a country," the new president goes on to say. "We do not accept this, and we will not allow it. Our unity, our union, is the serious work of leaders and citizens in every generation. And this is my solemn pledge: I will work to build a single nation of justice and opportunity. I know this is in our reach because we are guided by a power larger than ourselves who creates us equal in His image."

The satirical newspaper *The Onion* sums it all up with an immortal headline: "BUSH: 'OUR LONG NATIONAL NIGHTMARE OF PEACE AND PROSPERITY IS FINALLY OVER.'"

Still, he doesn't seem so bad, this new President Bush. I am in Washington that day, shivering in the rain, covering the inauguration as a twenty-six-year-old reporter. The ceremony does not seem to signal a change of power so much as a slight reshuffling of roles.

That afternoon, Bill and Hillary Clinton—now *Senator* Clinton—will hold a farewell rally at Andrews Air Force Base. "I left the White House, but I'm still here," the outgoing president tells his adoring staff. "We're not going anywhere." Then both Clintons board an air force jet and fly to New York, their future political base.

That night, I will attend the Texas Wyoming Inaugural Ball, where men in tuxedos and cowboy hats and women in ball gowns with big hair crowd around to watch Dubya and Laura show them a few desultory steps on the dance floor. The new president, a tee-totaler, will be back at the White House by 11:37, early enough that, if he chooses, he can flip on *Saturday Night Live* and catch the end of the opening sketch. In it, a wistful Darrell Hammond, as Clinton, refuses to budge from the Oval Office, much to the furrow-browed confusion of Will Ferrell, as Dubya.

It is not until later that we will be able to comprehend the consequence of this transfer of power.

At that moment, back down in Florida, a young Lebanese student is learning to fly. He has enlisted in a secret plot known as the "planes operation." His target will be the U.S. Capitol.

1

Zero Zero

No one yet knew how the twentieth century would truly culminate. Let's start at the beginning of the end: November 25, 1999. It was Thanksgiving Day in America.

That day, in Germany, a young man began a journey.

Ziad Jarrah had spent much of the autumn preparing for a long overseas trip. He had withdrawn from the university in Hamburg where he had been studying aeronautical engineering. He had given up the lease on his apartment. He had packed his bags, minding instructions to conceal his true intentions and making sure to bring along a sturdy pair of hiking boots.

He had endured many emotional conversations with his on-and-off romantic companion, Aysel Sengün, a German-born dental student of Turkish descent. She wanted to know where he was going. He told her he needed to return to Lebanon, to see his family, to think about the future of their relationship. They had been fighting about his aimless direction, his inconsistent affection, and his growing devotion to religion. Once a casual Muslim, a beer drinker and bong smoker, Ziad had drawn close to some friends from his mosque, a group of men Aysel didn't know. They exerted a mysterious pull on him. She couldn't understand it, but she could feel its power.

That fall, Ziad had told his classmates he was planning to continue his education in the United States. One of them would later recall that he appeared extremely nervous in the days before he disappeared from campus. He and Aysel packed up his apartment, storing some of his school papers with a friend. Ziad bid her farewell at the train station, and she returned to her own university, in a town a few hours away. He was the picture of a bright graduate student, bookish-looking, with his tousled hair, a neat beard, and little oval glasses. Aysel still loved him.

She was worried. She was already wondering if she would ever see him again.

On November 25, Jarrah boarded a Turkish Airlines flight in Hamburg. He was a rich kid, the product of a cultured Beirut family, but he was not really bound for home. What were his thoughts as he departed? Was he ecstatic? "The morning will come. The victors will come," Jarrah had written the month before, in Arabic, in scribbled notes that were later found among the school papers he had stowed. "The earth will shake beneath your feet."

He was twenty-four years old. Did he already know where his journey would end?

"Oh," Jarrah had written, "the smell of paradise is rising."

The cabin door closed behind him, and the plane took off, bound for Istanbul and points beyond.

THE YEAR 2000 was fast approaching: fewer than forty days away and counting. The millennium was coming to a close, and the whole world, it seemed, was moved by a spirit of departure. History seldom pays heed to round numbers, but sometimes it does converge in a time and place. That same November, as Jarrah set out, another group of voyagers made their way to a beach.

In the still hours before dawn, beneath the light of a nearly full moon, they followed a path through the mangroves to a spot on the marshy shoreline. It was a warm, windless Cuban night. There were fifteen in their party, most of them members of two extended families. The oldest was a sixty-five-year-old grandfather; the youngest, a boy of five. His mother had roused him from bed.

Finally, it was time to go.

She told the little boy that they were taking a trip to visit relatives, which turned out to be true in a way. On the beach, a rickety sixteen-foot aluminum boat was waiting.

The voyagers clambered aboard, carrying enough bread, cheese, cooked hot dogs, and fresh water for an unpredictable ninety-mile journey. Stealthily, a few of the men pushed the craft out through the waves, keeping the outboard motor silent to avoid detection as they set off to sea.

The little boy was excited, oblivious to any danger. The other passengers would playfully ask him, "Where are you going?"

"*Me voy para La Yuma*," the boy chirped back: "I am going to America."

The boat's passengers were fleeing Cuba for all the usual reasons: economics, politics, discontent, love. Some of them couldn't swim, or feared the sea. But they were willing to risk the journey because they believed they had a destiny, a better future, awaiting them in the United States. Their captain, Lázaro Munero, was an army deserter, cabdriver, and occasional black-market trader who had recently been beaten and imprisoned by Fidel Castro's security forces. He had made the sea voyage to Florida once before, returning because he missed his girlfriend, Elizabeth, who worked as a maid at a resort near their hometown of Cárdenas. This time, Lázaro was leaving for good, taking Elizabeth, his parents, a brother, and a few others from his neighborhood. Elizabeth had decided to bring along the boy, her son from a previous marriage.

Lázaro had built their boat himself, in secret, from salvaged metal and spare parts. An uncle had tried to talk him out of sailing the makeshift vessel. "This is not a boat," he'd shouted, after taking a look at the rusty hulk. "It's garbage!" But Lázaro was confident. From Cárdenas, you could easily catch the Gulf Stream current, which would whisk you right to Florida. It didn't take long, though, for the simple plan to go wrong. The boat's outboard motor broke down while it was still in sight of the coast. The voyagers rowed to an island. Lázaro, whose nickname around Cárdenas was "El Loco," was determined to continue. He had sold his cab, an antique Chevrolet, to finance the trip. He made repairs to the boat and waited to set out again beneath the cover of night.

On the second try, the boat managed to evade a Cuban coast guard ship and made it into international waters. But then a storm rolled in, and the engine died again. In the darkness, the voyagers frantically bailed out the boat as it was lashed by waves. Then it capsized. The voyagers held on to the hull all night. When the storm cleared, they moved to a couple of truck-size inner tubes they had towed along as life rafts and prayed for rescue.

The two tubes were joined together by a rope. Elizabeth placed her boy on top of one of them and put her jacket over him as a shield from the sun. Others held on to the sides of the tubes, half submerged, watching out for ships and sharks. Most of their food and water was lost. As the hours passed, they grew weak and delirious. Lázaro's brother, hallucinating, cried out that he saw land and swam away. Lázaro pursued him; neither man returned. Soon, others fell away.

The night after the wreck, the life rafts somehow came untethered. One of the tubes would wash up a day later in Key Biscayne, near Miami, carrying a pair of survivors, barely alive and stung all over by jellyfish. What happened during the night on the other tube is unknown. The boy dozed off to sleep, and his mother was there, but when he awoke, she was gone.

Early on November 25, Thanksgiving Day, a man set out from the dock behind his home on the Intracoastal Waterway, just north of Fort Lauderdale, for a holiday fishing trip with his cousin. Off Lighthouse Point, they noticed a piece of junk, a black inner tube, bobbing in the rough seas.

Then one of them saw it: a small hand.

JANET RENO SPENT the weekend after Thanksgiving at her family home on the edge of the Everglades. It was a rangy, rough-hewn ranch house, a relic of the strange Old Florida, built by her mother from cypress beams and adobe bricks, with a long screened-in porch looking out on a yard shaded by live oaks, gumbo-limbos, and red-blooming poincianas. A flock of screeching pet peacocks bobbled about. Visitors were always shocked to discover that *this* was the home of the attorney general of the United States. But for Reno, it was where she restored herself, sitting at the long cypress table out on the porch and soaking in the sultry warmth, watching the lizards skitter, catching up on the hothouse intrigue of Miami.

On this holiday weekend, the big news in the *Miami Herald* was a happy story. A five-year-old Cuban refugee named Elián González had been found clinging to an inner tube three miles out to sea. Television camera crews had been alerted, naturally, to be there when the fishermen brought him in to the dock. On Friday, November 26, Reno picked up the *Herald* and saw a front-page picture of the boy gazing up with a dazed expression from a stretcher. His face was angelic.

A spokesman for the Immigration and Naturalization Service, which Reno oversaw, tried to sound a cautionary note, pointing out that at least ten others, including the boy's mother, were presumed dead. "The ocean is a dangerous place," the spokesman told the *Herald*.

Little Havana greeted the rescue as a divine act. That Thanksgiving, on Miami's popular Spanish-language talk radio stations, the refugees were likened to the Pilgrims, and the boy's drowned mother was mourned as a victim of Fidel Castro's dictatorship. Wondrous stories soon began to circulate. It was said that the fishermen had found the boy encircled by magical dolphins, who had protected him, and that he had escaped his ordeal without a scratch. And it was true that Elián shocked his doctors with his fast recovery, polishing off a Thanksgiving turkey dinner.

"LITTLE RAFTER LEAVES HOSPITAL," read the lead headline in that Saturday's *Herald*, as the boy, looking gaunt and wearing a baseball cap, was released into the care of his extended family in Little Havana. "God wanted him here for freedom," his twenty-one-year-old second cousin, Marisleysis Gonzalez, declared to the TV cameras. "And he's here, and he will get it."

That was that; turn the page. At the top of A2 was a large graphic: "Countdown 2000 . . . 35." All over the planet, expectation was building for a once-in-an-epoch tick of the clock. *Two thousand*—it still felt odd on the lips. In the twentieth-century imagination, 2000 served as a milepost on the horizon, a marker of the future. In the year 2000, everything was supposed to be different.

In the year 2000, there would be rocket cars and interstellar travel.

In the year 2000, the earth would have six billion humans, and most would be starving.

In the year 2000, we would have a cure for cancer.

In the year 2000, the world's supply of oil would be exhausted.

In the year 2000, Jesus Christ would rise again.

Now the year was almost here, close enough to touch, making the futurism of the past look quaint. The late-night comedian Conan O'Brien spoofed it with a recurring bit in which he made goofy predictions over spooky music. ("In the Year 2000 . . . toilet paper will be totally computerized at last.") Still, even the smart alecks had to admit, there was a momentous feeling in the air. For the first time, the turn of a century would be experienced as a global, communal event. A few pedants pointed out that because there was no year zero, the new millennium would technically only begin with 2001. They were ignored. It had been decided long before that December 31, 1999, would be the most wildly important New Year's Eve anyone would ever see.

Governments were staging lavish festivities. A half-million people were expected on the National Mall, where President Bill Clinton would ignite a fuse to light up the Washington Monument like a giant pyrotechnic sparkler. In Great Britain, Prime Minister Tony Blair was spending a fortune on spectacles, including an event at his new $1 billion Millennium Dome in Greenwich, "the home of time." In a bit of tourism-driven temporal maneuvering, the tiny Pacific nation of Kiribati moved the International Date Line so that the first place to see 2000 would be its easternmost point, an uninhabited coral atoll it renamed Millennium Island.

Capitalism, marching out of the twentieth century unvanquished and unquestioned, operated in its customary way, as marketers promoted millennium concerts, millennium cruises, millennium fashions, millennium car sales, and for those who were tired of hearing about the millennium, millennium retreats. A Manhattan hotelier offered to rent out his entire Midtown building for $1 million. For the cost of $40,000, you could take a supersonic charter flight on the Concorde from a banquet in Paris to a party in New York, celebrating midnight twice. For those shopping at lower price points, there were package vacations, bottles of champagne, palms full of ecstasy.

For Reno, the nation's chief law enforcement officer, there was much to worry about. The kooks were on the move in their many crazy colors. In the words of one scholar of millennial studies, the world was becoming "apocalyptically aroused." Christian pilgrims were assembling in the Holy Land to witness the Second Coming. As the attorney general, charged with protecting America from all threats conceivable and inconceivable, Reno was seeing classified intelligence indicating that terrorists were eyeing the opportunity to stage attacks. Finally, there was this year-related computer glitch, the Y2K bug, which threatened to go haywire when the clock hit midnight. Technologists were trying to avert chaos, and a few prophets were predicting doom.

"SOMETHING'S COMING," Chuck Harder said. He was right about that, if nothing else.

Harder called himself "the man who sees tomorrow." For years, the radio talk show host had been issuing dire warnings from his base in White Springs, a small town in northern Florida. "They say Soviet-built nuke plants are not ready for Y2K," Harder said as he opened a broadcast of his show, *For the People*, in December. "In Italy, they have bunkers ready for Y2K. U.S. officials are worried about violence, and Times Square is planning a marathon of midnights."

In a time of good fortune, Harder was a determined pessimist. "It's interesting to watch this countdown," he said, "because nobody knows what's going to happen, even computer programmers. Most of the ones I know have a house in the country and a generator."

The Y2K bug was a real problem—a product of human error and lack of foresight. The software that ran most computers contained a basic flaw because the programmers who had originally written it, to save space, had used only two digits to denote the year. Apparently, they had assumed their code would be obsolete by the time 99 flipped over to 00, but instead, it had become the foundation for . . . well, everything. The technical details were fuzzy to most, but the potential nightmare was easy to grasp. "THE DAY THE WORLD CRASHES," read an alarmist headline on the cover of *Newsweek*. Computer experts were saying that the bug could cause problems, though whether these would amount to a nuisance or a crisis, no one knew.

During the late 1990s, the Y2K threat had given birth to a whole apocalyptic belief system, which held that the increasing interconnection of modern life contained a catastrophic risk—a hidden time bomb. Could you imagine what would happen, the doomsayers would ask aloud, if all the computers stopped working at once? Power plants would shut down, the stock market would crash, planes would fall from the sky. The most extreme scenarios foresaw accidental nuclear weapons exchanges, riots, food shortages, civil war. "You may be tired of Y2K, ladies and gentlemen, but I'm sorry to tell you, you better listen," Harder warned in late 1999. "Those who have goods put away will be laughed at by those who didn't. And then it'll hit, and then it'll hit."

On his website, Harder sold self-published books with titles like *Year 2000 Panic!*, describing what would happen when the power went out and "life reverts to 'Stone-Age' conditions." During the call-in segments of his show, survivalist guests and listeners traded tips on preparing for what Harder called "the coming dark times." He peddled mail-order gear. "Serious about preparing for Y2K? Listen closely," he intoned in one commercial. "If you want to order grain mills, solar panels, cases of yeast, books, Y2K videos, solar lanterns from $84.95 and up, crank-up free-play radios, solar-powered lights and radios, you best act now and get in line." Harder's own home, down a sandy rural road, was outfitted with three sets of generators and two thousand gallons of propane. He was growing vegetables in his greenhouses, and his swimming pool was filled with potable water. He had constructed a second tiny, self-sufficient house with solar panels on its roof and a water tank on a raised wooden platform. Listeners could purchase a manual for replicating his "energy liberty" home for the price of $49.95.

Harder's listeners certainly didn't trust the government to protect them. "Ladies and gentlemen, if you please," Harder said that December. "I do not believe either the Republican or the Democrat Party give a fig, that's *F-I-G*, about Mr. and Mrs. America. They are immersed in the champagne and caviar of Big Business." Harder's listeners were alienated, angry, and powerless. They had no place in the political system of the time and no way to talk to one another, except over Harder's phone lines. "We're only eighteen days away from Y2K, and a lot of people think it's a joke," Harder said. "The White House is going to release figures to discourage Y2K panic."

Around the country, authorities were preparing for unrest while calling for calm. In Florida, the government had unveiled a public service ad campaign with the slogan "Don't Be Y2Krazy."

"They're going to do whatever they can," Harder cautioned his listeners, "to keep you *asleep*."

AL GORE JUST couldn't win.

He was right about Y2K, just as he was right about so many other things. In July 1998, the vice president had given a speech forecasting that the bug "could cause serious problems for commerce and communications all over the world if we're not serious about fixing it." Coming from the most earnest, computer-literate public servant in the land, the warning acted as an effective prod. The federal government embarked on a massive reprogramming effort that, a little over a year later, seemed to have headed off the mass meltdown many feared. It was another victory for Gore in his long struggle to make government more efficient, functional, and rational. And so . . .

Q: What did all of America know about Al Gore's contributions to technology?
A: The guy claimed he invented the internet!

It seemed he would never live it down—that little, passing remark he made in a March 1999 interview with CNN. Gore would always protest that he really hadn't said he had *invented* the internet, but rather that, during his time as a senator from Tennessee, he "took the initiative in creating the Internet." *Took the initiative!* By which he meant, of course, he had labored to pass a piece of legislation known as the "Gore Bill," which funded the expansion of a rudimentary communications system originally developed by the Defense Department, hastening its evolution into what was then known as the "information superhighway," while also funding basic research that led to the creation of tools like the first Web browser. Like so much of what Gore did, his contribution was boring but important. ("He *did* invent the fucking internet," one of his policy advisers would complain in frustration years later.) But the joke was more fun than the truth.

The truth was that although Gore was a genuine prophet—more prescient about the future than any politician of his time—he was, at this critical juncture, unable to find his own way forward.

His likely opponent in the fall campaign, George W. Bush, had a dead eye for political weakness and a charming way with the national media. The Texas governor had sized Gore up, he told reporters, after reading a profile in *The New Yorker* in which Gore held forth on the subject of his favorite philosophers, mentioning Reinhold Niebuhr and Maurice Merleau-Ponty. Bush figured that a man with a brain like that would have trouble reaching America. When Bush was asked at a Republican primary debate in December 1999 who *his* favorite philosopher was, he was ready.

"Christ," the governor said. "Because he changed my heart."

It had to be maddening to Gore, because he could see what Bush was doing. ("He's not a dunce," Gore told a friend at the time.) Here was a man who was the son of a president, the incumbent whom Clinton and Gore had defeated, who was now presenting himself as a regular old Christian fellah. Here was a challenger running against a popular administration who was smudging out all ideological differences to pose as a candidate of continuity. "The times just don't call for major change," a Bush adviser assured a writer for the liberal *New Republic*.

In so many words, Bush was saying he would be Bill Clinton with his fly zipped.

There was Gore's problem, at least in his own mind, which admittedly was clouded by years of suppressing his expressions and his individual identity as he stood stolidly behind his rascal president. He was furious with Clinton and fixated on him. They had once been true friends, to the degree that anyone who competed in politics could be: a pair of New Democrats, both pragmatists from the South. They had looked so appealing, campaigning together eight years before. Then came the scandals, real and concocted: Travelgate, Troopergate, Filegate, the Paula Jones lawsuit, Hillary's billing records, Vince Foster's suicide, renting out the Lincoln Bedroom, all the fund-raising shenanigans of the 1996 campaign, some of which Gore had been dragged into, much to his legal discomfort. But those episodes all blended together now as a prelude to the main event, the investigation of Clinton's affair with White House intern Monica Lewinsky, which had culminated in his impeachment in the House. Although Clinton had been acquitted in the Senate and felt vindicated, Gore feared that voters would end up punishing him for the president's behavior. He would go days on the campaign trail without uttering Clinton's name. Gore had hoped to display independence and self-confidence, but Clinton was furious, and voters found the pose insincere.

Clinton and Gore needed to salvage the relationship. Late in the year, like so many estranged couples before them, they screwed on their smiles and took the family to Disney World.

On December 11, Clinton's limousine passed throngs of mouse-eared tourists as it carried him from a meeting with South African president Nelson Mandela, who was staying near Epcot Center, to a convention of the Florida Democratic Party, at another hotel on the park's grounds. Gore would be there for a rare joint appearance. The running mates were getting back together, for one day at least, for the sake of Florida. Gore's campaign strategists could already see that the state, and its 25 electoral votes, might prove pivotal in the coming year's election.

"You may have noticed that I can't run for anything this year, so I want to tell you how come I came down here," Clinton began in his familiar, folksy style. As he approached the end of the century, and the last year of his presidency, he was in a reflective mood. "In my whole lifetime there has never been a time when America had this much prosperity, this much social progress, this much national confidence, with the absence of crisis at home or a threat abroad," he said.

Clinton spoke about the great technological leaps of the 1990s: the mapping of the human genome, the explosion of innovation enabled by the internet. He said that many futurists were telling him that by connecting people, the World Wide Web might even bring an end to war. But he also saw something troubling. "Don't you think it's interesting," he observed, "that in this most modern of times, the biggest problem in the world today is the oldest problem of human society: We don't trust people who are different from us. We fear them. It's easy to go from fear to dislike, from dislike to hatred, from hatred to dehumanization, and then to violence."

Then Gore appeared, speaking in a different register. As a politician, he lacked Clinton's natural warmth, and he would often try to compensate with volume and energy. He prowled the stage with a cordless microphone. "Florida should be a battleground in this election next year," Gore predicted. "Florida can make a difference." Four years before, Clinton had won the state, becoming the first Democrat in decades to do so in a presidential election. But it wouldn't be easy for Gore to repeat that feat. Republicans dominated Florida. In 1998, the state had elected a hard-charging conservative governor—who just happened to be George's younger brother Jeb Bush.

Now, as if Gore's challenge in Florida weren't difficult enough, there was a new issue to deal with: the problem of the Cuban boy. At a press conference after his speech, Gore faced a barrage of questions about Elián Gonzalez. The boy's heartwarming story had taken an unexpected turn. It turned out that Elián's father, back in

Cuba, said he had had no idea that his ex-wife was planning to take their child to America. He wanted Elián returned to Cuba, but his own relatives in Miami were refusing to give his son up, saying the boy's mother had died for his freedom.

The family in Miami had the backing of the city's conservative Cuban exile leaders, who were rallying support from Republicans, including Bush. The day before, the Texas governor had suggested the custody dispute might simply be resolved if Elián's father came to see him in America and got a "whiff of freedom." At his press conference, Gore took a typically nuanced position. "I would insist upon due process of law within the appropriate tribunal to make sure the decision is made on the basis of what is in the best interest of that child," he said, adding that he also wanted "to make sure the views of the boy's father are honored in the process."

Elián was also coming to Disney World. The day after Clinton and Gore appeared in Orlando, the boy and his Miami family members arrived with an entourage of reporters for a theme park vacation. It was all paid for by an ambitious Cuban American politician who was the cochairman of George Bush's campaign in Florida. The boy, who had just celebrated his sixth birthday, rode on a carousel with his cousin Marisleysis as a group of onlookers chanted, *Elián! Elián! Elián!* On the "It's a Small World" ride, he stiffened with fear when he stepped into the little boat.

Soon, he recovered. Elián clapped along as the boat he was riding in progressed on its journey through many nations, shouting, "*Míralo!*"—"Look!" The press recorded the whole adorable scene.

Bill Clinton could see political peril ahead. One key to his success in Florida had been securing support—or at least nonaggression—from Cuban power brokers in Miami. When he arrived there for a fund-raiser after his Orlando speech, he was greeted by protesters shouting, "Freedom!"

Later, at the airport, as he prepared to board Air Force One for his flight back to Washington, Clinton pulled aside the Cuban American mayor of Miami-Dade County, Alex Penelas.

"Alex," the president asked urgently, "what are we going to do about this six-year-old boy?"

THERE WERE OTHER concerns weighing on Clinton that day, ones he couldn't utter out loud. Three days before, he had received a briefing from the CIA director and his top White House counterterrorism adviser. Through classified surveillance, U.S. intelligence agencies were picking up an alarming increase in activity among terrorist groups—most important, Al Qaeda. For several years, the Clinton administration had watched with concern as the group, under the leadership of the charismatic Saudi construction heir Osama bin Laden, had grown in its size, ambition, and capabilities. The day of the Orlando trip, the CIA produced a high-level briefing memo entitled "Bin Ladin [*sic*] To Exploit Looser Security During Holidays."

The millennium celebrations presented "unique opportunities for violence," in the laconic description of a CIA briefing presented that December: so many people, gathering in public spaces around the world. The Agency was predicting somewhere between five and fifteen attacks.

On December 14, a U.S. customs agent at a border crossing between Canada and Washington State intercepted an anxious-looking man who was waiting to drive his car off a ferry. Hidden in the spare tire well of his trunk were the raw materials for a fertilizer-based bomb, including timing devices and chemical accelerants concealed in medicine bottles and an olive jar. The suspect, Ahmed Ressam, was an Algerian-born petty criminal who had trained to make explosives at Al Qaeda camps in Afghanistan. His luggage contained a French-language travel guide to California and a map of Los Angeles, with circles around three airports. He was also carrying a scrap of paper with a name and a phone number on it, with a Brooklyn area code.

Suddenly, the holiday mood turned skittish. Some cities canceled their millennium celebrations. In New York, Mayor Rudolph Giuliani announced a massive operation code-named "Archangel," which would involve shutting down seventy-two blocks of Manhattan on December 31 and flooding the streets with police. Shortly before Christmas, during a visit to a Washington soup kitchen, Clinton warned that Americans should be alert for suspicious activity. In the *Chicago Tribune*, the great Jeff MacNelly drew an editorial cartoon depicting the Old Man 1999 and the Baby 2000 surrounded by police and FBI agents, guns drawn, shouting, "Freeze!"

The nation's law enforcement and intelligence agencies mounted what the CIA director, George Tenet, would later describe as "the biggest asses-to-elbow disruption operation in the history of the country." Usually, the CIA had a mistrustful relationship with its domestic counterpart, the FBI, but during the state of emergency, they put their intense rivalry aside and cooperated. Janet Reno slept on a couch at the Justice Department's headquarters so she could be available to authorize secret surveillance warrants at any time of the day or night.

At a crisis meeting, the head of Reno's office of intelligence held up a Grinch doll. "Christmas is cancelled," she informed the staff.

IT WAS TIME to get out of New York. The most famous businessman in America, the bloviating pseudo-billionaire Donald Trump, was headed to Florida, of course. Trump was planning to throw the biggest, the best, the classiest New Year's Eve party that Palm Beach had ever seen, at his club, Mar-a-Lago. Gladys Knight was singing. Sylvester Stallone was coming. Tickets cost $2,000. "I wouldn't be anywhere else," Trump told the newspapers. "It's going to be incredible."

New Year's Eve was a peak night of the Palm Beach social season, the swirl of galas and gossip that diverts America's wealthiest resort island through the winter months. Trump had hired the island's foremost party planner, Bruce Sutka, an impish impresario renowned for staging lavish spectacles involving elephants and llamas, or strippers and drag queens, or giants and dwarves, or Roman centurions with their bodies painted gold. Trump had a large white tent erected next to the mansion's pool, which Sutka decorated in Venetian fashion, with black and white drapery and large wooden blackamoors, exoticized statues of African servants, holding candelabras. Champagne glasses hung from the ceiling. There was a thirty-pound mound of caviar.

The moment had arrived: December 31, 1999.

Trump's guests started arriving early, around 7 p.m. They wore tuxedos and frilly ball gowns, and at least one socialite, the wife of a shoe store magnate, accessorized with a pair of novelty "2000" eyeglasses. Trump greeted everyone up on the terrace, by an ice sculpture that also served as a martini luge. He cast an appraising eye over his crowd. "That's Stephanie Seymour," he told one bystander, pointing to the supermodel, who was there with her husband, a rich art collector. Trump's latest Slavic model girlfriend, Melania Knauss, had come down with him for the holiday on his Boeing 727. His teenage daughter, Ivanka, an aspiring model herself, was also there, dressed in red satin. A satellite truck was parked in the driveway, so that Trump could duck out and share his profound thoughts on the millennium with TV news anchors.

Trump was happy to put the 1990s behind him. For much of the decade, he had struggled with ruinous debts. (In one year alone, he reported a $916 million loss to the IRS.) He had been forced to liquidate many of his trophy assets. And 1999 brought its own set of troubles. His father, Fred—his benefactor all these years—had finally died after years of senility. Trump's bitter divorce from his second wife, Marla Maples, had been finalized in June. Defying the adage that the house always wins, Trump had even somehow figured out how to lose money as a casino owner.

He had a plan to lift his spirits, though. Donald Trump was running for president.

THE MILLENNIUM DIDN'T arrive all at once but, rather, followed Earth's orbit as it spun forward. The first humans to reach midnight, reportedly, were sailors aboard a U.S. Navy submarine parked four hundred feet beneath the International Date Line, serving as an early-warning system for Y2K glitches. On Millennium Island, a few perilous feet above sea level, two dozen reporters were on hand to record midnight's first landfall, as grass-skirted islanders performed traditional dances and the president of Kiribati handed a torch to a young boy. At the South Pole, climate scientists popped open champagne bottles in subzero temperatures. In Auckland, the first baby of the new millennium, a boy, was born at 12:01 a.m. In South Korea, thousands attended a "DMZ 2000" ceremony, leaving folded peace wishes on a barbed wire fence at the border with the North. In Moscow, ravers danced on the street in front of the headquarters of the security service once known as the KGB, beneath an electronic billboard that read, "Internet. *Da!*" That evening, Russians would receive the shocking news that their first postcommunist leader, President Boris Yeltsin, had resigned, leaving a little-known former KGB agent named Vladimir Putin in charge.

In Jerusalem, two thousand Christian pilgrims walked in procession up the Mount of Olives, but Jesus was not there to meet them. In Egypt, a French techno artist staged a "cyberconcert" in front of the pyramids. But the Christian calendar's millennium was not celebrated in more devout corners of the Muslim world, where it fell in the midst of the holy month of Ramadan. In Afghanistan, the jihadis in the camps fell asleep beneath a winter sky splattered with stars. That night, an Al Qaeda operative was sitting on a flight from Kuala Lumpur to Bangkok, watching the cabin, counting the number of passengers in each section of the plane. It was just a reconnaissance mission. The next day, he flew first-class to Hong Kong on United Airlines, passing through security with a box cutter in his toiletries bag.

By the time Chuck Harder went on the air, at 2 p.m. on the East Coast, he knew the night was not going to end in catastrophe. His final hour opened on a downcast note:

"We're taking your calls on any subject," Harder said. "This is New Year's Eve. I wish you all a very, very prosperous and happy New Year's, and that said, I can only say we have a big, long, heavy, heavy, heavy future in front of us. We have a country that needs to be fixed."

Harder cued up the news headlines: "London marked the New Year with the ringing of Big Ben and a spectacular fireworks display on the Thames. Greenwich Mean Time reached midnight without any problems . . . President Yeltsin stepped down this past day. His prime minister, Vladimir Putin, is on the job as an interim. That's until elections are held in March . . . Soon it will be Americans' turn to celebrate. Millions from around the world are waiting in Times Square for the start of a new decade . . ."

A BRILLIANT 1,070-POUND crystal ball hovered above One Times Square, waiting to begin its midnight descent. Some hardy souls had camped out for days to secure prime positions around the neon-clad office tower turned advertising billboard. On New Year's Eve, they shivered through twenty-four hourly countdowns, one for each time zone, with culturally specific performances for every longitude. Many New Yorkers, who tended to avoid Times Square on the most placid days, were getting as far away as they could from ground zero. But some gravitated to the action.

That night, Kevin Ingram was high above the throng, in a condominium apartment overlooking the bedazzling spectacle. He had told his friends to get to the party early on New Year's Eve, to beat the cordon of twitchy New York City police officers who were locking down Times Square. The guests arrived in their New Year's finery, the women in their heels strutting past the cops on Eighth Avenue. After a ride up the elevator, they found a large apartment with a stunning view of the ball.

The apartment belonged to a close friend of Ingram from the world of investment banking. The party was for their crowd, what another guest later described as "the Black elite of New York"—the corporate executives, the power lawyers, the Wall Street players. Ingram, a compact, fashionably bald forty-one-year-old, was one of the brightest stars in the firmament. He was an MIT graduate, financially brilliant, and a master at reckoning the complexities of risk and reward. He had worked on the bond desks at Goldman Sachs and Deutsche Bank, where he had made his name as a trader in mortgage-backed securities, becoming one of the most prominent Black men in high finance. By night, Ingram lived fabulously, blasting Biggie Smalls out the rolled-down windows of his green Bentley, mixing it up at the clubs with hip-hop moguls and—always—many beautiful women.

On Wall Street, the decade was ending with a crescendo. Earlier that day, both the New York Stock Exchange and the tech-focused NASDAQ closed the millennium at an all-time high, driven upward by day traders sitting at their home computers and by the speculative mania surrounding the dot-com marketplace. Some said it was a bubble, and ready to pop, but that put no damper on the party. Ingram, who had recently left Deutsche Bank in a squall of contention, was now involved in an array of new ventures: real estate development in SoHo, a jazz club in Harlem. Of course, he also had an idea for a dot-com. He was certain it would transform the trade in mortgages, making it easy to speculate on the swelling debts of American homeowners.

There were other dealings, too, with some shady men down in Florida, where he kept his boats and his yellow Ferrari. Ingram didn't talk about that risky business with anyone . . .

Enough about that. Now it was time to drink and dance as Earth spun toward midnight. Out the window, a great mass of revelers was jostling shoulder to shoulder. The network news anchors—still the predominant source of information for the American public—were broadcasting live from Times Square, bringing updates from all over the globe. MTV—still the predominant propagator of pop culture to America's youth—was staging a New Year's Eve special hosted by veejay Carson Daly. At around 10 p.m., as the crowd counted down to midnight for Argentina and Greenland, Sean "Puffy" Combs took the stage in a tux and an open white shirt.

A few nights before, Combs—then known by the stage name Puff Daddy—had been involved in a gun battle at a Times Square nightclub, which he fled in a car with his girlfriend, the starlet Jennifer Lopez. He had been arrested on criminal weapons charges. It was a huge tabloid circus.

"Y'all ready for 2000 in here?" Puffy shouted, before launching into "Mo Money Mo Problems."

I'm the D to the A to the DDY . . . Know you'd rather see me die than to see me fly.

Over on pay-per-view, the Artist then known as ♀, who would soon return to being known as Prince, was staging a TV performance before an audience at Paisley Park, his residence and recording studio in suburban Minneapolis. The show was supposed to climax with what was promised to be the last-ever live performance of his classic hit song "1999." The song had been released seventeen years before, but its words now rang true in the moment. It had become the millennium season's anthem, once again inescapable on the radio and dance floors.

For the show's finale, the Artist, a shimmying pixie in a shimmering lamé outfit and big hoop earrings, was joined by a gaggle of guest performers. "Two thousand zero zero, party over, oops, out of time," the audience sang along, as purple balloons imprinted with the Artist's unpronounceable name symbol began to fall from the ceiling, and everyone partied, one last time, like it was 1999.

Perhaps the merrymaking masses joining the chorus failed to notice the song's dark, lyrical references to war, destruction, the Bomb, and Judgment Day. The Artist had been raised as a Seventh-day Adventist, and "1999" was about confronting the Apocalypse. That fall, he told CNN's Larry King that when he wrote the song, he was contemplating that "this system is based in entropy, and it's pretty much headed in a certain direction."

As usual, Prince got there first.

The pay-per-view special, *Rave Un2 the Year 2000*, had been taped earlier that year. That night, Mr. 1999 incarnate enjoyed a quiet dinner at an Italian restaurant in Minneapolis.

THE FBI AGENT running the millennium bombing investigation was watching Times Square from a police post, waiting to see if anything would blow up. His ultimate boss, Janet Reno, was monitoring the night's festivities from FBI headquarters. Reno had been early to recognize the threat of international terrorism. Weeks after she was nominated as attorney general, a group of Islamic fundamentalists had exploded a truck inside the parking garage at the World Trade Center, and Reno would sometimes talk about the dread she constantly felt, thinking about the next bomb.

During her tenure, the FBI had built a state-of-the-art facility called the Strategic Information and Operations Center—what Reno described as a "super-duper command post." It was a forty-thousand-square-foot complex full of banks of secure computers, video screens, phones, and fax machines. Reno and the leadership of the FBI watched as the clocks on the wall approached zero zero.

But the night was turning out to be peaceful. Near the White House, at the government's Y2K command center, bored technicians relaxed and popped in a video of *Apocalypse Now*.

At some point in the evening, Reno ducked out of the FBI building to pay a visit to the White House, where President Clinton was holding a state dinner to commemorate the end of the twentieth century. His guests included Elizabeth Taylor, Olympian Carl

Lewis, director Martin Scorsese, artist Robert Rauschenberg, and futurist Ray Kurzweil. Muhammad Ali gave Reno a kiss. Like Ali, Reno had Parkinson's disease. It caused her to shake, and the tremors were getting worse. She was trying to spend more time in Florida. Her natural habitat seemed to restore her health.

Dominating the room, as usual, was Clinton's political ally and spiritual adviser, the Reverend Jesse Jackson. Born to an unwed teenager in segregated Greenville, South Carolina, Jackson had marched with Dr. Martin Luther King Jr. in Selma and had barged to the front of the civil rights movement after MLK's assassination, which he witnessed. He was a TV celebrity who had twice run for president in the 1980s, rattling the white liberal establishment and winning votes across racial lines, showing how it might be possible one day for a Black candidate to win it all. "The moral arc of the universe is long," Jackson would often say in his speeches, quoting Dr. King, "but it bends toward justice." Now Jackson was closing out the century at the White House.

Shortly before midnight, President Clinton left in his motorcade and went to the nearby Lincoln Memorial to address the crowd waiting for the fireworks on the National Mall.

"The change of centuries, the dawning of a new millennium, are now just minutes away," he said at 11:53 p.m. "If we want the story of the twenty-first century to be the triumph of peace and harmony, we must embrace our common humanity and our shared destiny."

The turnout for the president's event was smaller than expected. His warnings about terrorism now seemed overblown. After the speech, from Clinton's limousine, his national security advisor called his top counterterrorism expert and said, "I think we dodged the bullet."

IT WAS A balmy night in the faraway winter paradise of Florida. In South Beach, thousands of muscled young men were dancing at an event that had been promoted as the "largest gay Y2K party on the planet." In a field in the Everglades, some seventy-five thousand Phish fans cheered woozily as the band took the stage before midnight, riding in on a giant motorized hot dog, and proceeded to noodle through a stoner rendition of "Auld Lang Syne." In Palm Beach, paramedics responded to an oceanfront party where an eighty-eight-year-old society matron had collapsed and died after choking on a piece of shrimp.

By a six-decade tradition, a highlight of New Year's Eve in Miami was the nighttime Orange Bowl Parade. The occasion brought together people of all ages, classes, races, and ethnicities in an old-time American ritual. Thousands gathered on the parade route, which ran along palm-lined Biscayne Boulevard, turned onto Flagler Street, and ended in Little Havana. The Goodyear Blimp hovered overhead as the crowd cheered on scooting Shriners and marching bands, the clomping Budweiser Clydesdales and a giant "Millennium Baby" balloon.

The Orange Bowl Parade was famed for its elaborate mechanized floats, extravagant follies confected out of chicken wire, burlap, hydraulics, and hundreds of pounds of glitter. Slowly, the floats rumbled past the festive crowd on the reviewing stand at Bayfront Park. One featured big jungle animals; another, alligators, herons, and a scale-model casino; a third, an ensemble consisting of Uncle Sam, a rocket, and a personal computer. The float for the grand finale, sponsored by the Miami International Airport, was dubbed "Gateway to the World." It was meant to promote the wonders of air travel. At its center was a gigantic globe surrounded by foam models of landmarks like the Eiffel Tower and the Sphinx.

At points in the parade, the Gateway to the World float would stop and shoot off fireworks, and its hydraulics system would open the globe like a flower, revealing the Statue of Liberty within. "It will welcome the United States into the new millennium," the parade program read. "As the globe opens and the Statue of Liberty rises two stories into the air, the world will become one." The float performed its spectacular animatronic routine in front of the reviewing stand. Then it turned left, crossing underneath the elevated tracks of the Miami Metromover train.

The float proceeded up Flagler, downtown's faded main street, where Floridians were crammed deep on the sidewalk. They cheered on the symbol of global unity. But then, suddenly, something malfunctioned. The float sputtered. The globe hissed and popped. Smoke spewed from inside the cavity where the Statue of Liberty was hiding.

The clock ticked forward and there, on the streets of Miami, the world broke.

2

Strange Land

...3...2...1...

BOOM!

Fireworks arced above Biscayne Bay, lighting the night sky in streaming colors, exploding without consequence as the new millennium began.

Near the stroke of midnight, the *Farallon*, a U.S. Coast Guard cutter patrolling the waters off Miami Beach, detected something on its radar screen: an unidentified floating object. The patrol drew closer and spied a shabby sixty-foot boat navigating by the light of the fireworks.

Suspicious, the *Farallon* tried to radio the boat. No answer. It tried to intercept it. It wouldn't stop. The *Farallon* issued a warning over its loudspeaker: *You're heading toward a reef!* The unlit boat kept motoring ahead heedlessly until it ran aground and nearly capsized.

The boat, a wooden island trader, turned out to be smuggling more than four hundred refugees from Haiti, packed in so tightly that a few down in the hold had suffocated. Now the dehydrated passengers sat, stuck, within sight of Miami's sparkling skyline. Most would be sent back to Haiti without so much as touching dry land. In Miami, the year began with cries of injustice.

The city's Creole-language radio stations spread word of the incident through Haitian neighborhoods. Protesters staged a New Year's Day sit-in outside the local Coast Guard station. Why was it, they demanded to know, that the Cuban boy, little light-skinned Elián, had been welcomed ashore while hundreds of Haitians suffered, and some died, only to be deported without even a court hearing? "Two things play against Haitians," a community leader told the *Miami Herald*. "We have no money and no vote."

But the protesting Haitians were missing the most relevant inequality. In the America of the twenty-first century, power would be distributed in different ways, by different means, to different people, although the America of the present didn't fully grasp the incipient transformation. Elián Gonzalez wasn't being treated differently just because he was from Cuba. Elián was special because he had the most valuable quality any person in America could possess in the year 2000.

Elián was famous.

THE STORY OF Florida is written in pavement. If you start at the Atlantic, at Brickell Point in downtown Miami, you can follow Eighth Street into Little Havana, where it becomes the fabled main drag of Cuban America, Calle Ocho. Stay on it and, outside town, it turns into the Tamiami Trail, a 1920s-era engineering marvel and environmental atrocity that cuts a concrete slash across the Everglades. The trail traverses the Big Cypress Swamp, swings north and turns into a traffic-choked suburban thoroughfare that runs up the Gulf Coast to Tampa. Past that, the same road continues on as plain old Route 41, a highway that meanders through North Florida along the path reputedly taken by the Spanish explorer Hernando de Soto. Near the Georgia border, Route 41 narrows into a country road and crosses a bridge over the Suwannee River, the inspiration for the minstrel tune that in 1935 became Florida's official state anthem.

There, way down upon the Suwannee River, in the tiny town of White Springs, the radio talk show host Chuck Harder awoke in the year 2000 and found that all was well.

"Hello, everybody," Harder said, as he started his show on January 4. "I'm *sure* it's just a coincidence, but our power has been going on and off here today. Don't know why, but it's been going on and off." The Y2K calamity had not materialized. There was no mass blackout, no famine. Harder's solar lanterns sat untouched; his cases of yeast, unopened. Late-night comics were already ridiculing the doomsday mania of Y2K. Optimists were crowing in vindication.

Harder took a breath and pivoted to the news headlines. "A particularly virulent strain of influenza has been sneezing and wheezing, coughing and gasping, eastward . . ." For Harder, there was always another disaster coming around the corner. His show, which aired across the country, was AM radio's foremost platform for radical paranoia, right-wing populism, pro-union protectionism, pseudoscience, and harangues about big bankers and "gun grabbers."

Talk radio was a powerful reactionary force in the culture, a discordant counterpoint to the era's soothing centrism. But even by the standards of his medium, Harder took a bleak view of the world, dwelling on hazards natural and unnatural: Pandemics. Hurricanes. Earthquakes. Geomagnetic storms emanating from the sun. Biological war. Nuclear war. Race war.

Most of all, Harder was a conspiracy theorist. He believed that an elite group of "maybe 3,000 people" controlled the U.S. government and the world economy, and he fulminated endlessly about the United Nations, the Council on Foreign Relations, and the "New World Order," a globalist cabal that was plotting "to grab power world-wide and enslave us all." He entertained feverish notions about a shadow government, mysterious "black helicopters," and alien visitors. (On television, the show *The X-Files* channeled some of these same ideas into popular entertainment.) During its 1990s heyday, Harder's show offered a sympathetic hearing to leaders of the antigovernment "patriot" movement, who were readying for a civil war between globalists and citizen militias. Harder defended the militias, suggesting they were mobilizing against tyranny.

Unlike Rush Limbaugh, his biggest talk radio competitor, Harder had no interest in aiding the Republicans. Harder hated both political parties, and he believed their leaders were all scheming to sell the nation for scrap. He was an exemplar of an emerging phenomenon *New Yorker* writer Michael Kelly described as "fusion paranoia," a "weird meeting of the minds" between the fringes of the right and left. The conspiracy theorist, Kelly presciently wrote, "is a stranger *of* a strange land, warped not against his culture but by it, and the curve of his warp follows the curve of the culture; it is only steeper and continues farther, off the edge of the graph."

On his show, Harder championed the American worker, railing against international free trade agreements, peacekeeping missions, and the United Nations. "These things came from the global elite, the people who want to own the world," he told his listeners. "And unfortunately, they're making excellent progress." In Harder's view, no one more perfectly represented this globalist elite than Bill Clinton, except perhaps his anointed successor, Al Gore.

In 2000, an admiring journalist described Clinton as "the first globalist president." In that year's State of the Union address, delivered with Gore sitting over his shoulder, Clinton celebrated globalization as "the central reality of our time," rhapsodizing about "the revolution that is tearing down barriers and building new networks among nations and individuals, and economies and cultures."

But Harder could see a reaction coming, through a glass, darkly. That day in January, he continued to shuffle through the news headlines as he waited for his callers. Senator Ted Kennedy was about to announce his endorsement of Gore. "Al Gore needs that help, if you can call it *help*," Harder said, acidly. "This is going to be a fascinating election year, ladies and gentlemen . . ."

"The BBC is reporting that an expert task force is being set up to monitor the threat of an asteroid strike on earth. Some astronomers say we're due one . . ."

"Monica Lewinsky was all over television yesterday and today. What a sad situation, huh? Unbelievable . . ."

"CBS News has kind of an interesting story that they're talking about that I want to share with you . . . By the way, the telephone lines are open now, 888-822-TALK . . . CBS is saying that more than one hundred angry Haitian Americans protested outside the U.S. Immigration office in Miami, criticizing what they called America's double standard . . . I gotta tell you that I think we gotta look at illegal immigration.

"I mean, the word *illegal* is in there, you know?"

AT FIRST, ELIÁN Gonzalez's immigration case looked to be straight-forward. Technically, he had entered the country illegally, but under the U.S. policy of the time, Cubans were treated differently from any other nationality, owing to the history of Cold War hostility with Fidel Castro and the diaspora community's political power in Florida. A Cuban intercepted at sea was subject to immediate deportation, but if a refugee made it to land, that person was designated as a "dry foot" and put on a fast track to U.S. citizenship. After Elián was rescued and brought ashore, his feet were deemed dry. Officials with the U.S. Immigration and Naturalization Service assumed the case would proceed routinely. "Kid is with relative," an INS official wrote in an email to a superior in Washington. "Kid paroled and will probably get 'green' card in a year."

Then Juan Miguel Gonzalez objected and asked for his son's return, throwing the immigration bureaucracy into unexpected confusion. Refugees seldom asked to go *back* to Cuba.

The INS initially treated the case as a normal custody dispute, to be decided in state court. A caseworker was dispatched to evaluate Elián's new home environment. The Miami branch of the Gonzalez family lived in a modest two-bedroom rental on a block of pastel-painted bungalows in Little Havana. The man of the house, Lázaro Gonzalez, was a chain-smoking body shop worker with a thick black mustache; his wife, Angela, worked as a seamstress in a textile factory. Elián was sharing a bedroom with Lázaro's daughter, twenty-one-year-old Marisleysis, who worked in a bank and spoke fluent English, unlike her parents. The family's household income was $29,000 a year.

The caseworker scrawled in her evaluation that the family was "very loving" and "determined to take care of [the] child." Her report on the visit described the family as "exhausted" by nonstop attention from politicians and the press, but nonetheless intent on assisting the boy's recovery. The family had already brought a psychologist in to visit Elián. Marisleysis had told the boy that his mother was in heaven. "The child is of very sweet and friendly nature," the caseworker wrote. "It seems he can manage what happened better than a man could." She concluded that Elián should "have a new start in a safe and loving environment with people who have stated that he is an angel, God sent [him] to them for a purpose, and that he is truly a miracle."

The evaluator signed off, "Best of fortune to cute Elián and his family!"

Meanwhile, in Cuba, Juan Miguel Gonzalez was frantic with concern. To him, it appeared that his relatives were trying to kidnap his traumatized child. Juan Miguel didn't really know his uncle, who fled Cuba during the mid-1980s. Lázaro maintained that he was upholding the dying wish of Elián's mother and questioned whether Juan Miguel was truly free to express his real opinion. If he just came to Miami, the relatives assumed, he would surely admit that he also wanted to defect. Juan Miguel would later recount that Fidel Castro himself offered to let him go. But he had remarried and had a new baby and a good job at a tourist hotel, and he had no desire to start his life over in America.

Twice in December, American diplomats in Havana met with Juan Miguel. They asked time and again what he wanted. "I want my son back," he said bluntly at the end of the second meeting.

Juan Miguel could reach his son on the phone and stayed in regular contact. But he feared that Elián was slipping away, into America's materialistic clutches. On Christmas Day, Elián narrated to his father as he opened his many presents, including a video game system. Juan Miguel was infuriated to see news photographs of Elián at Disney World and wrapped in an American flag at his sixth birthday party.

Castro was an expert when it came to outmaneuvering his enemies in the exile community, a group he maligned as the "Miami Mafia," and he seized on the case of Elián, claiming that the boy's American relatives were trying to "destroy his identity." Castro promised a "battle for world opinion." On Elián's sixth birthday, the dictator toured his elementary school in Cárdenas, where his classroom was fitted out as a shrine. The regime erected billboards with the boy's face on them and staged massive demonstrations where marchers carried signs reading, *"Liberen a Elián."* The state TV network launched a daily program, *Round Table*, devoted to analyzing the latest developments. One day, Fidel excused himself from a meeting with the secretary-general of the United Nations in order to take his customary seat in the show's studio audience.

Meanwhile, in early January, Elián appeared as an honored guest, wearing a paper crown, at the Three Kings Parade down Calle Ocho in Little Havana. There was a float commemorating his rescue, featuring a choir of children singing songs and one of the fishermen who had plucked Elián out of the ocean. The grand marshal, New York Yankees pitcher Orlando "El Duque" Hernandez, stopped to shake little Elián's hand. "I love you, and stay," El Duque said.

To the Cubans of Miami, the idea that Juan Miguel might deny his son a chance to live in freedom seemed abhorrent. "I think the dolphins love him more than his father," one parade-goer told the *Herald*. Some of the exiles had come to Miami as unaccompanied minors themselves, during the 1960s, as part of a church-sponsored mission called Operation Pedro Pan.

Outside Miami, however, the argument looked different. Polls showed that a majority of Americans nationwide took the father's side. Four out of five respondents in one poll said they were following the case closely. In January, a photo of a doe-eyed Elián appeared on the cover of *Time*, next to the headline "WHERE DOES HE BELONG?"

As a legal matter, the answer appeared straightforward. Elián's father retained custody, and he wanted his son back. Janet Reno had served as a prosecutor in Miami, so she understood, and sympathized with, the Cuban community's perspective. But as attorney general, she was bound to respect the law. This was America. There were rules. There was a system.

IN THE MID-1990S, the most beautiful man in New York City, John F. Kennedy Jr., decided to start a political magazine. He named it *George*—as in George Washington. It was a glossily superficial publication, dedicated to Kennedy's belief that the profession chosen by his martyred father was "another aspect of cultural life, not all that different from sports and music and art." There was a dawning sense, at this moment, that news and entertainment were merging. As if to prove his point, in the summer of 1999, JFK Jr. crashed his private plane into the ocean off Martha's Vineyard, inspiring a days-long marathon of televised mourning.

For what would be Kennedy's final issue, *George* sent an interviewer to the office once occupied by Attorney General Robert F. Kennedy, inside the monumental headquarters of the Justice Department, to interview RFK's successor, Janet Reno. It was hard to imagine a public figure less fitted for the flippant mood. Reno was six foot one and solid as a pillar, flinty, and allergic to frippery.

It was known throughout Washington that Reno was distrusted by her boss, the much-investigated Clinton, who thought her Justice Department was too independent. She was likewise disdained by the Republicans, who thought she was not independent enough. She was regarded with contempt by the Washington press corps and the punditocracy, which ridiculed her alleged political clumsiness and pinched public demeanor and called her a scold, a schoolmarm—all the coded language she was accustomed to hearing as a powerful, unmarried, unadorned woman.

"Ostensibly," the interviewer said, "you don't conform to the prevailing culture of the capital."

"I'm not one who conforms to the prevailing culture of any place," Reno replied.

In fact, Reno did belong in one place. She was not just *from* Florida; she was *of* Florida, the Old Florida. She grew up in Miami back when residents still pronounced its name *Mi-AM-aa*—a southern city, sunburnt and segregated. Her family's history told the weedy tale of the place.

Reno's mother, Jane Wood, moved down in 1925, as a twelve-year-old, during the first great Florida land rush. Miami's real estate promoters called it the Magic City. Jane later wrote that she found it "dumb, dull and flat." Miami's tiny population quintupled during the 1920s boom; nothing there had history, and everyone was green. The city was in the grip of one of its periodic bouts of speculative fever, its streets crawling with salesmen known as "binder boys," who stopped pedestrians to press them to buy property sight unseen. Then, in 1926, a massive hurricane roared through, devastating Miami. It blew away the bubble, but it enthralled Jane.

"I saw the hurricane as a great vandal, and that appealed to me," she later told her daughter's biographer. "After that, I loved Florida because the hurricane was part of it; it wasn't dull and dumb. It had force, all that great power. It was something I could feel."

Jane, too, was an untamed force. "She could storm and rage at what she thought were the wrongs of the world," her daughter later reflected. As a high school student, Jane started working for newspapers. During an early stint at the *Herald*, she met Henry Reno, a talented crime reporter who had also moved to Miami in the mid-1920s. For their first date, Henry took her on his boat to go diving for crawfish. They married in 1937 and had four children in quick succession. Janet was the eldest. The family called her "Janny."

When Janny was eight years old, the Renos purchased twenty-one acres on the border of the Everglades—"as far west as they could go before the land gets squishy," a family friend later said. Jane bought a pick at a local hardware store and started chipping away limestone and laying the foundation for a two-bedroom house. She knew nothing about construction, so she began writing a home improvement column under the pseudonym "Hal Hand," interviewing a carpenter here and an electrician there, building her project in bits and pieces. She erected a frame of Florida cypress. She salvaged the bricks for the chimney from the rubble of a burned-down house. She turned a hunk of mahogany driftwood into a polished mantelpiece.

Jane never completely finished her house—for years, there were no doors on the bathrooms. But the family moved in and populated the property with a menagerie of chickens, goats, and cattle. The children had ponies. One day, driving on the Tamiami Trail, the lonely highway that crossed the Everglades, Jane came upon a roadside stand with a sign: PEACOCK EGGS: $1. She bought two, brought them home, and hatched them under a duck. Thereafter, the Reno property was home to a gaggle of brightly hued, screeching birds, every one of whom the family called Horace.

The Reno family home was a sort of swampy salon. Henry was a well-connected reporter—his investigations of the Mob and gambling rackets helped win the *Herald* a Pulitzer Prize in 1951—and he knew a lot of judges and politicians. The Renos would throw regular parties on their porch, where the drink and gossip flowed late into the night. "What they would do is get two opposing people together," a Reno relative recalls, "and see if they could get them arguing."

Janny attended Cornell University and went to Harvard for law school at a time when women were still a rarity in the legal profession. But after that, she returned to Miami and continued to live in her mother's house, mixing with Jane's eclectic crowd as she entered into a life in politics.

During these years, Jane was exploring Florida's wild interior, taking excursions into the Everglades with a friend who owned a swamp buggy. She discovered that the vast sawgrass marshes were neither impenetrable nor uninhabited. One day, in the Big Cypress Swamp, she came across a band of Seminoles, descendants of native inhabitants of the Southeast and other oppressed peoples, including fugitive slaves, who had fought a decades-long guerrilla war against the U.S. government in the Everglades during the nineteenth century. The Seminoles said their children were falling ill with a mysterious sickness. Jane published a story about it, won a journalism award, and forged a lasting friendship with the tribe. She drank with them, kept writing about them, and advised them on public relations as they fought for better treatment.

The group of Seminoles who lived nearest to the Renos, known as the Miccosukee, adopted Jane as one of their own. They gave her a name in their language and told her it meant "Rumor Bearer." They taught her how to wrestle alligators. (The secret: if you hold them on their back for fifty seconds, they'll go limp and give up.) Jane would take young Janny to the tribe's all-night Green Corn dances. Around the campfire, Janny heard their legends and proverbs.

"When the world gets old," the Seminoles told Jane, "you see strange things."

This became a Reno family saying. And Janny did see some strange things in her time: the seedy racism of the state legislature, where she was a staffer in the 1970s and part of a group of idealistic young liberals who battled a segregationist cabal known as the "pork chop gang" over civil rights and constitutional reform; the violence and vice of Miami, where she served as the county prosecutor during the 1980s, at the height of the vicious reign of the drug gangs known as the "cocaine cowboys." But nothing was as strange to her as the ways of Washington.

When the Elián Gonzalez case landed on Janet Reno's desk at the Justice Department, she realized it was going to be trouble. "It's almost like," a former aide says, "Janet saw the end of the movie."

3

Kandahar

Kandahar smelled like shit.

Quite literally, it stank. The city was a labyrinth of dusty alleys and grayish mudbrick dwellings, few of which had indoor plumbing. Their toilets discharged directly onto the streets and sidewalks, which oozed with rivulets of raw sewage, creating a stench "so strong it was paralyzing," one city resident would later recall. Ziad Jarrah, as a refined native of cosmopolitan Beirut, must have found it all a shock to the senses: the sight of turbaned traders leading donkeys down potholed streets; the pleas of swarming beggar boys; the sulfurous black smoke of burning garbage; the cold, stony graveyards full of martyrs; the piercing call to the dawn prayer; the mornings of arduous training; the afternoon religious lectures; the brotherhood of belief.

To Jarrah and a zealous few others, Kandahar had the air of paradise.

You can see the thrill in his face as he rehearses for a propaganda video on a tape of raw outtake footage recovered by U.S. agents in 2002. Jarrah is bearded and grinning, his brown eyes dancing behind oval glasses as he sits against the blank wall of a safe house, an AK-47 rifle propped up behind him. Always vain about his appearance, he is wearing a pristine white *shalwar kameez*. He looks relaxed, high-spirited. He says something to the dour fellow traveler sitting next to him, Mohamed Atta, who cracks a brittle little smile.

Ziad was good company—that's what people would later say, the ones who didn't know.

How had he gotten to this place? Investigators would later retrace every step of his journey. It appeared to have begun on a grimy street near the Hamburg train station, at a storefront mosque that sat adjacent to a bodybuilding gym. There, as a twenty-two-year-old student, Jarrah fell in with a group of strident men who always gathered in the back corner of the turquoise-painted prayer room. They would sometimes meet at Atta's apartment, which they called the House of the Followers. They would watch propaganda videos celebrating the heroic cause of the Muslim mujahideen who fought in civil wars in the former Yugoslavia and the Russian state of Chechnya. They would discuss the glories of jihad and the rewards awaiting martyrs who died on the battlefield: an eternity spent reclining on jeweled couches, sipping wine, enjoying the attentions of seventy-two virgins.

The followers came from different nations and varied backgrounds. Jarrah was the privileged child of an affluent Lebanese family. His parents had given him a red Mercedes as a teenager and had sent him to exclusive Catholic schools. He had come to Hamburg to study engineering. Jarrah's closest friend in the group was a charismatic, penniless Yemeni refugee who went by the name "Omar." (His actual name was Ramzi bin al-Shibh.) He, in turn, sometimes lived with Atta, an Egyptian urban planner who led an Islamic study group at a Hamburg university.

What the followers who visited the apartment all had in common, besides Islam, was a sense that they were adrift in a world controlled by dark forces. They were conspiracy theorists, drawing from the same wellspring as the American far right. Atta, the group's ideologist and hardened core, was a virulent anti-Semite who preached that a globalist cabal controlled the world economy, the United Nations, and the White House. Looking, later, through some packed-away boxes belonging to Atta's study group, a German journalist would find a paranoid library. One volume, *The Global Conspiracy*, by an assassinated Palestinian cleric who had inspired Osama bin Laden, tied the jihad against the Soviets in Afghanistan to the struggle against a "Jewish octopus." The book's first page was neatly inscribed with the name "Ziad."

"We're ready to fight America, just as we fought Russia," *The Global Conspiracy* concluded. "We will attain one of two goals: a martyr's death or victory." Many men heeded that call. It is estimated that between 1996 and 2001, some ten thousand to twenty thousand trained at camps in Afghanistan.

A group of four left Hamburg in late 1999: Jarrah, Atta, Ramzi bin al-Shibh, and another one of Atta's roommates, a chubby Emirati named Marwan al-Shehhi. They flew to Pakistan separately, so as not to arouse the suspicion of the German police, who were monitoring some of the more visible militants at their mosque, and followed a well-trodden path through Pakistan's frontier provinces. From Karachi, Jarrah traveled to the western city of Quetta, where the Taliban operated a number of guesthouses under the all-seeing eye of the Pakistani intelligence service.

The guesthouse keepers arranged for Jarrah's transportation on the winding roads over the Toba Kakar Mountains, across the thinly patrolled border with Afghanistan, and on to Kandahar. There, Jarrah presented himself at another guesthouse, which served as an intake center for the camps operated by Al Qaeda—

although no one on the inside used that name. They called their organization "the Sheikh's group." The Sheikh, of course, was Osama bin Laden.

Upon their arrival, enlistees filled out a form; handed over their passports, money, and personal clothing; and adopted a *kunya*, a "battlefield name." They were told to "forget their pasts" and were discouraged from discussing their true identities. This was both a security measure and a bonding technique. Men who arrived as foreigners—Egyptians, Saudis, Uzbeks, Western converts— acquired a new jihadist family. They called one another Brother. Jarrah took the *kunya* "Abu Tareq," choosing the name of a general who, according to legend, burned his boats after invading Spain so his army would have no temptation to retreat. Maybe even then he was casting an uncertain glance over his shoulder.

Training typically began with an orientation talk at the guest-house. After that, the trainees settled into a dawn-to-dusk routine of prayer, exhausting exercise, meals of mushy lentils, and basic instruction on guns, guerrilla tactics, and Islamist ideology. Although the Taliban had outlawed television, the Sheikh's guest-houses operated outside the rules, so at night, the brothers would put Hollywood movies on the VCR, action blockbusters starring Arnold Schwarzenegger and Jean-Claude Van Damme.

In reality, the battle they were bound for was not cinematic. The main purpose of the camps was to supply troops to reinforce the Taliban, which meant most of the brothers were bound for Afghanistan's north, where the regime was fighting a dismal war against American-backed insurgents. It is likely that Jarrah originally intended to serve on the front lines, too, with the other mujahideen. But if this was indeed his plan, almost immediately, within days of his arrival in Afghanistan, it was diverted.

Al Qaeda leaders scouted the camps, looking for prospects for secret overseas operations. Besides the basic military training camp outside Kandahar, the organization had other facilities for terrorism. At these more specialized camps, explosives experts would offer instructions on making improvised bombs, referring to information from handbooks published by American survivalists. One mad bomb maker was trying to fabricate chemical weapons from simple materials like cigarettes and from poisons tested on rabbits, donkeys, and bin Laden's sons' puppies.

It was quickly apparent to Al Qaeda's leaders that the well-educated men from Hamburg had unusual potential. Jarrah and Atta were moved to a more isolated guesthouse, south of Kandahar, where they would room with one of Al Qaeda's public relations men. He arranged for them to meet bin Laden. They swore allegiance to the Sheikh, who gave them a special mission.

OSAMA BIN LADEN was living about a half hour's drive from Kandahar, on the grounds of a former government farm that had been used as an army barracks during the Soviet Union's rule of Afghanistan. The Taliban had offered him his choice of facilities, and he had picked this one because it was rough and remote, explaining that his group desired a primitive life. The complex sat in the middle of a flat sagebrush plain, surrounded by a ten-foot-high wall over which flew the black flags of jihad.

The CIA called the camp Tarnak Farms, but within Al Qaeda, it was known as al-Matar, or "the Airport," because of its proximity to an old military airfield. It consisted of a six-story office building and around eighty pink-shaded concrete houses. The complex had been damaged in the Afghan civil wars, but bin Laden, whose background was in construction, had overseen renovations, turning the dilapidated buildings into dormitories, a religious school, and a medical clinic. There was also housing for around fifty families, including some of bin Laden's wives and several of his children. The Sheikh himself slept in a house next to a thatch-roofed mosque.

Contrary to popular mythology, Osama bin Laden was not that wealthy; his family had disinherited him. Nor was he a brilliant mastermind. His lieutenants knew him to be egotistical, stubborn, and often irrational, placing great faith in signs and portents. ("Who had a good dream?" he would often ask his men after their morning prayers in the mosque.) The Sheikh's organization was shambolic, rife with dissension and infighting, scraping by on intermittent donations from abroad. His soldiers and children often went hungry. He didn't seem to care.

Bin Laden made up for all these organizational deficits with his genius for branding. He gave close oversight to Al Qaeda's media unit, known as As-Sahab, or "the Cloud," which produced his propaganda videos. He followed the news through digests prepared for him by operatives in Pakistan, and he listened to the BBC on a portable radio. He cultivated his image as a fierce, ascetic holy warrior, always carrying a small assault rifle he had supposedly taken off a dead Soviet officer in the 1980s. Spectacular terrorist attacks, like the 1998 bombings of the U.S. embassies in Dar es Salaam, Tanzania, and Nairobi, Kenya, served as marketing. Every time Al Qaeda blew something up, recruits flooded into the Sheikh's camps. Bin Laden would often pay them visits, arriving to a storm of celebratory gunfire and giving sermons in which he boasted of his high poll numbers in the Arab world.

Yet each success made new provocation more challenging. He had to keep topping himself. Bin Laden had promised to strike the United States at home and was desperate to figure out how to do it, but he faced a problem: a talent deficit. Most of the recruits in the camps lacked the sophistication to pull off a complex operation. A former CIA agent visiting Afghanistan on a magazine assignment in 1999 encountered some Al Qaeda fighters at a rebel prison and sized them up as "poorly educated peasants who'd stick out like sore thumbs at the security controls of a first-rate international airport." Recruits from Europe and North America were fairly rare and tended to be misfits or miscreants, like the failed bomber Ahmed Ressam, a former petty criminal.

The men from Hamburg, though, were different. "They seemed wily and intelligent," one of their trainers, a Yemeni named Abu Jandal, later wrote in a memoir. They were fast learners, used to living in Europe, comfortable with Western culture. The trainer recalled that Atta and Jarrah argued about Germany. Atta thought the country was decadent and irredeemable, while Jarrah said he liked it, found its people friendly and accepting. Yet when they were offered a chance to attack—to strike the enemy that bin Laden had called "Unbelief International"—they both enlisted. They knew it would be a suicide mission.

This was their most important qualification. They had to be willing to kill and to die.

"I came to you with men who love death just as you love life," Jarrah had scrawled in the notebooks he left behind in Hamburg. The Afghan camp experience propelled young militants toward the ultimate choice. "Talk yourselves into martyrdom operations," bin Laden would say in his sermons. "Encourage yourselves."

There was a process for volunteering for martyrdom. Candidates would usually seek out their trainers to offer themselves or leave a note in their camp's mosque. If they were accepted, they would be summoned to meet bin Laden. He would ask them to swear *bayat*, a loyalty oath modeled on a pledge Bedouin tribal leaders were believed to have given the Prophet. Usually, the audience took place in his dimly lit office at the camp, which contained little besides papers and the library of books he consulted on Islamic doctrine and geopolitics. (He liked to quote Fidel Castro and Richard Nixon.) A crudely drawn map of the Middle East hung on one wall. Bin Laden sized up his recruits quickly. "He had the beady gaze of a hawk," one of them later recalled in a memoir.

"He extended his right hand with his palm opened upwards and took mine," the Al Qaeda member wrote. "I noticed how long his fingers were and how soft his skin."

However Jarrah decided, it happened very fast, in a whirlwind of meetings and initiations that took place over the course of the holy month of Ramadan. After swearing the oath to bin Laden, he and the other men spent the rest of Ramadan preparing. They received advanced training, meeting frequently with a former Egyptian soldier who had expertise in explosives and commando tactics. Bin Laden had kept the "planes operation" secret from all but a tiny few within the organization. Fearing internal opposition, he had even excluded some members of Al Qaeda's ruling council, who would later claim they protested, too late, that the idea was madness. For security purposes, most of the men who joined the operation remained ignorant of the entirety of the plan until the day of the attack was near. Only Jarrah and Atta knew all the details at the time they enlisted. With astonishing speed, they had become the Sheikh's trusted soldiers.

That winter was a disappointing season for the Sheikh's group. It was not a unified force, but a franchise organization with affiliates in different countries, which varied greatly in their capabilities. Several affiliates had plans timed for the millennium, but the attacks fizzled. There was one terrorist plot that did succeed, though—a hijacking. A few weeks into Jarrah's stay at bin Laden's camp, an Indian airliner landed at the nearby Kandahar airport. Terrorists in red ski masks had stormed the plane's cockpit, threatening to crash the plane if its pilots didn't fly it to Afghanistan. The hijackers, with the tacit support of the Taliban and the ISI, Pakistan's intelligence service, held the passengers hostage, demanding the release of prisoners held by India, including a radical Muslim cleric. After a few days, on New Year's Eve, Indian negotiators complied. For the terrorists, it was a victory—and maybe, a tactical model.

Once the cockpit was under control, the rest was just a terrible leap of imagination.

In January, the leadership of Al Qaeda celebrated Eid al-Fitr, the feast marking the end of Ramadan, with bin Laden at his headquarters. Much of the leadership of the world's most murderous terrorism organization came to the camp in Toyota vans, as if for a company picnic. They were a minuscule group, really—maybe one hundred fifty barefoot, bearded men chatting amiably on prayer mats. A handful of little boys, the terrorists' children, scampered about. Jarrah sat in the second row, his head wrapped in a white turban. The Sheikh, tall and robed, brushed past him with a small retinue of armed men in military fatigues. He wrapped himself in a tan shawl and walked to a lectern set up in front of a wall pockmarked with bullet holes.

"The world infidels have united and ganged up against the Islamic people," bin Laden preached. "The blood of Muslims has become the cheapest blood." The Sheikh quoted scripture and parables and decried the presence of "American tanks, American soldiers, and even military Jewish and Christian womenfolk" in Saudi Arabia, the land of the Prophet.

"There is no room for hesitancy here," he said. "It is clear from the Koranic verses what are the reasons for tarrying behind instead of fighting for God: love of the world and dislike of death. . . . Love of the world and dislike of death. Error follows from that." Truth be told, bin Laden was not a great orator—he was dogmatic and repetitive—but to the men who had sworn to die for his cause, his message echoed with urgency.

"We have to free ourselves from our chains," he concluded. "God is greater than a strong and large nation. . . . Fear is linked to this jihad. Fear and awe are both linked with this jihad."

The operation was in motion. Soon, Jarrah would be traveling again, this time to America.

4

The Wall Street Project

You get out of the limo and the concrete glistens like diamonds. Wild rhythms of Brazilian dancers and live steel drums carry you into your elevator. One breathtaking minute later, you're 1,350 feet closer to heaven. The sounds of laughter lure you deeper inside as Kid Creole and the Coconuts and Tito Nieves y Su Orquesta have their way with your heartbeat. You present your American Express® Card and bubbles erupt from bottles of Veuve Clicquot. All around you, Russian Beluga. White and black truffles. 1982 Bordeaux. You feel a little lightheaded. Could it be the altitude? You turn a corner and all of a sudden, there it is. The greatest view of the greatest city on the greatest night of the century. No wonder they call this place <u>Windows on the World</u>.

—*American Express magazine advertisement, December 1999*

On a winter day in 1999, inside the celebrated restaurant at the top of the World Trade Center, the Reverend Jesse Jackson gathered in communion with the representatives of Mammon.

"Brother Zuckerberg," the reverend said in his symphonious

baritone as he brought a doughy partner from Goldman Sachs to a stage at the front of a Windows on the World banquet room. "Brother Fishman," Jackson said, calling up a man from Citigroup. The white financiers came forward to pay careful respects. Arrayed before the stage in plush red chairs were Black bankers and corporate executives, Black congressmen and cabinet secretaries, and Isiah Thomas, the retired NBA star and proprietor of the e-commerce start-up iSIAH.com. Jackson had convened the group, including some of the wealthiest and most important people in Black America, for his latest crusade: the Wall Street Project.

"The thrust, as you will hear over and over again, is access to capital," Jackson said as he opened the Wall Street Project's second annual conference. "Say, 'Access to capital.'"

"Access to capital," the audience murmured.

"Access to capital!" Jackson called out.

"Access to capital!" the congregation responded in unison.

"There are no budget deficits, there are no Communist threats, and yet we have more wealth in the hands of a few," the civil rights leader preached. "Someone once said that money does not grow on trees. And that is not true. Money does grow on trees if it's planted in money mud.

"Say," Jackson commanded, "'If it's planted in money mud.'"

"If it's planted . . ."

"In money mud," Jackson prodded. "In money mud."

". . . in money mud," the congregation responded.

Jackson had twice run for president, calling himself the candidate of "the desperate, the damned, the disinherited, the disrespected, and the despised." Now, in the latest of many reinventions, the reverend was fighting for a new cause: the right to get rich.

Jackson described the Wall Street Project as the continuation of the struggle he had joined in the 1960s. As a young civil rights activist in Chicago, Jackson ran an economic empowerment initiative called Operation Breadbasket. It pressured companies to do business with local Black-owned enterprises by appealing to their better angels and, when necessary, threatening boycotts. In sermons, Jackson would lead his audiences in a call-and-response routine, repeating the affirmation "I am *somebody*." Self-belief was his creed, and he deferred to no one—not even Martin Luther King Jr. At the end of King's life, his own economic views were moving leftward as he championed a multiracial social justice initiative called the Poor People's Campaign. Jackson spoke up in defense of capitalism; King was furious. "If you want to carve out your own niche in society, go ahead," he scolded the young upstart, "but for God's sake don't bother me!"

The two reunited for a protest in Memphis, where Dr. King sought to reconcile. One afternoon, at the Lorraine Motel, King called out to Jackson from his balcony, "Jesse, I want you to come to dinner with me." Then there was the crack of a rifle shot, and King fell dead.

And here Jackson was, three eventful decades later, at the top of the Twin Towers, looking down on the Financial District, which was shrouded in swirling snow. He was no longer the rhyming rabble-rouser in a dashiki, who flirted with Black nationalism and chatted with Dick Cavett during the 1960s and '70s. But the Wall Street Project was employing the same tools as Operation Breadbasket—moral suasion, the threat of protests—to target the nation's largest business institutions. They were prospering during the Clinton era; now Jackson was demanding an equitable distribution of the spoils. Whether out of genuine commitment or fear, many of corporate America's biggest names (Ford, Coca-Cola, AT&T) had contributed financially to the project. Behind Jackson onstage sat a panel of prominent guests, most of them white.

Brother Zuckerberg from Goldman Sachs spoke, and then Roger Ailes, the portly Nixonian who had just started Fox News, the new conservative alternative on cable TV. (Ailes began his remarks with an off-color ethnic joke.) Then Jackson called up the headliner, one of his project's most prominent benefactors and also its landlord.

"I now want to bring forth a friend who has . . . Well, he is deceptive, in that his social style is such that one can miss his seriousness," Jackson said. "For his success is beyond argument. When we opened this Wall Street Project and we talked about it, he gave us space at Forty Wall Street . . .

"He's created for many people a comfort zone. When I ran for the presidency in '84 and '88, and many others thought it was laughable or something to avoid, he came to our business meeting here in New York because he has this sense of the curious and a will to risk to make things better. And so, aside from all his style and his pizzazz, he is a serious person who is an effective builder.

"Donald Trump."

Trump walked to the microphone wearing a smirk.

"Jesse started off by saying most of the wealth in this country is in the hands of a few," he said. "And I thought to myself, 'Is that a bad thing?' What's wrong with that, Jesse?"

The reverend and his audience laughed along obligingly.

"I was just telling Roger," Trump went on, referring to Ailes, sitting behind him on the stage, "Jesse had an expression last year: 'the wall on Wall must fall.'" Like an emcee at a roast, Trump recounted an uproarious story about his rent negotiation with the similarly shameless Reverend Jackson. "He said, 'Listen, I want some office space in your building on Wall Street. Because the wall on Wall will fall.' And I said, 'It's okay, Jesse, I'll make a good deal with you. I'll get you some space; you'll pay about forty dollars a foot.' And he said, '*No no no*, I don't want to pay forty dollars.' I said, 'How about thirty?' No! It was the cheapest deal I made in the history of Forty Wall Street. He got it for *nothing*. He's a very tough negotiator. We know that, right? No, he's a terrific guy."

Jackson jovially reclaimed the microphone. "And with all that wealth," the reverend said, with a mischievous look, "Trump wants a free ticket to the affair tonight. A freebie!"

That evening, there was to be a fund-raising gala on the floor of the New York Stock Exchange. Maya Angelou was scheduled to appear, along with President Clinton, who had enlisted Jackson as his spiritual adviser—and a spirited defender—during his recent sex scandal. "We will go from discussing Monica to discussing money," Jackson proclaimed at Windows on the World.

Monica to money! his congregation chanted all together. *Monica to money!*

JACKSON WAS NOTHING if not canny in sizing up the ethos of the era. Social justice had enjoyed its day; now it was time for money-making. The stock market, once a gated community for brokers and bankers, had lately become accessible to anyone with an E*TRADE account. In white suburbs and Black neighborhoods alike, pastors were preaching the "prosperity gospel" at burgeoning evangelical megachurches, promising that God would shower wealth on the faithful. The rough-edged music of the early 1990s—the anticorporate grunge bands, the violent gangsta rappers—had fallen out of favor. Pop culture was now consumed with aspiration. Puffy Combs, the reigning king of hip-hop, was on the cover of *Forbes*. Puffy endorsed luxury brands and threw parties in the Hamptons where guests mimicked hoity-toity manners, dressing all in white. In the video for his 2000 hit "Big Pimpin'," the emerging superstar

Jay-Z cavorted on a megayacht with models in bathing suits as he rapped, "We doin' big pimpin', we spendin' cheese."

Yet, as Jackson realized, most of the profits of the boom time were accruing to the people who already had all the cheese. In an awkward moment at his conference, a questioner asked the man from Goldman Sachs how many Black partners his firm had. He fumbled and mumbled before disclosing that the answer was 1 . . . out of 220.

"As long as Wall Street had the comfort zone of our detachment, those kinds of numbers could exist," Jackson said. "Our partners need not feel shame about these bad records. Change them."

If a single individual could be said to embody Jackson's hope for change on Wall Street, it was a short, intense, mathematically minded, and impeccably tailored financial executive named Kevin Ingram. "Kevin was more or less the person that Jesse was pointing to," says a friend and coworker of Ingram's at the time. "He was kind of recognizing Kevin as a very successful Black executive on Wall Street." Ingram was at the stock exchange gala that evening, dressed in black tie. On his arm was his wife, a fabulously glamorous model of West Indian extraction. Her name was Deann, but everyone called her Sparkle. She was a fixture on the New York City hip-hop scene.

"Everybody was treating him like he was a god," recalls one of his wife's friends, who also attended the Wall Street Project party. "I just remember that when Kevin walked by, they were like, *Kevin is here.*"

Kevin was the guy who had made it on Wall Street, a bond trader who had climbed to the top ranks of banking. How much cheese did Kevin have? Donald Trump came to *him* for loans.

Ingram was a wizard at securitization, which was a jargony way of saying he traded in debt—another thing that Americans had lately been consuming with abandon. He managed billions, made millions, and was happy to flaunt his success. Unlike some of his Black peers on Wall Street, who kept their voices down as they assimilated into the white-dominated society of high finance, Ingram lived loud. "Kevin Ingram—he was like the Black guy who was still a Black guy, operating at the top of a firm," says a Black banking colleague. He was a new archetype.

"To us, he was the Black version of Gordon Gekko, that's how we saw him," says a music and entertainment industry executive who was friendly with Ingram at the time, referring to the financier played by Michael Douglas in the 1987 film *Wall Street*, who proclaims that "Greed is good."

Ingram came from Philadelphia—North Philly, to be precise. Over the course of his childhood in the 1960s and '70s, his row house neighborhood was hollowed out by drugs, crime, and neglect. But Kevin's family was upwardly mobile. His father, Nathan, was an army veteran who had been wounded in France during the Second World War. A brilliant but troubled man, he started out as a real estate appraiser, sizing up property values, and later went into investing. "Daddy, he owned a lot of real estate," says Karen Ingram, Kevin's twin sister. Nathan had restless ambition and hardly ever slept, but sometimes he was overtaken by dark moods and disappeared to the basement. He died when Kevin was just five years old. In later years, Kevin would hint to friends that there was mystery surrounding the circumstances, suggesting that his dad might have been murdered by mobsters as a result of real estate dealings. In fact, the cause was determined to be suicide.

After Nathan's death, Kevin's mother, Doris, took over the family's real estate business. The daughter of a midwestern doctor, she met her husband during the war, when she worked as a volunteer nurse. "I think we all got a combination of my father's brains and my mother's tenacity," Karen says. She and Kevin were in the middle of a pack of six children. Their eldest sister became a civil rights attorney and, later, a professional tap dancer. An older brother played briefly in the NFL. Kevin was a math prodigy. He went to Central High, an elite magnet school for top achievers. He hardly had to study; numbers came to him effortlessly. He also played the saxophone. As a teenager, he would stay out late performing at jazz cabarets.

Kevin benefited from the support of a series of older, white academic mentors who recognized his gifts. He went to MIT, where he majored in chemical engineering, and then won a prestigious scholarship for graduate study at Stanford. But after a while, he tired of laboratory work. A friend suggested a shift. Ingram switched to Stanford's business school. This was during the early 1980s, the dawn of Silicon Valley and supply-side economics. Technologies were being invented, fortunes were being made, and Stanford was the engine room of what *Time*, in a 1983 cover story, dubbed the "New Economy."

Ingram earned his MBA and went to Wall Street in 1984, the year Ronald Reagan declared that it was "morning in America." The stock market was just beginning a decades-long ascent. In the fifteen years between November 1984, the month of Reagan's landslide reelection, and the end of the century, the S&P 500 average would increase by almost ten times. But there was nothing challenging about betting on stocks in a bull market; any sap could win that way. The real excitement was in bonds. For traders in debt like Ingram, it was the beginning of a renaissance.

At the most elementary level, a bond is a debt instrument. In a traditional lending model, a bank offers a loan to a customer, to be paid back with interest over a fixed period of time. But by turning that loan into a bond and selling it, the lender can take an immediate profit, while also offloading the risk of the loan onto an investor. In return for taking the very small chance that the debt might not be repaid, a bondholder receives a steady, predictable return. Prior to the 1980s, the bond market was a boring place, concerned primarily with large loans to highly creditworthy institutions like governments, public utilities, and major corporations. But then people on Wall Street decided to get creative. Ingram arrived at this Promethean moment.

Every month, millions of homeowners were making mortgage payments to banks. These were small trickles of cash, but if you combined them into bonds, through the process of securitization, they totaled up to a torrent of trillions. Mortgage bonds contained inherent risks. Each loan was connected to an individual property and an unpredictable homeowner, who might either default if the economy went bad or refinance early if interest rates went down, thus wiping out their debt. But in the mid-1980s, Wall Street banks came up with a new type of security, called a collateralized mortgage obligation, or CMO, which allowed them to redivide the torrent of loan payments into new securities tied to various streams of cash, each with a different risk equation. In a simple model, one bondholder might get all the interest, while another took payments on the principal. Innovation followed innovation, allowing Wall Street to slice and recombine debt in an endless variety of esoteric ways. The market would eventually become so incomprehensibly large that a housing downturn would send waves of destruction across the whole world economy. But that was still twenty profitable years away.

Ingram started out at Lehman Brothers, but he soon moved to the mortgage-trading desk at Goldman Sachs. Wall Street's most storied firm was accustomed to dominating every market, but it had been slow to get into mortgages. Goldman's elite status was partly to blame. It traded Treasury bonds and financed corporate mergers; it didn't deign to deal with small-time home lenders. By the time Goldman realized the opportunity it was missing, it was lagging far behind the innovators, the so-called Big Swinging Dicks at Salomon Brothers, later immortalized in Michael Lewis's book *Liar's Poker*. "They were minting money," says a colleague of Ingram's at the time, "and somebody at Goldman said a lot of that money should be ours." When Ingram was hired, Goldman was trying to restore the natural order.

Unlike stocks, which were listed on a public exchange, bonds were created through financial engineering and bought and sold on an opaque marketplace. Pricing and trading bonds was about understanding math; Ingram excelled at it. He was particularly good at grasping the workings of the riskiest instruments, like derivatives, which were tied to complex probabilities. "He was as analytical as the most analytical people," says a friend from a competing firm, who shared Ingram's experience of being Black on Wall Street. "Being African American, you not only had to be good, you had to be much better than good, and he was much better than good."

Ingram was reportedly one of only six Black bond traders at Goldman, and the firm's leadership was acutely aware of its deficit. His career benefited from the support of high-level executives, including a legendary trader the firm had hired from Salomon Brothers, one of the original Big Swinging Dicks, who promoted Ingram to head the mortgage-trading desk. "People tend to think of this as a mystical area, but it's really a practice," Ingram told *Black Enterprise* in 1992, when the magazine included him in its special issue ranking the "25 Hottest Blacks on Wall Street." A friend later quipped that out of the twenty-five, Ingram "was *the* best dressed."

"Kevin was never fascinated so much with the money, because the money wasn't it," his sister Karen says. "I think that's the way it is with everyone in our family. It's the game itself. It's the challenge. It's 'Can you do it?'"

Ingram was charming, cocksure, and always game for adventure. He told *Black Enterprise* that he liked to go cliff diving. He raced around on motorcycles. One time, a Goldman colleague recalls, a group of bond guys went out to Jackson Hole, Wyoming, for a ski vacation. Ingram didn't know how to ski, but he picked it up quickly. In the evening, they all met at a place called the Million Dollar Cowboy Bar. "Kevin walks in—five-foot-not-so-many-inches of Kevin," says the former coworker. "With a full-length mink coat, a mink hat, and a tall blonde on each arm." (For the purposes of historical accuracy, Ingram believes that the fur was actually beaver or otter, and specifies that it would have been just one blonde—two wasn't his style.)

Ingram was married for part of the time he was at Goldman, to a woman who had worked as an accountant for the firm, but that didn't slow him down. "I was a bit flamboyant," Ingram recalls. "I was from my neighborhood, and I acted like a kid from North Philly. Didn't matter. And all the Black guys warned me, 'You can't act like this.' I was like, 'Yes, I can.'"

At the time Ingram was on the trading desk, Goldman Sachs was still a buttoned-up private partnership, not yet a publicly traded multinational leviathan. The firm culture discouraged outward displays of wealth. "When I started at Goldman," says an executive who oversaw Ingram, "I had bosses who told me if you were caught driving a nice car in the parking garage, you're fired." Ingram bought a green Bentley. Like all unwritten rules, the firm's norms were applied unevenly and often fell heavily on those who already stood out as different.

Ingram's superiors saw him as a rare talent, but also found him perplexing. He could be arrogant and demanding. He partied and womanized prodigiously. This hardly made him unusual on Wall Street, where firms would tolerate all sorts of laddish behavior so long as the lad in question was making money. But Goldman's leaders decided that Ingram was, as one put it, "difficult to manage." His bosses—mostly white men who had been conveyed through life on a cushion of privilege—wondered if the headstrong trader was really Goldman material.

In 1994, Goldman and its mortgage desk had a rocky year. Ingram had hoped to make partner, which would have given him an ownership share in the firm, which was on the verge of staging an immensely lucrative initial public offering. But he was told to wait. He was furious, and his resentment became fixed on another mortgage trader who did make partner that year: Steven Mnuchin. "I resented it," Ingram says. "To me, I was more talented than Steve Mnuchin in every respect. And it's true." Some Goldman colleagues agreed with Ingram's assessment, later recalling Mnuchin as a slithery character. But his father, Robert, had been a revered executive at Goldman, and so younger Mnuchin's name was already made at the firm.

"I guess I'm not the chosen one," Ingram said to a colleague. He stayed at Goldman, but his disenchantment was palpable. He was getting divorced and was socializing with a new set of friends, from the world of hip-hop. Former coworkers would later recollect that he sometimes disappeared from the office for long, unexplained stretches. (Ingram says that accounts of his absences were exaggerated.) After he was passed over again in 1996, Ingram quit. He recalls that he blasted out a mass email questioning Goldman's perception of itself as an elite meritocracy.

Ingram took a senior position at a firm that better suited his temperament: Deutsche Bank. And that is how he ended up playing an unwitting role in the rebirth and ascent of Donald Trump.

THAT'S ANOTHER STORY, and no surprise, it ended unhappily. Six months after the Wall Street Project gala, Ingram found himself back at the World Trade Center, unemployed and calculating his next move. He was working in the South Tower, in temporary space offered to him by an investment firm, and casting about in every direction for new business opportunities.

This brought him to Randy Glass. Ingram met him through Didi, his friend and tennis partner. Didi—his full name was Diaa Mohsen—was an Egyptian who was in the import-export business, whatever that meant. Didi talked a big game and purported to be related to Egypt's deposed royal family, but he lived in a modest brick row house in Jersey City, and he was always hustling. He had a gift for making connections. He had met Glass in Atlantic City, at a high-stakes table at the Trump Taj Mahal casino. Glass dealt in diamonds down in Boca Raton.

Ingram kept his forty-four-foot yacht, the *Ingee*, at a marina near Fort Lauderdale, not far from where Glass lived. One Monday night, Didi brought the diamond dealer over to meet Ingram on the boat. Glass seemed sleazy, but he definitely had the air of someone used to handling serious money. He presented himself as a wealthy entrepreneur who was seeking investment advice. He said he had partners, very private businessmen, who had "a certain amount of cash coming in every month." He said they needed help "cleaning it up."

As a man who made his career by analyzing risk and reward, Ingram should have known to flee right then. While Glass was vague about his business, it wasn't hard to size up the situation.

But Ingram was working on a variety of other business ventures: restaurants, a real estate development, a dot-com. They all had one thing in common. They needed money to get going. As always, access to capital was the key. In a follow-up call, Ingram told Glass to come see him in New York. "My offices are at Two World Trade Center," he said. "On the eighty-fifth floor."

One June day, Didi and Glass took the elevator up to Ingram's office. Didi was stocky and had a bulbous boxer's nose. Glass was oleaginous, with slicked-back hair. After preliminary talk, the details of which are in dispute, Glass handed over $100,000 in cash. Ingram wrote him a check from a corporate account at Chase Manhattan Bank for $91,000, taking a fee of $9,000. It was just a start. Didi said that Glass would need to take care of many millions.

After the meeting, Ingram got to work. He told Glass he was forming offshore shell companies. He drew up a prospectus for a new entity, the "IAM Global Money Fund." ("I am *somebody . . .*")

"He explained to me that we have an investor for two million," Ingram said in a phone call to Glass.

"Yes, a week, right," Glass replied. "Now Di said something about fifteen or twenty million; what is this about?"

"The fund has to be established with a minimum investment," Ingram said. "Look at the fund as a nonbank bank. That's what it is. It's a bank without bank requirements."

Glass said that his partners needed to meet with Ingram first. "In order for that to happen," he said, "you'll come down, just do a bank wire in front of their face while they're sitting there. And they'll start with whatever nominal amount of money just for that wire transfer."

Ingram said that was a "trivial" condition. "So, I'm going to assume we're moving forward, and I'm going to go ahead and get my accountants and my attorneys to set up the legal documents."

In another call, Glass told Ingram that he and his partners were about to close a lucrative sale. "It's going to be a very large transaction," he said. "Let me tell you, I am not a poor little boy."

"I know that," Ingram said. "I've heard."

"We're partners," Glass said. "We're on the same team now."

"They are aware of the numbers we're talking about," Ingram asked, "the setup numbers?"

"Yes, you said fifteen," Glass said.

"Give it twenty for starters," Ingram replied.

They agreed to meet again soon, back down in Florida.

5

Baseball Man

"It's King Kong versus Godzilla," Mike Piazza said.

It was midwinter, the depths of the baseball off-season, and the New York Mets catcher was doing color commentary for the 2000 edition of a made-for-television exhibition, *Big League Challenge.* The tournament's premise was brutally simplistic: in each round, two power hitters would face off and mash as many home runs as they could out of a Las Vegas stadium.

Playing the role of King Kong was Mark McGwire, the gargantuan red-bearded slugger who had recently shattered the all-time record for home runs hit in a single season, with seventy.

Across the diamond was Godzilla: the fire-breathing muscleman Jose Canseco, McGwire's former teammate turned resentful rival.

Thwack! Thwack! Thwack!

One after another, the baseballs flew over the fence.

"That may be the highest one he's hit yet!" an ESPN sports-caster marveled as one of Canseco's homers arced over five hundred feet, easily clearing the scoreboard in center field.

"Jose is just absolutely punishing the baseball," Piazza added.

Over the prior decade and a half, Canseco and McGwire had shaken up the sleepy national pastime, dazzling fans with their awesome feats of strength. As young teammates with the Oakland

A's, they had earned the nickname "the Bash Brothers." McGwire was enormous and quiet, an All-American athlete who had starred at the 1984 Olympics in Los Angeles. Canseco was Mr. Miami, a huge, handsome Cuban who had raced around in sports cars, cannoodled with Madonna, and spent his winters in South Florida, socking softballs in a league financed by his hometown's cocaine cowboys. Together, the two athletes had formed a fearsome duo, powering the A's to a World Series championship and transforming the look of the entire sport. Now every team in the league had at least one hitter who resembled the Hulk; even the little infielders were showing up to Spring Training with bulging biceps. The baseballs were soaring. Over the 1990s, the cumulative number of home runs hit across the major leagues increased by nearly 70 percent, reaching an all-time high in 1999. In the 2000 season, hitters would end up smashing that record again.

"Very few people in the world can do what we can do," Canseco said in an interview during a break in the competition, over B-roll footage of his mighty swings and his weight-training routine. "All the weightlifting that goes into it, the nutritional aspect, the hard work, the hours spent in that game and . . . That's what you're working for, to hit that baseball for a home run."

Canseco didn't mention the magical ingredient, but around baseball, everyone knew his secret. The other players called him "the Chemist."

Growing up in Miami, Canseco had been a skinny kid—a slap-hitting, one-hundred-eighty-pound weakling. He was a low-level minor-leaguer when a bodybuilder friend injected him with his first dose of steroids. He started with a mixture of testosterone and Deca-Durabolin.

The next spring, the twenty-year-old showed up at training camp with an added twenty-five pounds of muscle. By the following year, 1986, Canseco was in the major leagues. "Look at his arms," a baseball scout marveled aloud, seeing him hit for the first time. "I don't believe it." Oakland's marketing department touted the handsome rookie as "the Natural." Soon, he made himself a superstar and a self-educated expert in the surreptitious science of performance enhancement. Showing a rare combination of speed and power, in 1988, he became the first player ever to hit more than forty home runs while stealing forty bases, and he won the American League's Most Valuable Player award. He celebrated his accomplishment by buying a $225,000 Lamborghini with a license plate reading "40-40." He credited his success to the wonder drugs in his bloodstream.

Even as they both excelled, though, Canseco grew intensely envious of McGwire. He was a steroid user, too. Canseco would later claim that when they were young, he had sometimes injected McGwire himself, jabbing a needle into his backside in a clubhouse bathroom stall. But McGwire was favored by the press—because he looked like a wholesome white boy, in Canseco's opinion—while Canseco was considered a selfish prima donna. It was McGwire who ended up with all the records, the adulation, and the lucrative endorsement checks, while Canseco saw his career set back by injuries and his bad reputation. By 2000, Canseco had become a journeyman, bouncing around from team to team as his athletic skills deteriorated. All he had left was his power.

Thwack! Thwack! Thwack!

"I don't think I've ever seen him this intense," McGwire wisecracked to the announcers.

Canseco defeated McGwire and then destroyed the rest of the competition, putting on a stupendous display in the final round against Rafael Palmeiro of the Texas Rangers. His fellow sluggers watched with an appraising eye. Backstage, they gawked at Canseco's ridiculously ripped physique. "What the hell have you been doing?" the San Francisco outfielder Barry Bonds hollered across the locker room. Canseco would later claim that, after the tournament was finished, he and Bonds had a talk. "I told him everything I knew," he later wrote. "It was Jose Canseco's Guide to Steroids 101." Bond's once-lithe frame was in the midst of growing to comic book proportions. He would break McGwire's home run record in 2001.

At the close of the *Big League Challenge*, Canseco collected his $600,000 in prize money and flew home to Florida, where he would soon start Spring Training with his latest team, the woeful Tampa Bay Devil Rays. There, as usual, his teammates would discreetly seek out his expertise. Canseco was happy to share. He was a steroid evangelist. Although the drugs were illegal, and considered dangerous, he believed that, if used properly, they could make anyone strong and healthy. Someday soon, he predicted, everyday people would take them to fight diseases, to increase their sex drive, and to slow the aging process. For now, though, they were a secret elixir. Canseco offered clubhouse chemistry lessons, going over the properties of different substances and how they worked in combination.

For all his accomplishments on the field, it was Canseco the Chemist who played the larger role in history. Wherever he went, his teammates got miraculously bigger and better. They won games, delighted fans, sold seats, scored ratings, and made wealthy team owners even wealthier. Everyone won. But the formula worked to the particular benefit of one baseball man.

He was going to be the next president of the United States.

GEORGE W. BUSH knew something about personal transformation. His carefully crafted campaign biography began with a moment of awakening. According to the legend, in July 1986, after celebrating his fortieth birthday, Bush awoke with a ruinous hangover. He then and there resolved to quit drinking and to get right with God. The wastrel oilman known around the West Texas town of Midland as "Bombastic Bushkin" found himself, and a new direction, in baseball. With some rich friends, he put together a deal to buy the struggling Texas Rangers. Bush turned the team around, ran for governor, and won over the state with his chummy, bipartisan style of politics. His meandering life story and his frank admission of imperfection were central to his popular appeal.

"I never dreamed of being president of the United States. It was never really part of my deal," Bush told the young conservative journalist Tucker Carlson, who visited him in Austin in 1999 on a reporting assignment for the magazine *Talk*. "I am, I guess, comfortable enough with myself to know that I may succeed, I may fail, but that's okay either way."

This was, as they say in West Texas, horseshit. Though it was true that he gave up drinking—and who can say what happened in his soul—the real change that occurred around the time of George W. Bush's fortieth birthday was that he got into the family business and lifted his ambitions.

The Bushes were a national political conglomerate, with branch offices in several states. The founder of the line, Prescott Bush, was an investment banker who married the daughter of George Herbert Walker, a Jazz Age tycoon, and later won a seat in the Senate from Connecticut. His son George H. W. Bush expanded the firm down to Texas, where he made a fortune in oil before entering politics, rising to be vice president by the time his eldest son turned forty.

Dubya had tried to follow the path of his father, with less success at every step. He was a benchwarmer on the Andover baseball team, where his dad had been a standout; a middling student at Yale, where his father had been big man on campus; and a flyer with the so-called champagne unit of the Texas Air National Guard during Vietnam, while his father had been a war hero. Through his twenties, he "chased a lot of pussy and drank a lot of whiskey," as he once put it. He lived at a high-spirited Houston apartment complex called the Chateaux Dijon. At the age of thirty-one, he met his wife, Laura, who made him respectable. But accomplishment eluded him. Like his dad had, Dubya ran for a seat in Congress, but he lost. He tried the oil business, and failed. In 1986, though, his father was planning to run for president. It was at this time that the Bush family gathered for a political summit at Camp David, where Dubya met a man who changed his life.

Lee Atwater was a liquor-drinking, pot-smoking, skirt-chasing, blues guitar–playing, poisonous-as-a-viper political operative from South Carolina. Atwater was supposed to be Bush Sr.'s campaign manager, but some members of the family were wary of his eccentricities and egomania. They also knew that a partner in Atwater's consulting firm, Roger Stone, was working for a rival Republican.

Dubya confronted Atwater about his loyalty. "I said, 'How can we trust you?'" he would later recall. "And Atwater, who was doing this shuck and jive act, stopped and said, 'Are you serious?' And I said, 'I'm damn serious, pal. In our family, if you go to war, we want you completely on our side. We love George Bush, and by God, you'd better bust your ass for him.'" His younger brother Jeb, who was active in politics down in Miami, seconded Dubya's opinion.

"If someone throws a grenade at our dad," Jeb told Atwater, "we expect you to jump on it."

Atwater was smart. He thought it over and came back to the Bush brothers with an offer: if they were so worried, why didn't they come work with him on the campaign? "If I'm disloyal," Atwater said, "you can run me off." Jeb didn't want to leave Florida, where he was establishing himself in the real estate business, but there was nothing keeping Dubya in West Texas, where his oil-exploration company was hitting nothing. He moved to Washington. "He was itching to go," a Texan friend would later tell the *Washington Post*. "It was his hole card."

Dubya had no official title, but he was sometimes described as the family "enforcer." At the Washington campaign headquarters, in a dingy building that dated to the Taft administration, he had an office in between Atwater and Roger Ailes, the ruthless campaign advertising man who would go on to start Fox News. Dubya would spend his days sitting there with his boots up on his desk, spitting the juice from the Copenhagen dip he used into a trash can, keeping his door open, listening.

Bush and Atwater developed an affinity. They shared a swaggering style and a kill-or-be-killed strategic philosophy. "It became possible for people to call [Bush] and to know they were talking to Lee," says the operative Karl Rove, a friend of Atwater's, who also got to know Bush during the campaign. To some, a biographer would later write, it appeared that Bush was Atwater's "alter ego," so close to him that it seemed they could read each other's minds.

The 1988 campaign was arduous. As Ronald Reagan's vice president, George H. W. Bush faced the challenge of distinguishing himself after his years of standing behind a more charismatic, lovable figure. *Newsweek* summed up his struggles in a cover story with the memorable headline "FIGHTING THE WIMP FACTOR." (A furious Dubya called up the story's author, Margaret Warner, and told her the headline was "disgraceful" and that she ought to quit the magazine.) Over the summer, Bush fell far behind his Democratic opponent, the moderate Massachusetts governor Michael Dukakis. Then Atwater and his boys went to work.

Atwater was a specialist in finding pinpointed ways to scratch at the scabs of race and class. When it came to Dukakis, he locked in on the case of a murderer named Willie Horton, who had been given a pass to leave a Massachusetts prison under a state furlough program and escaped to commit more crimes. Horton, who was Black, was a perfect vehicle to exploit racist fears. Atwater later claimed that he realized the effectiveness of the attack when he overheard some white bikers talking about Horton at a restaurant in rural Virginia. The Bush campaign and allied political organizations evoked Horton constantly in advertisements. Atwater said he intended to tie the criminal so closely to Dukakis that he was going to "make Willie Horton his running mate." At a rally in California, the elder Bush declared, "No more furloughs for people to rape, pillage and plunder in the United States!" Meanwhile, Ailes and his advertising team were remorselessly redefining Dukakis as an effete liberal. They made a devastating ad from awkward footage of the Democratic nominee riding in a tank.

In the end, Atwater's war machine crushed the dork in the tank. The first President Bush moved into the White House, and Atwater became chairman of the Republican National Committee. (He died two years later, of a brain tumor, at the age of forty.) But Dubya left Washington and moved back to Dallas. Atwater had once cracked to a fellow campaign staffer that the junior George Bush could go either way: "chump or champ?" By the end of his father's campaign, the question had been answered.

"George went up as Sonny Corleone," a friend would later say, "and came back as Michael."

Some of Dubya's friends from Republican politics were already pressing him to run for office in Texas. But Bush decided that this would look too impatient, and besides, he needed to make some money. Within weeks of his father's election, Bush Jr. was in negotiations to buy the Rangers. The move was perfect. He was a genuine baseball fan, and as a team owner, he could introduce himself to the public without appearing to trade too blatantly on his father's office. Baseball was a manly business, and it would put his name in the newspaper every day, in the friendly confines of the sports pages. But politics was always the endgame. By this time, Rove had become the younger Bush's adviser, and even before the Rangers deal closed he was spinning it for the boss, telling reporters it "anchors him clearly as a Texas businessman."

The Rangers were a miserable franchise, without a single playoff appearance in their history and owned by an elderly, right-wing curmudgeon. The owner was a friend of Bush's family, so he was happy to entertain an offer. Bush assembled a consortium of other investors and bought the team for $75 million. He personally contributed just $600,000, which he estimated to be around one third his net worth.

Though his share in the Rangers was tiny, Bush made his presence large. As the managing partner, he would regularly attend games at the team's half-empty stadium, a rundown former minor league park that broiled in the summer. Instead of sitting in a luxury box, like most owners, Bush would sweat it out in the first row behind the Rangers dugout, munching on peanuts and chatting with the beer vendors. He peed at the same urinals as the fans. He dealt amiably with hecklers, apologizing for the pitching staff. He took the Rangers beat reporters golfing. He traveled the state, promoting the team and handing out baseball cards with his picture on them.

Bush also visited the clubhouse and got to know his players. He would practice his awful Spanish on the Latin American guys. One time, late in an extra-inning game, he called out to his All-Star first baseman, Rafael Palmeiro, ordering him to hit a homer so everyone could go home. Palmeiro did so, and tipped his cap to his boss as he crossed home plate. Bush became particularly friendly with Nolan Ryan, the veteran Texas-born pitching ace who was on his way to the Hall of Fame. He and Ryan would sometimes work out together in the weight room.

It was all another form of politics. The Rangers needed Bush's skills as a public ambassador, because he and his investors were planning to build one of those charming retro ballparks that were going up everywhere around the major leagues—at taxpayer expense, of course. Two years after Bush took over, the voters of Arlington approved a sales tax to subsidize the ballpark.

Still, Bush would need to fill that new stadium, and the Rangers were doing little to thrill fans. In August 1992, the front office pulled off a shocking move, a trade that the press celebrated as the biggest in the team's history, exchanging three good players for one of the biggest stars in baseball: Jose Canseco. "A blockbuster," Bush crowed to the press. Though Canseco was just twenty-eight, and seemingly entering the prime of his career, Oakland had reportedly tired of the never-ending chaos and controversy surrounding his private life. (There were also prevalent rumors that he was using steroids.) Bush was delighted to welcome the slugger to his team. "I think the fans will love him," Bush said. "He's a marquee player."

Canseco would prove to be a disappointment on the field. His most important contribution to the Rangers came in the clubhouse. Shortly after he joined the team, Canseco would later write, he gave one of his chemistry lessons to Palmeiro, whom he had known since their days playing high school ball in Miami, along with two of the team's most promising young hitters. With his three alleged pupils leading the way, the Rangers would bash more home runs than any other team in baseball the following season. "Before long," Canseco later wrote, "other players from all over the baseball world saw what was going on with me and my buddies from Texas."

Who knows what Bush observed in his frequent trips to the locker room? But anyone could see that the Rangers were a team transformed. They kept hitting long after Canseco had moved on, fielding a potent power-hitting lineup, a perennial playoff contender that always filled its handsome new stadium, the Ballpark in Arlington. The Rangers became one of the most profitable teams in baseball. In 1998, at the height of the team's on-field success, Bush's ownership group would sell the franchise for $250 million. With various bonuses figured in, Bush would receive around $15 million, a 2,500 percent return on his initial investment.

By that time, though, Governor Bush was playing in a bigger league.

THE GOVERNOR'S OFFICE, in the red granite State Capitol building in Austin, was a shrine to Bush's career as a baseball man. Its centerpiece was his personal collection of two hundred balls autographed by the game's greats. He also displayed a bat signed by Mark McGwire, wishing Bush good luck in 2000. On the trail, baseball was Bush's conversational lodestar—he used it as a way to connect, man-to-man, with other politicians, donors, and reporters. When Tucker Carlson asked who his greatest hero was, he replied, "Nolan Ryan." No one was ever going to accuse Dubya of being a wimp.

People did think he was stupid, but that was fine with him. "I have always been underestimated," Bush told a reporter. "You can understand why. People say, well, he's Daddy's boy and has never done anything of accomplishment. But that's good. I'd rather be underestimated than overestimated." No one had underestimated his daddy's brain, and look at what had happened to him—turned out of office by the fickle voters who swooned for a southern governor who said he felt their pain. Dubya was the rare politician who went out of his way to emphasize what he didn't know. "Nobody needs to tell me what I believe," he said on the trail. "But I do need somebody to tell me where Kosovo is." Al Gore knew where Kosovo was. It wasn't helping.

Bush had taken Gore's measure and knew how to fit him for a coffin. After all, he had been there back in 1988, in that office with Atwater, and he understood how hard it was for a vice president to display his own identity, to show his self-possession. "I know who I am and he doesn't know who he is," Bush told a friendly columnist from the *Texas Monthly*. He dismissed Gore as a fake. "The man dyes his hair," Bush would say. His message in 2000 would be that Gore was a politician without principles, a man who would say anything, do anything, to win.

Bush was better at deflecting attention from his ambition. He drew on an arsenal of self-deprecating jokes and anecdotes. There was the story he told about his tough-minded mother's reaction when he told her he was planning to run for governor against a folksy Democratic incumbent, Ann Richards. "George," she reputedly said, "you can't win." But he did win.

As governor, Bush was popular across party lines. He pressed for education reforms and cut property taxes. He championed "faith based" initiatives as a replacement for welfare programs, which appealed to evangelical Christians. He spoke out against racism and held a moderate view on immigration, declaring that "family values don't stop at the Rio Grande." (He also sent more than one hundred fifty convicts to the death chamber, but Texans liked that.) To describe his political philosophy, he adopted a phrase coined by one of his advisers: "compassionate conservatism."

Bill Clinton had perfected the defensive strategy of "triangulation," taking conservative ideas like overhauling welfare, scaling back "Big Government," and cracking down on crime and refashioning them into a form that was smaller and marginally more progressive. Bush was trying to take the same approach, but from the right. Speaking at a fund-raising event in 2000, Clinton would deftly sum up Bush's appeal: "'How bad can I be? I've been governor of Texas. My daddy was president. I've owned a baseball team. They like me down there,'" Clinton said. "'Everything is rocking along hunky-dory. Their fraternity had it for eight years, give it to ours for eight years.'"

It had become a cliché to say that politics was now just a game, a low-stakes competition between two parties that differed on little of substance. Pundits were calling this the "*Seinfeld* election"—a campaign about nothing. "I'm coming to learn," comedian Jon Stewart, host of the newly popular fake newscast *The Daily Show*, said that year, "that entertainment, politics, and the media are really juggling the same balls." This worked to Bush's advantage, leaving him free to campaign on his values, temperament, and character. He and Gore had similar biographies: they were both Baby Boomers, Ivy Leaguers, and sons of prominent politicians. But they had diametrically opposed personal styles: Gore was distant and cerebral; Bush, wry and physical.

This version of George W. Bush could disarm anyone. He would stride down the aisle of his campaign plane, razzing the traveling press, bestowing winks and nicknames, sometimes touching the guys he liked with masculine familiarity. A magazine writer would describe his method: "Bush brought both of his hands up to my cheeks and pinched them between his fingers, gently shaking my head forward and back. 'I just wanna head-butt you,' he said affectionately."

With women, Bush kept a respectful distance. One journalist described him as "the second-handsomest man" in most rooms. He was good-looking, with wiry graying hair, a cleft chin, and rugged lines in his forehead, but he was not sexy. He promised to restore "dignity and honor" to the Oval Office, by which he meant: *no blow jobs.* He was deliberately banal. When asked what he wanted written on his tombstone, he replied, "He came, he said, he accomplished."

Dubya shared his father's name and bushy-browed squint, but he was doing his best to dispel any suggestion of a resemblance. Everyone said he took after his mother, Barbara Bush, the family's fierce matriarch. He shunned veterans of the old Bush political organization. ("I'm not interested in the people who lost my dad's election," he reportedly explained.) He took care not to repeat the mistakes made in 1992, when he had been busy running the Rangers. Poppy, as Bush Sr. was now known in retirement, had infamously admitted in a debate that he did not know the cost of a gallon of milk. For every stop in this campaign, Dubya made sure his aides gave him a briefing book containing the local cost of milk, gas, and other necessities. He often deployed his mother as a surrogate, but he rarely used his father, who said he was proudly watching from the stands.

"I'm amazed—still amazed—at the way he's done," Poppy told the *New York Times.*

Poppy was more involved than he would admit. He played a headmaster's role when it came to schooling his boy—he was still apt to slip up and call him that—in the delicate art of foreign policy. The elder Bush might have had more experience in the realms of diplomacy and intelligence than anyone in the world. He had served as director of the CIA during the 1970s. He knew the secrets.

Long before Dubya decided to run for president, Poppy started arranging for his geopolitical education. He sent his good friend Prince Bandar bin Sultan, the Saudi ambassador, down to Texas to offer Dubya some lessons in realpolitik. ("In the big boys' game, it is cutthroat," Bandar reputedly told him. "It's bloody and it's not pleasant.") As his campaign took shape, Dubya would discuss world events with a group of foreign policy specialists from the first Bush administration, including Condoleezza Rice, who would become a campaign adviser. On military issues, he relied on his father's defense secretary, Dick Cheney, and on Cheney's former deputy, Paul Wolfowitz.

Still, Dubya was who he was. One day, in the midst of the New Hampshire primary season, he gave an interview to a local TV news reporter who surprised him with a pop quiz, asking him to identify world leaders.

"Can you name the general who is in charge of Pakistan?" the reporter asked.

"The new Pakistani general, he's just been elected—not elected, this guy took over office," Bush replied. "It appears this guy is going to bring stability to the country and I think that's good news for the subcontinent."

"Can you name him?"

"General," Bush replied. "I can't name the general. General."

The answer was "Pervez Musharraf." But come on! Who cared about the guy who ran Pakistan?

6

The Magic City

One Sunday in 2000, readers of the *New York Times* awoke to a front-page article headlined "TELEVISION'S NEW VOYEURISM PICTURES REAL-LIFE INTIMACY." It described a curious experiment in programming. Along with their usual dramas and comedies, TV networks were developing a new formula, placing regular people in extreme scenarios. "The shows range from examinations of people trying to survive on a desert island to people trying to get along while locked together in various settings of forced intimacy," the *Times* reported. Instead of depending on scripts and actors, "reality" shows could turn anyone's life into popular entertainment.

TV critics could cite precursors, including the long-running MTV series *The Real World*. But to see an even more powerful proof of concept, the network programmers needed only to flip the channel to CNN, or MSNBC, or Fox News, or Univision, or Telemundo—all of which were broadcasting something very similar from Miami: the Elián Show. The street outside the Gonzalez family's bungalow in Little Havana had come to resemble a twenty-four-hour carnival. A flotilla of TV trucks was lined up, motors thrumming, flying thirty-foot satellite masts. The reporters and cameramen on the stakeout called it "Camp Elián." They spent their days idling in folding chairs, keeping an eye on the yard, waiting for Elián to come out and play on the swing set or splash in a baby pool.

The viewers at home soon got to know all the characters in the Gonzalez household. His macho uncle Lázaro would sometimes parade in front of the cameras with Elián on his shoulders. Emotional Marisleysis took on the role of surrogate mother to Elián, speaking for him on TV, at press conferences, and even before a Senate hearing. One day, a newspaper writer found Uncle Delfín, a former political prisoner, sitting in a director's chair at Camp Elián, flipping through a magazine article about the child. "He's just a kid," Delfín said. "He doesn't know he is famous."

Later in the year, the cultural critic Frank Rich, in a *New York Times Magazine* essay, would describe the Gonzalez case as a prime example of a "new genre" of entertainment: "a relentless hybrid of media circus, soap opera and tabloid journalism." One study found that, in terms of the volume of television coverage, the Gonzalez case was the second-biggest celebrity story of the prior decade, behind only the O.J. Simpson murder trial. (O.J. himself, who had recently relocated to Miami, was unimpressed: "How many O.J. stories could there be?" he asked Rich.)

The show's self-appointed producer was a portly, white-haired political consultant named Armando Gutierrez. He was locally renowned, the *Herald* reported, for his "hardball tactics" and his mastery of "the dark campaign art of digging up damaging information" on opponents. But he claimed his heart was touched by Elián's rescue. He had knocked on the Gonzalez family's door soon afterward to offer his services and had since installed himself inside the house as the family's press agent, strategist, and liaison to the Cuban exile community. Its leaders immediately saw in Elián a potent public relations weapon. The previously anonymous Gonzalez family suddenly began issuing press releases attacking "the monster that tyrannizes the Cuban fatherland" and unveiled a website full of adorable photos, www.libertyforelian.com.

To the Cubans of Miami, Elián was a miracle child. A mural appeared on the family's street depicting his inner tube surrounded by leaping dolphins and bathed in celestial light. Miami's popular Spanish-language radio personalities held the boy up as a hero—maybe even a messiah. "He is surrounded by a divine halo," said a host on Radio Mambí, the most influential station.

Elián adjusted quickly to his place at the center of extraordinary attention. He would wave and call out to the cameramen through the yard's chain-link fence. Strangers would occasionally wander by with their kids, seeking a celebrity playdate. A Miami congresswoman brought Elián a bike. A congressman brought him a puppy, a black Labrador retriever named Dolphin. Illusionist David Copperfield showed him magic tricks. Senator Bob Smith, a Republican from New Hampshire, paid a call on the house and claimed that Elián had pleaded for his political help.

"Elián said to me, 'Ayudame, Señor Smith,'" the senator told the cameras.

The Justice Department, which oversaw the immigration service, was moving cautiously. The family dispute could harm the Clinton administration's efforts to improve diplomatic relations with Cuba. Florida's status as a potential swing state in the presidential election was never far from anyone's mind—especially Clinton's. In an internal email, a Justice Department official wrote that the decision-making process was being directed from "the highest levels."

The fate of the little lost Cuban boy would be determined by the attorney general herself.

JANET RENO'S FIRST exposure to the legal system came through her father. She grew up watching Henry Reno working the police beat for the *Miami Herald*, making phone calls in his underwear in the morning, collecting news of the previous night's crimes and arrests. He sometimes took little Janny to court. She would sit beside him as he covered trials. She was intrigued by the workings of justice and also took note of its accepted inequities—the way judges would punish white and Black defendants differently for similar offenses. Janny also noticed that, with few exceptions, all the lawyers in the courtrooms were male. She would be one of only sixteen women in her class of more than five hundred students at Harvard Law School. In all she did, Reno was always among the first. When she returned home to Miami in 1963, she would discover that some prominent law firms would not even consider hiring a woman, no matter what her qualifications.

Though, at times, there were men in her life, Reno never married. She lived with her mother in the house near the Everglades. She became close to a young liberal attorney with political aspirations and managed his successful campaign for the state legislature. They started a small law firm together. Reno later left it to work as a legislative aide at the State Capitol in Tallahassee. Although the Renos were Yellow Dog Democrats who had opposed segregation and Jim Crow, Jane disapproved of her daughter's turn to politics. She warned Janny about "getting bogged down in her foolery." But Janny was not easy to discourage.

In 1972, Reno ran for the state legislature and lost narrowly. Afterward, the elected state attorney for Dade County, which surrounds Miami, offered her a job. Reno would always say she was reluctant to become a prosecutor. She thought they were less concerned with justice than with jailing people. But she took the position and discovered she could do good: shaping lives, saving lives. One of her first tasks involved setting up a new juvenile court system. She became a champion of vulnerable children. When the state attorney unexpectedly announced he was resigning, the governor appointed Reno to serve out his term. She was the first female state attorney in Florida's history. "Whoever you are," Reno said at her swearing-in ceremony, "whatever color you are, whatever language you speak, I want you to feel at home here."

Reno served through a violent period in Miami's history. In the late 1970s, Colombian drug cartels started using the city as a transshipment point. Gangs fought machine-gun battles at shopping malls, and the county medical examiner rented a refrigerated truck from Burger King to accommodate all the corpses. Miami's public offices, including the police department, were rotten with corruption. Reno assembled a team of honest young prosecutors, many of them women, and drove them hard, tracking the progress of their cases in a small black notebook. In the office, Reno struck fear into her subordinates with her towering presence and cutting glare. At night, she would drive back to her mother's house in her green Ford Mustang.

Reno's tenure—and Miami's history—was shaped by a pair of convulsive events that occurred in 1980. That May, a group of Miami police officers who had beaten a Black motorcyclist to death were acquitted of his murder. The city was consumed by four days of race riots. White motorists were stopped and attacked by mobs. One man was burned to death in his car. Altogether, eighteen people were killed. The sky glowed orange at night. Although Reno's office had brought the case against the police officers, she was blamed for the acquittal and the unrest. In the streets, rioters chanted, *Reno! Reno! Reno!*

National Guard troops surrounded the Justice Building in downtown Miami, where Reno watched the smoke rise over the city from her sixth-floor office window. Some Black community leaders came to her office and advised her that the only way to quell the riot would be for her to resign. She refused. The Reverend Jesse Jackson flew down to lead a protest, calling Reno a "symbol of oppression to all of us." But Reno was nothing if not stubborn. After the riots were over, she visited Black neighborhoods, talking to people on street corners and in churches, and listening. She refused to accept police protection. She promised to learn from her mistakes.

Reno's outreach earned grudging respect, and she won reelection that fall. What really ended up converting her critics, though, were the actions she took in the following years: hiring Black prosecutors, setting up "drug courts" to redirect addicts facing jail for nonviolent offenses to treatment, and aiding single mothers by pursuing deadbeat dads for child support. This last policy inspired rapper Luke Campbell, of the ultra-filthy Miami hip-hop group 2 Live Crew, to write a song about her. In her deep Old Florida drawl, Reno would sometimes sing the chorus: *Janet Reno gonna getcha, gonna getcha . . .*

The riots were an indelible horror. But it was the second historic event of 1980 that forever altered Miami's political culture. That year, Fidel Castro opened the Port of Mariel and allowed some 125,000 Cubans to set sail for Florida. Miami already had a substantial Cuban community, but the Mariel Boatlift fundamentally upended the city's demographics and power structure. The city's "Anglos," non-Hispanic whites like the Renos, became a small minority of the population. A rising generation of Cuban American politicians took charge. They worshipped Ronald Reagan and competed to outdo one another in their opposition to Castro.

The Miami of the 1980s, Joan Didion wrote, resembled "a Latin capital, a year or two away from a new government." The city was teeming with two-bit paramilitaries and embittered veterans of the

CIA-sponsored Bay of Pigs Invasion, who expressed roughly equal amounts of hatred for Castro and the treacherous Kennedys. (It seemed no coincidence, Didion wrote, that Miami was the hub of conspiracy theories about the JFK assassination, the Watergate break-in, and the Iran-Contra scandal.) By 2000, however, the revolutionary passions had waned. Brigade 2506, a Bay of Pigs veterans group once dedicated to overthrowing Fidel, now functioned more like a local chamber of commerce. The militants had aged into graying, big-bellied insiders.

Meanwhile, Fidel, who had survived the Bay of Pigs, a crippling economic embargo, countless assassination attempts, and the fall of the Soviet Union, was now elderly. His regime had calcified. The fires of conflict that sustained both sides were burning low.

Then Elián arrived, followed by TV cameras.

RENO THOUGHT SHE understood Miami. She had been raised there, had won elections there. She knew its folkways and had a strong relationship with the city's Cuban community. Even though she had been off in Washington for years, she felt that perhaps she alone could resolve the mess at home. As attorney general, Reno was responsible for a vast law enforcement bureaucracy, with awesome powers and responsibilities that spanned the entire legal system. But she would make the Elián case her single-minded focus.

Reno knew the outcome the law dictated. Juan Miguel Gonzalez wanted to be reunited with his son, and in early 2000, the Immigration and Naturalization Service announced that it would respect his wishes. "He has a father," Reno said of Elián. "And there is a bond between a father and son that the law recognizes and tries to honor."

The response was ferocious. Disruptive protests broke out all over Miami. The demonstrations were coordinated from the Little Havana headquarters of Brigade 2506 and cheered on by Radio Mambí. "What we want is to paralyze the legal process," said one protest leader. "We hope we don't have to get to the point of paralyzing the city, but we have that ability."

The Gonzalez family could not change the law, but they could slow its implementation. Exile organizations assembled a legal team to represent the family and sued to overturn the INS decision in federal court. Elián applied for asylum in the United States, with the boy signing the legal document himself, in childish capital letters. To Juan Miguel, and most Americans, it seemed absurd to suggest that a six-year-old might be permitted to decide for himself where he wanted to live. But the Miami family's lawyers argued that returning him to Cuba would be immoral.

The protests calmed down as the case settled into a legal stalemate. The Gonzalez family invited the press into their kitchen, now cluttered with boxes of legal paperwork. An Associated Press photographer rode to school with Elián for his first day of kindergarten. Diane Sawyer, cohost of the ABC morning show *Good Morning America*, came to the school to interview Elián. They played on the floor, and he drew her a crayon picture of himself floating on his inner tube.

One day, in their routine surveillance of Elián's outdoor playtime, news cameras caught some breaking news. As a plane flew overhead, the boy appeared to shout, in Spanish, "I want you to take me back to Cuba!" A linguistic controversy broke out, as analysts dissected Elián's grammar to determine what, precisely, he had said and whether he'd really meant it.

That evening, Juan Miguel appeared via satellite on the ABC program *Nightline*.

"It has been suggested," guest host Chris Wallace said, "that the reason you do not come to Miami is because the Cuban government is afraid that once you get to Miami, you will defect."

"Who said that? Who said that?" Juan Miguel retorted. "I think I have been extremely clear. . . . Sometimes what I would like to do is go down there with a rifle—I don't know—to get rid of how many people."

"Are you serious about that, sir? It's obviously a very inflammatory remark."

"And what about it isn't inflammatory, what they are doing to my son!"

In Havana, Fidel was organizing an emotionally powerful response. Elián's two grandmothers led a one-hundred-thousand-strong "March of the Mothers" outside the U.S. diplomatic mission. The boy's maternal grandmother, already mourning her drowned daughter, said she didn't want to lose Elián, too. "What I want is to go and get him," she declared. "Just give me a date and time."

The proposal sounded like a breakthrough. The Clinton administration hastily arranged for a visit, and a few days later, Juan Miguel saw the pair of *abuelas* off at the airport as they boarded a chartered jet and flew to the United States to meet with Reno in Washington. Against all odds, the Elián Show appeared to be headed for a heartwarming finale: a grandmother summit.

RENO SPENT EIGHT years as attorney general and never got used to Washington. She had no time for its ostentation, intrigues, and petty vanities. She lived alone, in a furnished apartment in a building that specialized in short-term rentals, and paid little attention to cultivating social relationships. Most days, she walked two blocks to work at the headquarters building known as Main Justice and stayed at her desk late into the evening. She approached her job with a solemnity that bordered on corniness. Sometimes, when her day was done, Reno would tell her security detail she wanted to take a quiet nighttime stroll around the memorials of the National Mall. She'd wear a hat in the hope of going unnoticed, though it usually didn't work.

With the exception of Hillary Clinton, Reno was probably the most recognizable woman in Washington. This was partly a matter of her height and appearance. She kept her hair chopped sensibly and bought her dresses, formless and usually blue, off the rack at department stores. In popular culture, she was endlessly satirized as gawky, weird, and crotchety. On *Saturday Night Live*, the co-median Will Ferrell dressed in drag for a regular bit called "Janet Reno's Dance Party," in which he played the attorney general as a harsh, herky-jerky Amazon. The right-wingers, dispensing sub-tlety, just called her a lesbian. On the streets of Miami, one Elián protester's sign read, "Janet Reno Is a Man."

To her chagrin, Reno was compelled to address her sexuality in campaigns and even her Senate confirmation hearing, where she described herself, wearily, as "an old maid who prefers men." She had no interest in discussing her inner life, but society insisted that she be categorized. "At a certain point," the *Washington Post*'s Liza Mundy wrote in a 1998 profile, "the images of Janet Reno these days cross over the predictable borders of political partisanship and even the ordinary borders of American heartland paranoia, and slip into someplace else entirely—the realm of intense cultural anx-iety about women in power. There is something about her, rocklike and unbleached, that simultaneously fascinates and confounds and even terrifies the popular imagination."

Reno had not been Bill Clinton's first, or even second, choice for attorney general. He had offered her the post back in 1993 only after his first two picks, both women, were knocked out of contention by minor scandals involving nannies who were illegal immigrants. Reno was conveniently childless, but she had turned out to be endlessly confounding to Clinton. One of those closest to him reportedly referred to her as "the Martian." In Clinton's view, his attorney general was too willing to delegate political investigations to independent counsels who poked into every corner of his administration. The most maddeningly persistent of these prosecutors was Kenneth Starr, who was originally appointed to look into Clinton's real estate dealings in Arkansas, but soon ran rampant. Clinton watched as Starr sent his friends to prison, subpoenaed his wife, collected his DNA, revealed his affair, and ultimately recommended his impeachment.

Clinton was enraged, and it was no secret that he would have liked to have gotten rid of his troublesome attorney general. But the president didn't dare to fire Reno, for fear of political blowback, and she would never resign. So, Clinton was stuck with her as long as she wanted to keep the job.

And she loved the job. Reno spent her days in the wood-paneled office suite once occupied by Robert F. Kennedy, one of her heroes. RFK's tousle-haired portrait hung above a fireplace where, according to lore, he'd roasted hot dogs with his kids. (The suite also had a hideaway apartment, up a staircase, known as the "Marilyn Monroe bedroom.") Reno complemented the grandeur with a memento from Florida, a framed needlepoint of a quote from Adlai Stevenson: "The burdens of the office stagger the imagination and convert vanity to prayer."

Some White House advisers considered Reno a liberal obstacle to their efforts to position Clinton as tough on crime. They dismissed her as a "social worker." She didn't like the label, but it was true she favored addressing the root causes of social ills and talked about using the law to protect the weak and endangered, rather than simply prosecuting and incarcerating criminals.

Reno had a particular interest in the rights and well-being of children. Although she had none herself, she had exceptionally maternal relationships with her many nieces and nephews and with the offspring of several of the women who had worked for her in the prosecutor's office in Miami. In the years before Reno went to Washington, she often took the kids on outings into the Everglades or had them over to play hide-and-seek in her mother's overgrown yard. At night, she might tell them pirate stories. In her office at Main Justice, Reno kept a box of toys under her desk for occasions when families came in. She enjoyed reading to school groups, often from a favorite picture book, *Voyage to the Bunny Planet*, a story of a magical world where "children who had lost their way" could change what had gone wrong. It began:

> *Far beyond the moon and stars*
> *Twenty light-years south of Mars*
> *Spins the gentle Bunny Planet*
> *And the Bunny Queen is Janet.*

As is often true in politics, it was Reno's admirable qualities, as much as her weaknesses, that led her into trouble. Her sensitivity to interference could make her impenetrable to outside advice. She would agonize over hard decisions, refusing to be rushed—to the frustration of allies. She was a micromanager who was always handing subordinates small tasks she called "get backs," which were often problems affecting individuals with touching stories. Her insistence on "doing the right thing"—a refrain she repeated so often that it became the title of a biography—led to paralysis in situations where there was no obvious right thing to do, as in the case of Elián Gonzalez.

Many of Reno's old friends in Miami were advising her to stay out of the dispute. The attorney general's personal involvement would only escalate the case, emboldening the anti-Castro hardliners. But Reno plunged into the swamp, and no matter how lost she seemed, she insisted she could find a way out. "The things that went on behind the scenes were incredible," says one of these allies of Reno's, ruefully. "And every step she took was a mistake."

On a Saturday afternoon, Reno welcomed Elián's grandmothers into her office at Main Justice with double cheek kisses. They sat down to discuss the boy's custody in her high-ceilinged, ceremonial conference room, which was decorated with New Deal–era figurative paintings depicting *Justice Triumphant* and *Justice Defeated.* The women handed Reno a plaintive letter asking her to "return Elián to the normality of life with his father, [half] brother, family, friends at school, his toys, dog and parrot." Through a young Cuban American aide, who served as interpreter, Reno tried to explain that the matter was tied up in court. But the grandmothers couldn't understand. In Cuba, when the man in charge wanted something to happen, it happened.

The grandmothers begged Reno to return Elián that weekend. They cried. They wailed. They stayed two hours. Then they did a television interview on MSNBC.

RENO WAS SO moved by the grandmothers' appeal that she ordered the Justice Department to arrange for them to visit Elián. But Lázaro Gonzalez refused to bring him to Washington. "They flew to Washington to meet with politicians and bureaucrats when the person they love is here with the family that was waiting for them,"

Armando Gutierrez told the *Herald*. The grandmothers had sworn they would never set foot in Miami, the den of Castro's despised "Mafia." But after negotiations, they agreed to visit, so long as the meeting was held at a neutral venue.

That Monday, the grandmothers appeared on *Today* in the morning and then flew down to Miami. They arrived to discover that Lázaro was insisting on a new plan: a family dinner at his house. A feast of Cuban pork and rice and beans was ordered from a local restaurant. An activist leader brought a huge batch of red, white, and peach carnations, intending to carpet the street out front with flowers as a gesture of peace. A large crowd gathered at Camp Elián, chanting, *Abuelitas, welcome!* Elián came home from kindergarten and learned that his grandmothers were coming. As the family spruced up the house for a party, he put on a video, *Home Alone 3*.

Elián waited and waited, but his grandmothers didn't arrive. They were holed up at the airport terminal, watching televised images of a mob scene outside the Gonzalez house. They feared they might be in physical danger there. After a series of angry phone calls, the grandmothers decided to leave without seeing Elián. Lázaro raced to the airport, with Gutierrez narrating to a TV station as they drove, only to find their plane already taxiing to the runway. The grandmothers flew back to Washington.

The next day, CBS announced it was developing a miniseries about Elián.

Reno tried again. She contacted an old family friend, Sister Jeanne O'Laughlin, the president of a Catholic university in Miami. If reason had failed to sway the family, Reno thought, maybe religion could work. The Gonzalez family was devout; they had a priest who came to the house regularly to say Mass. Sister Jeanne agreed to host a mediation session at her residence in Miami Beach.

The grandmothers flew down again. The local news channels broke into their regular daytime programming to broadcast the summit live. Lázaro and Elián arrived in a motorcade, trailed by a carful of attorneys and the head of the Cuban American National Foundation, a lobbying group. To the grandmothers' alarm, a flag-waving throng awaited them outside the nun's house.

All sorts of sinister rumors were circulating around Little Havana. Some said that Cuban intelligence agents would be waiting inside the nun's house to snatch the boy. Others said that Fidel, under the sway of the black magic of Santería, planned to make the boy a human sacrifice. Sister Jeanne offered Lázaro a tour to assuage his fears, showing him that there were no secret agents hiding behind any trapdoors. The two sides of the family were to be kept separate inside the thirteen-room residence. Sister Jeanne introduced another nun, a Cuban, who would act as interpreter. Lázaro gave Sister Jeanne a note to pass on to the grandmothers, and the nuns took Elián upstairs.

The grandmothers were waiting in a soothing room overlooking Indian Creek. They kissed Elián and showed him an album of pictures of his family, pets, classmates in Cárdenas, and the empty desk waiting for his return. But Elián paid more attention to the food and toys the nuns kept bringing. He was cold, standoffish—not the same grandchild he'd been two months before.

"Well," Elián informed them, "they're going to make a movie about me here."

Three times, the nuns suggested that the grandmothers join Lázaro's family for dinner, but they rejected the idea of reconciliation. At one point during the visit, by prearrangement, Juan Miguel called his mother on her cell phone. He wanted to talk to Elián outside the presence of his Miami relatives, who were reportedly taping his calls for legal purposes. But the nuns confiscated the phone, saying the call violated the ground rules for the reunion. Elián was ushered out.

The grandmothers sobbed. Sister Jeanne was somber. There was no breakthrough.

As the family arrived back at the house in Little Havana, Elián and Lázaro held up their arms and flashed the V sign to signify victory. "I feel confident," Marisleysis told the cameras. "Now I feel that he is more on this side than on that side."

Elián called in to Radio Mambí. "Tomorrow, they're going to make me an American citizen," he said. The next day, Marisleysis flew to Washington on a private jet to lobby Congress to pass a Republican bill to grant the boy citizenship. The grandmothers also appeared on Capitol Hill. "My grandson is different," one said. "He must be saved—urgently." The grandmothers flew home to Havana, where Juan Miguel joined them on a sixteen-mile parade in an open-topped convertible from the airport to a tearful audience with Fidel. A delegation of seventeen hundred schoolchildren greeted them with chants of *Free Elián!*

Meanwhile, Sister Jeanne—the supposedly neutral mediator—announced that she was convinced that Elián should stay in America. She visited Reno at Main Justice to make her argument. After brief observation, Sister Jeanne had decided that Elián had experienced "the mystery of bonding" with Marisleysis. She was troubled, she wrote in a *New York Times* opinion piece, by what she described as the grandmothers' "trembling, furtive looks, ice-cold hands." She thought they were terrified of their handlers from the Cuban embassy and maybe even wanted to defect.

"I saw fear in Elián," the nun wrote. "I became a wiser woman at that moment, wincing at my own naivete. I considered what it would mean for this boy suddenly to be ripped away from his surrogate mother, how this second trauma might scar him permanently."

Later, Sister Jeanne disclosed another startling detail. In the stress of the meeting, she had forgotten to pass along the note Lázaro had written to the grandmothers. She found it in her pocket afterward and opened it. "I was shocked by what it said," she told the *Herald*. "The great uncle believed Castro would make a witchcraft sacrifice of Elián."

There was no hope for a reasonable compromise; it seemed that Miami was deranged by love and hate. One day, in the crowd outside the Gonzalez house, a new sign appeared: ELIÁN IS CHRIST. RENO IS LUCIFER. CASTRO IS SATAN.

7

For the People

Sometime in early 2000, I had my first conversation with Donald Trump. I had just started a new job, covering real estate and politics for a weekly newspaper called the *New York Observer*. For my very first story, I decided to write an article about the Trump World Tower, a seventy-two-story residential skyscraper that the developer was building next to the United Nations headquarters, with financial backing from Deutsche Bank. The tower had incited a lawsuit from a group of neighboring apartment owners, including Walter Cronkite. I called up Trump. In those days, any reporter, even a kid no one had ever heard of, could get him immediately. He went on the attack, of course, calling his opponents "a few wealthy people who have lost their views," and describing the most vocal of them, a dot-com financier, as a nobody.

After my first article was published, my editor congratulated me and gave me a rule for the future: "Anyone but Trump." No one wanted to read about him. Donald Trump was a joke.

This was four years before *The Apprentice* premiered, six years before Twitter was invented, sixteen years before Trump devoured everyone's minds. In 2000, he was a diminished creature, an irrelevant relic of the 1980s. He was rich, but not as rich as he'd once been, and nowhere near as rich as he claimed. During the 1990s, he had lost many of his trophies: the Plaza Hotel, the Trump Shuttle airline, the Trump *Princess* superyacht, Ivana and Marla. Trump had managed to restore his finances through some clever sleight of hand, taking his casino company public and shifting its enormous debts to shareholders, and he was once again building and naming things after himself in New York. But other developers dismissed him as a phony. They told me he didn't own anything, only fronted for other investors. They said, derisively, that Trump was just a brand name.

That brand lived on free publicity, and Trump wasn't too proud to beg for it. So, when he first floated the idea that he might run for president in 2000, no one took it seriously. The campaign was launched, appropriately, with a story in the *National Enquirer*, the Florida-based supermarket tabloid that had recently been taken over by a Trump buddy, publishing executive David Pecker. "GET READY FOR PRESIDENT TRUMP?" read the headline on a story that reported the "stunning result" of an *Enquirer* poll that put Trump in second place, with 37 percent, 2 points behind Bush and well ahead of Gore. The poll's sample size was just one hundred people.

Rumor had it that Roger Stone, the roguish political operative, was angling to run Trump for the nomination of the Reform Party. It was the third option on the ballot in that year's election, an organization cobbled together from the remnants of the populist movement led by Ross Perot, the eccentric Texas billionaire who had run as an independent in the two previous presidential elections. Perot had done well enough in 1992 and 1996 that the party, previously his personal vehicle, would start 2000 as a reasonably solid alternative to the two major parties. It would be eligible to receive $12 million in public financing under federal campaign laws, which was considered a lot of money back then. Perot said he wasn't interested in running again, though, which meant that the Reform Party was looking for a new leader.

In the summer of 1999, Stone had turned up at a big Reform Party gathering in Michigan, where volunteers handed out copies of the *Enquirer* article and plastered the venue with "Trump 2000" posters. "Everywhere you look," a reporter covering the event wrote, "you see The Donald's albino-caterpillar eyebrows and the hair that looks like an abandoned nest." Cynics said it was just another one of Trump's desperate plays for attention and speculated about Stone's motives. Was he just looking to dip into that $12 million honeypot of federal campaign funding? Was he on a sabotage mission from Bush, who blamed Perot's third-party candidacy for his father's defeat in 1992?

"The idea that I would torpedo the Reform Party because of its danger to the Republican Party? Just not so," Stone told me when we met for lunch in Fort Lauderdale in 2019, as he awaited trial on charges related to Russian interference in the 2016 election. "I really wanted Trump to run. I thought it would be an epically interesting campaign."

Trump and Stone had a long and twisted relationship. They had first gotten to know each other back in 1980, when Stone was running Ronald Reagan's campaign in New York and living at the apartment of Roy Cohn, Trump's attorney and life coach. Over the years, Stone advised Trump as a consultant, lobbying for his casinos and doing personal errands, like securing approvals for a dredging project that allowed him to park the Trump *Princess* at a New Jersey marina. At the time, Stone had one of the most powerful political consulting firms in Washington, where his partners included Lee Atwater and Paul Manafort. Even then, Stone was an outlandish character, a self-glorifying dandy known for his custom-tailored pinstripe suits, his bright yellow hair, his flexible morals, his fondness for dirty tricks, and his willingness to take credit for his opponents' misfortune. "If it rains," he liked to say, "it was Stone."

By the 1990s, though, Stone was marginalized. He had been banished from mainstream Republican politics after, ironically enough, the *National Enquirer* revealed that he and his wife were swingers. Trump was one of the few clients willing to be publicly associated with him after the sex scandal. He liked that Stone was a practitioner of the dark arts. At the same time as he was running the Trump 2000 campaign, for example, Stone was also helping Trump mount a sneak attack against a Native American tribe that was trying to open a New York casino that would encroach on his Atlantic City business. Through a front group called the Institute for Law and Society, Stone took out ads that accused the tribe of having ties to organized crime and drug dealing. (One ad featured a picture of a hypodermic needle.) After the subterfuge was exposed, Trump was forced to pay a rare fine and make an even rarer apology to Native Americans.

Trump and Stone were not friends. Another former Trump consultant recalls that the developer would ridicule Stone's foppish pretensions, calling him "butt boy." But they were a codependent pair. Stone was the brain; Trump had the name. Stone had great hopes for Trump's third-party candidacy.

"In many ways, the 2000 campaign has been airbrushed out of history," Stone says. But it happened. Trump hired a staff. He took campaign trips. He published a book entitled *The America We Deserve.*

"He always had this overarching belief that our leaders are stupid," Stone says. "That we're being taken to the cleaners by all of our trading partners, we're being abused in our foreign policy." Stone recognized, earlier than anyone, that this was a product Donald Trump could sell.

"OUR WAY OF life is ending—the American way of life is ending," Chuck Harder lamented to his listeners one afternoon around this time. "The Democrats under Bill Clinton took your jobs away, and your future . . . We, as a rule, are a trusting people, we are a good people, we have a good heart. But we have become 'sheeple.' We simply do as we are told by the media. Our children now have rings through their noses, studs in their tongues, all kinds of things hanging off their body that's pierced one way or another. They look like some kind of folks from another planet, because the media tells them to do that. We have become creatures of the tube."

Chuck Harder was a creature of the airwaves, with a voice made for radio and a broken body. He was a rotund, bearded grump who sometimes introduced himself as a "beach ball with legs." Since the summer of 1999, he had been mostly confined to a wheelchair, after a terrible slip and fall that dislocated his kneecaps, which had healed wrong. From his home studio overlooking the sluggish Suwannee River, he would sit with a rescued stray cat named Ghosty on his lap, delivering pained monologues about "soup line medicine" and profiteering health care executives.

Harder endlessly lamented the demise of American greatness. In his telling, his life story traced the nation's trajectory. He grew up in Northern Illinois, where his father owned a factory, and was raised in a big house near a country club. He started out as a disc jockey on rock stations as a teenager in the late 1950s and later got into film and television production. In 1968, George Wallace, the segregationist Alabama governor, hired him to shoot TV commercials for his presidential campaign. Harder followed Wallace around on the trail, listening intently.

Harder moved to Florida, got divorced, went broke, slept in his car for a while. In 1987, he began broadcasting his show, *For the People*, out of his garage in Tampa. He started out as a consumer advocate, lending an ear to scam victims and crusading against corporations. He was enthralled when Ross Perot mounted his first presidential campaign in 1992. The folksy businessman was an ornery coot best known for promoting a conspiracy theory about prisoners of war supposedly being held secretly in Vietnam. He ran on a message of budget austerity, political reform, and throw-the-bums-out anger and won 19 percent of the vote, the best performance by an independent candidate in eighty years.

"Naturally, the elite media barbecued both Wallace and Perot, pinning every negative name on them possible," Harder later wrote. "Outsiders are not welcome in politics."

Bill Clinton's election marked the beginning of talk radio's heyday. Harder was part of what you might call the anti-Clinton resistance. For three hours every afternoon, he offered scorching commentary, developing a following of devoted listeners who believed that only he was telling the awful truth. *For the People* aired on hundreds of stations around the country, mainly in the heartland states. "He is the king of grassroots airwaves," Morris Dees, the founder of the Southern Poverty Law Center, wrote in 1996, at a time when Harder's reach was second only to that of conservative powerhouse Rush Limbaugh.

Harder declined opportunities to take his show to corporate radio networks, choosing to remain in White Springs, a nineteenth-century spa resort town that by then had all but been abandoned. He ran his own nonprofit organization called the People's Radio

Network, which he described as the "workingman's PBS." His fans paid fifteen dollars a year to belong to the organization, which also sold books, published a newspaper, and hawked merchandise via a toll-free number. There was a national network of local *For the People* club chapters. At the peak of Harder's reach, in the mid-1990s, he renovated a Victorian-era hotel to use as his headquarters. Loyal listeners would come to White Springs to watch Harder do his show from behind bulletproof glass in a studio on the ground floor of the hotel.

In the years before the internet became ubiquitous, call-in shows like Harder's acted as primitive social networks, places where conspiracy theorists could gather and share their wildest notions about the New World Order. Harder came down with an acute case of what would later be described as "Clinton Derangement Syndrome." He obsessed over White House scandals real, dubious, and delusional. He delved into alleged corruption and cover-ups and suggested that those who crossed Clinton's path had a funny way of turning up dead. He sold a documentary video called *The Death of Vince Foster*, which suggested there was something that didn't add up about the much-investigated suicide of a White House lawyer. (There was no real mystery; he shot himself.) Harder often had on guests like Christopher Ruddy, the author of a book on the Foster case and the founder of the website Newsmax, who had made Clinton scandalmongering into a speculative industry. Harder was equally suspicious of "Lady Hillary," whom he believed responsible for ordering an IRS audit that caused financial problems that cost him the hotel and, eventually, the People's Radio Network itself.

As much as he despised the Clintons, Harder was not a Republican. He did not fit anywhere in the political universe of the time. Ideologically, he was way out in the Kuiper Belt, where the extremists of the left and right circle in irregular orbits. He had the anticorporate crusader Ralph Nader on his show as a frequent guest, and he was gleeful when massive protests against globalization broke out at a meeting of the World Trade Organization in Seattle in December 1999. At its furthest extremes, the paranoia aired on his show verged into realms of anti-Semitism and white supremacy. Harder always denied that he was a racist, but at the very least he was willing to give haters a hearing. His guests included gun nuts, militia leaders, and crackpots of all stripes.

In earlier times, Harder's listeners might have been called Know Nothings or John Birchers. In the future, they would evolve into Truthers, Birthers, Tea Partiers, Deplorables, the alt-right, QAnon, and ultimately, the Republican base. But in 2000, they were just called lunatics. To the extent that they had any home, it was Perot's movement. Although he was officially nonpartisan, Harder was deeply connected to Reform Party politics. "The wackiest people in the Reform Party all listened to Chuck Harder," one former party official recalls.

Harder was contemptuous of both Al Gore and George W. Bush, two lifetime members of the ruling class, and he expressed disgust with their "two-party, two-princeling system." But in order to mount a credible campaign, Reform Party leaders needed to find a candidate who could carry on Perot's populist cause. And it appeared they might have discovered the right man in a most unlikely place. In early 2000, Donald Trump invited the Reform Party to visit him at Mar-a-Lago.

WHEN TRUMP ANNOUNCED an exploratory campaign in the fall of 1999, the press snickered. "Why should his legacy be a skyscraper that casts a shadow on the U.N.," Maureen Dowd asked in her *New York Times* column, "when he could cast a shadow on the world?"

Trump gave Dowd a flirtatious interview. "To be blunt, people would vote for me," he assured her. "They just would . . . Maybe because I'm so good looking. I don't know. Larry King calls and says, 'Do my show. I get my highest ratings when you're on.'"

Adam Nagourney, a top political correspondent for the *Times*, obliged the would-be president with a visit to his corner office on the twenty-sixth floor of Trump Tower and pressed him to explain "the basic rationale for a Trump candidacy." Trump drummed his fingers on his desk, cast a glance at his long wall of magazine covers of himself, and responded:

"There has been a lack of spirit in the country with respect to what's going on. Obviously. Things are starting to look a little bit queasy. People are worried about the 2000 phenomenon. The Y2K. And I don't know that I am. Because I don't think that I am particularly. But you know, they think computers are going to come out and gobble and destroy the world."

On his desk, Trump had a tall stack of clippings, including the original *Enquirer* article placing him in second place in that sketchy one-hundred-person poll.

"Those are the real people," Trump said, referring to the tabloid's readers.

"That is the Trump constituency," Roger Stone added.

Comedians could hardly conceal their glee. "This is what this country needs and deserves," said David Letterman, who presented a Top Ten List of "Trump for President" slogans. (No. 4: "Friend of the working man and, even better, friend of the working girl.") Washington pundits agonized over America's shallow obsession with celebrity. One Sunday morning, Tim Russert, the host of the NBC talk show *Meet the Press*, invited on Jack Gargan, the Reform Party chairman, a Florida political gadfly who was a good friend of Harder's and a fellow Y2K prepper.

"Do you think Donald Trump could be the nominee of the Reform Party?" Russert asked.

"He could be," Gargan replied. "Our open primary nomination process allows just about anybody . . ."

"Anybody?" Russert interjected. *"Anybody* can become the Reform Party nominee?"

Trump did seem an odd fit for an organization officially committed to the principles of restoring honesty and frugality to Washington. The party's signature issue was curbing the influence of special interests and big campaign donors, while Trump was a caricature of a fat cat who openly admitted to giving money to politicians in return for favors. ("A lot of times," Trump explained, "favor is a positive thing.") The Reform Party even had an official rule against negative attacks, which threatened to render Trump completely mute.

Stone saw, however, that the party was ripe for a takeover. It was divided into squabbling factions. The party's most prominent officeholder, Governor Jesse Ventura of Minnesota, was a profane former professional wrestler and the leader of the moderates, which said something about his opposition. Ventura was urging Trump to seek the nomination. The businessman was talking about drawing on his fortune to mount a campaign, as Perot had, suggesting a budget of $100 million. If Trump got into the televised debates in the fall, who knew what might happen?

Still, it was hard to believe that Trump was actually going to do it. Many Reform Party members suspected his campaign was just a crass publicity stunt. To woo them, Trump held a reception at his Palm Beach estate, a 118-room Mediterranean Revival folly built by a Broadway set designer who, Trump claimed, was "the greatest architect of the 20th Century." The homespun party leaders scarfed down salmon canapés in the mansion's opulent White and Gold Ballroom. "There was so much double knit in the room," Stone says, "that if you had an open match, it would have blown up like *that*."

"It was hilarious and a blast," recalls a Reform Party member who attended. "It was Trump mixing with the unwashed masses." They all fawned over the candidate as he worked the crowd. But when Trump took the stage to give a speech, the air in the room went dead. He wasn't anything like Perot. He didn't talk about rooting out special interests or dislodging the elites who ran Washington, the insurgent party's only unifying ideas. He just recited platitudes. Trump didn't understand who these people were, had nothing to say to them. He was . . . dull.

"Looking back at this point, in retrospect, it was the perfect Trump audience," the party attendee says. "They were conspiracy-minded, they were white working class. They were the Chuck Harder crowd. Down the road, these people would become the core Trump supporters. At this time, he was not giving them the red meat that he would later deliver."

It was hard to tell what there was to Trump's candidacy beyond his celebrity. And the Reform Party was not just going to hand him the nomination. Trump had competition. His opponent left no confusion about where he stood. His platform called for tearing up trade agreements, forsaking alliances, deporting "illegals," building a wall. His name was Pat Buchanan, and he was one of Harder's people. He was campaigning on an old, loaded slogan: "America First."

8

The Life

At around eleven o'clock on a cloudy, sweltering South Florida morning, Kevin Ingram was zipping up I-95 in his yellow Ferrari Spider with his sidekick Didi stationed in the passenger seat, heading to Boca Raton to give a presentation to Randy Glass and his mysterious investors. Ingram called from the road to tell Glass he was stopping at an office supply store. "I'm a long-term, big-business guy, so anything I got to do, I'm not going to write it down on paper," he said. "You know those Magic Marker boards where you wipe it clean? I'm getting one of those."

Ingram promised Glass that his partners would be impressed with his investment pitch. "I'm a professional," he said. "I'm not going to do this for, like, a quick hit. I'm a lifelong manager."

"Kevin, listen, this isn't a onetime deal," Glass said. "Believe me when I tell you: this is for the long run. And this isn't some corporate executive board. You understand what I mean."

"There's not going to be any mysteries when I'm done," Ingram replied.

Ingram and Didi were bringing their tennis gear. That was how they first connected, back when Ingram was still working at Deutsche Bank. Ingram had moved from his New York apartment to a sprawling art-filled triplex across the Hudson River, in Jersey

City, with stunning views of the Manhattan skyline. He started frequenting the public tennis courts, where Didi was the local hotshot. They started playing, and one thing led to another. Now he and Didi were in business together.

Glass had challenged Ingram to a tennis match after the meeting. He had been talking a lot of trash about his game. That was Randy. He was a scamp.

Glass owned a jewelry store and was involved in the diamond business, a secretive international trade where deals were often done in cash. He also had tentacles in the underworld. Didi had come to Glass a few years before to sell some rough diamonds he had procured from the warring African nation of Sierra Leone. That deal failed, and Glass had also maybe stolen a few of the diamonds. But Didi didn't hold it against him. The two of them were into all kinds of crooked business: passing off phony Picassos, fencing a truckload of stolen Minolta copiers, trafficking plundered Egyptian antiquities.

Glass lived a charmed life. He had somehow finagled his way into marrying a wealthy woman from Palm Beach society. They lived in a Mediterranean-style stucco villa that backed onto an artificial lake in a recently constructed gated community called Seasons of Boca Raton. The tennis club was across the street. A little before lunchtime, Ingram and Didi pulled up in the Ferrari. Glass and his partners were waiting inside. Glass introduced Ingram to the guy in charge, a businessman named Ray Spears. He had flown in from the West Coast for the meet.

"I'm a financial engineer," Ingram told the group. He diagrammed on the whiteboard the structure of the entity he had devised, drawing arrows that showed how their cash, once committed to the IAM Global Money Fund, would move to accounts in the Cayman Islands controlled by Ingram, who would then direct the money into investments, paying out periodic dividends at his discretion. He never used the phrase "money laundering." This was money *management*.

Ingram proposed to launch the fund with a capitalization of $25 million to $30 million. Glass had already told him that his partners wanted to start with a modest transaction, to see how Ingram performed his financial acrobatics. Glass presented $250,000 in cash. Didi counted the money, taped it up in a plastic bag, and packed it into a piece of carry-on luggage. One of Spears's associates gave Ingram a bank account number in London. Ingram got on the phone and gave instructions to wire $227,500 from his account, subtracting his 9 percent fee. Then they went out to play tennis. As promised, Glass won.

Later in the afternoon, Ingram and Didi drove back to Turnberry Isle, the marina resort development where Ingram kept his boat the *Ingee*. Didi tossed the bag on, and they both climbed aboard. That night, they went out to a strip club, where Ingram bought a $3,800 bottle of Dom Perignon. He had cleared more than $2,000 from his day's work, and Glass had promised there would be much more cash on the way—tens or hundreds of millions. But he had an even better reason to celebrate. The next day, a judge in New York would at last finalize the settlement of a federal lawsuit.

Kevin Ingram had taken Deutsche Bank to the cleaners.

LATER ON, INGRAM'S friends would wonder what had possessed him to make the choices he did, to take such foolish risks. Was it drugs? Was he broke? Had he cracked under the pressure of expectations? "I wasn't particularly shocked," says a former banking colleague. "Not because of any criminal tendencies I saw in him, but because I believe he had gotten carried away with his success." The decisions were all his. But more than anything, his friends blamed the life, and the life began with a woman, of course.

Kevin Ingram met Sparkle in the early 1990s. His personal affairs were already disorganized. His wife, a former Goldman Sachs coworker, filed for divorce in 1993, the same year they had a son. (Ingram also had an older child from another relationship.) Regardless of his marital status, his nights were always a whirl. "He was a golden boy, spending his money and living the life," says a friend who met Ingram while managing an Upper East Side cocktail lounge where Kevin and his banking pals had a regular booth. Many other women came and went, but Sparkle was different.

Ingram first glimpsed her at the airport. He had gone to LaGuardia to pick up a different girlfriend. He was waiting for her, circling in his car, when his eye caught a striking sight on the curb: a tall, willowy young Black woman with full lips and high, chiseled cheekbones. She was just returning from a modeling shoot in Jamaica. She felt his gaze.

He was driving an expensive car, she noticed, and wearing some kind of exotic hat, like Crocodile Dundee. He drove past once, twice, and then stopped. "If you like what you see," she said saucily, "why don't you ask for my number already, and we can get to know each other?" She told Ingram her name. She had picked it up as a teenager on Long Island, and her agent had suggested she use it professionally. Sparkle gave him her digits. Kevin called that night.

Sparkle was barely twenty; Kevin was in his mid-thirties. "He was a little arrogant," recalls one of Sparkle's friends. "He was a *lot* arrogant, let me just be honest. But the generosity? Unparalleled. I mean, whatever we wanted. The champagne would just flow." Ingram would drop thousands of dollars without a thought. They dined at the finest restaurants, flew to Paris on the Concorde. "He would wake up one morning and be like, 'I want to buy you diamonds,'" says the friend. "And they would go to Fortunoff or Cartier, and he would buy her diamonds."

Even as Ingram lavished Sparkle with attention, he was secretive about himself. He was the kind of man who was cryptic and elusive in a way that made you want to know more. At first, Sparkle wondered where all his money came from, and it took her a couple of years to figure out he was a big shot at Goldman Sachs. The first use of *google* as a verb would not occur until 1998. By that time, they were engaged, and Kevin had moved on to Deutsche Bank.

The German bank was in the midst of its own hot pursuit. In an effort to transform itself into a serious competitor in global financial markets, it had lured a swashbuckling megalomaniac named Edson Mitchell away from Merrill Lynch and given him $2 billion to go on a Wall Street hiring spree. Mitchell brought in one of Ingram's mentors from Goldman, who in turn offered Ingram a job overseeing trading of mortgage bonds and other asset-backed securities at Deutsche Bank, doubling his salary to a reported $2 million. Ingram enticed other discontented Goldman traders to come over and work for him. "Let's kick Goldman's ass," he told them.

Deutsche Bank had a different cultural metabolism. Mitchell was trying to inject some American energy into its veins. "It was a totally cowboy mentality," says one of Ingram's coworkers there. "Everybody for themselves." Mitchell hired the most aggressive traders he could find and pushed them to be adventurous. He wanted to shake off the German institution's stodgy attitude about risk, particularly its aversion to speculative instruments like derivatives, which allowed traders to bet enormous sums on swings in the market. He encouraged his financial engineers to experiment with new forms of securitization. In theory, any steady cash flow could be turned into a bond: tolls on a bridge, payments on a credit card, royalties for a song. (Around this time, David Bowie turned the revenue stream from his back catalogue into "Bowie Bonds.") Ingram's mortgage department moved into an unexplored niche: securitizing commercial real estate loans.

Commercial financing was much riskier than home lending. Mortgages for properties like shopping malls and office buildings were enormous—many millions of dollars. The time frame for constructing new developments was years long, and if anything ugly happened to the real estate market before a loan could be securitized, the bank, as the lender, could get stuck with a huge default. Many banks were especially wary of lending in New York, which had only recently emerged from a commercial real estate crash. But Deutsche Bank was willing to take chances.

In 1997, Ingram's desk had a profitable year, and he received a multimillion-dollar bonus. "We were jet-setters; it was fabulous," Sparkle recalls. "It was like we were living the life. He was a dream boyfriend." Ingram made the money, and Sparkle had the social connections. She had worked for a time at Def Jam, the record label founded by Russell Simmons, and she offered Kevin entrée to the lavishly high-living hip-hop milieu. The two went to Puffy Combs's parties, where talent from his label, Bad Boy Entertainment, mixed with thugs, celebrities, and white CEOs seeking a frisson of danger. Sparkle was at Club New York, hanging in the vicinity of Puffy and Jennifer Lopez, the night of the 1999 gunfight that put the rapper in serious legal peril. (He ended up being acquitted of all charges at trial.) All Sparkle heard was a *pop, pop, pop*, before everyone ran.

"I felt like Kevin's life was a gamble," says Sparkle's friend. "She was a hot, beautiful young model who was *much* younger than him, and she opened up a world that he didn't necessarily have access to in that he was a big star in the finance world, but nobody really knew him."

Ingram made a silent investment with a nightclub owner who was renovating an old printing shop in SoHo. The club was called NV (pronounced "envy"). It became a hip-hop hot spot. "It was a ghetto fabulous place," says a party promoter who worked with the club's management and became friendly with Ingram. On big weekend nights at NV, the upstairs VIP section would be filled with rappers and NBA stars like Patrick Ewing and Allen Iverson. DJ Dee Wiz worked the turntables, spinning Jay-Z, Missy Elliott, A Tribe Called Quest, Busta Rhymes, Mobb Deep, Foxy Brown, Puffy, and all his Bad Boy Entertainment acts. And of course, Biggie Smalls, aka the Notorious B.I.G.—the late, great B-I-G-P-O-P-P-A.

Federal agents, mad 'cause I'm flagrant . . .

Ingram hung out with Simmons and Andre Harrell, another label boss. "Russell, and especially Andre, they were intrigued," Ingram says. "Because I was from such a different world, and so successful." As hip-hop became the dominant musical form, its moguls were learning to wield their commercial power and figuring out how to be rich. In 1999, Simmons and a partner sold Def Jam to a conglomerate for $135 million. Ingram and Sparkle attended Simmons's beach wedding to model Kimora Lee on the island of St. Barts, where Martha Stewart took snapshots and one of the grooms-men, a Kennedy family member, later enthused that the guests included "four supermodels, two billionaires, two princes, three movie directors, and a crackhead."

Sometimes, Ingram played in pickup basketball games where the hip-hop guys faced off against the Black finance guys. Ingram was small but tough—he would run into a hard foul and pop right back up. "We would always kick their ass, and that you can quote me on," recalls one of Ingram's banker teammates. "One minute you could be playing basketball with Puffy or Russell or Andre, and the next minute you could be talking to the CEO of an insurance company about his portfolio of risk and selling him a couple hundred million worth of securities."

Moving in the circles he did, it was inevitable that Ingram would cross paths with Donald Trump. Trump was in the flow, running around socially with Russell Simmons and fawning over his commercial acumen. ("Russell knows the market, he sees the future, and that's the ultimate businessperson," Trump told *New York* magazine in 1999.) Trump loved to tell a story, later to become Palm Beach lore, about the time his Mar-a-Lago guest Puffy Combs was supposedly discovered on the shore outside a snotty neighboring club, engaged in what a local gossip columnist described as the "horizontal rumba" with his girlfriend, Jennifer Lopez. Trump also had a romantic relationship with a Black model named Kara Young, who claimed he was "ignorant of Black culture before he met me."

Ingram never liked Trump. "He was a clown," he says. "Nobody cared about him. Nobody."

Clown or not, Trump was a real estate developer, and Deutsche Bank was looking for those. Ingram had recruited one of his former Goldman colleagues, Mike Offit, to build the commercial mortgage department. One day, Offit received a call from a real estate broker asking if he might consider a loan to Trump. No one else on Wall Street would, fearing what was known as the "Donald risk," as a consequence of his epic defaults during the early 1990s. But Deutsche Bank was willing to extend credit even to developers with iffy histories. Trump personally came to Offit's office to pitch him on a comeback project, the $125 million renovation of 40 Wall Street, a Gothic Revival skyscraper that had once been the tallest building in Lower Manhattan.

Ingram recalls that he went to meet Trump at his office during the deal negotiations. "I remember the look on his face when he saw a little Black guy was, you know, Mike Offit's boss," Ingram recalls. But nothing distracted Trump for long when he was pursuing money. Trump tried to ingratiate himself to Ingram, inviting him and his friends to dinner. "I would always joke, I would say, 'I bet you there's a boxer that's going to show up,'" Ingram says. "One day it was Mike Tyson. It was Evander Holyfield. And I was thinking to myself, 'This idiot thinks he's going to sit Holyfield next to me and it's going to impact my judgment.' . . . It was comical."

Ingram would later recollect that he was personally opposed to dealing with Trump, but the commercial mortgage department ended up making the loan in April 1998. "He never gave me even ten seconds of resistance," says Offit, who commemorated the transaction by commissioning a scale model of 40 Wall Street to display in Deutsche Bank's office. A couple of months later, the bank did a second deal, joining a consortium that extended a $300 million loan to construct Trump World Tower. It was the beginning of a tangled client relationship that would go on for decades. But by the time Trump came in, Ingram's career was already flaming out.

DEUTSCHE BANK HAD a gangland culture, and the hires from Goldman were constantly warring with crews that came from other firms. After about a year, Ingram's boss, his mentor from Goldman, got whacked. Ingram assumed his position, taking a greatly expanded role in the bank's trading operations. The job was international in scope, and he often traveled to London, where Edson Mitchell was based. Mike Offit recalls going out with Ingram to London's exclusive after-hours clubs, along with "a knockout girl" who was not Sparkle. "Kevin dated the most beautiful Black women you've ever seen," the former colleague marvels.

It was a gamble, and Sparkle inevitably discovered his extracurricular activities. She broke up with him and dramatically ripped off her engagement ring. But they made up, and Ingram bought her another ring—this one with a diamond so large and expensive she would never toss it away. Some of those closest to Ingram would have preferred it if the engagement had stayed broken. "She would run Kevin all night long," says Ingram's twin sister, Karen. "Kept him in the street all night, doing whatever else she had him doing."

The higher Ingram rose, the later his nights went. One of his friends recalls staying at NV until closing one early morning and then following Ingram's Porsche "at about a hundred twenty miles per hour through the Holland Tunnel to New Jersey with four girls" for an after party on one of Ingram's boats. "It was as decadent as you can imagine," he says of those days. "Then it would be me waking up and saying, 'What the fuck just happened?'"

Ingram levered up his personal risk. Cocaine was everywhere in the clubs, and many Wall Street guys, who had to be at work at the crack of dawn, were enthusiastic consumers. "Instead of having a couple of cups of coffee, they would have a couple of bumps," recalls the owner of NV. "There was a time when I was using it, but I wasn't addicted," Ingram says. "I was into it, but no more than most of the guys on Wall Street. That was the cocaine era. Everyone in my social circle for sure was using as much or more than I was."

Among his friends, Ingram was renowned for functioning at a high level on little or no sleep. He could go to work at 6 a.m., get off at 6 p.m., and stay out until last call. "Sometimes you're too smart," says a friend of Ingram's. "You feel invincible. You start to test yourself. You start to come into the office a little late, still hungover. And you come into the meeting, and these guys slept eight hours last night, had their coffee, had their sparkling water, and you're still the smartest guy in the room. Kevin was the smartest guy in the room. Anyone who doesn't tell you that is a liar." The problem was that, at some point, he was no longer making it into the room.

During his later years at Goldman Sachs, Ingram's coworkers had noted that he sometimes went absent from work for curious periods of time. At Deutsche Bank, the pattern reemerged. "He's making all this money, he starts looking good," recalls Offit. "And he starts doing Kevin stuff, disappearing for three days." Ingram contends that he was working constantly and says his subordinates had no need to know where he was at every moment. The bank was in an expansionary phase, trying to recruit talent, and that required many confidential meetings. Sometimes he had to fly off on a moment's notice. This was Wall Street. He was the boss.

Sometimes, though, Ingram needed quiet. "Some people like to call it depression," he says. "I just like to turn all the lights out, and I don't think about anything for a day or two." A psychiatrist would later give him a diagnosis of bipolar disorder. In a written evaluation, the physician noted that Ingram experienced "hyper" episodes in which he needed little sleep, was productive at work, and threw around money. It described his father's history of depression, which included a hospitalization and at least one unsuccessful suicide attempt before he killed himself.

In September 1998, Ingram and Sparkle had their long-awaited wedding. The ceremony was performed at a church in Brooklyn, followed by a reception at the Water Club, a restaurant on the East River. Ingram wore a tux and a goatee. Sparkle wore a lovely ivory-colored gown, a tiara, and a pair of diamond bracelets Ingram had sent over that morning as she got dressed with her many bridesmaids. The event brought together the worlds of modeling, urban culture, and high finance. The couple danced to the hit "Can I Get A . . . ," in which Jay-Z battles back and forth with an avaricious female rapper. Her lyrics raised some eyebrows in the Ingram family: *Can you afford me? My niggas breadwinners, never corny. Ambition makes me so horny . . .*

The party was meant to be a send-off. Ingram was about to move to London to work directly with Mitchell, a major promotion. But the same month as the wedding, the markets crashed, as economic turmoil in Asia and Russia turned into a global contagion. The Federal Reserve organized a bailout of a hedge fund called Long-Term Capital Management. The fund had used complex quantitative models to make enormous bets on the bond markets, and it was deemed "too big to fail." Trading in mortgage securities froze up, too.

The crisis passed, and everyone would soon forget all its lessons, but Ingram's department lost "a boatload of money," a Deutsche Bank source later told *Investment Dealers' Digest*. And just like that, as another source told the trade publication, "it was—bang, you're dead."

Mitchell asked for Ingram's resignation and cut loose about a third of his 120 employees. That was just the code of Wall Street, and Ingram could have submitted to his termination like a good soldier, taking a generous severance and walking away with his reputation intact. Instead, he fought back, telling Mitchell he would have to fire him and demanding even more severance.

Ingram was angry. "He was really hurt by that, the way it happened," says Sparkle. "It was a big position for him, that he worked for his entire life. To not have it, that was a devastating blow." Ingram blamed office politics for his ouster, and he believed that racial factors had come into play. Other executives who were closer to Mitchell—and were, of course, white—had lost more money and yet kept their jobs.

Ingram calculated that he still had some leverage. Despite its losses, Deutsche Bank still had ambitions to become a major player on Wall Street. At the same time as Mitchell was pushing out Ingram, he was negotiating a $10 billion merger with an American bank. Regulators threatened to block the merger, citing Deutsche Bank's lack of candor regarding its dealings with the Nazis. (It would soon apologize for its history, which included financing the construction of Auschwitz.) At this juncture, the bank could little afford a racial discrimination lawsuit. And Ingram could call on an intimidating ally. One day, a rumor ripped across the Deutsche Bank trading floor in New York:

Jesse Jackson is in the building.

Jackson was representing the Wall Street Project. Promoting Black-owned investment firms was only one facet of the project's mission. Another was, as Jackson put it, "challenging the finance culture." If asking nicely for equitable treatment did not work, the reverend was happy to make his disappointment known, using his proven talent for whipping up controversy wherever he went. Jackson was going to force Deutsche Bank to explain why it had fired one of the most successful Black executives on Wall Street. And he was going to make sure Ingram got paid.

Jackson later told a journalist that he acted as an "honest mediator" with the bank. "Rather than having a court battle or a street battle," Jackson said, "we sat around a common table, to look at a partial resolution." Deutsche Bank sent Mitchell and another top executive. The meeting went poorly. Ingram sobbed, according to a later report, and the mediation attempt failed. Instead of compromising, both sides filed legal actions. In reply to Ingram's claims of discrimination, Deutsche Bank alleged that he had been an irresponsible employee, citing his alleged absences and his investment losses, and claimed that he had charged $45,000 in wedding costs to his expense account.

The fight went back and forth for months, and during this stressful period, Ingram's erratic patterns turned more self-destructive. "Bad decisions," Sparkle says, summing it up in retrospect. "Bad financial decisions, bad friend decisions." Ingram was going through one of his "hyper" phases, devising and discarding numerous business ideas. He wanted to reopen an old Harlem jazz club called Minton's. He invested in reviving a beloved chicken-and-waffles joint. He formed a company called Mastermind Entertainment, hoping to break into the hip-hop industry. He flitted into real estate, striking a tentative deal to develop a property near Club NV in SoHo. He had an architect draw up plans for an eighteen-story condominium apartment building.

He and a former Deutsche Bank colleague were also collaborating on a dot-com start-up. Ingram imagined it could revolutionize bond trading, which at this point still happened mostly over the phone. By digitizing, Ingram could cut the big banks, his old bosses, out of the equation. He thought it was a million-dollar idea, maybe a billion-dollar idea. But it needed angel investors.

Ingram was expecting an enormous settlement from Deutsche Bank. News organizations later reported that he initially demanded $20 million from the firm, although Ingram recalls the figure was closer to fifty. In any case, while the dispute was tied up in litigation, he was burning cash. He was ignoring his lawyer's bills. Meanwhile, he was playing tennis with Didi, who had his own moneymaking ideas.

Ingram had originally taken up tennis for career purposes. "Kevin became a pretty damn good golf and tennis player," says a former colleague, who is also Black. "A lot of other guys figured they needed to learn those games in order to be accepted. 'Okay, I don't just need to get a house in the Hamptons, I need to learn how to play tennis, so people will come over and play with me.' But Kevin was different. The money that Kevin made gained him acceptance. Kevin's brilliance gave him entry to an exclusive club that played golf, tennis, skied, whatever. But Kevin wasn't going to stop at being in the club; he was going to be the best at whatever he undertook."

At first, Ingram and Didi would just hit around. Didi gave tennis lessons to Ingram's sons. But they became fast friends, much to the chagrin of Sparkle, who didn't understand their bond. ("I never liked him," she says of Didi. "He's such a bullshit artist.") Ingram and Didi started talking business and flying down to Fort Lauderdale, for reasons Sparkle could not begin to guess. Ingram often used to go to Florida to get away from the commotion. He liked to take his friends and his kids out fishing. But whatever he was up to with Didi, it wasn't relaxing.

Later, Ingram would claim he was motivated by compassion. He said Didi was scuffling through life and had a disabled son. "He was a very nice guy that I started caring about, simple as that," he says. "He's a guy who wanted so much more for his family than he could give them." Didi rejects this characterization of the relationship. "I am the main man," he said in 2021. "I am the real fucking character. . . . When I open my mouth there comes out a lot of bullshit. I didn't go to Harvard, I didn't go to Princeton. But I am more intelligent than anybody you can think of."

Ingram and Didi's business schemes ranged from the mundane to the mind-boggling. The pair partnered with a New Jersey contractor named Rocco to form a construction company called BIA. (The initials stood for "Black, Italian, Arab.") Through his business contacts, Didi would sometimes come across cheap merchandise, stuff that had fallen off a truck, and Ingram says he would offer occasional financial backing to what Didi called "closeout deals." (Ingram claims he did this as a favor, and didn't bother to ask too many questions.) But Didi's most ambitious ventures were international. He claimed to have represented Egypt in the Olympics, said his brother was a retired army general, and purported to have connections all over the world. He took Ingram on a trip to Egypt, where Didi was trying to put together a deal to invest money for the Libyan state oil company, which had recently been freed from international trade sanctions. Didi later claimed that Ingram attended a four-hour meeting at a Cairo hotel with a representative of the oil company, who ultimately answered to dictator Muammar Gaddafi.

Ingram claims he traveled to Egypt for purely "social" reasons and denies that he was aware of any business that Didi was discussing involving Gaddafi's regime. Didi later complained that Ingram cut his visit short despite his objections, and the oil deal never went anywhere. "Hi . . . from Africa," Ingram wrote in the subject line of an email to his architect, saying he was coming home from his trip early and pressing him to move on the plans for the building in SoHo. "Push, Push, Push!" Ingram urged.

Ingram appears to have viewed Randy Glass as a potential source of capital for his business ventures. Didi had introduced him as a high roller at the Atlantic City casinos. Somewhere along the line, Didi also indicated that Glass and his business partners were connected to a Florida billionaire, Wayne Huizenga, owner of the Miami Dolphins and the Blockbuster Video chain. Whoever they were, they were supposed to be coming into an enormous amount of cash. Didi later claimed that Glass suggested the figure could be as large as $300 million.

From his time at Deutsche Bank, Ingram understood how to

move large sums unobtrusively through the financial markets. It was easy to do it when you spoke the language of structured transactions and private wealth management, knew the offshore tax havens, and had the right bank accounts. Money was money. Glass told Ingram that his partners wanted their cash to be returned right away, in quick, clean transactions. But Ingram seemed to have a more long-lasting relationship in mind, in which he proposed to manage and invest the incoming funds.

But the enormous deposits Glass promised never materialized. Ingram grew frustrated and nervous, perhaps considering the stakes. Didi told Glass that Ingram was "shaking." Ingram started to doubt whether Glass and his partners were truly serious. "You know when you get a horse and you put a carrot in front of him and let him run?" Didi told Glass in a phone call. "You show the horse the carrot and the horse keeps chasing?" Didi told Glass that Kevin called him "the carrot man."

Then, just as Ingram and Glass finally seemed to be on the verge of closing the deal, Deutsche Bank agreed to settle the employment case. The terms of the agreement were never disclosed, but sources close to Jesse Jackson later said that Ingram received around $6 million. If so, it wasn't as much as he had initially demanded, but it was still a windfall. With the settlement money in hand, Ingram seemed to suddenly lose interest in chasing Glass and his carrot.

"I went to Florida because I thought I was going to meet guys who knew Wayne Huizenga," Ingram says. "When I kind of figured out what was really going on—because they did ask me to launder some money, right? That's why, after that trip, I stopped talking to them."

The morning after the meeting in Boca Raton, he started doing Kevin stuff again. He went missing. Didi speculated that he was on the yacht with a woman he had met the night before.

"Let me ask you a question," Glass said, "Kevin's not stupid enough to . . . I mean, he just met this girl, right?"

"What do you mean stupid?" Didi replied.

"I mean, he's got money lying around."

"No, no," Didi reassured him, saying he was holding on to the bag of cash.

"Not to beat a dead horse," Glass said, "but I'm looking forward to doing that other business."

The "other business" was the source of the cash. He and Didi were arms dealers.

INGRAM CLAIMS HE never understood where the money was coming from. He says that Didi told him it had to do with his dubious "closeout deals," and he did not ask further questions. He says that is because the sums involved were trifling to him, small enough to fit in a suitcase. Maybe he didn't really want to know the details. Glass later claimed that in their initial meeting at the World Trade Center, he mentioned arms deals and even showed off some snapshots of weapons. He said Ingram acted rattled, telling him to take back what he had said. Ingram denies this exchange happened the way Glass described it. Glass was always vague and roundabout, Ingram contends. "You never knew what he was talking about," he says. "He was talking in riddles all the time."

Glass urged Didi to make sure he kept his mouth shut about the arms deals around Ingram, who was supposed to be just the money launderer. He had no need to know about their other business.

"Listen," Glass cautioned Didi, "don't mix the two things."

For many months, Glass had been trying to unload a warehouse full of illegal military armaments. He had guns, grenade launchers, and even Stinger missiles, shoulder-fired weapons capable of bringing down an aircraft. Didi had been marketing the wares overseas. Shortly before the Boca Raton meeting, he hit on an interested customer.

"Remember the guy from Pakistan?" Didi said in a phone call.

"Yeah," Glass replied.

"He's very connected to the Taliban. You know who is the Taliban?"

"No," Glass admitted. "What are they looking to buy?"

"Every fucking thing! Whatever we have, they take."

"They got money? You know these people?"

"I don't want to mention the fucking guy's name on the phone."

"All of a sudden," Glass said incredulously, "you're not going to talk on the phone."

"Listen to me," Didi said. "You know who supplies him with money? Osama bin Laden."

9

The Force of Things

"This is a good place, if you want to start reading," the director said off camera.

Leaning against the window of a pickup truck, Ziad Jarrah scribbled a few final revisions on a sheet of paper. He was ready to record his last words. Martyrdom videos were a marketing innovation introduced in the 1990s by Al Qaeda's second-in-command, the Egyptian jihadist Ayman al-Zawahiri, as a way for suicide operatives to serve the cause from beyond the grave. They involved some stagecraft. Jarrah was filmed tromping across an Afghan plain, the wind whipping his hair and a red-checked keffiyeh draped over his shoulders. He sat down with his back to a vast, flat, rocky nothingness, with a rifle between his legs.

"As you know," said the director, "this speech requires passions and enthusiasm."

"Say that again?" Jarrah replied.

"Passion is essential for this speech."

Jarrah took a deep breath and began.

"Oh, Muslim nation, the infidels from all walks of life have ganged up against us, as they are led by the double-headed snake of the Jews and crusaders," he read in a monotone. "They suck the Muslim blood, and they are taking away our wealth and lands . . ."

CUT! The director stopped Jarrah. He was not hitting his notes with enough conviction.

"Repeat this again."

Jarrah tried to enliven his laconic delivery a little. "Let all the infidels know that Islam and Muslims are strong and able to destroy their kingdoms and to shake the ground beneath them. They hide behind the oceans, plotting against us, while their people enjoy their lives and our people are getting killed and slaughtered."

Jarrah's concentration kept breaking. He flubbed his lines, cracked up laughing, lost his place, got frustrated. "I am sorry, I made many mistakes," he apologized.

"Why don't you try a different approach," suggested another voice from behind the camera. "Do you have a will for the Muslim nation, a will to the Muslim youths, for the Muslim seculars? . . . In these last moments, which we are using to congratulate you and say farewell, we want to ask you some questions, and we would like your kind answer. First question: what motivated you to carry out this operation?"

"Praise God," Jarrah replied, "we only follow Him, we are ordered to do so!"

The interviewer was unsatisfied. He pressed for a better answer.

"What motivated you to carry out this operation?"

"Praise to God," Jarrah replied. "As we all know, we are now facing a New World Order led by the United States, which has enslaved Muslims and dominated their land and wealth. Nothing happens in the world without its approval, and that is the crisis which has befallen all Muslims. The U.S. is enslaving these regimes . . ." He halted midsentence.

"I had at first some idea I wanted to explain," Jarrah said. "But I lost track . . ."

He never did leave an explanation. Nothing in Ziad Jarrah's

life—no trauma, no injury—seems to have led to his choice to become a mass murderer. He was very different from Mohamed Atta, who was consumed by his hatred of worldly things. ("Joy kills the heart," Atta once instructed a member of his Hamburg study group.) Marc Sageman, a former CIA officer and forensic psychiatrist who has studied Al Qaeda, argues that the decision to turn to violence is less often motivated by specific grievances than by circumstances and group dynamics, that terrorists are swept along their path by what the French call *la force des choses*—"the force of things."

"What really explains 9/11," Sageman says, "is that they absolutely were flattered to be selected, to be in the vanguard."

But there was another force in Jarrah's life, one that kept pulling him back. In the early months of 2000, it tugged at him again. As isolated as Afghanistan was, it was still connected to the rest of the world, and word had somehow filtered to him that the woman he had left in Germany, Aysel Sengün, was looking for him. He had told her he was going to be visiting Beirut, but she now knew for sure that he had lied. She had been in touch with Jarrah's parents in Lebanon, and she had discovered that he had never gone home.

Aysel wasn't totally naïve. Jarrah had been talking about joining the mujahideen fighting in Chechnya. They had argued about it. She thought he sounded idiotic, that he was going to get himself killed for nothing. Now she had heard rumors that he and some friends had gone on jihad.

Frantic for information, Aysel started calling phone numbers Jarrah had used in Hamburg, and she reached some of his friends from the mosque. Soon, a letter arrived for her from Ziad, which was unusual. He wasn't the writing type. From the postmark, it appeared someone else had mailed it from Yemen. In the letter, Ziad told her to calm down and assured her that he would soon return. He had plans for their future, he wrote. He wanted to have a child.

Aysel was overjoyed to learn that Ziad was alive. She informed his family. A few days later, he followed up with a scratchy international phone call. He said he was on his way home.

BY THE TIME he called, Jarrah was likely in Karachi, where the plotters met with the terrorist who had devised their mission. His given name was Khalid Sheikh Mohammed, but to Jarrah—and everyone else in Al Qaeda—he was known as Mukhtar, which loosely meant "the head man." Mukhtar thought of himself as the brains of the organization. "While they use their muscles," he would later boast, "we use our minds." Mukhtar was not as religious as bin Laden. His motivations were more political and predated the founding of Al Qaeda. (His nephew Ramzi Yousef had coordinated the 1993 bombing of the World Trade Center.) He seems to have regarded bin Laden as something of a holy fool. He had so far avoided swearing the *bayat* oath of allegiance to the Sheikh. One of his operatives later told interrogators that Mukhtar treated Al Qaeda like a "general store," a place to find men and material for his schemes.

Mukhtar considered himself an artist of violence, and he painted in many hues. He hatched plots to blow up Big Ben, the New York Stock Exchange, and the Panama Canal; to assassinate Jimmy Carter and the pope; to attack nuclear plants; and to take down airliners with bombs hidden in shoes. He had first pitched the concept of the planes operation to Al Qaeda in the mid-1990s. Bin Laden initially dismissed the plan as impractically complex, but he changed his mind in 1999, purportedly after hearing the news that a commercial airline crash off the coast of Massachusetts had been attributed to the deliberate actions of a suicidal Egyptian pilot.

The difficult part was finding volunteers who could fly planes. The first four candidates bin Laden selected proved totally unfit. One of them, a one-legged Yemeni jihadi who went by the code name Silver (as in Long John), immediately caught the attention of Western intelligence agencies. When he took a trip around Asia to test airline security, he was searched and questioned at airports and secretly identified and tracked by the CIA. He and another operative were rejected when they applied for U.S. visas. The other two, both Saudis, managed to reach the United States, but they didn't get very far in flight school due to their poor English language skills. Within a few months, one of them was back in Saudi Arabia, and the other was working at a San Diego gas station. The plan likely never would have gone anywhere if it hadn't been for the appearance of the men from Hamburg.

They were perfect. Mukhtar had little time for complicated spy games. He liked to hide in plain sight, and he believed that simplicity was the key to success. The men from Hamburg could travel under their own names, as students. They would use a casual conversational code—what Al Qaeda called "cover language"— referring to their targets as if they were academic subjects. (The World Trade Center was the "faculty of architecture.") Mukhtar had been a foreign student at a college in North Carolina, and he thought Americans were mostly dumb and incurious. The country's prosperous complacency, its lack of fear, would offer all the cover they needed.

As for piloting planes, Mukhtar was under the impression that this part would be easy to figure out. He assumed that flying was something anyone could learn, just like driving. He delegated most of the detail work. Mohamed Atta was to be the operation's "emir," or boss, meaning he was in charge of implementing the general concept. After Jarrah left Karachi, on January 30, he likely never spoke to Mukhtar again.

Jarrah flew back to Germany, changing planes in Dubai. There, he was pulled aside by Emirati security officials, reportedly because his name had shown up on a CIA watch list. During a four-hour interrogation, the security men examined his passport and searched his bags, which contained jihadist tracts and tapes. Jarrah said he was training as a pilot, acknowledged he had been to Afghanistan, and said he would soon be traveling to the United States.

The CIA was alerted, but apparently it showed no further interest. Jarrah went on his way. At the Dubai duty-free shops, he bought some gifts for Aysel: clothes, jewelry, honey. Soon, he was back at her door. His beard was gone. He looked like the old Ziad again.

ZIAD JARRAH MET Aysel Sengün in 1996, on the day he moved into a university dormitory in Greifswald, a clammy, conservative town on the Baltic Sea. He was newly arrived from Beirut. At twenty, he was an indifferent student and an enthusiastic partier. He roomed with his cousin, who would settle in Greifswald and open a pizzeria. They frequented the town's bleak nightclubs, wobbling back home on their bikes. Aysel, who lived down the hall, was a child of Turkish immigrants who had been raised in Germany. She was vivacious, fun-loving, secular. They were both interested in studying to become dentists.

Within a month, Ziad and Aysel were a couple. She was in love; he was complicated.

The relationship was tumultuous. Aysel was willful and needy, while Ziad was emotionally distant, always noncommittal. They would fight, and he would vanish from her apartment for days. But he always came back, promising to do better. In 1998, he decided they should get married, and he asked Aysel's father for his blessing. The man threw Ziad out of the house. As a proud Turk, he didn't care for Arabs, and he wanted his daughter to be assimilated—a German.

It was around this time that friends noticed a change in Ziad. He abruptly decided he wanted to become an aeronautical engineer, saying he had always loved planes, and he moved away to enter a program at the Hamburg University of Applied Sciences. Aysel continued her studies at the university in Greifswald. He promised to visit every weekend, but he drifted away.

Ziad grew stubble, then a full beard. He started eating with his hands, as devout Muslims do. He talked more about religion, about Israel and the intifada uprisings. This was strange to Aysel, who had never heard him express political views. ("Without trying to judge," she later told police, "I can say Ziad watched the news to the same extent he watched animal documentaries.") Jarrah told one of Aysel's friends that he wanted to do something that mattered with his life and that he was willing to die for his beliefs if necessary.

When Aysel visited him in Hamburg, Ziad left her alone in his apartment while he went out to see his friends from the mosque. When she asked if she could meet them, he told her women were not allowed to go where he went. Their arguments turned intense as Ziad grew more severe and controlling. "He wanted to make a quiet, unobtrusive woman out of me," Aysel later said. He told her to quit drinking and smoking, as he had, and asked her to socialize only with other women. She placated him by dressing more modestly, but she refused to wear a headscarf.

They fought bitterly over her independence, and on at least one occasion, Ziad hit her. She would break up with him, and he would crawl back, repentant, professing his love.

Aysel was jealous. She felt as if mosque were her competitor. Ziad would fall out of touch for days or weeks at a time, and she would write plaintive letters explaining her feelings of love. "I couldn't sleep last night, and I thought for a long, long time," she wrote in one. "I just want to ask you one thing: Be honest to me, don't just say it, if you don't mean it with all you believe and if you think I would change my mind about jihad." Ziad insisted that they get married, despite her parents' disapproval. In March 1999, there was a quiet wedding—an unofficial religious ceremony in Hamburg. Aysel agreed to do it on the condition that Ziad sign a contract promising not to discourage her from continuing her dental studies. But Ziad immediately reneged. They fought, made up, separated, reunited. Even after she discovered he had lied about his Beirut trip, she held out hope that he would come back to her.

In retrospect, it would be hard for those who loved Ziad to explain how they had been so deceived. His behavior fit a familiar pattern of radicalization. But in the moment, it was easy to mistake it for a private crisis—Aysel referred to it as his "rebellious" phase. The truth was still impossible to imagine. "We came here to Germany so we could live better," his cousin would tell the *Los Angeles Times* in 2001, "not to die for some insane idea."

And for a while, after Ziad returned to Germany following his mysterious two-month absence, it seemed like his troubled phase had passed. The Sturm und Drang, as Aysel called it, were gone. Ziad was pleasant, no longer demanding. He didn't go to the mosque. He spent most of his time with her, in Bochum, the city where she was continuing her studies. He agreed to everything she said she wanted. He appeared to have a fresh direction in life. He said he was finished with Hamburg and his friends there. He wanted to fulfill a childhood dream by becoming a pilot. He bought flight simulator software. He doodled pictures of airplanes.

Still, Aysel wondered where Ziad had gone during his long absence, what he had done. She asked him the question many times, but he told her it was better if she didn't know the details. At night, lying beside him in bed, she lifted the blankets and examined his body as he slept, looking for a scar or some other telltale indication. But there was no clue, nothing to see from the outside.

"**THE HEARTS OF** freemen are the tomb of secrets . . ." This proverb was quoted in the second chapter of a 180-page manual entitled *Military Studies in the Jihad Against Tyrants*, a textbook Al Qaeda used in its Afghan camps. A good undercover operative, it taught, was patient and unflappable. He avoided mosques and never said anything that drew attention to his beliefs. He did not hastily break off relationships from his old life. He went about his ordinary routines.

Over the next five months, Jarrah and the other men from Hamburg made methodical preparations. They reported their passports missing, so they could get new, clean ones, without any stamps from Pakistan. They looked into flight schools, determining that European ones were too regulated, time-consuming, and expensive. They discovered that America was the place to go. Atta composed an email that he sent to thirty-one flight schools around the United States:

Dear Sir,

we are a small group (2–3) of joung [*sic*] men from different arab countries. Now we are living in Germany since a while for study purposes.

We would like to start training for the career of airline professional pilots . . .

Flipping through the listings in a trade magazine called *Aero-kurier*, Jarrah saw an advertisement for the Florida Flight Training Center, based in the town of Venice. On March 26, 2000, he flew to Munich to meet with Pascal Schreier, its German sales agent. Schreier talked up the Sunshine State: its year-round warm weather was perfect for flying, it had many small airfields, and compared to Germany, with its many rules and restrictions, America's skies were open to anyone. Renting a small Cessna, Schreier would tell people, was cheaper than renting a Jet Ski.

Jarrah struck the recruiter as "very educated" and "intelligent"—a good potential student. "He asked all the right questions," Schreier would later recall. They met for three hours, and Jarrah filled out an application for a full pilot training program, which cost around $20,000.

And then . . . he did nothing. There was a monthslong lag in his preparations, the first of several pauses in his activity. Several weeks after Jarrah's visit to Munich, Schreier called him to follow up on his application, leaving a message on Aysel's answering machine. This sparked another fight—it was the first she had heard of Ziad moving to America.

Aysel returned Schreier's call. She told him Ziad was no longer interested in flight school.

But something drew him back in. He told Aysel he had to go to America. As usual, she rationalized his decision. If he wanted to be a pilot, this was the quickest route. He could earn his license in six months. And at least he wasn't disappearing again. He was back to normal.

After this trip to Florida, they would finally be together, for good.

10

Oscar Night

The most honored film of that millennium year evolved from a chance encounter with inspiration, a haunting moment created by the Twin Towers of the World Trade Center. One day in the 1990s, a young graphic designer named Alan Ball was walking home after a brunch in Manhattan. As he told the story, it was a blustery afternoon, and as he was passing through the desolate concrete canyon between the towers, he looked up in the air and saw a white plastic bag twirling in the windy crosscurrents. The image stuck with Ball, and years later, after he became a screenwriter in Los Angeles, he incorporated it into a script as a central metaphor. His film, *American Beauty*, is about a depressed, free-floating suburban man, played by Kevin Spacey, who awakens his anger and finds new life in his lust for a precocious teenage girl.

"An amazing film," said reviewer Bill Clinton, who was good buddies with Spacey.

Though *American Beauty* had its detractors, who were repelled by Spacey's character and his leering fantasies, it was nominated for eight Academy Awards in 2000, more than any other film in a year filled with inventive contenders. There was *The Matrix*, in which a hacker named Neo takes a red pill and learns that the world he inhabits is just a technological illusion. There was *Being*

John Malkovich, a surreal comedy in which a nebbishy puppeteer discovers a secret portal that allows him to temporarily inhabit the character actor's body. There was *Magnolia*, director Paul Thomas Anderson's apocalyptic ensemble film, in which Tom Cruise gives an Oscar-nominated performance as Frank T. J. Mackey, a leather-clad motivational speaker whose misogynistic id brought to mind a certain third-party presidential candidate.

"I will not apologize for who I am," Cruise bellows in one scene, over his adoring audience's approving whoops. "I will not apologize for what I need. I will not apologize for what I *want*!"

Then there was *Election*, a political satire in which Reese Witherspoon plays an overachieving high schooler named Tracy Flick, who will stop at nothing to win her class presidency. Critics would note her more-than-passing resemblance to another ambitious blonde just starting her own political career. In February 2000, after months of careful preparation and Westchester home-shopping, Hillary Clinton announced her candidacy for an open U.S. Senate seat for New York. "I hope you'll put me to work for you," she said, channeling her inner Flick.

Some forty-five million viewers watched the Academy Awards that March, one of the largest audiences for any televised event that year. Billy Crystal emceed. Jack Nicholson presented the Irving G. Thalberg Memorial Award for Lifetime Achievement to Warren Beatty, who had been publicly mulling whether to run for the Reform Party nomination himself. "If you had your choice," Beatty said in his acceptance speech, "and you could get the Thalberg Award or the White House, I think I would stick with this." His beaming and very pregnant wife, Annette Bening, was up for Best Actress that night, for her performance as Spacey's adulterous wife in *American Beauty*.

She lost, as did Cruise, but *American Beauty* won Oscars for Best

Picture and Best Original Screenplay. Ball closed his acceptance speech by thanking "that plastic bag in front of the World Trade Center so many years ago, for being whatever it is that inspires us to do what we do."

If a common thread ran through the most memorable films of that Oscar season, it was an undercurrent of foreboding, an uneasy sense that something inexpressible was amiss. "Look Closer," beckoned the tagline on the *American Beauty* movie poster. Neo looks closer and discovers that humanity is secretly enslaved by computers. *Magnolia* ends with a biblical storm of frogs falling from the sky. Perhaps the film that expressed this disquiet best was David Fincher's *Fight Club*, which was initially reviled by many critics and denied any major Oscar nominations that year. Its disaffected male antihero ends up turning to terrorism, blowing up tall buildings to wipe out crushing debt.

The most commercially successful of the 2000 Best Picture nominees, though, was a moody supernatural thriller, *The Sixth Sense*. It stars Bruce Willis as a wounded child psychologist who is counseling a boy who can see ghosts. The movie was an unexpected blockbuster, propelled by word of mouth about its spooky plot and its shocking final twist, which in those days, before the internet spoiled everything, could still take its audiences by surprise.

Close your eyes if you don't want me to ruin it . . .

. . . The hero was dead all along but didn't know it.

NO SURPRISE HERE: Al Gore was a fan of *Being John Malkovich*. Who can say what the vice president saw in that parable of escape from the prison of identity? But in the midst of his 2000 campaign, Gore had his chief strategist call up the film's hipster director, Spike Jonze, to invite him to visit his family at his farm in Tennessee. Jonze brought a portable video camera and shot a short biographical documentary. It is a remarkable artifact, a shaky single-camera portrait of a relaxed Gore in his natural habitat, as raw and pseudo-intimate as one of those new reality TV shows—a viral video *avant la lettre*. The thirteen-minute film was shown once, to an audience at the Democratic National Convention, and immediately forgotten.

"I'm a little more reserved than a lot of people I know in politics," Gore says in one scene, sitting with a towel around his neck after taking a swim. "Trying to break through that is probably the most frustrating thing." The camera follows him as he walks in the woods and describes his youthful disillusionment with politics. He offers a tour of his farmhouse, showing off—to the evident discomfort of his wife, Tipper—a nude self-portrait she painted when she was pregnant. He sings an off-key bit of the song "Up on Cripple Creek" to himself. He makes ironic jokes about his stiff demeanor. He sits with his daughter Sarah and analyzes his deficiencies.

"Yeah, that's the guy who's been standing motionless onstage behind the president for eight years," Gore says. "What in the hell makes you think that *he* could be president?"

"Are all vice presidents that motionless?" Sarah asks.

"No, no," Gore replies, with perfect deadpan timing. "I did it *really* well."

Gore understood the perversity of his predicament. He was suffering from the comparison to Clinton with the president's admirers and suffering from his proximity to Clinton with his opponents. But mostly, he was just suffering. His rare capacity for self-diagnosis was matched by the futility of his attempts to remedy his ailment. He wanted to be seen for who he was. But the more he tried to fix his image, the more he appeared to be blowing in the wind.

He was widely thought to be a phony, a panderer, a desperate striver. It didn't help that he looked like a perfectly packaged politician, one assembled in a factory from poll-tested components: thick limbs, solid chest, strong chin, nose like a Roman statesman's, a healthy crop of black hair with a bald spot he took care to conceal. But for a man who had spent decades in the public eye, he displayed unusual vulnerability. "One suspects that, like many sober-sided and deliberate people, he is extremely brittle," a *New Yorker* journalist wrote in 1998. As vice president, he would sometimes give out copies of a book called *The Drama of the Gifted Child*, saying it offered deep insight. ("In everything they undertake they do well and often excellently; they are admired and envied; they are successful whenever they care to be—but all to no avail.")

He had been groomed for greatness by his father, Senator Albert Gore Sr., a New Dealer with a common touch. Senior was renowned for playing the fiddle and helping to create the Interstate Highway System. Even now, he was Junior's model. Gore's advisers called their candidate a "futurist populist."

Family legend had it that the first word little Albert ever learned to spell was *green*. He was a child of postwar Washington, raised in a suite at the Fairfax Hotel on Embassy Row. The downstairs neighbor was a segregationist Arkansas senator. On the first floor was a clubby restaurant where the Rat Pack hung out and where Robert F. Kennedy could be glimpsed at a regular table. Gore went to a top prep school and then to Harvard, where he was a popular, brainy jock. His senior year, 1968/69, he wrote his thesis on the subject of television and how it had reshaped presidential politics. ("I pointed out the growing importance of visual rhetoric and body language over logic and reason," he would write in 2007. "A lot of good that senior thesis did me.")

He opposed the Vietnam War but served in it anyway, out of

obligation to his country and, one suspects, his father's career. But Albert Sr., who had turned against the war, was defeated in 1970. Gore went through a time of disillusionment—the archetypal stage that mythologist Joseph Campbell would have described as the hero's refusal of the call. He smoked a lot of pot and listened to a lot of Dylan. He studied at Vanderbilt's Divinity School and did fine work as an investigative reporter at a crusading liberal newspaper, the *Tennessean*. He had married his high school sweetheart. As a young husband, Al swore to Tipper that he would never follow his father.

Then, in 1976, he received a phone call telling him the local congressman was about to retire.

"I'm going to run for Congress," he blurted out to Tipper. He immediately dropped to the floor and started doing push-ups like a boxer getting in shape for a fight.

He trained himself to be an adept public servant. He won his House race and was assigned a seat on a committee that did investigations, which he used to uncover corruption and scandals. He devoted his energy to arcane subjects like computer technology and nuclear arms control, impressing experts with his appetite for knowledge. He held the first congressional hearing on the then-obscure theory of global warming, featuring a professor whose class he had taken at Harvard, one of the first scientists to raise the alarm about rising concentrations of carbon dioxide in the atmosphere. He developed a reputation as a deep thinker at the vanguard of his rising generation. (The political columnist Michael Kinsley described him as "an old person's idea of a young person.") He won a seat in the U.S. Senate in 1984, then ran for president in 1988. He was only forty.

The 1988 campaign was a disaster. In a crowded Democratic field, Gore tried to stake out a position as the refreshing choice, and aligned himself with a moderate faction that called themselves the New Democrats. He anticipated that his most serious competition would come from one of his peers in the Senate—maybe Joe Biden, with whom he would have a long and rivalrous relationship. ("Gore comes off to me as a guy who has absolute confidence in what should be done and really isn't all that interested in what you think substantively," Biden told the *Times* in 2000. "Al operates on an intellectual assessment that doesn't accommodate much input.") Instead, Gore would find his route to the nomination blocked by a very different politician.

The Reverend Jesse Jackson was making his second run, after a surprisingly strong showing in the 1984 primaries. This time around, he was determined to prove he was not merely a Black candidate, but a serious contender for the presidency. Jackson went out to Iowa, the overwhelmingly white farm state, and ran on what he called "gospel populism," attempting to appeal to poor people of all races. "You hear folks who don't have dental care or health care, can't buy enough groceries or pay their electric bill, hear 'em talking 'bout they somehow got something in common with Reagan and Bush," Jackson said, speaking his exaggerated country cadences. "'Both of us is *conservative*.' Naw. Naw—one of y'all is rich, and one of y'all is poor."

As a southerner, Jackson cut into the support Gore had anticipated in his home region. What's more, he had a way of wickedly piercing Gore's intellectual pretenses. At a debate, after Gore offered one of his wonky monologues about pollution, Jackson brought down the house with a wicked wisecrack: "Senator Gore has just showed you why he should be our national chemist."

Gore tried to talk about his signature issues, like the environment, but no one seemed to care. Instead, it was Jackson's campaign that ignited the enthusiasm of the party's base. He swept the southern states that Gore was counting on and, for a brief moment after an upset victory in Michigan, became the front-runner for the nomination. *Time* put him on its cover, with a one-word headline: "JESSE!?" The Republicans were overjoyed. Jackson's egotism and prolix speaking style, full of riffs and rhymes and alliteration, made him ripe for parody and demonization. In the midst of the Democratic primary battle, George H. W. Bush attacked Jackson as a "hustler from Chicago."

Fearing defeat in the fall, the Democratic leadership rallied to beat back Jackson's insurgency. Gore served as their blunt instrument. In the New York primary, where he had decided to make a last stand, he allowed his campaign to take a racially divisive turn. Following the advice of his political consultants, he refocused on the polarizing issue of crime, going on the attack against both Jackson and the front-runner, Michael Dukakis. At campaign appearances, he stood by passively as New York City mayor Ed Koch, a Gore supporter, savaged Jackson, citing the reverend's criticism of Israel and his alleged anti-Semitism to say that Jews would be "crazy" to vote for him. (Jackson had never lived down referring to New York City as "Hymietown" during his 1984 campaign.) A little more gently, Gore questioned Jackson's qualifications. "We're not choosing a preacher," he said. "We're choosing a president." He was also the first candidate to raise what would become known as the "Willie Horton issue" against Dukakis.

Each night during the New York campaign, Gore would privately call Jackson to apologize for the attacks of the day. The preacher thought he was seeking absolution.

Gore was defeated in New York and ended his campaign. Jackson ended up winning some 7 million primary votes nationwide, second only to Dukakis, including 12 percent of the whites who voted. Gore would reach out to Jackson in later years, inviting him to high-minded dinner parties where his guests discussed issues of race. But neither of them ever forgot.

"Y'all know who my *real* hero is?" Jackson said to a gathering of ministers in 1995. "My real hero is Albert Gore. That's right, Al Gore. Father a senator—mine a janitor. He went to Harvard—I went to a little black college, North Carolina A&T. Albert was elected to the U.S. Senate—I was just in the movement, worked with Breadbasket and PUSH in Chicago. Then, in 1988, I beat him in Iowa, a state 98 percent white. He said it was 'cause of liberals and farmers. So, I beat him in New Hampshire. He said it was 'cause he was off campaigning in the South. So, I beat him in the South on Super Tuesday. He said Dukakis had split his support. I beat him then in Illinois, in Michigan. He said he wasn't really tryin'. I beat him then in New York. Said he ran out of money. But now, here I am this afternoon, talkin' to y'all in this church in South Central LA—and he's Vice President of the United States. How'd he manage to do that? *Amazin'.*

"Al Gore's my real hero, being able to do something like that. They attacking affirmative action now 'cause of what they call racial preferences.

"Preferences? Racial preferences? Don't be comin' to *me* talkin' about racial preference."

AFTER THE DEBACLE of his first presidential campaign, Gore went through a period of self-analysis, asking friends and advisers where they thought he had gone astray. He came to the conclusion that it was his consultants who were to blame. "I began to doubt my own political judgment," he later wrote of the 1988 campaign, "so I began to ask the pollsters and the professional politicians what they thought I ought to talk about."

He decided to go on a journey. He put a map of the world on the wall of his Senate office. His staff stuck pushpins into it, marking all the worst environmental crises, and Gore flew to see them on spartan military jets. He walked in a desert that was once a lake, rode on a nuclear submarine beneath the melting Arctic ice cap. In Washington, he started to deliver dinner party lectures, using an easel and a flip chart to demonstrate how global temperatures would rise in the future.

In the midst of this penitential moment, real tragedy struck. In 1989, Gore took his six-year-old son, Albert III, to a Baltimore Orioles game. While the two were walking back to their car with the crowd, the boy dashed away. Gore would later recall looking down, as if detached from his body, and watching his son's little hand slip out of his big hand. Then the boy was in the street, and then a car's brakes were screeching, and then he was in air, flying maybe thirty feet. He landed in a gutter.

Gore thought his son might die right there. But doctors operated on him, and he survived.

Tipper was devastated and went through a deep bout of depression. Gore set up an improvised Senate office in his son's hospital room and threw himself into a period of fervent productivity. A month after the accident, he introduced what became known as the Gore Bill, financing a $1.7 billion program that did, in fact, play a role in inventing the internet. He started to write a book about the environment. It was originally meant to be a bland campaign vehicle—he was thinking about running again in 1992—but after the accident, he set his mind to something more ambitious. He got rid of his ghostwriter and toiled over the manuscript himself, working late into the night in his father's unoccupied Capitol Hill apartment. He opted against running for president.

Gore's book, *Earth in the Balance*, was a philosophical polemic filled not just with scientific data but with ruminations on the Cartesian mind-body problem and humankind's relationship with the living planet. In it, he was sharply critical of America's political culture. "Increasingly, we concentrate on form to the exclusion of substance," he wrote. "Tactics prevail over principles. Too often, principles themselves become tactics, to be changed as circumstances warrant."

Gore swore to be true to his principles, and to prove he was serious, he took some seemingly suicidal positions. He proposed a new tax on carbon emissions, a radical idea at the time, and the phased-out elimination of the internal combustion engine. "I have become very impatient with my own tendency to put a finger to the political winds and proceed cautiously," he wrote. "Every time I pause to consider whether I have gone too far out on a limb, I look at the new facts that continue to pour in from around the world and conclude I have not gone far enough."

Some of Gore's friends read the book and wondered whether he was unconsciously trying to sabotage his political future. Then came the surprise twist: *Earth in the Balance* became a best seller in 1992 and landed on the bedside table of the Democratic presidential nominee, another smart young southerner. Governor Bill Clinton invited Gore to meet. They got together for a secret chat in a suite at the Washington Hilton and talked for hours about their ideas for the country. Clinton asked Gore to be his running mate. Gore stuck his finger in the wind and said yes.

NOW HERE HE WAS, some eight years later, campaigning ever so carefully, weighing his every word precisely for its impact. Today he was in New Hampshire, dutifully trying to fend off a pesky primary challenger, the former senator and basketball star Bill Bradley, who was running as a progressive. Gore spoke at a Manchester business group's "Politics and Eggs Breakfast" and then proceeded to Concord High School, where he was to address English teacher Joanne McGlynn's Media Literacy class.

Standing at the front of the school auditorium, he took off his coat and tried to act informal, attempting to connect with the kids by talking about his love of *The Simpsons*.

"I want to ask you a question," one student said to the vice president. "How do you get students to get involved in more politics?"

"Hmm," Gore replied. He searched his memory banks and pulled up a safe answer, an anecdote he had told many times before. In fact, it could be found on page 4 of *Earth in the Balance*: a story about a girl from a town called Toone, in a poor section of Tennessee.

"Twenty years ago," Gore told the students in his singsong baritone speaking voice, "I got a letter from a high school student in West Tennessee about how the water—her family was drinking from a well—tasted funny." This was back when he was just starting out as a young congressman. "We investigated," he went on. "What we found was that one mile from her home, a chemical company had dug a big trench, and they were dumping millions of gallons of hazardous chemical waste into the ground. It had seeped down into the water table and contaminated her family's well and the wells of other families in that rural area."

He explained that his congressional committee then investigated, looking at similar toxic waste sites, including a notorious one near Buffalo. "I found a little place in upstate New York called Love Canal," Gore said. "Had the first hearing on that issue. And Toone, Tennessee—that was the one you didn't hear of, but that was the one that started it all." He said his hearings inspired legislative action that ended up creating Superfund, the federal cleanup program.

"And it all happened," Gore concluded, "because one high school student got involved."

Great answer! Ms. McGlynn's students were impressed. But the Media Literacy class was not Gore's only audience. The actual media was also present, in the form of a traveling pack of Washington beat reporters. They had been listening to Gore drone on for years, and they were hyper-attuned to his tendency to preen about how he was smarter, better, righter, and first. The next day, the *Washington Post* and the *New York Times* both reported on Gore's lecture at the high school, with crucial elisions and one fateful misquote.

"I was the one who started it all," the articles had Gore saying. Not "*That.*" Not the small town, not the student's letter, but *I* started it. *I*, the most dangerous word in Al Gore's large vocabulary.

The *Post* noted that Love Canal was already nationally known before Gore's hearings and suggested his supposed boast was "reminiscent of earlier attempts to embellish his role in major events." The list was familiar by now: inventing the internet; claiming he'd been the model for the handsome protagonist of his Harvard classmate's novel *Love Story*; suggesting he had contributed, as a Harvard student, to Hubert Humphrey's 1968 convention speech; arguably exaggerating the dangers he had faced as a soldier during his tour in Vietnam. Gore making himself out to be the hero of a major environmental scandal fit the fabulist caricature.

"FIRST 'LOVE STORY,' NOW LOVE CANAL," read a headline in the *Washington Post*.

"AL GORE'S LOVE WHOPPER," squealed the *New York Post*.

"Gore, again, revealed his Pinocchio problem," George Stephanopoulos said on his Sunday morning talk show. David Letterman did one of his Top Ten Lists, of "other achievements also claimed by Al Gore." (No. 1: "Gave mankind fire.")

Never mind that Gore had been misquoted—later corrections were buried inside the newspaper. And never mind that his hearings actually *were* important, leading to the identification of 3,383 toxic waste sites. And never mind that, while we're on the subject, the author of *Love Story* actually *did* say he modeled his character, in part, on Gore. Ms. McGlynn's class tried to defend Gore, staying after school to write up a press release entitled "Top 10 Reasons Why Many Concord High Students Feel Betrayed by Some of the Media Coverage of Al Gore's Visit to Their School." None of it mattered. Love Canal joined the litany of Gore "lies."

Down in Austin, opposition researchers working for the Bush campaign were combing Gore's long history for every tiny inconsistency. Karl Rove, who described himself as Bush's "mad scientist," had a three-pronged strategy to define Gore as a fibber, a flip-flopper, and an out-of-touch liberal elitist. "It's not just the information," a campaign official later said, "it's finding that one little factoid that is just devastating." The guys who led the "oppo" team were both on the popular Atkins diet (lots of meat, no carbs), and they would spend their days wolfing down ribs and bunless hamburgers while cackling about their latest discoveries.

Gore was on the Atkins diet, too, and it made him constantly hangry. He had never been a warm employer, but as the 2000 campaign wore on, he grew frustrated and reproachful with his staff. For a man who was supposedly a systems thinker—one of the vice president's signature achievements was his technocratic "reinventing government" initiative—he was remarkably poor at managing an organization. His campaign staff was a mess, with competing circles of consultants fighting for influence and fees. Gore mistrusted them all and relied heavily on his family, especially his daughter

Karenna, who was twenty-six years old when she assumed an official position as one of the campaign's advisers.

It was Karenna's idea to secretly hire an unorthodox image consultant: Naomi Wolf, the author of the bestselling book *The Beauty Myth* and a proponent of what she called "power feminism." Wolf convinced Gore of her insight into the psyche of female voters, instructing him to wear soothing "earth tones" and telling him that women perceived him as a "beta male." She urged him to assert himself by spurning Clinton, a personality so dominating that he was commonly known within Democratic circles as "the Big Dog." Other factions of the staff eventually leaked the news of Wolf's consulting sessions, prompting what the *Times* described as a "full-blown tizzy."

Once again, Gore had been playing with his identity. "The heart of the storyline," one of his other advisers later wrote, "was that Gore the phony was letting a 'mystery' guru reinvent him."

Despite it all, he was still able to crush Bill Bradley in New Hampshire, and he wrapped up the nomination in March, in the Florida primary. Although George W. Bush held a decent lead in the polls, Gore had the advantages of incumbency and a strong economy to run on, and he had good reason to think that, once voters turned their attention to the general election, he would be able to close the gap. After all, Bush's own father had trailed at a similar point in his race with Dukakis in 1988, and the vice president had gone on to beat the governor handily in November.

Instead, during the spring, Gore's campaign plummeted into absolute disarray. Looking back, his advisers would place the blame on a single small person: Elián Gonzalez.

THE EMOTIONAL FAMILY dispute was perfectly configured to reveal Gore's political weaknesses. As a stubborn rationalist, he had trouble understanding how the plight of this one Cuban boy had developed into a national obsession. ("It is no longer possible to ignore the strangeness of our public discourse," he would write in a subsequent book, *The Assault on Reason*, reflecting on "a new pattern of serial obsessions that periodically take over the airwaves for weeks at a time.")

Knowing that he needed to win an overwhelming number of votes in Miami if he hoped to have a chance in Florida, Gore tried to take a carefully calibrated position, expressing vague sympathy for both sides during the negotiations. His contortions impressed no one. A *Saturday Night Live* skit portrayed Elián, played by a squeaky-voiced Chris Kattan, letting loose at an angry press conference: "To the crass opportunists like Al Gore . . . I say bite me."

In late March, not long after Gore's primary victory in Florida, the Cuban government announced that there had been a major change in Juan Miguel Gonzalez's negotiating position. He was now willing to come to the United States to retrieve his son. Reno told the family in Miami that when he arrived, they would be compelled to give the boy to his father. Miami once again erupted. Thousands of protesters rallied outside the Gonzalez home.

At an emotional press conference, Reno appealed for calm. "It is a community I love," she said. "And when it's hurting, it hurts me." But her legal position was unwavering. "We believe that the law is clear," she said. "The father must speak for the boy because the sacred bond between parent and child must be recognized and honored, and Elian should be reunited with his father."

Once again, Gore faced a choice. He stuck his finger in the sultry South Florida air. "Elian should never have been forced to choose between freedom and his own father," he declared. "Now we must take action, here on our own shores, to make sure Elian's best interests are served." He endorsed a congressional proposal to grant

Elián permanent residency, siding with Republicans and the protesters in Miami against Reno and Bill Clinton, his own president.

It was a horrendous mistake. Gore gained nothing with the Cubans of Miami, who were mostly Republicans anyway, while damaging himself with voters nationwide, who mainly backed Reno. The rationalist appeared to be playing to an irrational mob. The backlash was swift and scathing.

"Shame on Gore," scolded a *Los Angeles Times* editorial.

"Just when we needed Solomon in the Elian Gonzalez case," wrote *Washington Post* columnist Mary McGrory, "we got Al Gore at his crassest."

The support of Gore and other national political figures encouraged Elián's relatives in Miami to take an extremist position. They started to call Juan Miguel an unfit parent. With tears streaming down her cheeks, Marisleysis Gonzalez addressed the press outside the family home, asking, "What does this country want to do to Elián? Drive him crazy?" The next day, Marisleysis had an anxiety attack. Paramedics wheeled her out of a Little Havana restaurant on a stretcher.

11

The Siege

On February 1, 2000, the United States recorded its 107th straight month of economic expansion, making the Clinton-era boom the longest in American history. "ECONOMIC NIRVANA SETS RECORD," declared the front-page headline in the *Miami Herald*. Unemployment hit a thirty-year low that month. Consumer confidence was soaring. The Baby Boomers were entering their prime earning years. Accounting for inflation, their generation's median income was almost triple that of their parents'. The stock market had returned more than 20 percent for five straight years.

Technology, service industries, and creative fields, the sectors collectively known as "the New Economy," were in the process of becoming simply "the Economy." *Time*'s reigning "Person of the Year" was thirty-six-year-old Jeff Bezos, whose online bookstore, Amazon.com, was ruthlessly cutting its prices and profit margins in an effort to crush its competitors, becoming one of the hottest stocks on the market in the process. Microsoft's Bill Gates, the richest businessman in the world, held so much market power that the Department of Justice was trying to break up his company in an antitrust case. The developers of a search engine called Google—still an upstart competitor to the market leader, Yahoo!—were starting to experiment with selling advertisements tied to keywords.

Needless to say, Chuck Harder was a dot-com skeptic. "Every time that Jeff Bezos sells something, he loses money on it," he griped on his show. "Now, my question to you is, how can doing something like that get you named Man of the Year when anyone who has a lick of sense realizes that, at his current rate of burn—we call it burn rate when you use up your money—I don't know how Amazon can stay in business for another year."

Another day, he ranted, "Yahoo! Just a few years ago everyone went Yahoo—*tee hee hee hee*. They just jumped twenty-eight dollars yesterday to close at four hundred thirty-six dollars a share. Good grief! Can you imagine a computer search engine making so much money? Just absolutely incredible."

Harder complained that America didn't *make* anything anymore. Industry was dying as corporate bosses shifted jobs overseas and reaped rewards from their shareholders in the form of salary bonuses and stock options. Many working-class Americans didn't have any savings to invest in the stock market. A study published by the Federal Reserve in 2000 noted that while the middle and upper classes were getting much richer, the net worth of those nearer the bottom was stagnant or even declining.

"Is your job better than it used to be? Have you been downsized? Did the factory close?" Harder asked. "Well, pardon me for being gloomy and doomy, but I must tell you, while everyone is saying how great the economy is doing, I keep wandering around looking for somebody who is happy. The folks in New York City are very happy. You can find some folks who are members of the 'I've got mine club' that are pretty happy. *I've got mine! I don't care about you!*"

One morning in 2000, America Online, the dial-up internet pioneer, announced the shocking news that it was buying the media conglomerate Time Warner, the parent company of CNN.

"The *biggest* merger to date," Chuck Harder said. "Can you imagine a little computer company, America Online, now paying out over one hundred fifty-four billion in stock and debt?"

For the second hour of his show, when he usually talked to a guest, Harder had on a leftist professor of communications, a critic of media consolidation. "The thing that has really upset me and hurt me over the years is that I have taken what is called the populist view," Harder said. "The minute you challenge free trade or corporate growth, the minute you challenge any of these giant-mega-global corporations, the people who are out there to shut you up start pinning names on you. Like you must be anti-Semitic. You must be a racist. You are a homophobe."

The professor murmured something noncommittal. Harder glanced at a bank of television screens above his console, which were tuned to the cable news networks.

"Right now, CNN is having a supposed talk show, a spirited talk show, and MSNBC is supposedly doing the same thing. Guess what they're talking about?"

"JonBenet Ramsey?" the professor said, referring to the famous tabloid murder victim.

"No, that's pretty well worn out. CNN is talking about the little boy from Cuba."

AS THE STRUGGLE over Elián darkened, Janet Reno's thoughts were shadowed by a previous negotiating disaster. "She lives Waco," a confidante told *Newsweek* as Reno dealt with the case.

The siege of the Branch Davidian compound outside Waco, Texas, began two weeks before the Senate confirmed Reno's nomination as attorney general. On February 28, 1993, agents from the federal Bureau of Alcohol, Tobacco, and Firearms, acting on a tip that the apocalyptic religious cult was stockpiling weapons, attempted to arrest the group's leader, David Koresh. His followers opened fire on the authorities. Four law enforcement officers were killed, and the cult hunkered down in its fortified compound.

After weeks of negotiation, the FBI decided that Koresh would never surrender willingly, and it presented Reno with a plan to raid the compound. It proposed to use nonlethal tactics and tear gas to subdue Koresh and his followers. Reno was reluctant to approve the FBI's plan. She later said that she lay awake at night worrying, "Oh my God, what if he blows the place up?" There were more than eighty people inside, including many women and children. Reno believed that, whatever she decided, innocent kids would be in danger. There were reports that Koresh had been sexually abusing girls, taking them as his "carnal wives."

She gave the go-ahead for the raid. The wooden compound went up in flames as America watched on TV.

At first, Reno thought it was possible that the twenty children inside might have survived the fire in an underground bunker. During a break in a television interview, an aide called to say that the children were dead. "She found out on live TV," the aide recalls. Reno's reaction would define her tenure as attorney general. "I made the decisions," she told the press. "I'm accountable. The buck stops with me." The pundits praised her. "STANDING TALL," declared a headline in *Time*.

But the Waco debacle never really ended for Reno. Like a slow-acting poison, it seeped into everything. It was the first blow to her relationship with Clinton, who felt, a top aide later told *The New Yorker*, that Reno made him look "weak and equivocating by comparison." It made her into a villain of right-wing gun nuts, who saw nothing wrong with the cult having amassed an arsenal.

Chuck Harder posited that Reno was covering up the horrible

truth: that the FBI had set the fire, maybe through incompetence or maybe deliberately. Harder spent years working with other conspiracy theorists who scrutinized and questioned every detail of the official story. "The United States government started the fires and murdered the people," he told his listeners in 1999. "You're going to see the story get bigger and bigger and bigger and bigger."

A paranoid strain runs through American history, all the way back to the Founders and their secret societies, but Waco unleashed something virulent in the political culture. In 1994, with "Waco" as a rallying cry and talk radio as a propellant, antigovernment fury fueled an insurgency that gave Republicans control of Congress for the first time in decades, making the conservative firebrand Newt Gingrich the new Speaker of the House of Representatives. The following year, on the second anniversary of the Waco fire, a Gulf War veteran named Timothy McVeigh detonated a truck bomb outside a federal building in Oklahoma City, killing 168 people.

McVeigh and his accomplice, Terry Nichols, turned out to have connections to right-wing militias and an obsession with antigovernment conspiracy theories. They spent time before the bombing on the Michigan farm of Nichols's brother, a Chuck Harder fan who reportedly attended meetings of a local militia. The bombing inspired a national backlash against right-wing extremism. But within days, Harder was airing alternative explanations of the horrific event. He and his allies decided the bombing was an inside job—a "Reichstag fire" set to serve as justification for an FBI crackdown on militias and gun owners. He cast "Crazy Janet" as the villain in the plot.

"*Ooooh, we have to take those guns away,*" Harder said one day, doing an exaggerated imitation of Reno's voice. "This is a great country, but it is being pulled apart at the seams by a group of people who have taken this country over. Taken it from *us*."

THERE WERE INVESTIGATIONS upon investigations of the Waco inferno. Eventually, a government commission was appointed, headed by a former Republican senator. In 2000, as the standoff over Elián dragged on, the commission staged a reenactment of the raid. It would conclude that there was "overwhelming evidence exonerating the government." Still, the questions continued to bedevil Reno. On March 28, 2000, she gave a deposition in a Waco wrongful death lawsuit.

"What does 'the buck stops here' mean to you?" a hostile attorney asked her.

"It means I'm responsible," Reno curtly replied.

She needed no reminder of the costs of failure. For the rest of her life, she kept a picture of a one-year-old girl who was killed in the day care center inside the federal building in Oklahoma City.

Reno was worried about the direction of the Gonzalez family's custody battle. The two sides were now trading unsubstantiated allegations of physical and emotional abuse. "Elián is afraid of his dad," his uncle Delfín told reporters, saying the boy had cut back on his phone calls with Cuba. Juan Miguel wrote Reno a letter, saying he feared for his son's safety. Marisleysis kept checking herself into hospitals, complaining of "nervous exhaustion" and other nebulous ailments. One day, watching CNN, she was enraged to hear a psychiatrist say that the child would be better off with his father. She jumped up from her dining room table, stormed across the street to CNN's tent, sat down in a chair, and insisted on giving a live rebuttal. Meanwhile, Elián played on his slide.

His uncle Lázaro was volatile. He gave rambling, profanity-filled statements to the Spanish-speaking reporters camped outside his front door. He hadn't worked in months. One supporter described him sitting inside the house, watching Reno on television, and shouting, "That old bitch hag!"

In Little Havana, the boy's defense had taken a messianic turn. The devout began to see signs and wonders. A vision of the Virgin Mary was glimpsed in a smudge on a bank's window. The volunteer army around the Gonzalez house was swelling with recruits, as anticommunists were joined by the newly awakened: sales clerks, bankers, dentists, other regular folks. A group called Mothers Against Repression, led by a former secretary of Reno's, gathered for prayer vigils outside the Gonzalez family home dressed all in black. Street vendors sold hot dogs and peanuts. The activists staged hunger strikes and practiced tactics to thwart a forcible handover, such as forming a human chain around the house. "We are the only people protecting the life of Elián Gonzalez," a protest leader declared. "We are prepared to die."

A more menacing contingent, members of an anti-Castro paramilitary called Alpha 66, appeared on the streets surrounding the Gonzalez home dressed in combat boots and black attire. Some young men in the crowd had donned gas masks and wore T-shirts memorializing the siege of Waco.

On April 6, Juan Miguel arrived in the United States with his wife and infant son. "We are Elián's true family," he declared on the tarmac at Dulles International Airport. He then hunkered down at the home of a Cuban diplomat and waited for Reno to deliver Elián as promised. News cameras chased him through the streets of Washington when he went to visit the prominent Democratic attorney who had been retained to represent him. Jesse Jackson showed up, meeting with Juan Miguel and volunteering his services as a mediator. For a moment, it appeared there was a deal to hand over Elián at the Vatican's embassy in Washington. Then, late on the night before the handover was to take place, Lázaro came out of his house and announced that he was scotching the agreement. "The boy lives in Florida," he said. "The boy has a new home."

It was a stunning act of defiance. Reno was hesitant to give the order for force, but the pressure to act—from the White House, from the voices in the television studios—was growing.

"Janet Reno cannot make up her mind, and we need leadership," the conservative legal analyst Barbara Olson said on Fox News. "She has to sort of grandstand, set a deadline that she then knows she's going to have to back down from."

"Elián Gonzalez went eyeball to eyeball with Janet Reno," another Fox commentator said, "and Reno blinked."

12

One Florida

The geeky young governor of Florida, Jeb Bush, had an innovative way of communicating with his constituents. He made his email address public, so any concerned citizen could write to him. The governor devoted time to answering each of the one hundred or so messages he received each day, addressing matters of policy, complaints about government services, and requests for his views on every conceivable issue. In 2000, the governor's account was deluged with emotional messages pleading with him to intervene one way or another in the Elián Gonzalez case.

"He is God's child and seems to me to belong here where he has a chance to learn of God and good," wrote one of the governor's correspondents.

"*God's child* is a wonderful expression for little Elian," Jeb wrote back. "He lived while ten died. God's hand was upon him."

Jeb was supporting the Miami relatives, but his mind was elsewhere that spring, preoccupied by another crisis, one that came right to his door in Tallahassee. On March 7, 2000, the Florida State Capitol was the scene of one of the largest political demonstrations in Florida's history. As many as fifty thousand protesters, led by the ubiquitous Reverend Jesse Jackson, marched down the

Apalachee Parkway to the capitol complex, singing spiritual anthems and chanting, *No more Bush!*

The chant was double-barreled, directed at both the Bush who was running for president and the one who was running Florida. As the march arrived at the capitol, Jeb was inside, delivering an address in which he was unveiling his agenda for the year, including the item that had inspired such massive opposition: his proposal to repeal racial affirmative action programs.

Jeb had given his plan the deceptively unifying name "One Florida." Its most divisive element called for replacing affirmative action policies at state colleges and universities with a program that would offer automatic admission to the top 20 percent of graduates of all public high schools, regardless of their color. Bush argued that the program would admit just as many or more minority students without using race as a basis. But many Black people in Florida, all too familiar with their state's long history of officially sanctioned racism, were not buying the governor's color-blind line. At the protest, some waved signs reading, "Jeb Crow."

"Maybe when you inherit a name," Jackson preached to the throng in front of the capitol, "maybe when you inherit legal protections, maybe when you inherit wealth, maybe when you inherit skin color, maybe when you inherit your parents' friends . . . Maybe you just don't understand."

From the top of the State Capitol building, a charmless twenty-two-story skyscraper, a group of Bush aides looked down on the protesters disdainfully. "Maybe this isn't the way you change things anymore," one said.

Jackson could sermonize all he wanted, but the tide of events was moving against him. The political realignment that had begun with the civil rights movement and the election of Richard Nixon was all but complete. That very day, Super Tuesday, George W. Bush had a chance to lock up the Republican nomination with primary victories across the party's southern stronghold. The future appeared to belong to the conservatives. In Florida, Republicans ruled both houses of the state legislature. Jeb's election, two years before, had given them complete control.

The One Florida initiative, however, had inspired a fierce backlash among Black voters, who typically turned out in low numbers in Florida. The Bush campaign had reason to fear that it posed a real danger. "Can you imagine," a Black congresswoman shouted outside the capitol, "what it would be like on November 8 to wake up and open the paper and see that George W. is president of the United States? That is my worst nightmare. We have to go to the polls!" Another civil rights activist exhorted: "Register to vote and get your grandmother and grandfather to vote!"

The Republicans could see this was going to be a problem. Somebody would have to fix it.

FIXING THINGS WAS Jeb Bush's specialty. He was forty-seven, six years younger than Dubya, and was inevitably identified as the smarter one. Far more than either his brother or his father, he was an intellectual conservative, a proud policy guy, and an acronym dropper who loved to pursue what he called BHAGs, his abbreviation for "big hairy audacious goals." Jeb wanted to fix public schools by implementing "market-based" approaches to education. He wanted to fix the environmental degradation of the Everglades by collaborating with his political supporters, the polluters of Big Sugar. He was fixing government by, whenever possible, getting rid of it.

Tall and thickset, Jeb worked long, intense hours and was known for sprinting up the stairs to the top of the high-rise capitol building to burn off excess energy. Whereas Dubya exuded ease, his brother radiated impatience. The truth was, they were never that close. When Jeb was a baby and George was seven, a middle sister died of leukemia, and soon after that, Jeb's older brother was packed off to boarding school. Jeb was the oldest child of the second phase of the family, with three younger siblings born after the tragedy. They were a competitive gang, always trying to outdo one another in a family system called "the rankings." The ultimate competition was for Poppy's approval. "As far as I'm concerned," Jeb would later say, "my dad is as close to perfection as a human being can be."

In contrast to his older brother, though, Jeb was less bound to Bush traditions. He attended the University of Texas, a significant diversion in a family where the patriarch, Prescott Bush, was known as "the Senator from Yale." He married a girl from Mexico whom he had met on a high school trip, which caused his mother some agita, and he converted to Catholicism. By the age of twenty-eight, he had settled in Miami. He and Columba were soon raising three children out in the suburbs. When his father ran for president in 1988, he would introduce "Jebby's kids" as "the little brown ones."

Jeb spoke fluent Spanish, reputedly with a Cuban accent. He entered local politics during the *Miami Vice* era, the chaotic years that followed the Mariel Boatlift. In 1983, he became the chairman of the county GOP organization and set about registering all those newly naturalized Cuban Americans as Republicans. Over the next three years, the party's membership increased by almost 60 percent. Jeb cultivated the cigar-smoking power brokers of Little Havana, becoming an unofficial White House emissary. He championed the "freedom fighters" battling Communist regimes in Central America during the Reagan era. He would appear at rallies in a guayabera shirt, chanting, *Libre!*

At the same time, he got into the commercial real estate business, partnering with a Cuban American millionaire he had met through politics. Miami was booming, flush with wealth licit and illicit. When Lee Atwater invited him and his brother along on the adventure of their father's 1988 campaign, Jeb turned down the opportunity to move to Washington, choosing to stick to his business in Florida. "He is probably the most serious of us," Dubya said at the time. Jeb was in a rush to make his fortune so he could run for office. His father's career was hardly dead and buried when he embarked on his own. As soon as the 1992 election was over, he started running for governor on a theme of redemption.

"I want to be able to look my father in the eye," Jeb said in one speech, as Poppy looked on approvingly, "and say, 'I continued the legacy.'"

The 1994 midterm elections were looking promising for the Republicans. Florida's incumbent governor, Lawton Chiles, was an aging southern Democrat who appeared to be headed toward extinction, like the rest of his breed. Jeb described himself as a "head-banging conservative" in the mold of the ascendant Newt Gingrich. "My father saw politics as service," Jeb said in 1994. "You can be far more effective if you view it as a mission, like a religion."

No one could miss the contrast with his brother. "Jeb will always seem more thoughtful," Dubya said delicately. The comparison annoyed Jeb to no end. He never wanted to be the foil. There were rumors that he was displeased with Dubya's decision to also run for governor in 1994. "It turns it into a *People* magazine story," he complained to Maureen Dowd, the *Times* columnist and unofficial family psychoanalyst, but he said he had "no control" over his brother. Dubya just shrugged off any tension. "Jeb's my little brother," he said. "He's done what I've told him to all his life."

While Dubya surprised many people—even his own mother—

by running a strong campaign against an incumbent Democrat, Ann Richards, it turned out that Jeb lacked his natural gifts. He was more introverted and self-conscious, and while he could overcome it, the exertion showed. (In this respect and others, he resembled Al Gore more than he did his own brother.) Governor Chiles, a crusty Old Florida cracker, caricatured his inexperienced opponent as an entitled outsider who didn't know the ways of the state. That Election Night, Jeb watched in disbelief as Republicans all over the country won in landslides, won shocking upsets, won both houses of Congress—and he lost.

"Can you believe *this*?" Barbara Bush said at a victory party in Texas. She was astonished; Poppy, crestfallen. "The joy is in Texas," he told reporters. "My heart is in Florida." Dubya, watching the returns in a hotel room in Austin, stepped into the bathroom to take a call from his father, who was in evident anguish. "But, Dad," he said, plaintively. "*I* won."

The morning after the election, Chiles kept to a long-standing tradition of traveling around the state to thank the public. Maybe it was happenstance, but as Chiles stood along a major roadway in Miami, Jeb drove by with his family. He stopped his car and shook hands with his opponent. "It was the right thing to do; it was the polite thing to do," Jeb later wrote. He was going to fix this. He soon founded a policy think tank. He teamed up with the head of the Miami chapter of the Urban League to start a charter school in the poor neighborhood of Liberty City. He cowrote a book called *Profiles in Character*, advancing a softened, values-based agenda.

In 1998, when Chiles had to step aside due to term limits, the new Jeb easily won the governor's office. (He even took a large percentage of the Black vote for a Republican.) He efficiently set about advancing his conservative agenda. "Bush governs like a man making up for lost time," the capital bureau chief for the *Miami Herald* wrote in early 2000. Many observers believed that if Jeb had not blown his winnable race in 1994, he might have been the one running for president. But now here he was, always a step behind his older brother, who expected him to be helpful to the cause.

Using his knack for mechanics, Jeb had assembled an effective party machine in Florida. "We had a blind dumb faith," Karl Rove would later say, "that no matter what happened, Jeb Bush would pull it off." And he might have pulled it off easily, if not for the controversy over One Florida.

FROM JEB'S PERSPECTIVE, the crisis arose from out of nowhere. It had started back in January, over the Martin Luther King Jr. Day weekend. Jeb spent the holiday in New Hampshire, campaigning for his brother, who was facing an unexpectedly vigorous primary challenge from Senator John McCain. In subfreezing temperatures, he and a group of other Florida officeholders, including Secretary of State Katherine Harris, went door-to-door in Manchester, handing out bags of oranges and boxes of strawberries for Bush. On Tuesday, when government offices reopened, Jeb went back to work at the capitol in Tallahassee. That was when all hell broke loose.

Two Black state legislators were sitting in his lieutenant governor's office, and they were not leaving. The pair, Kendrick Meek of Miami and Tony Hill of Jacksonville, were backbenchers, not part of the Democratic leadership with which Jeb had worked fairly collaboratively during his first, highly productive year in office. The legislators had sought a meeting with the governor to make the case for preserving affirmative action. Jeb's office had rebuffed them, instead sending them to the lieutenant governor. Now the pair had planted themselves on the striped couch in his office and were vowing to stay until they talked to Jeb.

Jeb, annoyed, poked his head into the lieutenant governor's office. "If you expect me to rescind my executive order," he said, "you better go get some blankets."

The state legislators said they would do just that.

"I hope you're comfortable," Jeb snapped and then left.

Meek and Hill knew what they were provoking. "By then," the Florida political reporter S. V. Dáte would later write in a biography of the governor, "all of Jeb's weaknesses—his stubbornness, his quickness to anger, his need to win *everything*—were well known." His brother, in his dealings with the Texas legislature, was known to occasionally destabilize an adversary by surprising him with a friendly kiss. Jeb was a fighter, but he had a glass jaw.

The civil rights sit-in created a spectacle at the capitol. Alerted to the confrontation, nine reporters crowded into the lieutenant governor's office, along with a feminist activist who just happened to be passing by. Bush and his aides were furious. TV news cameras caught the governor yelling at a press office staffer. "Your life's going to be a living hell," he said. "Kick their asses out." He later explained, not entirely convincingly, that the eviction order was meant to be directed at the reporters, not the protesting Black legislators. In the end, they all stayed.

Jeb convened a press conference at which he gave an impatient statement. "We are not going to waver," he said, calling the act of civil disobedience "childish, sophomoric, and unbecoming an elected official." Then the governor packed up his laptop and went home for the evening, leaving a group of state police officers to monitor the demonstration. The protesting politicians worked a cell phone all night, calling reporters and radio stations.

"African-Americans are tired of being dictated to," Hill told the *Palm Beach Post.*

By morning, the scale of the debacle was becoming clear. A

group of around a hundred Democratic legislators, activists, and Black students from Florida A&M University staged a sympathy sit-in outside the governor's office, singing "We Shall Overcome." The affirmative action debate, previously not much of an argument at all, was suddenly on the front pages of all the Florida newspapers. Jeb went back to the office where Meek and Hill were still waiting, along with the reporters who had spent the night stretched out on the floor. "If you need more water, I'll get you water," Jeb offered. "There's a way to resolve this. You can go out like other people. You can go to a restaurant. You can go home." They still would not budge.

Finally, Jeb offered a hasty compromise. He met with the legislators, sitting at the head of a table in an awkwardly packed conference room, and announced plans to hold a series of public hearings on the One Florida plan. The Republican leader of the state house of representatives, one of the politicians who had been campaigning with Jeb in New Hampshire, was disgusted, grousing that the "whine fest" had rattled the governor and his staff. "I always believed that white men can't jump," he joked at a reception, "until I started working around Kendrick Meek."

None of this was going to be helpful to George W. Bush. The day of the sit-in, someone from his campaign called his brother's office, alarmed, trying to find out what was happening in Florida. Jeb was supposed to be the one solving problems, not creating new ones for the campaign.

DUBYA, THOUGH, WAS facing his own crisis, in New Hampshire. McCain, the cussed Vietnam War hero, was mounting a defiant stand, refusing to give up even as the entire party leadership fell in behind the front-runner. McCain was riding around the first primary state in a bus called the *Straight Talk Express*, campaigning against special interests and the influence of corporate donors. McCain also romanced the press, with whom he would chat for hours on his bus, making ribald jokes and sharing unvarnished opinions. To Bush, a candidate who was campaigning on his authenticity, McCain's even more authentic authenticity posed a mortal threat.

Bush's allies in New Hampshire warned that he was headed for disaster, but Rove, his brainy strategist, assured him of victory. "Rove had the charts to prove it and everything," another Bush adviser told a reporter. When McCain whupped him by 19 points, it threw the Bush organization into temporary disarray. Bush called his staff "crybabies" and ordered them to stop bickering. "I'm looking forward to going down South," he told the press. "And pretty soon we'll be getting into big states and eventually maybe we can get on down to Texas . . . and Florida."

The next battle, though, would be in South Carolina. Outwardly, Bush was serene. "People are seeing whether I've got what it takes," he told a journalist who was following him around the country. "But you know who else is seeing whether I got what it takes? *I'm* seeing whether I got what it takes." His confidence may have been bolstered by the fact that South Carolina was favorable territory—Lee Atwater's home state. Dubya knew how to win there, Atwater's way.

During the two weeks leading up to the primary, South Carolina voters were bombarded with anti-McCain advertisements. A group called Keep It Flyin' accused McCain of backing a movement to remove the Confederate flag from atop the state's capitol dome. (Neither he nor Bush took a firm stance on the issue, but McCain had dared to call the segregationist symbol "offensive.") Callers flooded the phone lines of talk radio hosts like Chuck Harder, repeating conspiracy theories that McCain, a former prisoner of war, was a traitor and a Manchurian candidate and that he had an illegitimate half-Black daughter. (She was actually an adopted Bangladeshi orphan.)

Bush claimed he had nothing to do with any of these scurrilous personal attacks. But he could not so easily disavow his own decision to speak at Bob Jones University, a fundamentalist Christian school founded by a racist preacher who believed that the pope was the antichrist and that Black Americans should be grateful for slavery because it had rescued them from "the jungles of Africa." The school maintained a controversial ban on interracial dating, which made some Bush advisers uncomfortable, but the campaign's top operative in South Carolina, a childhood friend of Atwater's, had argued that the candidate's going there would send a heartening signal to the state's conservative Christian voters.

Bush beat McCain soundly in South Carolina, effectively stamping out the brief rebellion. His brother, meanwhile, was having a more difficult time with his racial uproar. Jeb personally attended an affirmative action forum in Miami, where thousands of Black citizens waited in a long line in the rain to file inside an auditorium and voice their opposition to his One Florida plan.

"This is an attempt to return to the dark days of the past," one female activist shouted at the governor, as he listened impassively. "We have been bought, sold, raped, beaten, executed, and excluded. The word *unfair* isn't adequate to explain our plight."

Jeb was shaken, but his mind was set. "What I concluded was that the things that were being said were not particularly rational," he said later, reflecting on the meeting. "It was raw emotion." In his view, his critics were all mixed up—it was racial preferences that were unfair. "It is wrong to discriminate. It is wrong," he told the *Herald*. "I'm going to keep at this and the emotions will subside at some point. People will see this for what it is, and when they do, they will embrace it."

The opposition had no hope of stopping the repeal. Their rallying cry, instead, was "Remember in November." Outside the Miami forum, local Democrats were registering people to vote as they stood in line. Al Gore was campaigning in Black communities all over the state. "I am for affirmative action because it's still needed," he said at a town hall in Tampa, held as McCain and Bush were battling in South Carolina. "I'm not like these Republican candidates who say they're scared to say anything about the Confederate flag." Jesse Jackson would return to lead a voter registration bus tour through ten cities, including Miami, Fort Lauderdale, West Palm Beach, and Jacksonville. Gore's path to victory, if there were to be one, followed the same route.

Of course, registering people to vote was one thing. Actually voting could be quite another.

THE BLACK COMMUNITY'S traditionally low rate of electoral participation in Florida was not a historical accident. Since the Civil War, many state laws had functioned to assure that Blacks would remain disenfranchised and disengaged. The most enduring of these was a provision in the state constitution, dating to 1868, which prevented anyone who had been convicted of a felony from voting for life. Vote suppression was not a by-product of the constitutional provision; it was its explicit intention. It had been adopted during the Reconstruction era as a way to counteract the newly passed Fourteenth Amendment, which gave freed slaves citizenship and equal protection under the law. At the same time as Florida's legislature created the ban, it also reclassified minor and vaguely defined crimes as felonies, so they could be used as pretexts to deny suffrage.

The law was indifferently enforced during the 1980s and '90s, though, when Democrats retained some control over the state government. Then, shortly after winning the state legislature, the Republicans passed a broad electoral reform bill, inspired by a fraud-marred mayoral election in Miami. The bill appropriated $4 million to scour the registration rolls for ineligible voters.

The legislation was passed before Jeb Bush was elected but implemented after he took office. The state's Division of Elections initiated a massive purge led by a Republican Party loyalist. (He would go on to become general counsel to the state GOP.) The division contracted with a database technology firm associated with a conservative organization called the Voter Integrity Project. Internally, there was no need to employ euphemisms like *integrity*. Employees of the database firm casually referred to the voters they were disenfranchising as the "dirtbags of the nation." The firm compiled a huge list of names of people with past felony convictions, not only in Florida but in other states as well, and then cross-referenced it against the more than eight million names on the state's voter registration rolls. The parameters of the firm's contract called for it to "cast a wide net," a federal commission later found. Republican officials encouraged the firm to be aggressive, even at the risk of misidentifying voters as felons.

On January 19, 2000, the State Capitol was paralyzed by the One Florida sit-in. The next day, the officials overseeing the voter registration purge drew up a new version of the project's guidelines. The tweaks loosened the parameters further, leading to the identification of another 65,776 alleged felons, including many more false positives. This list, like the previous one, was sent on to county election boards, which were responsible for maintain-

ing registration rolls under Florida's decentralized system of gover-
nance. The local elections officials were shocked. Many voters were
to be purged simply because their name bore a passing similarity
to that of a felon. Some county employees discovered the names of
coworkers and family members on the list. Because of a data entry
mistake, some 8,000 voters who had committed misdemeanors in
Texas were incorrectly classified as felons. That screwup was belatedly fixed, but an analyst would estimate that more than 20,000
other voters were "erroneously identified." Some of them never discovered this until Election Day.

"I had a sense," says Bob Graham, a Democrat who served in the
Senate at the time, "that this was not just a casual, independent action, but part of a larger plan to shape the voting rolls." By the end
of 2000, a study would find that Florida had more disenfranchised
ex-felons than any other state. Nearly one in five voting-age Black
males would be ineligible to cast a ballot. Black voters accounted
for 10 percent of the registered population, but they made up
40 percent of the felon list. People who had been voting for years
were cast off the rolls based on long-ago convictions. "This was a
first," one official later said in a civil lawsuit deposition. "It was the
accumulation of names, some of them going back 40 years." One
Black man in Tampa had his right to vote rescinded because, in
1959, he had been convicted of vagrancy for sleeping on a bench.

The way the system was set up, voters would be tagged as felons,
and unless they objected, they would be deregistered. Little noti-
fication was required. Many voters who were purged later claimed
they never received so much as a form letter. County officials had
broad latitude to decide how to handle appeals. In some places,
voters who said they had been wrongly identified as felons had to
supply proof that they were not criminals. Officials would send a
reply letter with an enclosed card that voters could use to submit

their fingerprints to law enforcement. Because the process was carried out unevenly on the county level, there is no definitive estimate of how many Florida voters were purged. But one newspaper analysis would later manage to find nearly 20,000 citizens who were knocked off the rolls. Of these, more than 2,500 appealed and managed to reverse their disqualification, although some did not win back their right to vote until after the election was over.

One day in June, the *Palm Beach Post* published a short article on the "glitch" that was causing a storm of complaints. "I understand it can be a shocking thing as a citizen to say that we've identified you as a possible felon," the director of the Division of Elections told the paper. "But we're not accusing anybody of anything." It was just a one-day story, though, another case of government dysfunction, one more item on the list of things for Jeb Bush to fix.

Jeb was busy that week, however, campaigning with Dubya across Florida. The Bush brothers did a fraternal comedy routine, making competitive jokes about their heights—Jeb was three inches taller—at a series of campaign events and fund-raisers. A news photographer snapped an endearing photo of the pair engaging in a playful staring contest across the aisle of Dubya's campaign plane. Wearing matching gray suits, blue shirts, and red ties, they appeared at a flag-draped reception for war veterans at a hotel near Disney World.

"You're about to hear from my older, smarter, and wiser brother," Jeb said in his introductory speech, "who I hope and pray will be the next President of the United States."

Hope and prayer would have little to do with it.

13

Palm Beach

"Sometimes you play dirty in life," said Donald J. Trump. "So I snatched it."

He was speaking, of course, of Mar-a-Lago—his home, his castle, his clubhouse, and weekend base of operations. Trump would lie about anything, but this story was true. He had bought the place for cheap back in 1985, preying on a bottom-feeding opportunity. The woman who built the 60,000-square foot mansion, a cereal heiress, had willed it to the National Park Service upon her death, with the modest intention that it be used as the winter White House. It had turned out to be ruinously expensive to maintain, so Congress gave it back to her estate.

That was when Trump swooped in with an offer of $10 million for everything, including the antique furnishings. He took the books out of the library and made it into a bar, where he hung an oil painting of himself in tennis whites, entitled *The Visionary*.

Trump may have made his name and fortune in New York, but it was in Palm Beach that he honed his political method. The island, sixteen miles long and just a few blocks wide, was perhaps the most concentrated strip of wealth and snobbery in the world, separated by three drawbridges from the rest of Florida. At first, Trump was shunned by its social set, who considered him hopelessly déclassé.

Mar-a-Lago, as a lavish example of the island's Moorish-fantasia architectural style, was a landmark, beloved by the widows who ruled its matriarchal society. They wrinkled their noses at Trump's plans to turn the historic estate into a private club. For years, he battled the local government over zoning and other issues related to Mar-a-Lago. Trump relished these conflicts. They seemed to be how he kept himself entertained.

He posed as a democratizer and delighted in outraging the society crowd with his vulgar displays of wealth. He heckled the blue-blazered toffs, mimicking their upper-class accents to reporters. He attacked their existing private clubs, which admitted only the right kind of millionaires, ones with good bloodlines and old money. He charged his opponents with anti-Semitism and made sure everyone knew that Mar-a-Lago welcomed Jews. In 2000, Palm Beach was up in arms over his plans to build a new ballroom, a fight that had culminated in Trump's calling the head of the local civic association a "loser." This in turn had sparked a revolt against Trump-compliant members of the town council, who would end up being tossed from office.

"It's an entertainment club with a razzle-dazzle showman at the helm, and it boils down to the dollar," one anonymous "Old Guard socialite" sniffed to the *Palm Beach Daily News*—the party-picture paper known as "the Shiny Sheet"—around this time. But by 2000, Trump's war with the socialites was mostly over. He had fought them, insulted them, and over time, he had worn down the resistance. In the end, it was Palm Beach society that had changed, bending in his image.

Mar-a-Lago memberships were open to anyone willing to pay the $100,000 joining fee. A visiting writer for *George*, which put Trump on the cover of its February 2000 issue, described the club as "a kind of real-life *Love Boat* for status-hungry businessmen

you've never heard of." It was a hangout for guys like Bernie Madoff, the little-known financial genius who had helped to create the
NASDAQ and who very quietly ran a hedge fund that somehow
always made money. (In the summer of 2000, some crazed financial analyst was running around saying he had mathematical proof
that Madoff was running a Ponzi scheme, but no one was paying
attention.)

From Thanksgiving to Easter, the Palm Beach season, Trump
performed as Mar-a-Lago's master of ceremonies. Everywhere else,
he was ridiculed, but within his domain, he ruled. In the mornings, he could be seen strolling the grounds, munching on bacon,
and inspecting the landscaping. At night, he presided over the social festivities. Out late with a reporter one night by the pool, he
was boozily greeted by club members as "President Trump."

Everyone was laughing but him.

"Running for president is no stunt," Trump assured the reporter.
"If I do, I'll do it right."

Trump was acting like a genuine candidate, more or less, conducting a Rose Garden campaign from Mar-a-Lago. He unveiled a
snazzy website that featured his face superimposed over the White
House and released position papers, coming out in favor of social-
ized medicine and a repeal of the inheritance tax. (His family was
in the midst of dealing with the estate of his father, who had died
the year before, leaving a fortune in intricate tax shelters.) Trump
was on TV constantly, discriminating little between *Meet the Press*
and *Access Hollywood*. He leaked tidbits to Page Six, the gossip desk
of the *New York Post*, and blasted out statements by fax. He floated
the idea of asking Oprah Winfrey to be his running mate.

Trump invited journalists to fly to Palm Beach on his Boeing
727, the one with a full-size bed and the dubious Renoirs, with
his gang of sybaritic cronies and their girls. "On takeoff, Trump

usually prefers to sit in the cockpit with his crew of three," the *Washington Post* reporter Robin Givhan wrote. "To see Manhattan from the control room of your own 727 has to do something strange and terrifying to your head. In this overwrought world in which gray-haired men swagger about barking commands and waving giant cigars—because accepted decency prevents them from displaying their Freudian obsessions—anything seems possible. Even the presidency."

Christopher Byron, the *George* writer, did an interview with Trump at Mar-a-Lago that was interrupted by the intrusion of Melania, "a half-naked fashion model wrapped in a towel about the size of a dinner napkin." He concluded, "At the dawn of the third millennium, Donald Trump *is* America—a creature of limitless possibilities, ever reinventing itself, bold, noisy, juvenile, shallow, obsessed with material gain, but with a smile to the world as wide as all outdoors."

Dan Rather came to Mar-a-Lago to do a segment for *60 Minutes*, checked out Trump's new golf course and his blue Lamborghini, and came to a similar epiphany: "If there would be a poster boy to represent America at the turn of the millennium—the celebration of celebrity, the rich almost reeking of prosperity, continuing proof that the American Dream exists—then Donald Trump's picture might best fill the frame . . ."

In the year 2000, the possibility that Donald Trump might actually *become* president was so remote that it was safe to enjoy him entirely at the level of metaphor.

TO BEGIN WITH, Trump's chosen political vehicle was a sputtering clown car. His entry into the race had driven the Reform Party into chaos—although, to be fair, it didn't need much of a push. It was split into two factions. The old guard, clustered around Ross Perot in Dallas, wanted to keep the party true to the founder's vision. Trump's candidacy had the support of an opposing contingent, which was gaining influence after notching the party's biggest-ever win.

That victory belonged to Governor Jesse "The Body" Ventura. A hulking, bald blunderbuss, Ventura was famous from his days on the professional wrestling circuit, where he played the heel. (His motto was "Win if you can, lose if you must, but always cheat.") After retirement, he had returned home to Minnesota, where he hosted a popular radio talk show and got elected mayor of a suburban town. Then, running on the slogan "Retaliate in '98," he had shaken the state and delighted the media by scoring an upset in a three-way race for governor.

Ventura was something new to politics: a populist who had honed his outrageous style in the WWF, entertaining fans with the phony spectacle of carnival combat. "You control," Governor Ventura told a journalist, reflecting on the experience. "You're the manipulator." He was also a gun enthusiast and conspiracy theorist who expressed the belief that the military-industrial complex had orchestrated the Kennedy assassination. His ascent thrilled fans on the fringes.

"Jesse Ventura, in my mind, could be presidential timber," Chuck Harder said on his show in 1999. "Ventura has been able to get people that normally don't vote to vote, and he has really, really energized the young Americans." But Ventura had promised to serve his full term as governor, so he decided to back Trump, whom he had first met at a *WrestleMania* event.

Really, Trump was just a proxy—a handy weapon for Ventura to use in his grudge match with Perot. The Reformers called themselves a "cyberparty." They had little formal structure, and most of their political activity happened online, via mass emails that often degenerated into name-calling between Ventura's partisans and Perot loyalists, known as "Perotbots" to their detractors. The Perotbots were determined to prevent Trump and Ventura from taking over.

They turned to a right-wing insurgent. Pat Buchanan, a squinty Catholic pugilist, was the longtime cohost of CNN's *Crossfire* and a two-time candidate for president. In 1992, he had helped to doom the first President Bush's reelection by mounting a quixotic primary challenge, doing well enough to force his way into a prime-time appearance at the Republican National Convention, where he delivered an inflammatory call for a "cultural war." Running again four years later, Buchanan upset the Republican front-runner, Bob Dole, in the New Hampshire primary. "The peasants are coming with pitchforks!" he declared, earning the nickname "Pitchfork Pat."

In the 2000 cycle, Buchanan tried to run for the GOP nomination for a third time, but he found that the right lane had already been savvily blocked by George W. Bush, who had learned from his father's defeat. So, Pitchfork Pat started to flirt with the Perot faction of the Reform Party, who shared his protectionist positions on trade and his pessimistic view of the Clinton era. ("It's almost the late empire," Buchanan told the *New York Times Magazine*. "I think we are an unserious people in an unserious time.") Talking to Sean Hannity on Fox News, Buchanan offered a jovial mock confession of "impure thoughts" about straying from the Republican Party.

From the campaign trail in Iowa, Buchanan called up Harder to remind *For the People* listeners of his opposition to trade deals, the United Nations, and globalism. "I think they should remember that there was only one candidate in 1996 and 1992 that was telling them that this New World Order was a betrayal of everything our Founding Fathers stood for," Buchanan said. "That we were not to abscond in search of monsters to destroy, that we were to stay out of foreign wars that were none of our business."

Although Pitchfork Pat was born in Washington and lived in a pillared white house across the street from the CIA's headquarters in Northern Virginia, he talked like a rebel, promising to "drain this swamp." He called the Confederate flag "a banner of heroism" and welcomed the support of white nationalists. "I believe, and I hope, that one day we can take America back," he declared in a 2000 speech at Bob Jones University, the racist South Carolina school. In another speech around the same time, at Richard Nixon's presidential library in California, Buchanan claimed that "mass immigration" was creating "linguistic ghettoes" and warned that "America is Balkanizing like never before." Declaring that "a country that cannot control its borders is not sovereign," he called for building a fortified fence along the Rio Grande. He promised mass deportations of "illegals," although he made an exception for Elián Gonzalez.

Buchanan announced his shift to the Reform Party at a rally near his home in Virginia. "Let me say to the money boys and the Beltway elites who think that, at long last, they have pulled up their drawbridge and locked us out forever," he said: "You don't know this peasant army!"

Ventura, a libertarian who had recently given an interview to *Playboy* in which he called organized religion "a sham and a crutch for weak-minded people," viewed Buchanan as an opportunist and a wingnut. But Pitchfork Pat commanded the loyalty of dedicated volunteers, known as the "Buchanan Brigades," who were ready to take over state chapters of the Reform Party. Looking at polls that showed Buchanan could win about 10 percent of the vote in a three-way race, the Bush campaign was worried. It looked like Buchanan could cost them the election.

Then, for some reason known only to him, Buchanan decided to bring up the Nazis.

BUCHANAN'S CAMPAIGN SLOGAN, "America First," was a call back to an isolationist movement of the late 1930s that had been disgraced by its association with anti-Semitism and its sympathetic attitude toward Adolf Hitler. Buchanan set out to rehabilitate his predecessors with a revisionist history book. *A Republic, Not an Empire: Reclaiming America's Destiny* was published just as he moved to the Reform Party. Buchanan's opponents combed the book for objectionable passages—and found many. In it, Buchanan argued that the Allies were partly responsible for starting the Second World War. He claimed that Germany posed "no physical threat to the United States." Afterward, he wrote, "Jewish influence over foreign policy became almost an obsession with American leaders."

Chuck Harder welcomed Buchanan on to his show to promote *A Republic, Not an Empire.*

"I want to tell you," Harder told him, "you have written one heck of a book."

"The book is getting bashed all over the place," Buchanan replied, "but I'm very proud of it."

"Why are they bashing it?"

"I don't know," Buchanan said with a laugh. "They said it supports Hitler!"

Now, finally, Donald Trump had material he could work with. He fired off a bellicose fax. "Pat Buchanan's stated view that we should not have stopped Adolph Hitler is repugnant," he wrote, misspelling the Führer's given name. And with that, Trump skipped off happily on the warpath. In a *Wall Street Journal* column headlined "AMERICA NEEDS A PRESIDENT LIKE ME," Trump accused the other candidates of being slow to "denounce a man who winks at barbarism." He called Buchanan's supporters "little wacky people." He assailed Buchanan's political views as "medieval" and "prehistoric." He called him a "Hitler lover."

"He doesn't like the blacks, he doesn't like the gays," Trump told Tim Russert on *Meet the Press*. "It's just incredible that anybody could embrace this guy."

EVEN TRUMP'S OWN campaign staff could never tell how serious he was about politics. It was in these moments, drawing blood, that he seemed to be developing a taste for it. He reveled in provoking outrage and saying the unspeakable. He gleefully questioned Bush's intelligence and the heroism of John McCain, a former prisoner of war. ("Does being captured make you a hero?" Trump asked in his interview with Dan Rather. "I don't know, I'm not sure.") In a bylined essay in the *National Enquirer* entitled "Why I Should Be President," Trump predicted that voters would soon be "bored to death" by the other candidates. "I'm not plastic. I'm not scripted. I'm not 'handled,'" he wrote. "Maybe the voters would find that refreshing. I guarantee one thing, they'd find it interesting." Perhaps revealing its institutional bias, another story in that issue of the *Enquirer* was headlined "AL GORE'S DIET IS MAKING HIM STUPID."

One night, MSNBC host Chris Matthews gave Trump an entire episode of his show, *Hardball*, taped before a raucous audience at the University of Pennsylvania. Trump started off by proudly introducing his son "Donny," a student at the Wharton School of Business.

"Where's my supermodel?" he said, proudly pointing all eyes in the direction of Melania.

Trump batted off a few hardballs from Matthews.

Was he really running for president?

"I am, indeed."

When was he going to release his tax returns?

"They're very big, they're very complex."

Who was going to be his First Lady?

"I believe in the institution of marriage, there's nothing better. It beats being the world's greatest playboy by a million. But sometimes you don't have a choice."

Then Matthews lobbed him a big, fat softball.

"Who would you say, positively, would be your hero for this whole century?"

"Well," Trump replied, "I think Pat Buchanan would choose Adolf Hitler."

The candidate of tolerance and moderation had a warning for the voters. "He's got to be stopped," Trump said. "I mean, I've never seen anybody that could polarize like this."

14

Sugar

Three miles and an incalculable social distance from Mar-a-Lago, down by the railroad tracks in West Palm Beach, stood a small, shabby warehouse. This was where Ray Spears and Randy Glass sold their illegal weapons. Glass was the marketer; Spears was his supplier.

In contrast to his voluble partner, Spears would offer little to his customers about himself or the sources of his merchandise. He dressed well and talked like he had been in the military. He said he had inherited the arms business from his father. When pressed, he would imply that some of the goods were stolen from the U.S. Army or diverted by corrupt manufacturers. He said he kept his inventory down in Mexico and used the warehouse as a showroom. One Tuesday morning, Diaa Mohsen—Kevin Ingram's talkative friend Didi—brought a pair of Pakistanis there to shop.

The visitors had flown down the day before with Didi. For months, the Egyptian had been working with Glass to find arms buyers. These looked like serious customers. They told Didi they had connections to the Pakistani military and the ISI, the nation's spy service.

"They're the central intelligence of Pakistan," Didi had explained to Glass in a phone call.

"Do they have hooks into the government?" Glass asked.

"They *are* the fucking government!"

When they arrived in Florida, the Pakistanis gave Glass and Spears their business cards, identifying themselves as R. G. Abbas and M. A. Malik, the directors of a prepaid calling card company called Close to Home Communications. As Spears drove them in his Cadillac to a Radisson hotel in Boca Raton, Malik said his contacts back in Pakistan had instructed him to be careful about what he said over the phone. The preliminary discussions continued at the hotel. Didi introduced Malik and Abbas as "the real guys." They said they were acting as procurement agents for the ISI, serving multiple end users—not just the Pakistani military, but also Islamic militants in Afghanistan and the Indian state of Kashmir, groups that ISI covertly supported.

The Pakistanis particularly wanted to buy Stinger missiles. During the 1980s, Stingers supplied by the CIA had served rebels in Afghanistan very effectively against the Soviet Army. Many missiles were left over after the civil war ended, but that supply was old and dwindling, and Stingers were rare to find on the black market. So, the ISI was very interested, Malik said. But he cautioned that, for reasons of security, they would want to move cautiously. The arms trade was full of thieves and con artists. Glass and Spears promised them that all doubt would be dispelled once they saw what was in the warehouse. The next morning, Spears picked them up at the hotel.

At the warehouse, a tough-looking man opened a gate topped with razor wire and directed the customers inside. They entered and beheld an arsenal. M16 machine guns were propped up in a row against one wall. There was a large box filled with blocks of C-4 plastic explosives. The dealers opened up nine large black cases, displaying the Stingers inside. Abbas said he was familiar with the weapon. The tubby Pakistani picked one up and put it on his shoulder, and Glass took a Polaroid, so Abbas could show his contacts back home that the missiles were genuine. Spears said the price for the Stingers was $150,000 apiece, or $125,000 if they placed a large order.

The Pakistanis flew back to New Jersey, where they were based. A week later, Abbas called Glass to tell him he had been in conversation with top officials in Pakistan. They were excited. Abbas asked Glass if it would be possible to purchase two hundred to three hundred of his "toys," by which he meant the Stingers. Spears later called him back to say he could probably do one hundred to start.

Abbas flew to Pakistan to negotiate the terms of the deal. It took a while, and during this time, Malik, who lived with his family in New Jersey, stayed in the United States and acted as a messenger. In February 2000, Malik flew to Florida to meet with Spears, bringing him a copper serving dish as a gift from Pakistan along with a nineteen-page list of helicopter parts he said his nation's military wanted to order. They went to lunch at a steak house in Fort Lauderdale. Malik said that he and Abbas were talking not only to the government of Pakistan, but also to representatives of Iran and "private people," middlemen who, he indicated, were associated with potential purchasers in the "north"—in other words, Kashmir and Afghanistan.

Malik and Spears discussed how to get the illegal shipments past customs inspectors. The plan was to conceal the arms as farm equipment and to ship them via a roundabout route through Dubai or China. Keeping up the agricultural ruse, the Pakistanis proposed to employ a simple code in their negotiations. Tank ammunition was to be referred to as "tobacco." Antitank rockets would be "tomatoes." And the most desired items, the Stinger missiles, would be the "sugar."

RANDY GLASS HAD first approached Didi about selling arms in late 1998. He told the Egyptian he had come across a supplier, who turned out to be Spears, and said he needed someone who could reach the international black market. Didi was delighted to help, offering to tutor Glass in the violent ways of the world. "It's always fucking boiling. Fanatics from both sides," he said. "That's how our factory works." Didi referred to himself as "overseas.com." He tried to peddle the merchandise in various war-torn countries, getting a few nibbles from potential customers purporting to represent Serbian paramilitaries and Chechen rebels and coming close to a sale to an embattled Congolese dictator. But the Pakistanis were Didi's best prospects yet.

At first, Glass found it difficult to believe the Pakistanis were serious. M. A. Malik—"Mike" to his American friends in Jersey City—looked like a striving immigrant, not a secret agent. In addition to his phone card company, Malik owned a couple of liquor stores and a laundry business. He served on the local zoning board. But Didi, who knew him from the tennis courts, told Glass that this seeming normality was a diabolical disguise. Glass flew to New York, and he and Malik went out to dinner at the Tribeca Grill, actor Robert De Niro's trendy bistro, where Malik introduced him to Abbas, a visitor to the United States and his partner in the phone card business. (Didi said it was a front.) Over dinner, Glass later claimed, the Pakistanis spoke of working with Osama bin Laden and other enemies of the United States, indiscreetly confiding that they wouldn't mind blowing up the entire restaurant.

"Who exactly am I dealing with here?" Glass asked Didi in a phone call soon afterward.

"You're dealing with a country," Didi replied. "Central intelligence."

"I mean, he told me he said that he was dealing with bin Laden, he said he was dealing with Iran," Glass said uncertainly. "So, this guy's for real, right?"

"Randy, they're for real," Didi replied. "Trust me."

Malik and Abbas told the arms dealers that the ISI had various intertwined agendas, all of which traced back to a single imperative: countering Pakistan's neighbor and archrival, India, in a long-running regional confrontation. In 1998, India and Pakistan had tested nuclear weapons, breaking an arms control treaty and incurring harsh U.S. trade sanctions. As a result, the Pakistani military could no longer buy replacement parts for its American-made fighter jets and helicopters, which presumably explained why the ISI would be looking for them on the black market. The Pakistanis were also trying to harass India through unconventional strategies. The ISI regarded militant Islamist groups in Kashmir and Afghanistan as useful proxies in this larger struggle.

When Pakistan had its military coup in late 1999, Malik assured the arms dealers it was a positive development. "Now we have our own people in power," he said. General Pervez Musharraf depended on the support of a handful of other top military commanders, the most important of whom he put in charge of the ISI. The new spy chief, an urbane military history buff, was also judged by the CIA to be a devoutly religious Muslim, with an "evident personal enthusiasm for the Taliban" that went "well beyond considerations of Pakistani national interest." The ISI was already riddled with Islamist sympathizers. Through its clandestine Directorate S, the Pakistani agency dealt closely with the Taliban, which in turn was sheltering Al Qaeda. According to a former member of bin Laden's inner circle, ISI operatives facilitated the movement of jihadis into Afghanistan and even sent instructors to work in the training camps.

The Pakistani government officially claimed it was trying to stamp out the terrorists. But Musharraf's regime was apparently playing a double game, offering cooperation with one hand while keeping the other behind its back. Malik said the ISI had a secret budget for black-market arms purchases. The deals would have to be approved by top military leaders, up to perhaps even Musharraf himself. But once it "clicks," Malik assured the dealers, there would be "never ending business."

In March 2000, though, the talks hit a temporary obstacle. Abbas reported that the generals had gone quiet. The CIA station in Islamabad was on high alert, because President Clinton was preparing to pay a visit.

Through his own spy agencies, Clinton was well aware of the ISI's duplicitous behavior in Afghanistan. He was trying to pressure Musharraf to crack down on Al Qaeda. On March 25, 2000, he traveled to Pakistan for an unusual summit. Because the CIA had intelligence that terrorists might try to shoot down the president with a Stinger missile, Air Force One was used as a decoy while Clinton flew in on an unmarked jet. The streets of the capital were cleared, and he was whisked in an armored car to meet Musharraf. In an intense conversation, Clinton pressed the general to use Pakistan's influence to convince the Taliban to expel Osama bin Laden. But Musharraf assured the Americans, with a straight face, that he had little leverage over the Taliban. The next day, Ziad Jarrah took his trip to Munich to sign up for classes at the Florida Flight Training Center.

RAY SPEARS WAS losing his patience. "We want to do business with you," he wrote in a letter that he faxed to the Pakistanis. "You and your people now need to show me that you are serious about wanting to do business. We are ready NOW." He underlined the last word three times for emphasis. "You know what merchandise we have and what the costs are. The next move must be made by you and your people. I suggest you bring someone in authority to the U.S. so that we can get the first container on the water."

On April 14, more than two weeks after Clinton's visit, R. G. Abbas faxed Spears a four-page handwritten reply from Pakistan. "LOVE LETTER," it read at the top.

"Mr. Ray," the letter said. "We are very much close to the deal of 50 sugar bags. You know very well these deal [sic] take a time. I send you inspection proforma on behalf of this I fix the price with inspectors of PK." He then listed many additional technical questions about the merchandise and asked about new items, such as air-to-air missiles for helicopters.

Spears faxed a letter in reply. "You must understand this: All of the sugar items have been performance tested in every way," the arms dealer wrote. "The U.S. military would not accept the sugar items if they were not tested 100%! All of the sugar items are completely assembled and ready to use. You and your people will not need any additional parts to make these items function. Do I make myself clear?? The items are ready now!!

"The answer to all of your questions on the sugar items for questions number 1 through 31 is YES! . . .

"Abbas, it is now the time for you to place an order."

Abbas made a series of calls from Pakistan pleading for more time. He said that many generals had to approve a purchase of this magnitude, and he assured Spears that the military trusted him because his own father was a retired general. One day, Abbas called Spears with someone he introduced as a military officer named Farid. Farid assured Spears that the project had "special funding" and had now worked its way up the chain of command to the "top man." He added that Pakistan had been allied with the Americans for fifty years and that it had helped them defeat the Soviet Union in Afghanistan. "We are a proven friend," Farid assured Spears, "just the friendship is on hold."

In the next breath, the officer added that Pakistan had other weapons suppliers. There was a cheaper, competing bid from the French. The ISI had a team currently shopping in North Korea.

As long as the sale hung in limbo, Spears and Glass had no money to launder. For months, Kevin Ingram had taken no part in their schemes. Ingram and Glass had argued and were no longer speaking. "I think by that time," Ingram says, "I had realized that these guys were bad news."

Glass claimed that Ingram had lost interest when it became apparent that his promises of an imminent investment of $10 million or $20 million was, in Ingram's words, "way off." Ingram counters that Glass was "creepy" and lied about everything. Ingram and Didi did try to patch things up with Spears and another of his partners, his accountant, at a restaurant in Boca Raton. At some point, Didi forgot about compartmentalizing and lapsed into talking about the arms deals at the table. Spears noticed that when this happened, Ingram seemed to tune out the conversation, striking up a parallel chat about money with the accountant.

Shortly after that lunch meeting, Ingram also cut off contact with Spears. "Of all the targets, he was the most circumspect," the man he knew as Spears recalls of Ingram. "He was intelligent. I had the feeling this was a guy who did well for himself, but still maintained his street smarts."

Ingram was right to be wary. Ray Spears was not an arms dealer, and he was not named Ray Spears. He was an undercover federal law enforcement agent. And Randy Glass was a rat.

Ingram had walked right into a sting operation.

So had the Pakistanis. Abbas soon reported that the generals had approved the purchase of five hundred Stinger missiles. If everything went as planned, he said, the first shipment could be on the water by June.

15

Go Time

Parkinson's disease is a degenerative nervous condition, and Janet Reno knew it would take everything from her in the end. At first, her symptoms were just an annoyance. When her medication kept her from getting a decent night's sleep, she would cut it back, dismissing the concerns of her press secretary, who worried that the attorney general would look weak to the news cameras. "So, I'll be an old lady who shakes," Reno said. As time wore on, the tremors grew pronounced. They were exacerbated in periods of stress, such as the Elián standoff. Her voice would quaver. She would clasp her hands tightly on her lap to keep them still. Nonetheless, she kept working, thinking, scribbling lists and plans in looped and wiggly handwriting, trying for a negotiated solution.

Legally, Elián's family members in Miami had no right to resist the attorney general's order to turn the boy over. They had lost every round of their fight in court, and though they kept appealing, Reno had the power to take the boy into custody. After all, Elián was an undocumented immigrant. Still, Reno waited and waited, hoping a little more conversation would somehow yield a settlement. "Obviously, it was because it was a little child," says Maggy Hurchalla, Reno's younger sister. "She saw a little boy in a situation with a bunch of stupid, angry grown-ups—no matter which side they were on—that might turn unnecessarily into death and disaster."

The morning after Lázaro's declaration of defiance, Reno spoke to Sister Jeanne, who said there might be one last hope. She ordered her staff in Washington to ready a plane.

"I'm just going to go," Reno said. She wanted to see Elián herself.

At a crucial moment, Reno was improvising, heading to the nun's residence in Miami Beach without a clear idea of her endgame. Choppers hovered over her Lincoln Town Car, broadcasting live on the evening news, as she made a surreal trip through the streets of her hometown. Reno was grave as the car cut through a jeering crowd outside the nun's house. Inside, after an exhausting day of shuttle diplomacy, Sister Jeanne had gathered Elián and his guardians.

Reno met the family in the dining room, where they were joined by a small delegation of her aides and a child psychologist. Elián dribbled a soccer ball and watched cartoons in another part of the house as the adults closed the door to talk. In her shaky hand, the attorney general took detailed notes. Marisleysis, she observed, was "very weak, very fragile." She had come straight from the hospital, where she had been convalescing. With the braces on her teeth and her high-strung demeanor, she looked more like a teenager than a surrogate mother. But she vowed to give her life to raising Elián as if he were her own son. Marisleysis said Elián had begged her not to let him leave, telling her, "My mother drowned. I don't want to go back." She claimed he had told her he was afraid of his father. She feared he would be "brainwashed" by Castro.

"In his eyes," she said, according to Reno's notes, "you will know what he really wants."

Elián would barge into the dining room from time to time, hopping onto the laps of the adults. A witness later described him to the *Herald* as "hyperkinetic." He bit the psychologist.

Reno came out of the meeting wearing a crestfallen expression. She had tried to explain the law to the family, saying they were out of options and had to give the boy up to the authorities. But the Gonzalez clan seemed impervious to reason. Close to midnight, as he left Sister Jeanne's house, Lázaro gave a threatening statement to the cameras, calling Reno's ultimatum "a traitorous act."

"Our position is that we will not turn over the child—anywhere," he said, adding ominously, "I want you all to know, the whole world to see, they are preparing to take a child from my home. They are training federal agents to attack my house."

Late that night, Reno set a deadline, saying Elián had to be turned over at the airport at 2 p.m. the next day. A nervous mood settled over Camp Elián, where activists kept watch all night. In the early morning hours, Armando Gutierrez came out and handed the news crew from Univision a videotape. It contained a forty-second statement from Elián, speaking in Spanish from his bedroom.

"Dad, did you see that old woman who went to the home of that little nun? She wants to take me to Cuba," he said, shaking his finger. "I tell you all now that I don't want to go to Cuba."

Soon the video was airing everywhere. Elián watched it the next morning in the family's living room with a crowd of supporters. The tiny house was crammed with local dignitaries: the mayor; actor Andy Garcia; Gloria Estefan, the beloved Miami pop singer. One of the men who rescued Elián, a house cleaner named Donato Dalrymple, also stopped in. He had lately become a regular visitor and a cable TV celebrity, even traveling to Washington for an awkward meeting with Elián's father. ("You know, I've never felt important in my life," Dalrymple, who called himself "the Fisherman," told the *Washington Post*. "He makes people feel important and loved and powerful.")

Elián ran around the house with his arms outstretched, imitating a plane. Outside, a swelling crowd readied themselves for the federal marshals, chanting, *War! War! War!*

Just before her 2 p.m. deadline, Reno made a televised statement: there would be no raid. She was backing down, giving negotiation even more time. An FBI official told the *Herald*, "The last thing Janet Reno wants to see on the front page of every paper in the country is a picture of a crying little boy being carried from that home by a federal agent."

The picture would be so much worse.

BILL CLINTON WAS ready to put an end to the ordeal. "I have done everything I could to stay out of it, to avoid politicizing it," he said on Reno's deadline day. "But I do believe it is our responsibility to uphold the rule of law." Publicly, he expressed sympathy to his attorney general in her "very painful situation." Off the record, though, his aides said they were "fed up" with the Miami relatives and added to the pressure on Reno. An anonymous presidential adviser told the *New York Times*, "A lot of us think she cannot make a decision on this to save her soul."

The press questioned Reno's fathomless faith in dialogue. "The resolution of the Elián case hinges on Janet Reno's inner conflicts, her Waco flashbacks, and her post-traumatic-stress syndrome from the Miami riots during her time as prosecutor there," columnist Maureen Dowd wrote in the *Times* on April 19. "The harder the attorney general tries to come to the rescue, the more elusive the rescue becomes. The more compassionate she is, the more endangered the object of her compassion. The tougher she talks, the deeper the other side digs in.

"You can feel her loneliness."

That day, Reno had to attend to a solemn obligation. April 19 was the anniversary of the Oklahoma City bombing, which of course was also the anniversary of Waco. In the afternoon, she flew to Oklahoma City on a government jet to attend the dedication of a national memorial. While her plane was en route, she learned of a surprise setback: a federal appeals court in Atlanta had issued a ruling that not only prohibited Juan Miguel from taking Elián out of the country while the family's lawsuit was being considered, but also appeared to accept that a six-year-old might be granted asylum against his father's wishes. In Little Havana, people were celebrating in the streets, although nothing in the court order prevented the INS from taking custody of Elián.

Reno revisited the scene of the terrorist attack. The street where Timothy McVeigh had parked his truck bomb was now a reflecting pond. She spoke just before Clinton. "We have come to rededicate ourselves to the belief," the attorney general said, "that we can build a better, stronger society, where conflicts are resolved peacefully, where laws are enforced justly."

Reno's plane had experienced a mechanical problem on the flight from Washington, and she ended up returning with Clinton on Air Force One. On the flight, the president summoned the attorney general to his cabin for a tense forty-five-minute conversation. He pressed her to act.

The next day, at Main Justice, the department began to make final preparations for what it was calling "Operation Reunion." Reno's preference had been to move calmly, during the daytime, but undercover agents, disguised as newspaper photographers, were doing surveillance in the crowd, listening to conversations in which protesters argued among themselves about whether to resist with force. Armed guards were reported to be in the house, and members of the paramilitary group Alpha 66 were in the crowd outside. A group of ten to twenty men, some of whom had criminal records, had camped out in an adjoining yard to provide added security.

There were rumors that guns were stashed in neighboring houses. That Thursday night, Marisleysis was alleged to have told an INS official, "You think we just have cameras in the house? If people try to come in, they could be hurt." The undercover operatives also tried to figure out, from sources who had visited the house, whether Lázaro was drinking.

The safest course, Reno decided, would be one she had been trying to avoid at all costs. She would go in with heavy force, in the dead of night, with a military-style raid. The operation would be set in motion over the approaching Easter weekend, when crowds outside would likely be thinner.

Yet, even now, Reno hesitated, consulting a group of Miami civic leaders who were trying to mount a last-ditch mediation effort. Negotiations continued through Good Friday as the operation waited for her signal. With tensions rising around the Gonzalez house, the Washington attorney representing Juan Miguel faxed a letter to all the television news networks, asking them to cut away from the scene once the raid began. "We believe that to broadcast to the public what will doubtless be an extremely difficult and emotional moment in this young boy's life," he wrote, would only "increase the damage and deepen the emotional suffering." Rather than considering the request, Fox News reported about the letter on the air. "I think the kid would rather have had a camera pointed at him than an automatic weapon," Roger Ailes would later tell the *Times*.

A team of around one hundred fifty federal agents mustered around midnight. The Miami mediators continued to plead for patience over the phone, saying a breakthrough was near. Reno polled the half-dozen or so key advisers sitting with her in the private office at Main Justice. It was time.

At around 4 a.m. on Holy Saturday, Reno called Miami. "It's a go," she said.

IT WAS ALL over very quickly. At about 5:10 a.m., the reporters at Camp Elián, dozing in chairs and sleeping bags, were awakened by commotion at the police barricade at the end of the block. A convoy of trucks and vans roared up the street, and members of a Border Patrol tactical unit sprang out, dressed in body armor. Some were armed with rifles, some with tear gas guns and pepper spray.

"They're here! They're here!" a cameraman shouted as everyone grabbed equipment.

Around back, another group of agents leaped the fence and took control of the yard, shouting, "Down or I'll shoot!" Armando Gutierrez heard the commotion and slammed the back door. "They're coming!" he screamed. Lázaro was sleeping on the couch with Elián beside him. Donato Dalrymple, the fisherman, was also sleeping there. Dalrymple scooped up Elián, who was screaming, and rushed him into Lázaro's bedroom. Meanwhile, Gutierrez opened the front door to let in a friendly Associated Press photographer, who had vaulted the chain-link fence in front of the house as soon as the convoy appeared. Roughly two dozen protesters also managed to make it into the front yard before the agents. They were subdued with tear gas.

An entry team rushed through the melee toward the house. They beat at the doors, then used battering rams to knock them down. A federal Border Patrol officer, wearing military-style tactical gear and carrying a 9-mm submachine gun, led the way to Lázaro's bedroom, where the fisherman was hiding in a closet with Elián in his arms. The AP photographer was there, too.

"*Que esta pasando?*" Elián asked the adults—what is happening?

The Border Patrol officer entered brandishing his submachine gun. The photographer snapped a picture. And just like that, in a frozen instant, the future shifted a little.

"Back off!" the officer yelled at the photographer. He grabbed Elián and handed him back to another member of the entry team, a female agent in an INS windbreaker who spoke fluent Spanish. She wrapped him in a blanket and rushed him through the living room, where other agents were holding Lázaro down on the couch. She carried the boy out the front door, through the tear gas, and climbed into a white van. The team was inside the house for just fifty-seven seconds. "We're taking you to see your papa," the female agent whispered to Elián.

He never saw Lázaro, Marisleysis, or Miami again.

Protesters hurled rocks, plastic chairs, and other objects at the van as it pulled away, and news cameras captured Marisleysis, in the backyard, collapsing in paroxysms of sobbing.

"God, how could you have performed only half a miracle?" she cried out in anguish. Soon, though, she recovered enough to show reporters around her ransacked house and to attack Reno. "She lied to this country," she said. "To me, she doesn't have a heart."

Reno addressed the press that morning, looking visibly relieved. She was asked about the stark photo, immediately indelible, of the federal agent with his gun pointing in the direction of a terrified child. "One of the beauties of television is that it shows exactly what the facts are," Reno replied. "If you look at it carefully, it shows that the gun was pointed to the side and that the finger was not on the trigger." Of course, Reno was wrong. No one—least of all the voters of Florida—would remember the precise angle of the gun's barrel. They just saw the show of force.

The truth was Reno really didn't care how it looked. It was over. Elián was on a plane to Washington. Reno went back to her apartment, lay on the couch, and slept for the first time in days. In the mid-afternoon, she was awoken by a call from her sister, Maggy. "Quick, look at the television," Maggy said. Now there was a second photo, of the boy in his father's arms.

"There was Elián Gonzalez, with the most radiant smile on his face that you can imagine," Reno recalled later. "And I knew I had done exactly the right thing."

Two days later, Reno saw President Clinton at the White House for the annual Easter Egg Roll. She read her favorite book, *Voyage to the Bunny Planet*, to a group of children. Clinton was happy with the outcome for Elián, but as always, he was thinking about political consequences. "I was confident that we had followed the only course open to us," he later wrote, "but I was still concerned that it could cost Al Gore Florida in November."

16

Earth Day

Al Gore's office in the West Wing of the White House was crammed with books and decorated with a framed poster, a photo of Earth as viewed from the moon by the Apollo astronauts. He told visitors it offered him a constant reminder of the "overview effect," the feeling of cosmic insignificance experienced by those few people who have ever seen the planet from that distance. The image, which had helped inspire the first celebration of Earth Day in 1970, also served as an apt metaphor for Gore's approach to his earthly business. He was an unabashed globalist, a holistic thinker. When he faced political adversity, his inclination was always to elevate.

On Friday, April 21, as Janet Reno engaged in her feverish final negotiations over the fate of Elián, Gore flew to Detroit to celebrate the thirtieth annual Earth Day. The visit was hastily thrown together, over the misgivings of some Gore campaign advisers, who were of the belief that the environment was a losing political issue, especially in the swing state of Michigan. But Gore insisted, and so there he stood, in a chilly, cavernous truck depot, decrying "the politics of environmental irresponsibility." He renewed his call, first set out in *Earth in the Balance*, to phase out the internal combustion engine. "I remember the fierce criticism I got eight years ago," he said. "I expected that criticism then, and I wear it as a badge of honor today."

Campaigning against the motor in the Motor City was a counterintuitive strategy, but Gore was trying to escape to a higher plane. He wanted to do something—anything—to change the subject from his mundane missteps. The environment was his touchstone: the one subject, perhaps, on which no one doubted his urgent conviction. A ten-year federal study released that spring had found that temperatures were already rising steadily and projected a further increase of five to ten degrees during the twenty-first century under a "business-as-usual" scenario. Gore knew time was wasting. The initiative he unveiled on Earth Day called for a new federal program to produce fuel-efficient engines for commercial trucks—the kind of practical, mechanical innovation that ignited his Gore-like enthusiasm. It was part of a $125 billion package of proposals that Gore rolled out over the course of the spring and summer, an ambitious agenda that stood in stark contrast to the drilling plans of the former oilman George W. Bush.

After the Earth Day event, Gore held his first press conference in two months. The reporters wanted to ask about Elián, about a never-ending federal investigation into the 1996 reelection campaign's fund-raising—about anything, really, other than carbon emissions. "While hammering Mr. Bush on policy matters," the *New York Times* reporter covering the campaign wrote the next day, "he is still struggling to overcome a problem that has dogged him since early in the campaign: how to demonstrate that he has a warm and human side, a passion for the presidency and ideals that are not tossed by political winds."

"EARTH DAY GIG NOT EXACTLY EARTHSHAKING," read the headline of a news analysis in the next day's *Detroit Free Press*.

Then, within twenty-four hours, the lightning raid in Miami would knock Gore's campaign off balance again. Although polls showed that a majority of Americans backed Elián's father's custody claim, Reno's use of force and the shocking photo of the seizure of the boy provoked a swift and bipartisan backlash in Florida. A Republican congressman from Miami called the raid a "monstrous crime," akin to throwing "a 6-year-old boy over the Berlin Wall." Senator Bob Graham, the highest Democratic elected official in the state and a potential Gore running mate, did a Sunday-morning talk show interview outside the Gonzalez home in Little Havana and said he felt betrayed by Clinton, who had promised him that the boy would not be taken away in the night. Graham called April 22, 2000, "another day that will live in infamy."

Cuban community leaders organized a one-day general strike, closing businesses and emptying schools. In an unusual show of political protest in sports, the many Cuban baseball players around the major leagues—most prominently, slugger Jose Canseco of the Tampa Bay Devil Rays—announced their decision to sit out a game in solidarity. Six players on Miami's team, the Marlins, stayed home. They lost in extra innings after running out of pinch hitters.

In Washington, Republicans accused Clinton and Reno of behaving like tyrants. "This could only happen in Castro's Cuba," said Trent Lott, the Senate majority leader. "I was ashamed of the United States government," said Tom DeLay, the most powerful Republican in the House of Representatives, who likened the federal agents who carried out Reno's orders to "jackbooted thugs." Mayor Rudy Giuliani of New York City, who was running against Hillary Clinton for the Senate, called the agents "storm troopers." George W. Bush, now the party's certain nominee, declared that the "chilling picture of the little boy being removed from his home at gunpoint defies the values of America and is not an image a freedom-loving nation wants to show the world."

Gore released a short statement appealing for calm and declining to endorse or condemn the raid.

At the White House, Bill Clinton was seething. For the first time in almost three decades, he was not running for anything himself. But he still held strategy sessions in the Yellow Oval Room, near his living quarters in the East Wing, where he would chew on an unlit cigar and game out the 2000 campaign. "Clinton is obsessed with Florida," a prominent Democratic senator told the *Times* that May. Even after Elián, Clinton thought the state was in play. But Gore had no interest in listening to Clinton, about strategy or anything else. From mid-May to mid-October, he never once entered the White House. He was out of there now, in his own distanced orbit.

CLINTON AND GORE made a handsome couple back in that first flush of the 1992 campaign, but they were never as compatible as they superficially appeared. Clinton described their initial chemistry as "correct, but not warm." Off camera, they were the opposite of their caricatures. The great empathizer, Clinton, was self-centered and often flew into rages; the robot, Gore, was funny and could disarm his boss with a wisecrack. "Gore was much more linear in his thought process, much more male, if you will," his policy adviser Elaine Kamarck later said. "Clinton was much more female, intuitive . . . Clinton essentially picked, in Gore, his wife. He picked Hillary." And that was where the tension began.

There was always a seesawing dynamic to the Clinton-Gore relationship, which was complicated by the reality that there was a second Clinton on the other side of the lever. Hillary and Al fought for influence over the president through their White House staffs. "There was a sandbox intensity to the struggle," Joe Klein, the court chronicler of the Clinton administration, wrote in *The New Yorker* in 2000. At first, Hillary was up. The president treated his wife as a partner in governing and let her take control of his health care reform plan, while Gore spent the tumultuous first two years of the administration toiling down in the bowels of the federal bureaucracy on his "reinventing government" initiative. Then Newt Gingrich and the Republicans humiliated Clinton in the 1994 midterms, partly by demonizing Hillary, and Gore was on top, helping to lead the counterattack, which involved embracing "small government" policies that Hillary and her allies hated.

Clinton and Gore were easily reelected, only to find themselves embroiled in a scandal over their campaign fund-raising, in which Gore had played a central role. "Mr. Vice President," one of his advisers had told him, "the bill is coming due for Bill Clinton, and you are going to pay for it." Actually, that was just the first installment. On January 17, 1998, the Drudge Report, a weird little gossip page on the brand-new World Wide Web, published an item about Clinton's rumored affair with a White House intern. The ensuing uproar threatened to destroy his presidency. Gore stood behind Clinton through his months of impassioned denials and then, in the face of DNA evidence, his confession. Gore read the independent counsel's novelistic report on the affair with prurient fascination. ("Is the cigar story really in there?" he asked his staff.)

"The women in the White House had absolutely *no* illusions about Bill," Kamarck said, but what was truly shocking was his lapse in political judgment. "The assumption was that Bill was a horndog, he wasn't going to change, he hadn't changed. But the thing that was so brutal about '98 was that the woman involved was not somebody to be trusted. It was an intern, a kid."

Gore grew convinced that he was the one who would end up paying the price for Clinton's disgraceful behavior. As his estrangement from Clinton grew, though, the president's relationship with his other partner pulled closer. Though the Lewinsky scandal was a personal humiliation to Hillary, it also made her indispensable to her husband. Losing her support was the one thing his presidency probably could not have survived, but she chose to persist. In the summer of 1999, Hillary appeared on the cover of the inaugural issue of *Talk*, the buzzy new magazine that editor Tina Brown had started with Harvey Weinstein, the movie producer and friend of the Clintons. "Is he ashamed? Yes," Hillary told the magazine. "Is he sorry? Yes. But does that negate everything that he has done as a husband, a father, a president?

"What is so amazing," Hillary said, "is that Bill has not been defeated by this."

It turned out that Americans liked Hillary when she was humbled, and her popularity soared. As her husband faced his trial in the Senate in 1999, Hillary considered whether to join it. She spent those months making exploratory forays to New York, where a Senate seat was open in 2000. She and Bill purchased a house in the suburb of Chappaqua, where she lived separately from her husband for much of the time, prompting rumors of a split. But she would later describe her Senate campaign as a form of marital therapy. "Bill and I were talking again about matters other than the future of our relationship," she wrote. "We both began to relax." Bill was popular in New York. Hillary wanted her husband at her side and was eager to deploy him as a fund-raiser.

Hillary had to overcome two obstacles. One was her probable opponent, Mayor Giuliani, who had proven appeal with blue-collar Democrats and a biting personality tailored to New York City's tabloid culture. The other problem was that she had never lived in New York. So, the First Lady began to learn the ways of the natives. In March, a month after announcing her candidacy, she attended the Inner Circle Dinner, an annual charity event put on by the New York City press corps, where local politicians pretended to enjoy satirical skits lampooning their vanities and scandals.

The theme of that year's dinner was "Livin' la Rudy Loca." Giuliani was the star of the show. Hillary swanned into a grand Manhattan hotel ballroom wearing jewels and black satin. As she made her way to her table, where she was sitting as a guest of the publisher of the New York *Daily News*, the First Lady tapped the mayor on his shoulder to offer an unintimidated hello.

"I hope that, as someone who isn't from New York, she doesn't miss the jokes," Giuliani told reporters covering the event. Hillary obligingly laughed along to routines that made fun of her carpetbagging and her husband's infidelities. ("Chappaqua . . . That's Indian for 'the Land of Separate Bedrooms.'") The highlight of the show, though, was a series of short films in which Giuliani, reprising a skit from previous years, dressed in drag, wearing a blond wig and a lavender gown. In one scene, shot in a department store, Giuliani encountered a good friend.

"You know, you're really beautiful," Donald Trump said, making his approving, purse-lipped expression. Giuliani, affecting a squeaky female voice, acted flattered and spritzed on some perfume. Trump nuzzled the mayor's neck and buried his face between his large fake breasts.

"Oh, you dirty boy, you!" Giuliani said, slapping Trump. "Donald, I thought you were a gentleman."

The audience groaned. *Donald Trump?* That joke was so tired.

Everyone expected to be very entertained, though, by the coming confrontation between Rudy and Hillary. (They were both on a first-name basis with the tabloids.) The *National Enquirer* was full of speculation over the state of the Clinton marriage. The conservative Clinton-outrage factory was busily churning out new material. Republican lawyer Barbara Olson, a veteran of the Clinton investigations who was now a TV commentator, published a biography called *Hell to Pay*. It portrayed Hillary as both a corrupt "aider and abettor" to her husband and a radical seeking to "foment revolutionary changes from the uniform of a pink suit."

"Now she is inventing a career beyond her husband, to make her own place in history—to find a path to ultimate power," Olson wrote. "But serving as the junior senator from New York will not provide a stage big enough for such ambitions. Like Eleanor Roosevelt before her, Hillary Clinton seeks nothing less than an office that will give her a platform from which to exercise real power and real world leadership." The Clinton era, Olson concluded, "is far from over."

Rudy was picking up his own attacks on the "Clinton Machine," and Bill Clinton soon replied in kind, calling Giuliani a tool of a "right-wing venom machine." But just as the show was starting to hit its stride, the plot fell apart. In April, Rudy disclosed that he had been diagnosed with prostate cancer, putting his campaign in doubt, and then in May, he held a press conference to announce he was leaving his marriage to be with his new girlfriend, much to the surprise of his wife, who was given no warning of the separation.

Rudy's supporters deserted him, with the lonely exception of Trump, who endorsed the mayor at a public event in the midst of his marital meltdown. "You're the best," the developer said. Nonetheless, Rudy dropped out, leaving Hillary to face only token opposition.

They'd get her next time.

AS BILL CLINTON watched his wife, a first-time candidate, navigating her way to the Senate, he was concerned that Gore's campaign was adrift. When Gore stopped talking to him regularly, Clinton grew passive-aggressive, calling up mutual friends to offer undermining strategic criticisms, in the apparent hope that they would filter back to the candidate. This gossip reached the press, as Clinton must have known it would. When he learned that the *Times* was preparing to publish a story about his private opinion that Gore seemed "listless," the president called up the reporter himself. "It is true," Clinton confirmed, "that I have urged him to go out there and enjoy this."

Clinton still had many friendly ears within the Gore campaign organization, and he bent them frequently. He complained that Gore was misusing him, and he agitated to take a more active role—traveling the country, playing their old songs. But Gore had no desire for a reunion tour. He could cite data to support the decision, but it was basically emotional. Karenna Gore, who was the same age as Monica, was vehemently opposed to allowing Clinton to get too close to her father. ("She felt that would kill him," a former adviser to Gore says, "and he bought it.") Clinton, in turn, was shocked to learn that Gore was taking guidance from a daughter young enough to be his mistress.

Clinton did not believe that the Lewinsky scandal had damaged his standing as much as Gore thought. He felt forgiven, and Hillary's success only vindicated his conclusion. But Clinton would later write that he called up Gore to tell him that if it helped, he would "stand on the doorstep of the *Washington Post*'s headquarters and let him lash me with a bullwhip."

"Maybe we ought to poll that," Gore replied.

Clinton swore that all he wanted at this point was a Gore victory, which would secure his presidential legacy. Gore had reason to be skeptical. Hillary was drawing attention and donor money away from his campaign and creating the impression that, far from fading into retirement, the Big Dog was going to be running around the yard in Washington. Almost from the moment Clinton was elected, people in Hillary's orbit had been whispering about the possibility that she might one day succeed him. In 1994, the First Lady dismissed this scenario as "beyond imagination." Now it seemed very imaginable—and Gore knew that if he lost, it would open the way for her to run in the future.

"He always felt very strongly," says a campaign official who discussed the matter with Gore, "that Bill Clinton wasn't interested in him winning the presidency, because he wanted a defeat, because he wanted Hillary to run the next time out. He was absolutely convinced of it."

Gore rarely voiced his suspicions of Clinton explicitly. "Al is not a person who likes conflict," a longtime friend says. "Especially conflict where you can only cause trouble."

Gore did not think he needed Clinton's advice. "Once I focus on politics," he told a writer for *George*, "I think I'm pretty damn good at it. It just takes time for perception to catch up with reality. We'll come to a point where the conventional wisdom changes, where people talk about the presidential candidate Al Gore rather than Vice President Al Gore . . . *struggling to escape.*"

In May 2000, though, the *Times* released a poll that showed Gore trailing Bush by 8 points nationwide. It indicated that voters favored Gore's stands on the issues, but they just liked him less. The summer presented two obvious, and perhaps final, opportunities for Gore to change the dynamic. One was the Democratic National Convention in Los Angeles. Gore knew his acceptance speech would offer him a rare window of time to speak directly to the public, and he obsessed over it with his speechwriters, trying to figure out how to introduce the real Al Gore. He remembered how much readers liked the earnest nerd who wrote *Earth in the Balance*. One of his ideas involved having quadriplegic British astrophysicist Stephen Hawking appear onstage, so Gore could tell a story about how he had come to befriend the smartest man in the world.

Gore's advisers were not sure that this facet of the real Gore would appeal to voters. But they were more enthusiastic about Gore's newfound desire to strike a populist chord, which would hark back to his father's brand of New Deal liberalism. That summer, Gore rolled out a new slogan: "The people, not the powerful." Clinton hated it. He thought it smacked of "class warfare" and of defeated Democrats of the past. He resented the implication that *he* had forgotten the people.

The second potential inflection point was Gore's selection of a running mate. The short list came down to the usual collection of senators and governors. Gore insisted on the inclusion of one name: Joe Lieberman. The senator's home state, Connecticut, was not electorally important, and Gore's advisers worried that Lieberman's hangdog demeanor would wear poorly. But Lieberman had been one of the few important Democrats who had broken with Clinton during the Lewinsky scandal, condemning the president's "immoral and harmful" behavior in a speech on the Senate floor. By picking him, Gore would send a statement of separation. That is what he wanted. So, Lieberman it was.

And for once, a Gore stratagem worked. The Lieberman pick met with instant acclaim. It was bold and historic: he was the first Jewish politician to be selected to run on a major-party ticket. Gore reasoned that the potential for anti-Semitism was outweighed by the implications in Florida, the state with the third-largest population of Jewish voters, many of them retirees who had been waiting their whole lives for an opportunity to pull the voting lever for someone like Lieberman.

"I think it's a way to say 'screw you' to Bill Clinton," one of the president's advisers told him when news of Gore's decision reached the Clintons while they were vacationing on Martha's Vineyard.

"I'm glad someone agrees with me," Hillary chimed in.

Personally, a source close to Clinton would later tell a *Talk* profile writer, the president considered Lieberman a "self-righteous, sanctimonious . . . pain in the ass." But as a strategist, even Clinton had to admit that the pick made some sense, especially in Florida.

"No, no, you're wrong," Bill told Hillary. "It's a great choice."

17

The Breakup

The Reform Party candidate Donald Trump had no particular ideology and showed little interest in acquiring one. To present the public with a platform, Roger Stone hired a ghostwriter to whip up a book about what Trump would do if he became president. The writer would later say his first thought was "Well, this is going to be my first published piece of fiction."

The ghostwriter came to see Trump at his office, which was staffed by a remarkable number of beautiful women. ("What office has a receptionist that is absolutely gorgeous," a former Trump Organization executive says, "but doesn't speak a word of English?") Trump spent an afternoon rambling about his ideas. He was very worried about terrorism. He loved Oprah. He wanted universal health care and a onetime tax on the rich to retire the national debt.

The ghostwriter filled in the rest. Donald Trump's campaign manifesto, *The America We Deserve*, came out just as Bush and Gore were in the midst of locking up their respective nominations. Trump launched the book with a signing event in the atrium of Trump Tower, sitting at a large desk on a stage fitted out to look like the Oval Office. The reviews were as one would expect. Walter Kirn, the literary critic for *New York* magazine, declared that *The*

America We Deserve proved Trump was "America's greatest living comedian."

There was, however, one critic who was more intrigued: Kirn's colleague, *New York* media columnist Michael Wolff. As the self-appointed voice of the city's knowing cultural elite, Wolff was dismissive of both major-party candidates. (After following around Al Gore on the campaign trail, listening as he searched for the "infinitely uninteresting middle ground" on every issue, he declared, "It is a sort of torture.") In Trump, on the other hand, Wolff saw great promise.

"I think it would be wrong to underestimate the inclination to cast a vote for pure entertainment value," he wrote. Trump, he went on, "is entertaining himself and the media and the electorate (and even making a certain sort of sophisticated political point, which is that an entrepreneur and public figure is larger than politics and politicians). This is performance art."

Whatever it was—art, a joke, a stunt, a dry run—Trump 2000 wasn't a normal campaign. For one thing, it didn't involve much campaigning. Trump didn't like the idea of driving around Iowa and begging for votes. He had an aversion to some basic aspects of human interaction, like shaking hands. "I think it's barbaric," he told an interviewer during his 2000 campaign. "Shaking hands, you catch colds, you catch the flu . . . you catch all sorts of things."

"You know," Melania told an interviewer, "there are a lot of germs from colds and flu, and nobody is really talking about this."

Nonetheless, running for president in 2000 would require Trump to meet some conventional expectations. He grudgingly hit the trail. For his first event, he, Melania, Roger Stone, and the rest of his campaign staff piled onto the Trump jet in Palm Beach and flew to Miami, a distance of seventy miles. From the airport, a fleet of police cars escorted Trump's limousine motorcade to the Bay of Pigs Museum, on a shabby street in Little Havana. Out front, Trump sat in his limo for nineteen minutes, waiting for a lagging bus full of press to arrive. When he finally got out, accompanied by Melania, he was greeted by an elderly Cuban fan. The man stuck out his hand.

Trump gave him a handshake. Shutters clicked. Challenge surmounted.

Inside, members of Brigade 2506, the Bay of Pigs veterans' group, guided Trump through a tour of exhibits about their cause. Trump attacked Castro as a "killer" and a "criminal" and confided that he often passed up deals to do business in Havana, though "it may be to my detriment financially." (This was a lie; he had recently paid a consulting firm to explore opportunities in Cuba for his casino company.)

"Viva Donald Trump!" the veterans cheered.

Afterward, Trump held a reception for a group of Reform Party leaders at a Radisson near the airport. He met his press corps—mainly tabloid reporters. (The *Miami Herald* sent its humor columnist, Dave Barry.) Trump compared himself favorably to Bush and Gore. "Let me ask you," he said. "Did they make billions of dollars in a short period of time? No. *Could* they make billions of dollars in a short period of time? I don't think so."

Trump claimed he was worth $5 billion, though this—his main campaign credential—was surely a huge exaggeration. ("Evaluating Donald's riches was like trying to bottle smoke," wrote his biographer Tim O'Brien, who reported that executives with "intimate knowledge" of Trump's finances around this time estimated his net worth was between $150 million and $250 million.) For Trump's purposes, the truth hardly mattered, so long as people *thought* he was a billionaire. According to a Gallup poll, Trump was recognized by 98 percent of the public, making him America's best-known businessman—more famous than its richest one, Bill Gates.

Trump's fame had its political disadvantages. In another poll, by CBS News, the percentage of people who viewed him unfavorably was the highest ever recorded for any public figure. It was curious to think that a man who was held in such contempt by so many Americans could imagine he had a future in elected office. But such was Trump's boundless capacity for self-delusion.

Trump's political advisers thought they saw a path to a respectable general election showing. A growing number of voters were independents. Trump could appeal to those who saw little difference between the major-party candidates, whom he sometimes called "Bore and Gush." It was no accident that Trump was campaigning in Florida, a state with a large number of independent voters, or that he was visiting a group of Spanish-speaking immigrants. The campaign's internal polling showed that while voters on the whole disdained Trump, working-class whites and minorities were more receptive to his message.

Trump polled especially well with Black voters. He bragged about his friendships with Puffy Combs and Russell Simmons and told the *New York Post* that the hip-hop tycoons had promised to raise $10 million for his campaign. Simmons immediately demanded a correction from the paper, though, saying that what he knew of Trump's politics "scared" him.

Beyond the New York tabloids and the *National Enquirer*, few news organs took Trump's candidacy seriously. Trump 2000 was covered as an amusing diversion from the real race. In those days, when access to the public's attention went through the strictly controlled channels—newspapers, magazines, television networks—it remained possible for the powers that be to shunt aside disagreeable voices. The internet was still in its infancy; the massive social media networks of Facebook and Twitter had yet to be invented. Trump had a talent for attracting media attention, but that coverage always came on the condition that he would be dismissed.

Even Trump had trouble taking himself seriously. "It was strange," says one 2000 campaign adviser. "It was like one minute you'd be on a conference call having a serious conversation, and the next minute, Trump would be in bed with Melania calling into Howard Stern."

Reader, this actually happened—on the very day that Roger Stone was planning to roll out Trump's proposal for a wealth tax on every person worth more than $10 million. In sultry accented English, Melania told Stern she was hardly wearing any clothing and described Trump's prodigious sexual appetite.

"She is actually naked," Trump assured Stern. "It's a thing of beauty." He asked, mischievously, "Is this your average interview, Howard, for a presidential candidate?"

Melania was on prominent display throughout the campaign. "Her primary function," Dave Barry wrote, "appears to be to stand around looking Babe-O-Licious." *Talk* gave her a two-page photo spread in the magazine: Melania, in a bikini and heels, sprawled across a rug with an eagle seal on it, like the one in the Oval Office. The attention Trump drew was good for her modeling career. Her day rate had doubled since they started dating. And that, in turn, was good for Trump, as he took a cut through the modeling agency he had recently started. This did nothing to dispel the suspicion that the entire campaign was just one big adventure in marketing.

Trump hardly even bothered to argue otherwise. "I'm the only one who makes money when he runs," he boasted repeatedly. He told any reporter within earshot that he was scheduling his campaign trips to coincide with a series of conferences organized by the self-help guru Tony Robbins, for which he claimed he was being paid $100,000 a speech.

The "Results 2000" motivational tour took Trump to ten cities, including Hartford, St. Louis, and Los Angeles. For the California trip, he invited along a delegation of political reporters and a crew from *60 Minutes*. Trump held a press conference near the rooftop pool of a Beverly Hills hotel, where he jostled for space with a TV crew that was shooting an interview with Whoopi Goldberg. ("She's a *real* celebrity," the crew said dismissively.) Stone looked on, wearing a double-breasted pinstripe suit and "Nixon Is the One" cuff links. The campaign staff had set out a glass bowl filled with little bottles of "Trump 2000"–branded hand sanitizer for the reporters.

Trump went on *The Tonight Show with Jay Leno*. ("I consider Leno a friend, and I think he's going to take me seriously," Trump had assured the press in Miami.) Now, as Trump waited in his dressing room with a reporter, Leno popped in for a pregame chat. He took a gander at Stone.

"Hey, Donald," Leno said. "You brought your bookie!"

When the cameras rolled, though, Leno was gently deferential. He introduced Trump as "the next president of the United States," and his band played "Hail to the Chief."

"Do you feel," Leno asked, "you'll be able to restore dignity to the office of president?"

The next morning, Trump brought the cameras along to the Simon Wiesenthal Center's Museum of Tolerance, a visit that would offer him another opportunity to disparage Pat Buchanan as a Nazi sympathizer. Walking through exhibits displaying the horrors of the Holocaust and other atrocities, Trump threw around off-key superlatives. ("Fabulous" . . . "extraordinary" . . . "outstanding.") "This morning was nothing less than brilliant," he told the press, before whacking Buchanan as a "racist" and connecting him to Hitler. Then everyone got on the plane for a fifteen-minute flight to Long Beach and Trump's appearance at the Results 2000 event, where he offered wiseguy wisdom to an audience of 21,000. "Get even," he said. "When somebody screws you, screw 'em back, but a lot harder, folks."

After the speech, Trump continued to a VIP tent, where he took some questions.

"How do I go about creating the capital that I need to start my business," one woman asked, "when all I have is my knowledge and my dream?"

"Meet a wealthy guy," Trump replied. The crowd erupted in hoots and laughter.

It was a bizarre phenomenon. The more loathsome Trump acted, the more his audience was entertained. People didn't even seem to mind when he mocked their cherished values. At one point in the Los Angeles trip, he hosted a gathering of Reform Party activists at his hotel. As the polyester people drank his wine and ate his goat cheese hors d'oeuvres, Trump attacked U.S. trade policies and said he was "opposed to new people coming in" via immigration. But he also expressed contempt for some of the party's basic tenets, like campaign finance reform. He told the New World Order nuts in the audience that he loved the United Nations. ("I'm building a ninety-story building next to it," he said, exaggerating the height of the Trump World Tower considerably.) He responded to a question about a national sales tax by saying, "How do I feel about sales tax? I try to avoid paying it whenever possible."

Someone asked Trump whether he would even support the Reform Party platform.

"Nobody knows what the Reform Party platform is," Trump replied, not inaccurately.

Matt Labash, a writer for the *Weekly Standard*, watched in awe. "It's a virtuoso performance," he would write of the event. "Trump has disagreed with, chided, even insulted his constituency, and yet they mob him afterwards, won over by either his Merlot or his candor."

Even Chuck Harder, who called Buchanan "a longtime friend of ours" on the air, found himself intrigued by Trump. One day, in the heat of the race, he had on a guest named Terry Reed, a supposed former CIA operative who claimed to know all about a conspiracy involving Bill Clinton and a drug-running ring that operated out of an airport in rural Mena, Arkansas.

"I certainly like what Donald Trump is saying," Reed said. "Which is amazing, to think that here we have a person who hasn't really served in politics but is certainly making the right noise . . ."

"Umm-hmmm," Harder said, concurring.

". . . in terms of the attitudes I think we're going to have to develop as we go into this new millennium. We have to complete Jefferson's experiment in utopia."

"I guess a lot of people are just tired," Harder said. "And I am—I think I'm tired of politics. Again, I don't back any particular candidate. I talk about issues and policy. But I think most people are just *burnt out*."

IN APRIL 2000, as a newspaper reporter, I covered a premiere event for an independent film called *American Psycho*. Directed by Mary Harron, it starred a chiseled young Christian Bale as Patrick Bateman, a wealthy and handsome Manhattan investment banker who likes to murder and dismember women. The party was held at the SoHo offices of Pseudo.com, a then-hip, soon-to-be-defunct video-streaming start-up, and as I recall, it featured a lot of dry-ice smoke. Critics had been confounded by the film, which was based on a violent and sexually explicit novel by Bret Easton Ellis. Was it a horror movie? A satire of misogyny and materialism? A shallow piece of "man-hating misandry," as one male movie critic suggested? It was only later that Harron's work was recognized as a feminist classic and that Bale's stomach-crunching, body-hair-free, porn-addicted, morally vacant serial killer would come to be seen as an omen.

In retrospect, there were Patrick Batemans all around us. The paper where I worked, the *New York Observer*, chronicled what our charismatic editor liked to refer to as the nation's "power elite," the cast of characters who created the political and cultural discourse. The dominant figure in the New York film industry was Harvey Weinstein, a friend of the Clintons and a major Democratic fund-raiser. The king of network television was CBS executive Les Moonves, the programmer behind the new reality show *Survivor*. The highest-rated voice on Fox News belonged to Bill O'Reilly, who was employed by Roger Ailes. Matt Lauer, the *Today* anchor, was the most popular face on morning TV. Russell Simmons was the father of the hip-hop industry.

American Psycho ends on an unsettling note. Patrick Bateman loses control, committing over-the-top acts of murder, but no one pursues him; he tries to confess, but no one cares. This, too, reflected reality. All the real-life characters in the previous paragraph were, eventually, brought down by allegations of sexual harassment or abuse, but in the year 2000, they were celebrated. In March of that year, the *National Enquirer* reported that a twenty-year-old actress had filed a police complaint against the comedian Bill Cosby in New York, claiming that "America's Dad" had sexually assaulted her. Cosby's lawyers threatened a $250 million lawsuit against the tabloid, and the story disappeared.

The most powerful man in the land, Bill Clinton, had gotten away with it, too. His supporters had rationalized the president's affair with a young intern as a mere folly, or an element of seductive charm. Monica Lewinsky, meanwhile, was a figure of national scorn, mercilessly mocked.

In the novel *American Psycho*, which takes place in the 1980s, Patrick Bateman particularly venerates one real person, whom he constantly cites as an inspiration: Donald Trump. Here, the satire breaks down. No fictional Trump could possibly top the real one's up-front misogyny. He wallowed in his piggishness and regarded women as another form of personal branding—an advertisement for his virility. Besides his modeling agency, he also ran a beauty pageant. As a candidate for the presidency in 2000, Trump told the *New York Times* that, in his view, the problem with the Lewinsky scandal was not Bill's behavior, but Monica's appearance. "I mean, terrible choice," Trump said. Had she been a supermodel, he added, Clinton "would have been everybody's hero."

Trump regarded his sexism as a political asset. Around Valentine's Day, he published a first-person essay on his presidential aspirations in *Gear*, one of the many so-called lad mags that proliferated during that last prosperous gasp of print journalism. (The cover of the issue featured the barely clothed seventeen-year-old starlet Jessica Biel.) The magazine's editor, Bob Guccione Jr., remembers the article's composition this way. It went without saying that someone would have to ghostwrite it, so the editor came around to Trump Tower for a chat. Trump introduced Guccione to Melania before he and the editor repaired to Trump's office to talk about his views. "He then immediately speed-dials two women on his speakerphone and makes dates with them," Guccione recalls.

"I'm not a judgmental guy, but it was clear that this was to impress on me that he was a stud."

Trump's *Gear* essay dismissed the "whinnying culture critics and media hacks" who acted as if they were repulsed by his celebrity and unapologetic womanizing. "Is there something wrong with appreciating beautiful women?" it asked. "Don't we want people in public office who show signs of life? I am who I am, and I make no bones about it."

Trump claimed he couldn't help it that the women all loved him, and he made sure none said otherwise. When he announced his campaign, his newest ex-wife, Marla Maples, made some threatening noises, warning in a British tabloid that she felt it was her "duty as an American citizen to tell the people what he is really like." Trump's lawyers accused her of breaking a confidentiality agreement, going to court to try to withhold $1.5 million in alimony, and she ended up keeping quiet. But it was not as if Trump's behavior were a secret.

When Trump was on the prowl, he would often run around with a wolf pack of wealthy pals down in Palm Beach. The media cheerfully recorded his exploits. For instance, after his first divorce, from Ivana, Trump celebrated by throwing a "Bachelor Ball" at Mar-a-Lago, to which he invited an ABC News crew, a *National Enquirer* reporter, and three busloads of models from Miami. The *Enquirer* reported that some of Trump's party guests copulated on the lawn.

"It's a fantasy," Trump told Maureen Dowd. "Certain guys tell me they want women of substance, not beautiful models. It just means they can't get beautiful models."

One weekend in 2000, to promote a new golf course he was building in West Palm Beach, Trump invited a writer from a magazine called *Maximum Golf* down to Mar-a-Lago. The resulting article noted that they were joined at LaGuardia Airport by another member of the developer's Palm Beach crew, a silvery New York financier named Jeffrey Epstein, and his companion Ghislaine Maxwell, a British-born heiress in sunglasses and "fashionably tight pants."

Epstein, a reputed math genius and a man of mysterious means, owned a compound on a quiet cove at the end of El Brillo Way. He and Maxwell would often socialize with Trump there and at Mar-a-Lago. "They seemed to be awfully chummy," recalls Abraham Wallach, a top Trump Organization executive at the time. Sometime that year, Maxwell would allegedly spot a beautiful teenager working as an attendant at the club's spa. The girl was reading a book on massage. Maxwell allegedly invited her to come over to the house and meet Epstein.

("Terrific guy," Trump would say of Epstein in 2002. "He's a lot of fun to be with. It is even said that he likes beautiful women as much as I do, and many of them are on the younger side. No doubt about it—Jeffrey enjoys his social life.")

"I just find women very vital to life, to my existence," Trump told the writer from *Maximum Golf* as they played a round at his new course. "They like the most obvious thing," he added, blustering as always about his sexual prowess. "And if they don't like that, I don't give a fuck how much money you have." On the seventeenth hole, Trump missed a putt and tossed his club some twenty-five yards. Afterward, though, he cheered up as he enjoyed a drink on the club's veranda and spotted a fetching girl.

"There is nothing in the world," Trump marveled, "like first-rate pussy."

CHUCK HARDER HAD news: "And the Donald, who is running for president—well, sort of—has dumped her. Stunning fashion model . . . MELANA . . . no . . . MELAYNA . . . I should say, MEL-ANIA Knauss is heartbroken after getting the axe from the Donald. Gee, gosh!"

That was not exactly how the breakup had transpired, but at any rate, Trump was single again.

Melania would put up with a lot of shenanigans, but there were limits even to her understanding. Their breakup played out in the gossip pages. One morning, the *Post* reported, Melania arrived at Trump Tower moments after another model left. She then found evidence of infidelity in the bathroom. (In one version of the story, reported in the *Post* at the time, it was a towel smeared with makeup; in another, it was an incriminating hair.) There was a fight, and Melania stormed out of Trump Tower. This presented a problem, because both of them were scheduled to fly that day to Minnesota to campaign with Governor Jesse Ventura.

Trump invited his son Donny to come along instead. "Rather than being upset," someone else on the trip remembers, "Trump was ebullient." He was thrilled that two models were fighting over him. He was invigorated. Liberated. His campaign was shot full of testosterone.

On the plane to Minnesota, Trump gave an interview to Jerry Useem, a *Fortune* staffer who had come along to write a brief, lighthearted feature. It gradually dawned on Useem that Donald Trump really thought he could be president. "He seemed like he meant it," Useem says.

In Minnesota, at another Reform Party rally, Trump performed his insult comedy routine, calling Pat Buchanan a "loser" and George W. Bush "no Einstein." He also brought up North Korea—"Run by some very bad people"—and suggested he would attack it to keep it from acquiring nuclear weapons. "That kind of sent a shiver," recalls Useem.

When asked what might deter him from running, Trump replied, "Death."

From Minnesota, he flew straight down to Mar-a-Lago to celebrate his newfound freedom. A gossip columnist would soon report that he had been spotted with three "surgically enhanced beauties" in the VIP room of a West Palm Beach club owned by a Mafia associate who was awaiting trial on murder charges. The *New York Post* caught up with Trump at a Manhattan promotional event for his beauty pageant, where he posed with Miss Florida, Miss Montana, and Miss Arizona. "She meant a lot to me," Trump said of Melania as he kissed the beauty queens for the cameras.

He really did seem to love Melania, in his way. Before long, through anonymous representatives, Donald and Melania were engaging in a weirdly touching back-and-forth in the gossip pages.

"She's a great girl, but Donald has to be free for awhile. He didn't want to get hooked," a source close to Trump told the *Post*.

"She's a one-man woman," a source close to Melania replied. "When she's with someone, she's only with that person and she expects the same."

"Donald already has spent a lot of time on the campaign and he's getting more and more serious, preparing and studying," a source told the *Daily News*. "I don't think either one of them ever thought he'd be this busy." However, this very well-informed individual added, "They're still checking in, saying, 'How are you? I miss you.' It's not like they had a big fight."

The magazine *George*, which was going to feature Melania in a "Meet the First Babes" photo essay, reached her for an updated comment on Trump's campaign. "I will have to follow the election a bit more closely," she said, "and listen to *all* the candidates."

Trump was chastened. He took Melania to a candlelit dinner at Le Cirque 2000. "When you see them together, you can tell that he loves her company," a source told the *Post*, "and she's head-over-heels about him." Who knows what was said? But there was a sudden weakening in Trump's interest in politics. There were no more campaign trips, no more events where Melania was paraded for the ogling masses like a boxing ring girl.

"In retrospect," Roger Stone says, "I was more excited about his running than he ever was." There were many obstacles to mounting a credible third-party campaign. It looked like the major parties would be able to shut the Reform candidate out of the debates. Buying TV advertising was expensive. The party's $12 million in federal funding would not go very far, and there was no easy way to tap the public for small contributions. Trump would either have to beg other rich guys, a humbling prospect, or dig into his own pocket, which might have been impossible.

Trump had publicly suggested he was willing to spend $100 million on his campaign. He gave Reform Party leaders the impression that he might sell his publicly traded casino company in order to finance the costs. But in reality, he was in no shape to do that. Useem, the *Fortune* writer, set aside his original conception of his Trump-for-president feature to do a deeper investigation. Trump's finances turned out to be even shakier than Useem had imagined. The bond rating of his casino company had recently been downgraded "from junk to junkier," he wrote. Shareholders were upset that Trump had borrowed $26 million from the company to pay off a personal loan. He reported that Trump was going to pay back the public company by mortgaging Mar-a-Lago. Trump denied it and threatened to sue *Fortune* prior to publication.

Not long afterward, though, he took out the mortgage.

"SO, WADDYA THINK, should I run?" Trump asked a visiting newspaper reporter one night as they sat next to a fire in a sitting room at Mar-a-Lago. There was never any subtext with him.

"If I set a goal of, say, 20 percent of the vote, I could run and still not fail?"

The reporter stammered that 8 percent seemed more realistic for a third-party candidate.

"I don't like to fail," Trump replied.

All around the country, Buchanan partisans were taking over state Reform Party chapters. In the South, his foot soldiers were members of the Sons of Confederate Veterans. Up north, he relied on an unlikely alliance with a Black psychotherapist and neo-Marxist activist from New York City who wielded significant influence in the Reform organization.

At a large party gathering in Nashville, local police intervened to stop scuffles between Reform factions. "I am ashamed of this party!" a big-haired woman in a red dress covered with Trump and Ventura buttons hollered as she wrestled over a microphone with a Reform official. The party chairman, a Ventura fan, was ousted and replaced with someone who was aligned with Ross Perot and Pat Buchanan. The new chairman denounced "exploiters such as Donald Trump," calling him a "hustler" who was just out to promote his book and his hotels. Ventura appeared at a press conference wearing a jacket emblazoned with the Rolling Stones tongue-and-lips logo and announced he was quitting his "hopelessly dysfunctional" party.

That weekend, Trump was far away in Palm Beach. He was happy. Melania was back. Mar-a-Lago held a pro-am tennis tournament, and Trump won at doubles, beating the convicted felon junk bond financier (and future Trump pardon recipient) Michael Milken and his partner in the final. That night he threw a party at the club. Trump and Melania, wearing a slinky black number, snapped a picture with Jeffrey Epstein, who had his arm around the bare waist of Ghislaine Maxwell. Epstein's friend Prince Andrew, the Duke of York, also attended. Trump told a gossip columnist that he and the prince played a round of golf that weekend. "Doesn't that sound more fun than making dumb speeches in the Rose Garden?" the columnist asked.

Yes, running for president was a gas, but there were other ways to entertain himself. The morning after the party, Trump issued a statement saying he was ending his campaign. As justification, he cited the news that the ex-Klansman politician David Duke had joined the Reform Party to support Buchanan. "This is not company I wish to keep," Trump declared. He published a column in the *New York Times*, decrying the "fringe element" in the Reform Party and recounting the reception in Los Angeles full of "Elvis look-alikes, resplendent in various campaign buttons and anxious to give me a pamphlet explaining the Swiss-Zionist conspiracy to control America."

Trump also sat down on *Today* with a friendly interviewer, Matt Lauer. Trump told Lauer he had been at Mar-a-Lago, watching the other candidates on television, thinking about how *hard* they were working, out there beating the streets. "And I said, 'You know, it's not such an easy life they have,' as I'm sitting in, you know, seventy-five-degree weather."

And with that, the hilarious, absurd, soon-to-be-forgotten presidential campaign of Donald Trump came to an end. It was fun. He was beaten. He had learned some things.

Lauer asked, would he do it again?

"Well," Trump replied, "I always flirt."

18

Circus Town

If Donald Trump had a historical forebear as a public persona and a flimflam man, it was nineteenth-century freak show impresario P. T. Barnum. Like Trump, Barnum was a populist politician, frequent litigant, and a hoax artist. He was a notorious liar, known throughout the land as the "Prince of Humbugs," and he was beloved for it. "Contrary to popular belief," the historian Daniel Boorstin wrote of him, "Barnum's great discovery was not how easy it was to deceive the public, but rather, how much the public enjoyed being deceived."

In 1871, beneath a big tent in Brooklyn, Barnum unveiled his most enduring creation: his "Grand Traveling Museum, Menagerie, Caravan, and Circus." It later merged with an enterprise run by the Ringling Brothers to become what was known as "the Greatest Show on Earth." After Barnum's death, his circus would make its home, as came naturally, in Florida.

For many decades, the off-season headquarters of the Greatest Show on Earth was its winter camp on the Gulf Coast island of Venice. Every year, a train would pull into its rail station, and elephants, big cats, and feathered women would parade over the Circus Bridge to an arena and clown college located next to the island's small airport. It was the sleepy town's foremost tourist attraction. There were winter performances and elephant rides and a flying trapeze school.

By the late 1990s, though, the circus was in the midst of a long financial decline, the train station was rotting, and the winter camp was abandoned. The clowns packed into their jalopy and split town. The cavernous arena sat vacant. A new cast of entrepreneurs started to set up around the Venice airport: flight instructors. The airport, a decommissioned Second World War military base, had a pair of mile-long runways and little air traffic, which made it ideal for training purposes. The instructors set up flight schools in hangars along the airstrip.

Many days during that summer of 2000, a young Arab student would zip over the Circus Bridge, past the dilapidated legacy of P. T. Barnum, in his sporty red Mitsubishi. To all outward appearances, he was having a wonderful time in Florida. Ziad Jarrah was on his way.

ON JUNE 28, Elián Gonzalez finally returned to Cuba. His relatives in Miami fought to the bitter end. Through their latest pro bono lawyer, a young conservative named Brett Kavanaugh, the family petitioned the Supreme Court to issue an emergency injunction while it decided whether to hear the boy's custody case. But they could not convince the justices, which was unsurprising, because the Supreme Court was universally known to be an institution that prized its lofty position above partisan politics. The Miami relatives were praying at a Catholic church when they received the news of their loss. Outside, Lázaro tried to fight a cameraman.

Janet Reno learned of the decision as she was in transit to an appearance in Orlando. "I hope everyone will accept the Supreme Court's decision," she said in a statement to the press. At the White

244 | THE YEAR THAT BROKE AMERICA

House, President Clinton conceded that he wished the boy's return had "unfolded in a less dramatic, less traumatic way for all concerned," and he halfheartedly dismissed the effect on Al Gore's campaign. "It's still more likely than not that he will win," Clinton said. Gore, meanwhile, was in Ohio, sitting on a stack of drywall at a suburban construction site, pitching his proposal for a $2,000 tax credit for purchasing an energy-efficient home.

Once again, his environmental plan would be overshadowed. Cable news channels broadcast five straight hours of coverage of Elián's departure. As soon as the Supreme Court came down with its decision, Elián and his father headed in a caravan to Dulles International Airport. All the major networks broke into their regular afternoon programming to show live helicopter shots of the white SUV carrying Elián to his chartered plane, images reminiscent of the famous O.J. Simpson car chase.

"I don't want to call it a Bronco, but it certainly looked like a Bronco," one cable news executive told the *Times*. "In the cable news business," another said, "a day like this is what we live for."

Elián's plane took off around 5 p.m. At the Gonzalez home in Little Havana, which had been converted into a shrine to the betrayed child, a small group of die-hard protesters watched the moment on TV, shouting, *No! No! No!* Three hours later, the plane touched down in Havana, where Elián was greeted by a photogenic group of flag-waving schoolchildren.

THAT SAME DAY, as TV coverage of Elián's departure droned on in the background, Ziad Jarrah arrived at the Florida Flight Training Center. He had passed through U.S. border controls a day before, at the Atlanta airport, getting a cursory stamp in his passport. Typically, one of his flight instructors recalls, the school's routine was to get a new student into the air immediately. "I'm trying to demystify it," he said of his method decades later. "'This is a great feeling: I'm flying.'"

Jarrah took his first lesson that day, in a little blue-and-yellow-painted single-engine Cessna. He crammed his legs beneath the dashboard, put his feet on the rudder pedals, and strapped on his harness seat belt. The propeller on its nose whirred to a deafening roar, and the instructor taxied the plane out to the runway, passing alongside a municipal golf course. The instructor would have guided Jarrah through the takeoff routine: pushing in the throttle, pulling back the control yoke, leaving the ground, ascending over the Intracoastal Waterway, bouncing through the air.

There were two competing flight schools in Venice, both coincidentally run by immigrants from the Netherlands. The flying Dutchmen were echt Florida characters. The owner of the school Jarrah attended, Arne Kruithof, was a handsome former bodybuilder and global vagabond who had spent his youth bumping around the resort towns of Europe and Morocco. His rival, Rudi Dekkers, was a businessman who had left behind a huge tax-evasion case back in Amsterdam. He would later be imprisoned in Texas on federal drug-running charges.

The flight schools marketed themselves primarily to inexperienced foreigners. Around this time, Kruithof shot a video in which he stood in front of his fleet of Cessnas wearing a starchy pilot's uniform. "In the pilot world," he said, "we look for stable, reliable, and loyal people who don't make mistakes once they're sitting in the cockpit of an aircraft. But for this, you don't need to be a superman." The skies over Florida were full of wobbly beginners, and headlines about crashes, collisions, and midair mishaps were a regular feature in the local newspapers.

The foreign students stuck out as an odd presence in the town, which was otherwise populated mainly by middle-class retirees from the Midwest. "It's newlyweds and nearly deads," a British student told the *Venice Gondolier* in 2000, for an inquisitive article headlined "VISITING PILOTS ANSWER QUESTION: WHY VENICE?" The foreign students roomed together in cheap apartments, trying to earn their licenses as fast as they could. "Pilots work short hours and make a lot of money," an Austrian told the *Gondolier*. "And the stewardesses aren't bad, either."

Jarrah was the first of the men from Hamburg to arrive in Florida. Mohamed Atta and Marwan al-Shehhi were still in New York, staying in a tenement apartment on the fringes of the Brooklyn neighborhood of Park Slope while they waited for some money from Mukhtar, the coordinator in Karachi. Mukhtar had a nephew who ran an electronics business in Dubai. He kept around $100,000 in cash in a laundry bag in his apartment, which he would distribute on his uncle's orders. On June 29, the nephew wired $5,000 to al-Shehhi, who picked up the money at a Western Union location at Fortieth and Broadway, just south of Times Square.

By July 4, when Venice had its big annual fireworks show on the beach, Atta and al-Shehhi had made it to Florida. The pair rented a little pink bungalow for $550 a month and enrolled in Rudi Dekkers's school. There, they interacted little with the other students, or with Jarrah.

Arne Kruithof's flight school was maybe five hundred yards from Rudi's, and Jarrah must have often run into his coconspirators out on the tarmac or at the Cockpit Café in the terminal. But whether for reasons of security or personality, he maintained his distance. Jarrah was a personable man, and he soon made new friends. They would go out to a bar next to the airport, the 44th Aero Squadron, although Jarrah drank rarely, if ever. He played golf on the course at the end of the runway. He talked about French soccer with his school's IT guy, who was from Togo. He smiled broadly behind his sunglasses in pictures the school tacked up on a photo-filled wall.

Arne Kruithof first met Jarrah in the lounge of the flight school. "I sensed pretty quickly that I was dealing with a very special young man," Kruithof later wrote in a memoir. "He radiated a good aura." Jarrah had a pleasant demeanor, was talkative and considerate. When Arne had surgery to repair torn ligaments in his knee that summer, Jarrah paid a visit to his house, carrying a plant and a six-pack of Budweiser. "From under his little John Lennon glasses," Kruithof wrote, "he looked at me with pity and asked if he could start doing things in the house for me."

Kruithof would often get all his students together for barbecues and beach volleyball, and Jarrah would come. The other students would make fun of his "pimp car," the speedy Mitsubishi coupe he had bought for his Florida adventure. Jarrah would laugh along. One time, he visited one of his instructors at home and made a delicious Lebanese dinner for the man's family. He charmed the women at the school. Jarrah told the one who worked the front desk that he had a girlfriend back in Germany, but he confided that they were having problems in their relationship. Aysel called him constantly. She was jealous, and resentful of his long absence. She thought he was living the high life—the *Saus und Braus leben.*

In fact, Jarrah was working hard, trying to figure out how to play his role in the planes operation. Mukhtar had underestimated how difficult it would be to learn to fly a passenger jet. Airline pilots trained on expensive simulators, and you couldn't just walk in and rent one. You had to get a private pilot's license, starting out on single-engine planes. Then you were supposed to work your way through the many tests and certifications necessary to become a commercial pilot, and only after all that could you get on one of those simulators. It was going to take some time.

Meanwhile, there was also the problem of the fourth pilot. Jarrah was supposed to have a companion at flight school, his close friend Ramzi bin al-Shibh. He tried to smooth the way for Ramzi's application by talking to Kruithof and his office manager, Rachel Davis. They were happy to have another student's tuition. But unlike Jarrah and the others, Ramzi was having trouble getting a U.S. visa. He was from Yemen, a country Davis had never even heard of—a place so comically remote to most Americans that the hit show *Friends* had recently made an entire episode that culminated with Chandler flying to Yemen to get away from his annoying ex-girlfriend, Janice. So, anyway, Ramzi was going to be delayed.

Jarrah spent the sticky Florida summer living with classmates in a ranch house off Alligator Drive. He shared a bedroom with a European student. Every day, he drove to school along the Tamiami Trail, the main drag through Venice, passing the Frosted Mug and Beef 'O'Brady's; a Blockbuster Video and a RadioShack; a bingo hall and a Big K Mart; Geier's Sausage Kitchen and Paul's Gunworks; a Walmart and the Books-A-Million, where kids lined up at midnight on July 8 to buy the latest *Harry Potter* book; and the Regal Cinema, which was showing *The Patriot* and *Mission Impossible 2*. He passed palm readers and porn shops and many, many churches. There were the American flags out everywhere for July 4: hanging in front of houses, flying over car dealerships, flapping from the hands of a mannequin outside a tanning spa.

In the air, though, Jarrah could escape. By early August, he had passed the first of the many stages in the process of earning his commercial pilot's license. (His instructor, in handwritten notes, counseled him to work on "collision avoidance.") Jarrah had amassed forty hours of flying time, ten of them solo. He was comfortable in the cockpit of a small plane. From above, he could take in the puddled landscape of the Gulf Coast, flying along the course of the Intracoastal Waterway, which was always dotted with pleasure boats. Down below him were planned developments of tile-roof houses on curlicue streets. Banking over the barrier islands, he could zoom low over white sandy beaches and vacation mansions.

The whitecaps moved in chalky lines across the turquoise waters of the Gulf of Mexico, toward the jutting wooden Venice pier. On a calm day, the fishermen would be out in boats, casting for grouper and tarpon. That summer, though, was a particularly bad one for sharks. The waters off Venice were full of menacing ten-foot bulls, hunting in packs. From the air, you could see their dark forms clearly as they prowled ominously close to unsuspecting swimmers.

19

TruMarkets

The federal criminal investigation known as Operation Sphinx was the creation of a con artist. Randy Glass was a brazen grifter, the kind of thief who could trick you into handing over your wallet while you thanked him for taking your money. Born Randy Goldberg in Baltimore, he had lived a colorful life—dancing in and out of crime, running car washes, managing a 1970s singer-songwriter, and smuggling hashish from Morocco—before finding his way to Florida and the wholesale jewelry trade. He served a year in jail for cocaine possession and had a record of arrests for small-time scams, like the one where he convinced some gullible marks to trade their house for supposedly "rare" postage stamps. Glass was shameless. He later described his philosophy to *Dateline NBC*: "If I couldn't talk you out of it," he said, "you got to keep it."

In 1998, Glass got pinched on federal fraud and money-laundering charges. An indictment alleged he had bilked wholesale dealers out of consigned jewelry cumulatively worth $6 million. Glass told one victim that his diamonds had been taken by "Mafia-connected" people. He told another that he had been robbed by "two Black males in camouflage clothes." He tried to pass off fake diamonds to a third. Glass was also charged with scheming with a narcotics trafficker to funnel $1 million in drug proceeds into diamond purchases. Facing serious prison time, he did what came naturally. He started scheming—this time, in cooperation with law enforcement.

Glass began to work with the federal Bureau of Alcohol, Tobacco, and Firearms. Although the ATF designated him a "confidential informant," he did much more than merely pass on information. Glass told the ATF he could bring in international arms dealers, and then he went out and created a network to penetrate. He called up Diaa Mohsen, the dodgy tennis player, and spun a tale about stolen weapons. "Listen, between me and you," Glass confided, "they have a warehouse full of shit." Didi fell for his ruse immediately. He boasted he could sell anything.

In their first conversation, Didi brought up Osama bin Laden as a potential buyer. "You don't know these fucking people; they are terrorists, they are organized," he told Glass. "They're going to war with this country." The ATF agents handling Glass were initially skeptical. "We thought it was bullshit, too," says one. But then Didi started to bring in customers.

Glass threw himself into the sting, spending hours on the phone, coaxing and wheedling with the same manic energy he had once used for grifting. "Randy was a wild man," says Dick Stoltz, the now-retired ATF agent who posed as his partner, "Ray Spears." "He was a con man, and an excellent con man." Stoltz surmised that Glass had a "two-pronged" strategy: "One was to get out from under the criminal charges. Two was to make himself some kind of a media star." Glass secretly dubbed copies of the cassette tapes of the phone calls he made as an undercover informant, amassing an archive of many hours of conversations that he may have hoped to use for a book or movie project. He saw himself as the hero of the caper.

"I was a rogue, a scoundrel," he told a newspaper in 2002. "When

I realized the magnitude of what I got involved in, I realized I had to stand up, do the right thing and be a patriot."

As a cooperating felon, Glass was supposed to operate under tight supervision, but his handlers could not control him. He was a "force of nature," another ATF agent later wrote, "and he was constantly coming up with side deals through the Egyptian." Glass paid out of his own pocket for Didi to travel to overseas meetings with purported arms trade contacts. Through Didi's black market network, he procured a fake Venezuelan passport, using the alias "Robert Blake," after the lead actor from the 1970s detective series *Baretta*. He asked Didi if he knew anyone who might be capable of handling the huge sums of money they expected to fetch from their arms sales. "Randy tells him right off, 'We're going to be laundering three hundred million,'" Stoltz says. "That precipitates problems down the line." Didi immediately thought of his friend from the tennis courts, Kevin Ingram.

Didi talked up Ingram's influence, saying that he had once been *Time* magazine's Businessman of the Year—he hadn't—and that he was tight with Jesse Jackson. Glass asked Didi how to spell Ingram's name, so he could do a search on AOL. Didi said Ingram was funding his travel to Switzerland to work on a "money deal" involving $500 million in frozen Libyan assets and a Saudi prince. Glass warned Didi that the scheme sounded like an obvious scam. Glass was unsure about whether to involve a Wall Street banker. Wouldn't Ingram be scared to get involved in their business? Didi reassured Glass, saying that his plan was to lie to Ingram. He could always say that arms-dealing cash came from the other thing with the Saudi prince. He would tell Ingram that Glass served as a conduit for international money.

In 2021, Mohsen contended that Glass entrapped Ingram. "They set him up," Mohsen says. Mohsen claims he innocently believed his arms deals were sanctioned by the U.S. government, "like Nicaragua and Oliver North," and that Glass told him they were working as secret agents.

"I didn't know he was a crook," Mohsen says of Glass. "Motherfucker."

In closed-door sentencing hearings, federal authorities praised Glass as a unique asset: "one of the most prolific informants the world has ever seen," the assistant U.S. attorney handling his case told a judge in May 2000. "There is a pattern to fraud guys, in terms of their soulless ability to not care who they hurt," the prosecutor said two decades later. "Randy, he was one of the best. . . . It was unbelievable. And that kind of ability is what makes a great informant. A guy who can play the role and not get deterred and not get screwed with." Still, the judge in the fraud case expressed skepticism about the whole scenario. "What we have so far," he told prosecutors during sentencing proceedings, "is talk."

The arsenal of weapons inside the warehouse was mostly from an ATF stockpile. The Stinger missiles were unarmed dummies, lent to the bureau by the Department of Defense. The warehouse itself had been seized by the government in a drug-trafficking prosecution. Every dollar in cash that Glass presented to Ingram belonged to the U.S. government. There were no illicit proceeds to launder because there were no arms deals. For all of Glass's efforts over two years—"a cavalcade of negotiations," according to an ATF history of the case, "with a litany of representatives of the world's hotspots"—by mid-2000, he had still not completed a single sale.

"None of it was real," Ingram claims. "It was con men conning con men, and one of them conned me." He said there is little question in his mind about why he was targeted, out of all the money-hungry men on Wall Street. "Why would they focus in on me?

What could it have been? Why spend two years looking at me? I had hot girls and a Ferrari and a boat. And I was Black."

INGRAM WAS STILL blissfully unaware of all this in the summer of 2000. As far as he knew, his dealings with Randy Glass were in the past—just some unpleasant business he had left behind down in Florida. He lived his life in chapters, proceeding from episode to episode, abandoning the last thing, finished or not, once he moved on to his next obsession. (It is tempting to see this as a symptom of his bipolar disorder.) "I've always asked myself, 'What's the hottest thing now?'" Ingram once said in an interview for a business publication's annual "40 Under 40" list. "That's what attracts me." And in the year 2000, nothing was hotter than the tech market.

Since the 1995 initial public offering of Netscape, the developer of the first commercial Web browser, internet start-ups had been going public at a dizzying rate. The most successful IPOs swiftly appreciated many times over, turning pimply programmers into paper millionaires. Some of these dot-com phenoms, like the online bookstore Amazon, would come to dominate the twenty-first-century economy. Others would later look as if they had been conceived in an irrational frenzy. There was eToys.com, which was Amazon for toys; and Pets.com, which was Amazon for pets; and Kozmo.com, a quick-delivery service that was basically Amazon for dudes who were so high they could not venture outside to buy a bag of Doritos. Some of the most notorious failures—like Pseudo .com, the streaming video website, or theGlobe.com, a website that aimed to connect friends and strangers in a primitive social network—would turn out to be both doomed and inevitable.

Ingram started a tech company called TruMarkets. It sought to capitalize on another emerging trend: the explosive growth of global financial markets. U.S. trade deficits, a product of global-ization and the decline of domestic manufacturing, were sending trillions of dollars flowing overseas, which returned to Wall Street in the form of investment capital. All that money had to go some-where. At first, global investors mainly put their capital in the safest place: U.S. Treasury bonds. But soon, in search of higher yields, they moved into mortgage securities. This gave Ingram's old col-leagues the incentive to become ever more inventive in creating new debt products. The bond market's voracious demand in turn incentivized banks to loosen their lending standards, which caused Americans to take on larger mortgages. By the end of 2000, home-owners would owe around 46 percent of the value of their homes to lenders, on average, the highest level of leverage on record.

The mortgage bond market, though, was still technologically primitive. In contrast to stocks, which any day trader could buy and sell on a home computer, bonds were usually exchanged in trans-actions brokered by human dealers at Wall Street firms. During his tenure at Deutsche Bank, Ingram had experimented with online trading, introducing a new internal system that cut the time it took to trade a bond from 38 seconds to just 2.1 seconds. After Ingram was fired, he and another Deutsche Bank veteran decided to adapt the concept into an open commercial trading platform that any buyer or seller could access via the internet.

They pitched the idea to a Silicon Valley venture capitalist named Gary Morgenthaler, who was enthusiastic. "It was the NASDAQ for bonds," Morgenthaler said two decades later. "This was a he-retical idea in 2000." In early 2000, he dashed off a memo ex-plaining the logic of the investment to his partners. "Today's bond market is an inefficient, 19th Century backwater, where investors get quotes by calling from broker to broker," Morgenthaler wrote. "Price data and transparency are minimal. A tight oligopoly of Wall

Street brokers and dealers controls prices. . . . An 'E-Bond Revolution,' enabled by ubiquitous access and universal acceptance of the Internet, is poised to overturn Wall Street's hegemony over this $13.5 trillion market."

Morgenthaler's venture capital fund invested an initial $6.2 million in the start-up. TruMarkets soon assembled a formidable roster of early investors. The best known was Jon Corzine, a former chief executive of Goldman Sachs, who was in the midst of spending a fortune on a campaign for a U.S. Senate seat in New Jersey. Corzine, a Democrat, had met Ingram when he worked for him at Goldman, and he put a reported $1.5 million into the venture. Other TruMarkets investors included a former top executive at Merrill Lynch and the asset management firm BlackRock, which was run by a famed mortgage bond trader who took a keen interest in the technology. Ingram, who had recently finalized his settlement with Deutsche Bank, contributed an initial $2 million to the company. He ended up putting most of his personal wealth into it, against the advice of some of his investors.

"They basically said, 'Don't go all-in,'" Ingram says. "And I went all-in anyway."

TruMarkets hired about fifty employees and leased an office across the street from the Empire State Building. Ingram was there every day, working long hours on the project. His cofounder, the other former Deutsche Bank trader, oversaw sales and operations. Ingram handled strategy. "Kevin was kind of the pie-in-the-sky guy," says a former TruMarkets employee. "Kevin would talk about world domination. He had this sense of drive and just did not want to lose." He appeared to be driven by a desire to get even with his old bosses on Wall Street.

"This was a $26 billion gross revenue market to Wall Street at that time," Morgenthaler says. If TruMarkets could capture even a fraction of that bond-trading activity on its platform, it could potentially upend the financial industry. Over the summer of 2000, TruMarkets started to pitch its technology to potential clients. That July, Ingram paid a visit to the New York headquarters of Nomura Securities, a Japanese financial brokerage, accompanied by Morgenthaler and another business associate, an investment banker who was also involved with the Wall Street Project. In a conference room off the trading floor, Ingram gave a live demonstration of the trading platform to a group of Nomura executives, including the head of the firm's mortgage securities department. He took them through a series of interactive screens, showing how the system could be used to auction off securities in a more transparent fashion, without human middlemen.

"Kevin was really brilliant at describing the vision of where he thought the technology was going," says the former TruMarkets employee. "We didn't use the term back then, but he knew it was going to disrupt the industry."

Everyone in the marketplace understood the problem TruMarkets was seeking to address. "You never knew who had what, you never knew what had traded," says someone who heard the pitch. "It was this idea that if eBay can do it with Beanie Babies, then we can do that with bonds." The question was whether the bond market would allow itself to be disrupted. Though it was opaque and sometimes treacherous, the existing system was also extremely profitable for the humans in the middle. "Wall Street is notoriously smart, aggressive and unscrupulous in its competitive tactics," Morgenthaler wrote in his initial memo. The big banks and brokerages would surely try to destroy anything that threatened their dominance. Morgenthaler says friends who knew the financial world told him, "You will be found facedown in an alley dead before this goes down."

"This was a flaming spear aimed at the heart of Wall Street," the venture capitalist says.

BACK IN FLORIDA, Randy Glass was still waiting to close his first arms deal. It turned out that a phony business could be just as frustrating to run as a real one. From Pakistan, R. G. Abbas was reporting another delay. In June, he said French arms dealers had undercut him, and now he had to come back with a whole new pitch. Abbas put together a sales proposal, addressed to the "Chief of the General Staff, Pakistan Army, General Headquarters, Rawalpindi, Pakistan," and faxed a copy to the undercover agents in West Palm Beach. The sales pitch offered a comparison between the Stinger missile and its French equivalent and promised "delivery to Pakistan through unconventional and Clandestine means."

Several weeks later, the agents in Florida received another update from Abbas, who sent them a twenty-four-page sales brochure for his company, Close to Home. It had a cartoonish front cover featuring the U.S. and Pakistani flags. Inside were pictures and charts listing the specifications of various armaments. He assured the sellers in Florida that the brochure was on the desk of the army chief of staff. But no order came, and the deal languished.

Through U.S. intelligence agencies, the federal investigators had checked out Abbas. He really did appear to have ties to the ISI. Still, they had to wonder, was he stringing them along?

Up in Jersey City, Mike Malik was also getting annoyed with the delays. He told "Ray Spears," Stoltz's arms-dealing alter ego, that he thought it was "crazy" that Abbas was wasting so much time in his bureaucratic back-and-forth with the Pakistani military. Didn't he understand this was all extremely illegal? In fact, Abbas would later tell Malik that he had gotten tied up because the ISI suspected he was a double agent working on behalf of the American government—which wasn't far from the truth.

Malik told the undercover ATF agents that he was negotiating with a second group of "private" buyers, whom he described as black-market dealers in Dubai. He said these merchants would deal with anyone, be it Pakistan, Iran, the Taliban, or rebels. And he said that they wanted to buy everything the Florida suppliers had to offer. On August 10, Malik faxed a fifteen-page weapons wish list to West Palm Beach. The list included the usual guns and missiles, but the Dubai buyers also wanted something more unconventional.

One page of fax, labeled "<u>URGENT</u>," listed highly dangerous nuclear materials, like Iridium-192 and Cesium-137, radioactive elements that could be used to fabricate a crude "dirty bomb." Malik said the Dubai group was particularly interested in buying a substance known as "heavy water," which was used as a coolant in nuclear reactors that produced plutonium.

All along, Randy Glass had been pretending that his suppliers could obtain anything, even nuclear weapons. "I'm scared to death," he told Didi, feigning moral agony, in one of their first conversations. "I'm petrified of doing something like this . . . If it falls into the wrong hands . . ."

Now the customers were calling his bluff. The long con had somehow wandered into the shadowlands of international nuclear proliferation. Glass and Spears sent a message back to the mystery buyers in Dubai: nuclear materials could be procured, for a price.

20

Remote Control

Ralf Panitz was a native of Germany, but he was a Florida Man.

A forty-year-old housepainter, Panitz had a complicated personal life, which he shared with the world on a Web page called "Wolfie's Home." First, through the internet, he met and romanced an older woman named Nan. They married and moved to Sarasota. There, Panitz took up with a local belly dancer whom he'd met in an AOL chat room. The affair threw Wolfie's Home into turmoil. Panitz and Nan divorced, but they couldn't quite stay broken up.

The situation required a mediator, and Ralf thought he knew the man for the job: Jerry Springer.

Springer, a frizzy-haired former mayor of Cincinnati, was the self-styled "ringmaster" of what he called "the most outrageous show on television," where fools and weirdos would lay out their lurid domestic conflicts before a blood-lusting studio audience. It was one of the highest-rated syndicated programs on daytime television. And it was there, on *The Jerry Springer Show*, that Ralf proposed to put his romantic life in order. He told Nan he loved her and that he wanted to get rid of the belly dancer for good. He asked her to reunite with him on the show. This sounded good to Nan. The episode was to be titled "Secret Mistresses Confronted."

Ralf and Nan met up in Chicago, where the show was taped, and stayed at a hotel together in a room paid for by the show's producers. Then they went to the studio.

Surprise! When Nan walked onstage, alone, the other woman was already there, waiting. It was an ambush. Ralf and the producers had tricked Nan. He wasn't getting back together with her. He had married the other woman. She was his wife, and *Nan* was now the secret mistress.

While Nan had been isolated in the studio's greenroom, waiting to go on camera, her rival for Wolfie's affections had been telling Springer's audience her side of the dispute, describing Nan as a "crazy" stalker. Now the new Mrs. Panitz got right up in the old one's face.

"You redheaded bitch from hell," she shouted. "I want a normal life."

"No, you don't," Nan retorted. "Neither does Ralf. He loves the excitement."

"He doesn't want you, Nancy. You're old. You're fat."

After a commercial break, Ralf was brought on. He kissed both women. The audience booed.

"I had sex with my ex-wife yesterday," Ralf admitted, "but I did that to keep her illusioned."

"Why?" Springer asked. "Why is it important to keep an illusion that you love her if you don't?"

"I wanted Nancy to go on the show," Ralf explained. "I thought she might be humiliated enough to realize it was over."

Springer addressed Nan. "He's telling you," the host said, "he doesn't want to be with you."

"That's fine. Bye," Nan said, and stormed offstage. Ralf gave his new wife a high-five.

THAT WAS THE end of the episode but not the conclusion of the story. After the taping, amazingly, Ralf and Nan reconciled. They moved into a low-rent bungalow off the Tamiami Trail. It was not a happy household. He continued to carry on with his second wife. On July 24, 2000, Nan appeared before a Sarasota County judge to seek an emergency injunction against Ralf, claiming that he was "frequently violent," had threatened to kill her, and had chased her from the house with a knife. The judge awarded Nan exclusive use of the rented home, kicking Ralf out. A sheriff's deputy escorted Ralf to the house to retrieve his belongings. That afternoon, the *Jerry Springer* episode featuring the love triangle aired. Panitz went to watch it at a local bar.

Ralf got drunk. Afterward, he returned to the house. Police would find Nan's bludgeoned body in the kitchen. A bloody footprint on her disfigured face was matched to one of Ralf's sneakers. He would be sentenced to life in prison. "To Jerry Springer and his producers," a judge said at Panitz's sentencing, "I ask you, 'Are ratings more important to you than the dignity of human life?'"

The question was merely rhetorical. In the year 2000, the makers of television were just awakening to the engrossing power of reality. Springer's schlocky formula—regular Americans, in staged confrontation, with a sizzle of real danger—was migrating from the malarial swamps of daytime television to the heights of prime time. That May, CBS debuted a new game show called *Survivor*. Based on a Swedish series, *Expedition: Robinson*, the show had a premise fit for an adventure novel. In its first episode, sixteen contestants were "marooned" on a tiny Pacific island, a onetime refueling station for the Imperial Japanese Navy, where they were to coexist under the eye of surveillance cameras. Over the course of the summer, usually doldrum months of sitcom repeats, the castaways would compete in a thirteen-episode elimination competition, with the winner to receive $1 million.

The show's creator, a former British soldier and boardwalk T-shirt salesman named Mark Burnett, had pitched his concept to the networks by showing off a mock *Survivor*-themed cover of *Newsweek*, boldly promising the show would be a hit. And he was proved right, immediately. It was only over time, though, that the new series grew into a cultural phenomenon, as the secret to its appeal revealed itself. At first, most *Survivor* contestants thought they were there to compete against one another in physical challenges. Only one seemed to realize that the nature of the game, in which the contestants would vote one of their own off the island each week, was about winning elections.

Richard Hatch, a paunchy, bearded, middle-aged white man, was identified by producers as a "corporate trainer." He was also an openly gay man at a time when that was still unusual to see on television. At first, he seemed unremarkable, save for his habit of unsettling his competitors by walking around the island naked. But over the first seven weeks of the show, he gradually revealed himself to be the antihero, scheming and treacherous. He formed an alliance with a few other contestants to vote strategically, methodically eliminating his strongest rivals.

"Outright lying is absolutely essential," Hatch said into the camera at the opening of Episode 9, which aired on July 26, two days after Nan Panitz's murder. That was the week that Hatch really took over the show. His enemies were plotting, but he was arrogantly confident. "They're not voting me off," he bragged, "because I'm not letting them." Every episode of *Survivor* concluded with a hokey "tribal council," at which the contestants would cast their ballots around a blazing campfire. That week, in his closest brush with death, Hatch avoided elimination by one vote.

The tribe had spoken, and the public was riveted. Some twenty-seven million viewers watched that week's episode. It won a stunning 36 percent share of viewers in the most important advertising demographic. All over America, people were gathering around office cubicles to talk about the show's plot machinations. *Newsweek* really did end up putting *Survivor* on its cover.

Burnett would later describe *Survivor* as "Machiavellian politics at their most primal." The show was carefully edited, and its events sometimes distorted, to heighten the conspiracy. Burnett coined a term, *dramality*, to describe his method. His neologism didn't catch on, but his genre did.

"It's quite a mean game," Burnett said on CNN, "just like life is a mean game."

MEANWHILE, THE REPUBLICANS and Democrats were busy creating their own dramality. August was the convention season, when the parties gathered for speeches, gossip, and open-bar drinking. It had been decades since the conventions played any function in deciding the nominations. They were, instead, made-for-television events, staged to entertain viewers with carefully crafted themes, storylines, and "spontaneous" moments. But they really did matter. At a time when a large population of swing voters could still conceive of supporting either party, a successful convention could produce a polling "bounce" that propelled a candidate to victory.

The Republicans held their convention in Philadelphia, where George W. Bush mandated an uplifting tone and a message of inclusion. General Colin Powell gave a stirring speech, calling Bush the candidate who could "bridge the racial divides." The star of the week was George P. Bush, the nominee's nephew, a half-Mexican heartthrob who was held up as a symbol of the party's attempts to appeal to a diverse new generation. Even the attacks on the hated Clintons were deliberately muted. (Although, the New York delegation, in a bid for pop-cultural relevance, did sell a T-shirt bearing the slogan "Vote Hillary Off the Island.")

The Democratic National Convention had all the entertainment. The party had decided to hold its event in Los Angeles. *George* threw a bash at a mansion in the hills, where Michael Douglas hobnobbed with Harvey Weinstein, who was organizing a gala at which Barbra Streisand was to perform. Chelsea Clinton showed up at a soiree held on the Oval Office set of the hit show *The West Wing*. Bill and Hillary kicked off their week with an event called the "Hollywood Tribute to President William Jefferson Clinton," drawing a panoply of celebrities (John Travolta, Brad Pitt, and Jennifer Aniston) and demi-celebrities (O.J. Simpson's lawyer Robert Kardashian).

There was no place for nobodies. An Illinois state legislator named Barack Obama was in Los Angeles that week, wandering the convention hall with a lousy credential, but he ended up leaving disheartened because he couldn't get on the list for any of the exclusive events.

Gore was reported to be less than thrilled with Bill Clinton's busy schedule, which included numerous parties and fund-raisers for Hillary's Senate campaign. The Gore camp felt that Clinton was drawing unhelpful attention to himself with his buckraking. Clinton, for his part, was still annoyed that Gore was keeping a reproachful distance from him. Gore would not even be in Los Angeles for the first night of the convention, when both Clintons were speaking.

The Clintons made the most of their role as the opening act, turning their night into a pageant of shared ambition. Hillary appeared first, taking the stage to the "Theme from *New York, New*

York," and speaking, with her usual leaden earnestness, of her generation's "rendezvous with responsibility." Then it was Bill's turn. He had told friends he wanted to go out like Babe Ruth, who, as the (slightly inaccurate) legend had it, smacked three home runs in his final game. Working with his longtime friend and image consultant, the Hollywood producer Harry Thomason, Clinton had come up with a showstopping entrance. He had kept his plan secret from Gore's advisers and had declined even to share a copy of his speech with them beforehand.

Thomason had choreographed a long tracking shot, capturing the commander in chief as he walked alone to the stage through the bowels of the Staples Center. As he waited for his cue, Clinton threw one of his wicked tantrums over some last-minute logistical changes—he wanted every step to look perfect. When the lights went on, though, he performed flawlessly, entering the arena like a conquering hero as a list of his accomplishments rolled across the bottom of the screen: LONGEST ECONOMIC EXPANSION IN AMERICAN HISTORY . . . LOWEST INFANT MORTALITY RATE IN AMERICAN HISTORY . . . HIGHEST HOME OWNERSHIP IN AMERICAN HISTORY . . . LOWEST POVERTY RATE IN 20 YEARS.

"My fellow Americans, this is a *biiiiiiiiiiig* election," Clinton said, in his Arkansas drawl. With his unparalleled explanatory skill, he made the case for the Democrats. "More than anybody else I've known in public life," he said, "Al Gore understands the future." That night, Gore picked up 5 points in his internal polling. The Babe had delivered. Bill celebrated by taking Hillary and Chelsea to yet another party, held in front of a fake New York City streetscape on the Paramount Studios backlot, where singer Michael Bolton serenaded them.

The second night of the convention belonged to the liberals, with appearances by various Kennedys and a rousing speech by Jesse Jackson, who mocked the "inclusion illusion" of the Republican convention. (Offstage, he was less enthusiastic about the ticket. "If it means we have to hold our noses and take castor oil, do it," he told a meeting of Black leaders at the convention.) Gore and Clinton had met that day in Michigan for a symbolic torch-passing rally. On his way to Los Angeles, Gore told reporters that he had been toiling over his own convention speech, working from ideas he had scribbled on poster-size sheets of paper.

This was not true. A team of speechwriters and consultants had painstakingly assembled the text, videotaping Gore's practice sessions and cutting them into bite-size segments to be shown to his pollster's focus groups. Each focus group participant would turn a dial to register positive or negative reactions, allowing the campaign to analyze the persuasiveness of every passage in the speech. Clinton was aware of the process and furtively lobbied the speechwriting team, advising them to tone down the populism and to stress his favorite themes: opportunity, community, and responsibility. Gore was still pressing the speechwriters to include a long, earnest anecdote about the astrophysicist Stephen Hawking, which horrified some of his advisers, who thought it would reinforce the impression that Gore was an elitist smarty-pants.

Finally, at a practice the morning of his speech, Tipper intervened. "Al, take Hawking out," she said.

"You, too?" he replied. He made the cut.

The convention was scripted to emphasize Gore's common decency, portraying him as a steady and reliable family man. Karenna Gore gave his nominating speech and feigned surprise as her father came out to offer his congratulations in a carefully scripted "unplanned" appearance. Tipper, a gifted photographer, introduced her husband with candid family photos. Lest anyone miss the point, Gore, as he took the stage, grabbed Tipper and gave her a big, long, uxorious kiss.

"I stand here tonight as my own man," Gore said in his acceptance speech, "and I want you to know me for who I truly am." He offered credit to Clinton for building a prosperous economy, but questioned whether the profits were reaching everyone. "Together, let's make sure that our prosperity enriches not just the few, but all working families," Gore said. He pledged to "challenge a culture with too much meanness and not enough meaning." He spoke directly to the many voters who thought the two major parties were presenting them with no real choice.

"That's the difference," Gore said. "They're for the powerful. We're for the people."

Robert Shrum, the political consultant who had authored much of the speech, would later say that Gore "gained more in forty-five minutes than anybody ever has at a convention." His late-summer convention bounce was huge, somewhere between 16 and 22 points.

After the convention, Gore and Joe Lieberman embarked on a cross-country tour, ending up in Fort Lauderdale, where they received a rapturous greeting from retirees at a Jewish community center. Lieberman gave a speech sprinkled with Yiddish, and the elderly crowd kvelled over him. "He's a rock star, like Barbra Streisand," an enthusiastic local congressman said. Gore was surging in Florida and everywhere else. On TV, Bush went on the offensive.

"There's Al Gore, reinventing himself on television again," said the narrator of a Republican campaign advertisement that started airing in Florida after the convention. The ad played an out-of-context snippet of audio, suggesting that Gore had claimed he had invented the internet.

"Yeah," the attack ad concluded, "and I invented the remote control."

CLICK!

ON AUGUST 23, the day that Gore and Lieberman made their triumphant visit to Fort Lauderdale, Americans turned to CBS to learn the result of that summer's most talked-about election. An estimated fifty-one million viewers watched the two-hour finale of *Survivor*, the largest audience for any event other than that year's Super Bowl. (In celebration, CBS programming chief Les Moonves sent Mark Burnett a champagne-colored Mercedes.) The last two contestants were Richard Hatch and Kelly Wiglesworth, a twenty-three-year-old river rafting guide.

The series had been edited to give their confrontation moral overtones. Richard played the unabashed villain. "Maintaining a thumb on all these personalities that I care very little about is exhausting," he complained. Kelly was the nice girl, conflicted about her betrayals. "How do you stay true to yourself and maintain integrity and still play this game?" she asked in one of the later episodes. "You can't." Kelly had assured her place in the finale by winning a series of physical challenges. Many critics pointed out that her showdown with Richard had a familiar workplace dynamic, offering up a choice between a high-achieving woman and a less-qualified man.

The winner was chosen at a final "tribal council," with a group of previously eliminated contestants serving as the jury. In the episode's most memorable moment, one of the losers, a midwestern truck driver named Sue Hawk, delivered a scathing diatribe against Kelly, with whom she had been friendly before Kelly cast the decisive vote against her. "This island is pretty much full of only two things: snakes and rats," she said. "We have Richard, the snake, who knowingly went after prey, and Kelly, who turned into the rat."

By a single vote, Richard was awarded the $1 million prize. In reality, the snakes often win.

ON A HAZY early September day, Bill Clinton was sitting in the rear of Marine One, the presidential helicopter, playing a card game called Oh Hell, which he had learned from Steven Spielberg one summer in the Hamptons. "Shit, shit, shit!" the president cursed cheerfully, as someone else threw down a trump card. The chopper swung around the Twin Towers of the World Trade Center and descended onto a riverfront helipad, where the president's bulletproof limousine was waiting to whisk him into Manhattan. He had come to attend the Millennium Summit of the United Nations, where he was to give a farewell speech to his fellow world leaders.

Clinton had business he wanted to finish at the United Nations— items he hoped to add to his ledger for the reckoning of history. That evening, he would be seeing Ehud Barak, the prime minister of Israel, and Yasir Arafat, the leader of the Palestinians. Clinton was planning to make one last push for peace in the Middle East, and he believed the two sides were within reach of a final settlement.

At the same time, he was plotting to eliminate the region's most dangerous troublemaker. As Clinton spoke to the Millennium Summit, the CIA was preparing to conduct the first test of a highly classified new program, code-named Afghan Eyes. Clinton had approved the secret project the month before, seeking "proof of concept" for an experimental aircraft called the Predator. The technology would allow CIA officers working out of a command center in Virginia to fly an unmanned drone by remote control on the other side of the world. On its first mission, scheduled for late that night, the Predator would conduct surveillance of one of Osama bin Laden's training camps, the complex near the airport in Kandahar.

The drone program had emerged out of Clinton's growing frustration with the struggle against international terrorism, which he had identified four years before as "the enemy of our generation." As president, he commanded the world's most powerful army. His intelligence agencies possessed awesome electronic surveillance capabilities. Yet these weapons were ineffective against a protean force like Al Qaeda, which was as much an idea as an organization.

Clinton had tried diplomacy earlier in the year, in his fruitless meeting with Pakistan's military leader, General Pervez Musharraf. And he had tried using brute force. In 1998, after Al Qaeda pulled off a coordinated suicide bombing attack on the U.S. embassies in Kenya and Tanzania, the president had launched cruise missiles at targets in Sudan and Afghanistan, including a camp where bin Laden was reported to be holding a meeting. The barrage proved ineffective, missing bin Laden by a few hours, and ended up only enhancing his outlaw image. Now Clinton was taking a fresh approach. He was getting inventive.

For years, the CIA had tried to develop informants inside Al Qaeda, with little success. The Predator drone, Clinton's national security advisor wrote in an August 2000 memo, could provide a technological solution to the intelligence failure, promising "live and prolonged coverage of locations where bin Laden and his leadership are known to travel." On its maiden test flight, the hovering drone beamed a video feed to a large screen for an audience of spies and national security officials. What they saw, one of Clinton's advisers later recalled, was "truly astonishing." The Predator spotted an extremely tall, thin man dressed in white robes, surrounded by bodyguards, walking from a residence that had been identified as bin Laden's to the camp's small mosque. Right there on the screen, they could see him as he lived and breathed.

Now the question was: could Bill Clinton kill him?

WITHIN THE ADMINISTRATION'S secret councils, the idea of using covert force against bin Laden had a powerful opponent. Janet Reno was the lawyer in the room, and she was more than willing to offer her blunt opinion. It was not just a question of whether a given action was legal. Reno would also ask, "Is it stupid?" In 1998, she had been a strong dissenter when Clinton decided to launch the strike in retaliation for the embassy attacks. She felt the evidence linking Al Qaeda to one of the targets, a plant in Sudan that the CIA suspected was being used to manufacture chemical weapons, was shaky. Reno had a screaming match with Clinton's national security advisor over the issue, arguing against the attack even as coordinates were entered into the cruise missiles. The Sudanese target turned out to be a pharmaceutical plant. Stupid, very stupid.

After the failure of the air attack, Clinton's national security team had started to develop plans for a ground operation. "You know," the president suggested to one of his generals in 2000, "it would scare the shit out of Al Qaeda if suddenly a bunch of black ninjas rappelled out of helicopters into the middle of their camp." But satellite photos showed the group's compound near the Kandahar airport was well fortified and situated on a flat desert plain. There would be no cover, no element of surprise.

The CIA director at the time, George Tenet, needed Reno's approval for any drastic action to neutralize bin Laden. "We all wanted him dead," Tenet later testified, but he added, "you must put it on paper." There was a legal issue: assassination was banned by a presidential order issued during the 1970s, after the public exposure of previous CIA misdeeds. But was Al Qaeda a criminal organization or an army at war with the United States? If it was the latter, Clinton could justifiably give an order to kill its leader in the field. Reno resisted this interpretation. She took the position that a decapitation strike would be legal only if an Al Qaeda attack were "imminent," though she never defined precisely what that meant. "She had a very high threshold," Tenet said.

Tenet thought that Reno did not understand what the CIA did. She annoyed the spy agency by barraging it with questions that delved deeply into tactical details of its plans. Her objections were legal and practical. In a briefing on one potential operation, the CIA told Reno it estimated the chances of success at 30 percent, and even then, bin Laden was likely to be killed, not captured and brought to justice. If arrest was just a pretext, not a realistic objective, the operation would verge on assassination. Because the assassination ban was set down in an executive order, not a law, Clinton could always rescind it. But Reno opposed this course on principle. She wanted bin Laden to be tried as a criminal in the United States. There were rules, she argued. There was a system.

She felt that even if killing bin Laden were lawful, it might be stupid—the first step down a damning path. Bin Laden and other Al Qaeda leaders housed their families in the complex. "I was concerned about women and children, and the specificity . . . of what they could do to protect innocent people," Reno later said. "It would be perceived as an assassination, and we ought to be very sure of what we were doing, because it would have a dramatic impact on the world's view of us as a nation, and our willingness to use democratic principles and the processes of justice."

Similar ethical reservations weighed on Clinton. The president was haunted, in particular, by a spy satellite photograph of bin Laden's camp on which he could see a child's swing.

By Clinton's order, nuclear submarines were continually stationed off Pakistan's coast, armed with cruise missiles that could be launched at bin Laden's camp at any time. But he never fired them, for fear of collateral damage. This was why he wanted the Predator.

After the drone's first test mission, Tenet brought a videotape of the footage of the man in white to the White House and screened it for the president. Over the next few weeks, drones flew nine more test missions, giving the intelligence agency a tantalizing view of daily life in Al Qaeda.

The men in the camp trained and prayed, and in the afternoons, they would sometimes play volleyball, with bin Laden captaining a team against his most trusted lieutenant, a similarly tall Egyptian who went by the name Abu Hafs al-Masri. But bin Laden was restless, always on the move in his Toyota pickup truck. "It was very much the O.J. thing," a witness to the test flights later told the journalist Steve Coll, "with a helicopter following a car down the freeway."

The CIA believed it sighted bin Laden on at least two occasions. Clinton never fired his missiles. Even in flawless circumstances, hours would elapse between an order to launch them and their impact at the target, during which time bin Laden was likely to move. Already, some within the national security apparatus were talking about the possibility of arming the Predator, to offer what they called a "see it/shoot it" option. Reno was sure to oppose that as outright assassination.

But after the Afghan winter, the drones could fly again, and there would be a new president, a new attorney general, and perhaps, new rules of engagement.

THEY KNEW THEY were being watched. On September 29, 2000, an Al Qaeda public relations man made an entry in his diary. Two times that day, once at around 7 a.m. and again after the noon prayer, the organization's military commander, Abu Hafs, had spotted a small surveillance plane hovering high above the camp. Bin Laden was also present at this time, meeting with around twenty-five of his senior operatives. The Sheikh warned his men that vigilance was necessary.

"In October, an event may occur," the propagandist recorded in his notes of a meeting conducted by bin Laden. He urged the brothers, who had been feuding among themselves, to get ready for "huge waves" of recruits. "We have shifted from a period of uncertainty to a period of expansion and preparation," bin Laden said, according to the notes. A climactic battle was coming.

Fearing enemy surveillance, bin Laden now took evasive action: moving around, sleeping in safe houses, varying his routine. It would be more than a decade before the CIA could fix his location again. Meanwhile, the airport camp was organizing for an influx. The brothers would soon be busy practicing on its rifle range, shooting at paper targets bearing the face of Bill Clinton.

21

Black September

"Eight months after landing on the FBI's Most Wanted list, terror kingpin . . ."

Chuck Harder fumbled with the unfamiliar name. ". . . *OZMA BIN-LAYDEN* has become one of the most popular figures in the Middle East, with thousands of fanatics ready to do his bidding."

Another day on Harder's radio show, another scary new thing for Americans to worry about. This time it was an international terrorist organization he referred to as "Awl Quay-ADA."

"U.S. officials," he intoned, "fear that the millionaire Saudi expatriate bunkered down with his four wives and fifteen children in a remote mountain region in Afghanistan is set to activate his followers for a series of new attacks on U.S. interests, including financial centers in New York.

"Am I making this up? No! I am reading to you, ladies and gentlemen, from the *New York Post*."

Even for the paranoiacs, it was hard to believe—the idea that the deadliest menace to the United States of America was some comic book evildoer who issued declarations of war against the world's lone superpower from a primitive compound without reliable electricity.

"There is a lot of movement," Harder continued, quoting the

assessment of a Washington terrorism analyst. "It's like a volcano just before the explosion."

Harder knew that no one was paying heed. "So, there we go, ladies and gentlemen, the big happy world we heard about is not doing that well," he said. "Now, my friends, all I'm going to say to you is that I know you've tuned out. Many of you don't want to hear this stuff anymore, you don't care about it, everything's okay . . . and what the heck? Somebody else will take care of it. But I still believe this is a great nation. I still believe that I have the duty to make sure that my children and my grandchildren have as good a country to grow up in as I did. And right now, they do not.

"You have to admit to that, don't you?"

SOME OF THE most frantic alarmists worked inside the White House. Richard Clarke, the president's counterterrorism czar, was busy drawing up an urgent plan for covert action against Al Qaeda, of which the Predator drone program was just one component. "This cannot be episodic or spasmodic," Clarke wrote in a classified memo to National Security Advisor Sandy Berger in early 2000. "Within the U.S., we have let a variety of terrorist groups take root. . . . These groups form 'sleeper cells' that do planning and can then support attacks or conduct attacks on order." That year, Clarke addressed a summit of FBI officials in Tampa, where he described Al Qaeda as a "worldwide political conspiracy masquerading as a religious sect" with a network inside the United States. He thought that Justice Department rules on policing political and religious groups, designed to protect constitutional rights, had put the FBI "in a straightjacket" when it came to monitoring radical elements within Muslim communities. (Janet Reno later said she didn't want agents to go "blindly from one mosque to another.")

278 | THE YEAR THAT BROKE AMERICA

In the wake of the terrorism alert surrounding the millennium, Clarke had drafted an "after action review," analyzing what intelligence and law enforcement agencies did right and wrong. All the agencies involved in protecting national security got together for a meeting in March 2000, where they agreed that they needed to improve when it came to collaborating and sharing intelligence, but nothing really changed. At the root of the dysfunction was an antagonistic relationship. There was supposed to be a clear delineation between the missions of the FBI, which handled domestic security, and the CIA, which operated overseas. But where their spheres overlapped, the cops and the spies feuded and worked at cross-purposes. The FBI catches bank robbers, the adage went, and the CIA robs banks. They both hoarded secrets. Most notoriously, the CIA failed to alert the FBI when two Al Qaeda members the Agency was watching flew from Bangkok to Los Angeles in early 2000. The pair, dispatched as part of the planes operation, would burrow into the Muslim community on the West Coast, where they interacted with Saudi diplomats, a radical imam, and an FBI informant, all without triggering any alarm. This was one of at least eleven opportunities the CIA had to disrupt the plot. "The agency missed every one of them," national security scholar Amy Zegart writes in her history *Spying Blind*, "for the same reason: longstanding organizational weaknesses in the CIA made it likely, even unavoidable, that smart people would do dumb things."

Meanwhile, Ziad Jarrah, Mohamed Atta, and Marwan al-Shehhi were going about their lives in Florida, taking flight lessons and shopping at Walmart. Even if the FBI had been looking for "sleeper cells," it probably would not have identified the three students from Hamburg. They committed no crimes and took care to follow the undercover tradecraft that Al Qaeda taught in its camps. They used free email accounts and hard-to-trace prepaid telephone cards and kept electronic communications to a minimum. They avoided mosques and places where Muslims congregated. They were clean-shaven and dressed like Floridians, in khakis and collared shirts.

They were on their own in America. Atta, as the "emir" of the group, was in charge. What little communication he had with Al Qaeda leaders went through intermediaries, in brief, coded conversations. (He was "a very serious man on the telephone," one of his contacts would later tell interrogators.) Atta and al-Shehhi lived a disciplined existence, spending all their time together, sharing a single cell phone and a joint checking account, opened at a bank a few blocks from their house, a tiny rented bungalow next to a drainage canal. Classmates at their flight school idly speculated about the nature of the odd couple's relationship. (One rumor was that Atta was an Arab prince slumming it as a student and that al-Shehhi was his servant.) Atta was stone-faced—an "asshole first class," in the subsequent recollection of the school's owner, Rudi Dekkers. His heavyset companion was friendlier, fond of dirty jokes, though his command of English was shaky.

Around 80 percent of the flight school's students were foreign, and enough of them were from the Middle East that Dekkers provided prayer mats for the Muslims. Atta and al-Shehhi never used them or prayed openly. They blended in, eating hamburgers at the airport's Cockpit Café, drinking coffee silently in the break room, surfing the World Wide Web in the flight school's computer lab. Mostly, they practiced, usually sharing a plane. They were diligent in carrying out their mission.

None of the wild stories that would later become part of their Florida fable—that they went out carousing at strip clubs, that they told their instructors they didn't care about landing—seem to be based in fact. Indeed, they *had* to know how to land if they wanted to earn their private pilot's licenses, so they could progress to more advanced courses, and ultimately to their goal of taking lessons on a commercial jet simulator. If anything, they were too enthusiastic: the flight school received a complaint about Atta and al-Shehhi doing "touch-and-gos," a landing practice maneuver, one evening on an airstrip in Clearwater that was supposed to close at dark. They were in a hurry. They said they had pilot jobs waiting for them in the Middle East.

Atta's impatience and gruff demeanor soon grated on everyone—including Jarrah, who chafed at his controlling and abrasive personality and avoided his "emir" as much as possible in Venice. When Atta's instructor refused to clear him to take a check ride, a final step on the way to his private pilot's license, he threw a loud temper tantrum, accusing the teacher of carrying a personal grudge. That instructor refused to continue teaching him after the outburst. But Atta kept working with other teachers and managed to pass the test in September. Immediately afterward, he and al-Shehhi informed Dekkers that they were transferring to another flight school, in nearby Sarasota. One instructor at the school in Venice would later recall that there "was a collective sigh of relief" when Atta left.

"I called him 'the little terrorist,'" the school's office manager would testify.

Of course, no one thought Atta actually *was* a terrorist. A manual used in Al Qaeda's camps instructed its operatives not to fall into "the enemy's excitement trap." Following procedure, Atta and al-Shehhi kept their political and religious views quiet. They were social misfits, but that was not so unusual at the school, which was full of lonesome foreigners with dreams of flight. True, there were hints. A student from the Middle East would later recall al-Shehhi showing him political websites that were banned back home. A school employee once saw al-Shehhi looking at an odd Web page that played Arabic music and had pictures of men waving flags. He told her the people in the pictures did not like Americans. He said some angry things about the oppression of the Palestinians. But these clues appeared conspicuous only in retrospect.

They talked little but watched closely. Back in Hamburg, in his study group lectures on Islam and the New World Order, Atta's conspiracy theories had demonstrated a preoccupation with American politics and the workings of its empire. (He believed that Monica Lewinsky was a Zionist agent sent to compromise Bill Clinton.) Now, living in America, Atta would be witness to a great power struggle. "The nation that wants to achieve victory over its enemy," the Al Qaeda manual instructed, "must know that enemy very well." In Florida, the enemy would come to him.

ON SEPTEMBER 17, 2000, Mukhtar's nephew in Dubai wired $70,000 in cash to Atta and al-Shehhi's account at SunTrust Bank in Florida. They immediately started on the second stage of their training to become commercial pilots, enrolling at a school called Jones Aviation.

"They brought a roll of money," recalls one of their flight instructors, Kendall Coleman, "and said, 'We need this much training.'" Atta and al-Shehhi were in a rush to amass the hours of flight time required to take their next test, which would certify their ability to control the plane by its instruments, a skill necessary for flying in bad weather or other conditions of limited visibility. Every day for the next few weeks, they drove their maroon Pontiac Grand Am to the Jones Aviation hangar at the Sarasota-Bradenton International

Airport, a half hour north of them on the Tamiami Trail. When they weren't in the air, they would practice on the school's flight simulation system, a mock cockpit with a yoke and a computer screen over the instrument panel.

Two days after they showed up, on the morning of September 22, the airport received another visitor: Governor George W. Bush. His arrival would have been impossible to miss. Traffic was snarled along the Tamiami Trail as several thousand Republicans waited in long security lines in the blazing one-hundred-degree heat for a campaign rally out on the tarmac. A band called Two Phat Cats played bluegrass, and a local Republican led the crowd in chants of ¡Viva Bush!

"He doesn't lie, he doesn't change the truth or flip-flop like Gore," a Bush enthusiast wearing a button reading "Annoy a Liberal" told a student journalist from a local college. "Gore wants to do away with the internal combustion engine. It's right there in his book, you can read it."

Bush was flying in from Nashville, on the final leg of what his advisers were calling his "metaphor of life" tour, a high-concept weeklong trip designed to showcase his plans for Americans "from the cradle to the grave." Florida was naturally the end of the line. The Republicans cheered with their eyes to the heavens as Bush's campaign plane descended for a landing and taxied to the stage. Bush came out into the swelter with his tie cinched tight.

"My little brother said if you come to Sarasota maybe a few folks will show up," he shouted out to the crowd on the tarmac. Jeb would be meeting him in Tampa later that day, as part of what was being billed as a "Bush blitz" involving five family members, including Poppy, and ten campaign events in various locales around the state. The whole gang would wind up at a rally that night in Miami, where the Bushes would share a stage with the Cuban community leaders who had organized the Elián Gonzalez protests. Dubya would promise: "¡*No mas Clinton!*"

The Bush blitz was an acknowledgment of an unexpected reversal. The campaign was lagging, and nowhere was its poor performance more noticeable than in Florida. The latest poll showed Bush trailing Gore by 3 points in the state. This caused some consternation for Jeb, who admitted that he had been "almost reclusive" during his brother's campaign. Some Republicans in Washington were starting to grumble to reporters, under the cover of anonymity, about the uninspired effort. It seemed the Bushes were blowing it, just as they did in 1992.

"I read something quite amusing the other day," Dubya told the crowd in Sarasota, referring to the reports of his campaign's struggles. "It's wishful thinking on behalf of our opponents. They said they think they can carry Florida. They don't understand what's about to hit 'em in Florida."

Switching to Spanish, Bush vowed to triumph. "¡*Vamos a ganar!*"

ONE OF BUSH'S advisers called it his "Black September." Suddenly it was Dubya, not Gore, who was stumbling, and the press was scrutinizing every little misstep. At a Labor Day event in Illinois, an open microphone caught Bush referring to a reporter from the *New York Times* as a "major league asshole," an unguarded comment that the press treated as a shocking affront. Next there was a fracas over a Bush campaign ad that, for one-thirtieth of a second, flashed animated text reading RATS across the screen. The Gore campaign complained that Bush was attacking by subliminal message. These were silly controversies, but they fed the perception that Bush was a callow dimwit at the very moment that his preparation for the presidency was facing a test.

In October, he and Gore were scheduled to meet for three debates. Gore was eager to match wits, and Bush's advisers were nervous. To get ready, the governor had been holding mock debates with a Republican senator who stood in for Gore. "I beat his brains in," the stand-in recalled of an initial session. During the week of the Democratic convention, Bush convened an intensive training camp at his ranch in Crawford, Texas. In the searing heat, he and his advisers crowded into a small, stuffy bunkhouse, and his sparring partner pummeled him some more. "It doesn't matter," a Bush aide scrawled in a note to a colleague. "We're doomed."

To make matters worse, Bush soon discovered there was a spy in his camp. In mid-September, a package from Austin was delivered to a Washington lobbying firm run by one of Gore's friends. Inside was a videotape, 120 pages of briefing material, and a note signed by one "Amy Smith," promising to call in the future to "find out what other materials can be useful to the VP." Gore's friend, who had been running his debate preparations, popped the tape into a VCR. There was Bush in one of his mock debate sessions. A participant recalls that the practice in question was held on a particularly scorching day at the ranch, and Bush was dressed casually in shorts and a "Curious George" T-shirt. He was in a peevish mood and blew up at the moderator.

In the hands of a rival, the leaked video was potentially devastating intelligence. But Gore's adviser wanted nothing to do with the stolen goods, and he turned the package over to the FBI. The newspapers referred to the scandal as "Molegate." The Bush campaign went on a hunt for the source of the leak. They speculated that the Democrats might somehow have broken into their campaign office. The Democrats countered that the leak must have been disinformation planted by Karl Rove. The spy-versus-spy plot went on for a few days, until it was reported that the FBI had identified a clerical employee of an advertising firm used by the Bush campaign as the culprit. (She later pleaded guilty to a federal mail fraud charge and was sentenced to a year in prison.)

The tape and the briefing materials were secret documents—the equivalent of Bush's war plan. They could have offered a crucial edge to Gore. But Gore would never stoop to collusion.

Then again, maybe Gore just felt that cheating was unnecessary. He had a reputation for destroying debate opponents. The July issue of the *Atlantic* featured a cover story on his ferocious style, illustrated with a portrait of the vice president with a single fang peeking over his bottom lip. "We felt the first debate would be his moment," a senior Gore campaign adviser later said. "That people would see two candidates on stage, but only one president."

IF THERE WAS ever a high point for the Gore 2000 campaign, it was that weekend before the first debate. For his debate preparation, he returned to Florida. Four years before, he had held practice sessions for his vice-presidential debate at the Mote Marine Laboratory and Aquarium, on the Gulf Coast island of Longboat Key. That debate had gone well, and Gore, as a matter of strategy and superstition, had told his aides he wanted to reproduce his prior preparations exactly. They had the aquarium staff mount a stuffed shark on the wall of Gore's practice room, just where it had been the last time. For extra luck, they hung a talisman from his 1992 debate preparation sessions, a horse bridle, on the shark. Gore was gonna ride that metaphor.

On the afternoon of September 30, Gore flew down to Sarasota on Air Force Two. The debate camp was supposed to be a low-key retreat, with little of the customary campaign hoopla, so it was a smaller-than-usual crowd that greeted Gore at the airport. Local

Democrats passed through a security checkpoint and stood outside a cluster of aluminum-sided buildings belonging to Jones Aviation. Airspace was closed for the vice president's arrival, grounding all planes, and many of the flight instructors and students took a break to come out and see the front-runner up close. There is no firm evidence that Atta and al-Shehhi were present, but Coleman says "they were around, at least, once to twice a day" during this period. Al Qaeda offered instruction on assassinations in its camps. Another man might have been tempted, but Atta stuck to the plan.

As Air Force Two landed, snipers kept watch from the roofs of the school's buildings. The plane rolled up to the chiming chords of U2's "Where the Streets Have No Name." Gore followed his usual entrance routine. He waited on the plane for a few minutes, listening to the crowd chant, *We want Gore!* Then he emerged, dressed in an open-necked linen shirt he wore tightly tucked into his high-waisted, pleated green slacks. He descended the plane's steps and then . . . *ran* at a dead sprint toward his audience while waving with vigor. He climbed up onstage and spoke in front of a sign that read, "Florida Wins with Gore." His remarks were brief, touching on Florida-centric issues. He introduced a group of guests he had brought with him, a panel of carefully selected "average Americans," including a Pennsylvania steelworker and an Atlanta firefighter, whom he claimed he would be consulting for feedback and ideas.

As an ironist, Gore could wink at the artifice of politics. "I'm not planning any gimmicks," he said that weekend, in an interview with two reporters from the *Times* conducted as the candidate took a barefoot stroll on the beach, simulating the act of vacation. "If something comes up that looks like a gimmick, you'll know it's spontaneous." He stopped to chat with well-wishers, including a man who introduced his little boys, Dylan and Wesley. Recalling his hazy pot-smoking days, Gore sang them a verse of Bob Dylan's song "John Wesley Harding."

But the funny thing was, as much as it might have looked like a stunt, Gore was truly serious about the whole listening-to-average-Americans thing. After debate practice, he took his panel of a dozen regular folks out to lunch at a place called Charley's Crab Shack. The restaurant's manager, a registered Republican, was inspired to slip the vice president a three-sentence note, telling him about overcrowding at his daughter's high school. He wrote that it didn't have enough desks for all its students. He enclosed a newspaper clipping that included a picture of his child standing in her science class.

Gore would later read the father's note to his advisers as he flew to Boston for the debate on Air Force Two. *This* was the kind of material he wanted. He filed the anecdote away for future use.

THAT WHOLE WEEKEND, Air Force Two sat outside the flight school at the Sarasota airport. "I remember the plane being on our ramp at night," Kendall Coleman says, "and somebody guarded that plane twenty-four/seven." Even if they somehow missed the rally, there was no way that Atta and al-Shehhi could have ignored the presence of the vice president. It was right there on the tarmac: that majestic blue-and-white Boeing jet painted with the words *United States of America*.

The foreign flight students would also have noticed the heightened security. The Secret Service "went through a lot of records," Coleman says. "They were there, they were checking us out. They were going through everything." Maybe this spooked Atta, because for whatever reason, during Gore's visit, he and al-Shehhi experienced an abrupt change of heart about Jones Aviation. They were ready to take a test, but instead of driving to Sarasota as usual, they asked Coleman to fly the plane down to meet them at the Venice airport. The exam tested their ability to control and navigate the plane while wearing a hood that limited their vision. Coleman flunked them. "It wasn't off by a little," he recalls. "They were really off by a lot."

Coleman told the students to polish up their skills. The failure was a routine setback. But Atta was furious. He called up a manager at the school and complained that Coleman was a "redneck." Atta and al-Shehhi had already alienated other staff members with their aggressive behavior. One instructor later told the FBI that on multiple occasions, the students had fought with him when he attempted to take control of their training flights.

"So, they took their money and left," Coleman says. "I never saw them again." The following weekend, Gore would fly back to Sarasota to prepare for his second debate. But by that time, Atta and al-Shehhi had quit the school. They had seen enough of Bush v. Gore.

22

Hurricane Season

"I love Florida," Bill Clinton said as he rode aboard Air Force One, chomping on an unlit cigar.

Was it really any wonder? The heat, the golf, the high kitsch, and the plunging necklines—it was his kind of scene. Most of all, Clinton loved those 25 electoral votes. Politically, Florida had a split personality. The north of the state was southern in culture, while its south was northern—an ethnic jumble of immigrants, white suburbanites, and Yankee retirees. In 1996, Clinton had shown how a Democrat could win the state: run up huge margins in Miami and the rest of South Florida; limit the damage up north, along the "Redneck Riviera" of the Panhandle; and slug it out along the Interstate 4 corridor, a swing-voting belt of suburban communities running from Tampa to Orlando and Daytona Beach. Now, four years later, he was back in Florida, not running for anything, just winging around and fund-raising, soaking up its northern money and southern hospitality.

Truth be told, it was hard to love Florida that day. This was early October, the hurricane season, and a nameless subtropical depression had just howled in from the Atlantic, bringing lashing winds and sheets of rain. But Clinton kept going, campaigning for its own sake, oblivious to the turbulence in the air or the elements on the ground. In Jacksonville, he was backed up by a gospel choir as he spoke to an auditorium packed with rapturous faces, most of them Black. They clapped, swayed, shouted "Hallelujah!" Then the president flew on down to Miami for a couple of fund-raisers for Hillary's campaign at the mansions of wealthy supporters. Through it all, the storm kept raging.

By the afternoon, Miami was flooded. At the airport, where the storm would end up dumping some fourteen inches of rain, Clinton tried to forge onward. He boarded Air Force One for a scheduled hop up to a fund-raiser in Jupiter. But not even the leader of the free world could defy the force of nature. He would be grounded in Miami for the most anticipated event of the 2000 campaign. That evening, Al Gore and George Bush were going to meet for their first debate.

The storm whipped the banyan branches canopying the avenues of Coral Gables as Clinton's motorcade rushed toward the Biltmore Hotel, the gargoyled Jazz Age landmark where he would spend the night. He settled into his suite, intending to watch the debate on TV. But on the screen there was nothing, just gray lines. The storm had knocked out the whole city's cable reception.

Trailed by his Secret Service detail, Clinton rambled off in search of a working TV. He looked downstairs, at the cigar bar on the Biltmore's seventh floor. He tried the marble-columned lobby, where he found a group of equally frustrated White House reporters. "I wish I had my wind-up, solar-powered radio," Clinton mused, before launching into one of his meandering stories about a gift he had received on a trip to South Africa. This led, in time, to a lecture on a landmark moment in political history, the 1960 Kennedy-Nixon debate, which Vice President Nixon won with listeners on the radio but lost with viewers on television, who remembered only his jowly, glowering face.

Clinton called up Hillary's brother, who lived in Miami. "Hey, buddy, you got a satellite?"

No dice.

"Let's do the debate right here," Clinton suggested, poking his skinny fingers at the reporters. "You can be Bush, and you can be Gore." The president playfully offered to moderate.

Finally, his stressed-out traveling staff managed to locate a wealthy Democrat with a working big-screen TV. Sirens screaming, the presidential motorcade forded the swamped streets, passing strip clubs, tattoo parlors, and a Blockbuster Video. Clinton listened to the beginning of the debate on an AM radio station. So far, so good, it sounded. Gore was scoring points, hitting Bush's tax-cut policy and touting the administration's signature accomplishment, saying it was "important to resist the temptation to squander the surplus." Bush was mangling his words.

Clinton was spirited into the house, as the sodden press pool slogged behind him across the squishy lawn. He took a seat on the couch next to the home's owner, an old pal, and settled in to watch Al Gore, the great debater, squander his best opportunity to win the presidency.

JESSE JACKSON WAS there to see it in person. The reverend had a knack for popping up in the middle of the action. Though he had a complicated history with Gore, Jackson was a party man and a celebrity surrogate. Despite his personal doubts about the ticket, he was in Boston to flack for Gore in the post-debate "spin room," where the campaigns tried to shape the media's verdict.

As he waited for the debate to start, Jackson stood next to a foosball table in the Budweiser-sponsored press tent, absorbed in a playoff baseball game. "I'm having a sacred moment," he told a reporter as he watched his Chicago White Sox bat with the score tied in the ninth.

"Blacks in Seattle are cheering for a white pitcher to strike out a Black man playing for the White Sox," Jackson philosophized aloud. "Just as whites in Chicago are cheering for a Black hitter to get a hit off a white pitcher. Why are we able to overcome race in sports?"

The reporter interrupted to ask Jackson for his pre-debate take. "Bush's résumé begins at age 45," he replied, without missing a beat. "Everything before that is just youthful indiscretion."

Bush was happy to let the Democrats set low expectations. Karl Rove had described Gore as "the world's preeminent debater" in his pregame spin, and Bush aides kept bringing up that magazine cover that depicted Gore as a vampire. If Gore had taken a sneaky peek at Bush's debate-preparation materials, he might have learned that his opponent's campaign had compiled a thick dossier analyzing every previous Gore debate, focusing on his fatal weakness: overconfidence. "He was like some steroid-crazed football player running around dying to put a lick on anything that moved," a Bush aide later wrote. Gore's advisers were worried that he showed a "raw, unbridled contempt" for Bush. At Gore's rehearsals in Sarasota, they had told him to keep a grip on himself, to control his aggression and his tendency to overstate the facts.

Gore should not have needed any reminder about the importance of appearances. In his Harvard thesis *The Impact of Television on the Conduct of the Presidency, 1947–1969*, he had examined how "visual rhetoric" kept voters from making "judgments on the basis of logic and reason." Gore understood that images and perceptions could be stronger than arguments. He knew the history lessons from the Kennedy-Nixon debate. Even so, he crammed right up to the final moments before the showdown, taking rapid-fire questions from his staff in his trailer while guzzling Diet Cokes and stuffing his face with power bars. He was late to reach the stage and rushed through his session with the makeup artist. The two candidates came out to the cameras in identical blue suits and red ties, but that was where the similarities ended. Bush looked relaxed, if a little vacant. Gore was hyper, hepped up on sugar, his face tinted a shade too orange.

In reply to the moderator's first question, about Bush's lack of experience, Gore segued into a sharp critique of his opponent's tax policy. "He would spend more money on tax cuts for the wealthiest one percent," Gore said, "than all of the new spending that he proposes for education, health care, prescription drugs, and national defense all combined."

"Let me just say that, obviously tonight, we're going to hear some phony numbers," Bush said in rebuttal. Gore smirked, looked down and scribbled something, and then lifted his eyes to give the moderator a skeptical sideways glance.

"Look," Bush went on, "I fully recognize I'm not of Washington. I'm from Texas . . ."

Gore was off-screen, but the microphone caught him emitting a loud sigh. He butted in.

"Jim, if I could just respond," he said to the moderator. "The governor just used the phrase 'phony numbers,' but if you look at the plan and add the numbers up, these numbers are correct. . . . I agree that the surplus is the American people's money, it's your money. That is why I don't think we should give nearly half of it to the wealthiest one percent, because the other ninety-nine percent have had an awful lot to do with building the surplus."

"New question," the moderator said.

"I hope it's about wealthy people," Bush replied with a grin.

The question was about Medicare.

"The man is running on Medi-scare," Bush drawled.

Huhhhh! Gore exhaled theatrically as Bush talked about his great compassion for senior citizens. Gore had a response ready. During his debate prep in Sarasota, his advisers had told him to make sure he stressed the contrast between Bush's plan, which would partly privatize the health care program, and his own proposal to create an untouchable trust fund to ensure Medicare's continued solvency. Gore called this fund the "lockbox." Hit that harder, his advisers said.

"If I could respond to that," Gore said, speaking slowly and methodically, as if explaining the clouds to a four-year-old. "Under my plan, I will put Medicare in an ironclad lockbox and prevent the money from being used for anything other than Medicare. . . . I would be interested to see if he would say this evening he'll put Medicare in a lockbox. I don't think he will."

Gore went on to describe, in his usual minute detail, how his health care plans were designed.

"Look, this is a man who has great numbers," Bush replied. "I'm beginning to think not only did he invent the internet, but he invented the calculator. It's fuzzy math."

Gore arched his eyebrows and gave the moderator a look that screamed, *Can you believe this?*

The debate went on like this for ninety minutes. Watching in the audience, the *New York Times* reporter covering the Bush campaign thought to himself that the governor was in the process of blowing the whole election. Outside, in the Gore campaign's trailer, his aides were cheering lustily. But in the trailer next door, Bush's aides were equally elated. They didn't care about scoring debating points. They were watching Gore's demeanor. It kept growing more exasperated and overbearing. He huffed and puffed. He grimaced. He laughed derisively. He shook his head and pounded the lectern. He rolled his eyes and threw his hands in the air.

Back in Austin, Bush's bloodthirsty opposition research guys were listening to every word, ready to pounce on anything that came out of Gore's mouth that resembled a lie or a tall tale. In a novel innovation, the campaign had set up a website, www.debatefacts .com, to identify any misstatements in real time. When Bush mentioned a wildfire he had dealt with as governor, the vice president couldn't resist one-upping him, saying that *he* had flown to survey the disaster with the head of the Federal Emergency Management Agency. Bush's research staff sprang to action. In fact, it turned out that Gore had visited the Texas fire, but with a different FEMA official. Another Gore fib! That went up on the website.

When Bush brought up his signature issue, education, Gore told a story from his trip to Florida, about the man who worked at the crab shack who slipped him a note about school overcrowding.

"He has a fifteen-year-old daughter named Kailey who is in Sarasota High School," Gore said. "Her science class was supposed to be for twenty-four students. She's the thirty-sixth student in that classroom. They sent me a picture of her in the classroom. They can't squeeze another desk in for her, so she has to stand during class. I want the federal government, consistent with local control and new accountability, to make improvement of our schools the number one priority, so Kailey will have a desk and can sit down in a classroom where she can learn."

Watching in the Bush campaign's trailer, one staffer snapped, "I bet that's a lie."

In the hall, it appeared that Gore had soundly beaten Bush. But Bush won the competition in the spin room. "We're going to ram this debate right up his ass," a Bush aide told the liberal comic and commentator Al Franken. "The sighing, the interruptions, the exaggerations." Bush's spokeswoman Karen Hughes expressed outrage at Gore's mistaken memory over the wildfire. "The president of the United States cannot do that," Hughes told the press. "The president cannot go into a meeting with a foreign leader and simply make things up that aren't true."

The principal of Sarasota High School soon came forward with his own rebuttal, saying that while the girl Gore referenced did have to stand one day, the situation was quickly remedied. "The missing desk was not a metaphor for decay," the principal wrote in a column in the *Wall Street Journal*. He did acknowledge that classes were crowded, blaming "deep cuts in this year's budget," thus affirming Gore's main point on education. But that mattered little. Gore had become, one journalist covering the campaign wrote, "the pumpkin-headed sigh master."

That weekend, *Saturday Night Live* did a wicked debate parody sketch. Darrell Hammond played Gore as a condescending know-it-all, opposite Will Ferrell's befuddled Bush. The sketch fixed on a term Gore had managed to mention seven times in the debate: *lockbox*.

"In my plan," Hammond said, mimicking Gore's slow, up-and-down cadence, "the lockbox would also be *camouflaged*. Now, to all outward appearances it would be a leatherbound edition of the *Count of Monte Cristo* by Alexandre Dumas. But it wouldn't be. It would be . . ."

Pregnant pause.

". . . the lockbox."

AFTER THE DEBATE came the deluge. In Florida, the rain kept falling all day and night. By the time Bush and Gore met, for a debate in which the words *climate* and *warming* were not uttered and where the only mention of the environment came in reference to gas prices, vast parts of Miami were underwater. A thousand homes were destroyed, streets were flooded hip deep, kids Boogie Boarded on sidewalks, and a truck turned over on the interstate, spilling its cargo of twenty-six stuffed alligators.

Scientists knew there would be more floods to come, as the oceans warmed, glaciers melted, and tides swelled. The peninsula of Florida, once the flat bottom of an ancient ocean, might someday go under again. That November, world leaders would be gathering for a climate summit in The Hague, where they intended to hammer out details of a treaty requiring nations to greatly reduce greenhouse gas emissions by 2012. Al Gore was a champion of the accord. The stand did him no good in the election. Conservatives despised the treaty, and the rest of the electorate was more or less indifferent to the issue. Climate change was something to worry about tomorrow.

But a splinter of the Democratic coalition *did* care and was threatening to desert Gore for the environmentalist Green Party. Its nominee, the sepulchral consumer activist Ralph Nader, was touring college campuses, decrying corporate power and saying there was no difference between Bush and Gore, whom he called "Tweedledee and Tweedledum." This claim was absurd: one of them wanted to drill for oil in the Arctic National Wildlife Refuge and the other wanted to ban the internal combustion engine. But polls showed that the challenge from the left could cost Gore in some key states.

Shortly before the election, the Gore campaign sent a delegation to Miami for a secret meeting with environmental activists. Gore wanted to hold a rally to promote his plans to preserve the Everglades, which were being despoiled by development and agricultural pollution. But the activists were unsatisfied. They vowed to picket the rally. They were furious that Gore had refused to take a position in a local debate over the redevelopment of a decommissioned air force base. The week before the election, Nader campaigned against the airport project in Miami. "Al Gore is waffling as usual," he declared. "He refuses to take a position as usual."

Local hard-liners formed a group called Environmentalists Against Gore. One of the leaders of the movement to save the Everglades blasted out an email to his friends and allies. "From crisis comes opportunity!" the environmentalist wrote. "Force the crisis!"

That fall, General Motors introduced its latest luxury line to the marketplace, unveiling a gargantuan, gas-guzzling, military-style vehicle called the Hummer.

EVERYONE WAS A critic, including Bill Clinton. After the debate, he called up Gore's staffers to offer some more unsolicited advice, telling them they should force Gore to watch that lacerating *Saturday Night Live* skit. They tried it as they were preparing Gore for the next debate. The idea was to get him to laugh at himself, to loosen him up a little, but the viewing had the opposite effect. It just made him even more self-conscious. At the second debate, he overcorrected.

Gore was so passive, he seemed almost sedated. Bush responded to a question about gun control with a paean to the "larger law" of the Bible. "I also believe in the Golden Rule," Gore replied. "And I agree with a lot of the other things that the governor has said." He offered no objection when Bush suggested that scientists were "changing their opinion a little bit on global warming." He kept a respectful silence as the governor described his foreign policy philosophy.

"If we're an arrogant nation, they'll resent us," Bush said. "If we're a humble nation, but strong, they'll welcome us. And it's—our nation stands alone right now in the world in terms of power, and that's why we have to be humble. And yet project strength in a way that promotes freedom."

Gore did not deign to question Bush's inexperience with national security, an area where his own expertise was unquestioned. Gore was a military hawk and an arms-control wonk. He was the administration's point person in its delicate effort to convince the rulers of Saudi Arabia to assist in the effort to neutralize Osama bin Laden. He had chaired what was known as the Gore Commission, which identified threats to aviation security, including the "changing and growing" danger of attacks on airlines within the United States. But terrorism did not come up at all.

After Gore finished the second debate, he spent the night near the site of the event in North Carolina, where he was roused from his sleep by news from the other side of the world.

In Yemen, at around 9 a.m. local time, a navy destroyer called the U.S.S. *Cole* had docked in the port of Aden for a quick refueling stop. A fiberglass fishing boat around thirty-five feet long and six feet wide puttered up to its port side with two men aboard. They waved to the sailors on deck. The crew waved back. Then the boat exploded with such force that the blast was felt miles away. The bomb blew a forty-foot hole in the ship's hull and tore through the mess hall, where sailors were lining up for lunch, killing seventeen and wounding dozens more.

Gore left the campaign trail immediately and returned to Washington for emergency meetings at the White House. It was the first time he had been inside the building since May.

Clinton was already dealing with another foreign policy crisis, in Israel, where his hopes of brokering a peace deal had been dashed by an uprising in the Palestinian territories. With this shocking attack on the U.S. Navy, violence now threatened to engulf the Middle East. But Clinton's mind was still on domestic politics. Flying on Air Force One to a memorial service in Norfolk, Virginia, the *Cole*'s home port, he told Janet Reno—and everyone else within earshot—that he was disappointed that Gore was not putting him to work on the campaign trail.

At the service, Clinton gave an emotional eulogy to an audience that included thirty-six wounded sailors, some still on gurneys, and families of the dead. "To those who attacked them, we say, 'You will not find safe harbor,'" Clinton vowed. "We will find you, and justice will prevail."

In Afghanistan, Osama bin Laden waited for the battle to come. He wanted it: Bring the cruise missiles, bring the invasion, bring the apocalyptic confrontation. *Force the crisis!*

No attack came. The Sheikh was disappointed and vowed that his next operation would be impossible to ignore. His media bureau was already at work on a video about the *Cole* bombing—the most effective recruitment film it ever made, in the view of the Al Qaeda propagandist who produced it. It included cameo appearances by a number of the men who would participate in the planes operation. The hijacking teams were now starting to train for their mission, honing their skills at a camp next to the airport compound, under the tutelage of a veteran Jordanian jihadi. They were slaughtering sheep and camels, learning how to slit throats.

23

Chasing Ghosts

The spying was the part of the job that Janet Reno had been least prepared for when she assumed the office of attorney general. When it came to investigating and trying criminals, Reno could look back on her long experience as a big-city prosecutor. But the Justice Department did much more than simply seek justice. Less known to the public was its national security mission. The FBI was in charge of intelligence gathering within the United States. The full scope of the government's ability to monitor national security threats was classified, known only to those with the proper clearances. But once you put on the magic glasses, what you saw was terrifying: the background radiation of danger that surrounded everyone else as they went about their daily lives in blithe ignorance.

The U.S. government could intercept and eavesdrop on telecommunications on a global scale through the National Security Agency, its signals intelligence organization. (The intelligence community joked that the NSA was so clandestine that its initials stood for "no such agency.") But there were strict regulations on the use of such surveillance powers within the United States. In 1978, in response to the revelation of rampant abuses by the FBI during J. Edgar Hoover's long tenure as director, Congress had enacted the Foreign Intelligence Surveillance Act, or FISA, which was designed to prevent law enforcement agencies from spying on Americans. Under the law, the FBI could only use its domestic intelligence capabilities against individuals suspected of acting as agents of a "foreign power." In most cases, FISA warrant applications had to be signed by the attorney general herself. Reno would personally review two or three a day on average, before sending them up to a secret court on the sixth floor of Main Justice for a judge's approval. Reno took her oversight responsibility seriously. She said she was determined not to allow the FBI to become the "Bureau of Intelligence." She felt there had to be protections against overreach.

"My job was to balance that," Reno later said. "The FBI has some agents who are superb at putting a case together and getting a conviction. At the same time, it has the tendency to make some assumptions with respect to information that says two plus two equals five when, indeed, it equals four." Reno set up regulations that were meant to ensure that surveillance evidence gathered by the FBI's intelligence programs was not used to gin up criminal investigations. This was known as "the wall." Reno personally guarded the wall. "In the end," she said, "I was the gatekeeper."

The government's spy powers were awesome. But there were rules. There was a system.

Reno was not a civil libertarian, though. She made her life in law enforcement. After the 1993 bombing of the World Trade Center, she told her subordinates that she didn't want to investigate future terrorist attacks; she wanted to prevent them from happening in the first place. The FBI's use of FISA surveillance greatly increased during Reno's tenure.

Reno's efforts to turn the Bureau to face the threat of international terrorism met constant bureaucratic resistance. She had a prickly relationship with FBI director Louis Freeh, who jealously guarded the Bureau's turf. Freeh was on even worse terms with Bill

Clinton, a tension that traced back to the FBI's aggressive pursuit of the Whitewater case, a real estate fraud investigation down in Arkansas that had uncovered no wrongdoing on Clinton's part, but had nonetheless dragged on forever, generating endless legal drama and, ultimately, the Lewinsky scandal. (Before the *Cole* bombing, Freeh had not spoken to the president in almost three years.) Even though Clinton had declared counterterrorism a national security priority, only about 6 percent of FBI personnel worked on the issue, and most of its resources remained directed toward its traditional targets: drug gangs, Mafia bosses, and white-collar crooks.

Investigating terrorist networks required foreign-language skills and international expertise, two things that were lacking within the organization. FBI agents were men (and, increasingly, women) of action. They busted criminals. But counterterrorism operations were defensive. They succeeded if nothing happened. The Bureau's institutional culture also disdained deskbound analysis. The prevailing attitude, one FBI official later said, was that "real men don't type."

Terrorists used the internet for communication and propaganda. But most FBI agents still worked with pen and paper, and many had computers that were so old they could not even access the World Wide Web. The Bureau's internal computer system was, in the words of one top official, "the joke of Washington." It allowed agents to search by only one keyword at a time—so "flight" or "school," but not "flight school." Freeh didn't even have a computer in his office. During the period of heightened security surrounding the millennium, Reno had noticed that the FBI struggled to translate and analyze all its incoming surveillance. Afterward, she issued a series of directives ordering Freeh to "immediately develop the capacity to fully assimilate and utilize intelligence." But when the millennium crisis passed, so did the FBI's urgency. "I did not feel that the FBI was putting it together," Reno later said. It didn't know what it knew.

The FBI's shortcomings would be brought into sharp relief in the aftermath of the *Cole* attack. The Bureau sent a seasoned counterterrorism expert to Yemen, a bullheaded bon vivant from the Manhattan field office named John O'Neill. He had spearheaded the response to the millennium threat, but he was not prepared to operate in the hostile foreign environment. He clashed with local authorities as well as the U.S. ambassador, who feared the FBI's confrontational approach might undermine a tenuous strategic alliance with Yemen. The CIA issued a warning that there was a "high" probability of further terrorist attacks on U.S. personnel, and at one point, armed Yemeni men gathered in a menacing formation outside the FBI's hotel. The American investigators had to evacuate and relocate to a navy warship. The bombing investigation hit a wall. O'Neill returned to New York, much to the relief of the ambassador.

Behind the internal infighting was the politically charged question of retaliation. The *Cole* bombing had all the hallmarks of an Al Qaeda attack. But Bill Clinton wanted certainty before he launched cruise missiles at bin Laden. The FBI could not provide him with proof.

Once again, the administration broke into a secret debate about whether to treat Al Qaeda as a criminal organization, as Reno and the FBI regarded it, or as a military adversary. White House adviser Richard Clarke wrote a classified memo arguing that because "criminal investigations of terrorism in other countries can be lengthy," Clinton should not be "constrained to await the results." He suggested that the president could strike at Al Qaeda based on an "intelligence case."

The CIA had already concluded that the *Cole* attack "likely had support" from Al Qaeda. The Agency knew that around the time of the millennium, Yemeni militants associated with the group had attempted to mount an identical attack on another U.S. destroyer. (The attempt failed when a skiff overloaded with explosives got stuck on a beach.) But the CIA would not make a definitive determination, either. The spies just weren't sure, and when it came to retaliation, no one wanted to be wrong. "History is written through a rearview mirror," Clinton's national security advisor would later say, "but it unfolds through a foggy windshield."

So, Clinton held his fire. He was thinking about the election, which was now less than a month away. He knew that any attack on Afghanistan was likely to be greeted with a chorus of criticism from Republicans, who had previously accused him of using military strikes to boost his personal political standing. (This was known as the "*Wag the Dog* scenario," after a 1990s movie satire.) If the attack went wrong, it could hurt Al Gore. Clarke later said he got the sense from Reno that the president "didn't really want to know" who had perpetrated the attack.

"Who the shit do they think attacked the *Cole*, fuckin' Martians?" one national security official vented, according to Clarke, after an inconclusive meeting at the White House. "Does Al Qaeda have to attack the Pentagon to get their attention?"

MOHAMED ATTA AND Marwan al-Shehhi were back at their old flight school in Venice that October. The school's owner, Rudi Dekkers, would later write that one day around this time, a student observed a jarring outburst. The pair was in the computer lab, tapping away quietly, when suddenly they erupted in cheers and started hugging. This was out of character for Atta, who was always so sullen. It seemed he had received joyous news from the internet.

Ziad Jarrah was in Germany when he learned of the *Cole* bombing. He had flown back there in early October, possibly to consult with the fourth member of his group, Ramzi bin al-Shibh, who was still having trouble getting approval for a U.S. visa. But Ziad spent most of his time with Aysel. They took a trip to Paris, staying with his sister, who worked in a bank there. Ziad and Aysel saw the sights and had their picture taken at the Eiffel Tower.

A few days later, Jarrah returned to Tampa, where another flight student picked him up in one of his school's Cessnas and flew with him back to Venice. Jarrah knew the *Cole* bombing was a practical setback for his operation. Ramzi was a Yemeni. He was never going to get that visa.

WHILE THE FOREIGN flight students went about their training in Venice, federal law enforcement was fixing its attention on West Palm Beach. The ATF's long-running sting operation had now cast its invisible net to cover Kevin Ingram, his Egyptian buddy Didi, a couple of Pakistanis who said they were affiliated with the ISI, and most recently, a shadowy group of "private" black marketeers based in Dubai who said they were interested in buying materials used to make nuclear weapons. Even Dick Stoltz, the undercover ATF agent who was running the case, was having trouble making sense of all the moving pieces. "I kept thinking that at some point this case would be taken away from us," he says. "These are intelligence matters, and that supersedes any kind of a criminal case." He waited for a call from above, but it never came.

Stoltz was a veteran undercover agent who had worked international cases before, most recently a long-term investigation of a Chinese gun-running network in California. But this was beyond his ken. CIA operatives who worked in places like Pakistan were familiar with the phenomenon. Domestic law enforcement agents would often stray into the realm of spooks, coming up with some zany story, a load of slag from the underworld that might contain a few nuggets of real intelligence. The ATF was good at busting cigarette smugglers and biker gangs, but it strained credulity to think that it had somehow stumbled across a previously unknown international criminal syndicate with connections to terrorists and foreign spy agencies.

The logical move would have been for the FBI, as the nation's primary domestic intelligence organization, to take over the case. But the Bureau was skeptical. Early on in the sting operation, an ATF supervisor had a contentious argument with the FBI's counterterrorism chief in Miami. "You're chasing ghosts," the FBI official dismissively told his counterpart. The FBI often treated the ATF like a mangy half-sibling, and its higher-ups had no confidence in the wild-eyed criminal informant Randy Glass. Glass claimed that in his meeting with the Pakistanis at the Tribeca Grill, they had brazenly talked about their connections to both the ISI and Osama bin Laden. But an audiotape of this meeting was curiously inaudible.

The ATF agents had never heard the Pakistanis mention Al Qaeda explicitly. They were oblique, speaking of "private" parties, "neighboring countries," and "rebels." Didi did suggest that Osama bin Laden was behind it all, but then again, he also said the world was controlled by Freemasons. The FBI higher-ups were unconvinced. They refused to designate the case as a counterterrorism matter, which would have given it more resources and access to classified intelligence.

Still, the ATF agents reported the operation's progress up the chain of command and involved all the "three-letter agencies," as they called the spies. The NSA, through its foreign electronic surveillance, managed to confirm at least some aspects of what the ATF was hearing. The Pakistanis did seem to be acting on behalf of the ISI in some capacity. The ATF agents on the case were told that U.S. intelligence agencies had determined that Pakistani government funds really were budgeted for black-market arms deals, in amounts that matched what their contacts had indicated. Some of the items they were asking for, like helicopter parts, corresponded to real needs of the Pakistani military. "This was not bullshit," says one of the ATF agents. "It was the ISI. We pretty much documented that."

"These were ISI agents," says the ATF case supervisor. "It was a full-blown ISI operation."

Was it possible that the sting operation was like a Ouija board in a B-grade horror movie, a preposterous game that had somehow managed to summon real demons? Even the most fantastical-sounding part of the conspiracy, the customers' interest in nuclear material, was impossible to summarily dismiss. For decades, Pakistan had been developing a covert network to procure the designs and ingredients necessary to build the bomb, an effort that had culminated in two successful nuclear tests in 1998. For its plutonium reactors, Pakistan needed deuterium, colloquially known as "heavy water," a substance that was difficult to fabricate and very much in demand on the black market. During their conversations with Glass and the undercover agents, Mike Malik and R. G. Abbas had repeatedly expressed interest in obtaining "sweet water," a coded reference to deuterium. (The dense liquid is reputed to have a sugary taste.) The Pakistanis had also dropped the name of their supposed contact in the nuclear program: a physicist named Dr. Abdul Qadeer Khan. He was a national hero in Pakistan for his contributions to building the "Islamic bomb."

Dr. Khan also had a side business that sold equipment, plans, and expertise to pariah states that were trying to develop nuclear weapons, like Libya and Iran. It operated out of Dubai, a port city that had long served as the hub for Pakistan's nuclear-procurement efforts, under the guise of a wholesale electronics dealership. Khan's activities were the subject of public speculation—and were already well known to the U.S. government, which confronted Pervez Musharraf's regime with evidence that it was supplying North Korea in 2000—so, it proved nothing that Mike Malik and R. G. Abbas had mentioned the scientist's name. But the pair did seem to know how the nuclear black market functioned. They mentioned intercepted shipments that U.S. intelligence confirmed.

The nuclear smuggling discussions continued after Malik shifted the focus of the negotiations to a group of mysterious private arms merchants in Dubai. During the fall of 2000, Malik assured his suppliers in Florida that the Dubai customers were on the verge of placing a $32 million order for heavy water, Stinger missiles, and night-vision goggles. The money would come in by wire, disguised as a payment on a phony contract for computers. On October 10, Malik told the undercover agent that the talks were "very smooth and very active," and that he planned to meet soon with the prospective buyers in person. He said they were just middlemen for "the government or whoever." Once the "money talk" was completed, the Pakistani assured the ATF agent, they would all meet in Florida to close the deal.

FIVE DAYS AFTER the *Cole* attack, Al Gore and George W. Bush met for their third and final debate. The candidates opened with condolences for the families of the murdered sailors. But the word *terrorism* was uttered only once during the debate, by Gore, in passing. When Bush was asked about unrest in the Middle East, he diverted into a discussion of Iraq, a side issue that happened to be a preoccupation of his foreign policy advisers. "Saddam Hussein still is a threat in the Middle East," he said. "The man who may be developing weapons of mass destruction."

The third time around, Gore finally found a balance between hot and cold. But the damage had been done. Bush had not just survived the debates—he had improved his standing in the polls.

Now, in the final stretch, the campaign would return to more favorable terrain for Bush. After the last debate, Dubya was embraced by several family members in attendance, including his brother Jeb. "It looked like I was kissing him," Dubya joked in a television interview a few days later, "but what I was really doing was whispering in his ear, 'We better carry Florida, buddy.'"

THREE WEEKS LATER, at 9:55 on a Tuesday morning, Dick Stoltz called Mike Malik in Jersey City for an update. Everything was clicking now, the Pakistani assured him. He would soon be flying to London and Hong Kong to negotiate with the prospective buyers face-to-face.

Who *were* these people? Stoltz still didn't know. He was looking through a foggy windshield.

The agent ended the call, stated the time of termination onto the tape, and popped the cassette out of his recorder. He sealed the tape in an evidence envelope, labeling it with the date: 11/7/2000.

Election Day had arrived.

24

The Numbers

It was midnight in Miami Beach, and Al Gore's motorcade was moving slowly past the neon-lit façades of the Art Deco district as a mob throbbed along Ocean Drive. *Let us in!* the overflow crowd chanted, clamoring behind barricades along the beachfront.

A limousine disgorged Gore, and the vice president headed down to the beach, trailed by his entourage of campaign advisers—the whole backstabbing brain trust. They had all piled onto Air Force Two for one final twenty-four-hour marathon trip through Iowa, Michigan, and Florida. Already woozy from exhaustion, they brushed past boxes of complimentary multicolored flip-flops and galumphed through the soft white sand in their shiny dress shoes. The clock had turned, and it was now November 7. The polls would be opening once the sun rose.

Everyone was converging on Florida for Election Day. *Look!* There was Jesse Jackson, who had spent much of the last month riding buses around the state, registering new Black voters and helping to make good on the One Florida protesters' promise to "remember in November."

Look! It was Harvey Weinstein, the artful ogre, who had rustled up a group of celebrities to fly down from New York City to lend their star power to Gore's late-night get-out-the-vote event. *Look!* Ben Affleck, Robert De Niro, Glenn Close.

Jon Bon Jovi was playing. Stevie Wonder was swaying.

The talent was assembled on a stage in front of a sand dune, beneath an array of bulbs that lit up to read, "FLORIDA VICTORY." And there was Gore, bounding onstage with his white sleeves rolled up, bleary and punch-drunk, his voice hoarse, his breath smelling of cough drops. He had hardly slept in weeks, just running on adrenaline and ambition. He was getting a little loopy.

"The moon is over Miami!" he shouted. "I want to fight for you and your families and your future and your communities, not the wealthy, not the well connected. Are you with me?"

The crowd, estimated to number in the tens of thousands, erupted in an enormous cheer.

"Florida," Gore said, waxing raspy and rhapsodic, "is the place where the future is being born!"

IF ONLY HE knew. Across the causeway in Little Havana, a bit earlier that day, there was another get-out-the-vote event. Uncle Lázaro and Uncle Delfín, of Elián fame, stood with their political consultant, Armando Gutierrez, in front of the Gonzalez family home. "It's important to remind people that this is how you get even," Gutierrez told the press. "At the polls."

On his own final swing, two days before the election, George W. Bush barnstormed through South Florida with Jeb and Mayor Rudy Giuliani. A popular host from Radio Mambí had introduced Bush at a rally in Miami, vowing to "punish the enemy with our votes," as some people in the crowd waved signs reading, "Remember Elián . . . Vote Bush."

Karl Rove called a reporter for the *New York Times* from the Miami rally. "It's going pretty wild!" he shouted. He assured the newspaper that Bush appeared to be headed toward a landslide victory. Rove said the campaign's polls showed him winning by 6 or 7 points. He had been telling Bush the same thing, saying the campaign even had a shot at some Democratic strongholds, like California, where Bush had spent a few precious hours campaigning during the homestretch. Bush really seemed to believe Rove's predictions. When reporters asked the governor what he was getting Laura for her birthday in November, he quipped, "New Jersey."

Gore's advisers saw another, craftier motive in Bush's travels to populous Democratic states. While the polls said Bush had a sizable national lead, his margin was tighter in many swing states. This presented the possibility that Gore could put together 270 votes in the Electoral College while losing the popular vote to Bush, a split outcome that had not happened since the election of 1888. It was rumored that Bush was trying to increase his national margin in case he decided to pressure electors to switch sides. He would cite the popular will. America was a democracy, after all.

Or maybe the baseball man just wanted to run up the score. He spent his final day swaggering through Tennessee and Arkansas, two states that were light in electoral votes but heavy in emotional symbolism for Gore and Bill Clinton. By the time Gore was on Miami Beach, Bush was hitting his pillow at the Governor's Mansion in Austin, supremely confident of victory.

Sure, there was an embarrassment for him in the final days: a local TV station in Maine dug up a police report describing a drunk-driving arrest from back in his wayward 1970s. And yes, Jeb's people down in Florida had been raising hell, trying to warn Rove that the state was going to be close. The math said Bush stood little chance without Florida and its 25 electoral votes.

This was not a scenario, however, that the Bush family wanted to consider. "I would never live it down if my brother didn't carry Florida," Jeb told reporters in August. At a gathering at the Republican National Convention, he said, "I don't want to live the rest of my life with the humiliation." But Jeb had been dealing with sniping about his campaign efforts, some of it from his brother.

In an interview the week before, Jay Leno ribbed Dubya about the rumors of family tension.

"I think we're going to be fine down there," Bush assured the *Tonight Show* host. "Little brother, he recognizes that Thanksgiving might be a bit chilly if things don't go right." Bush narrowed his gaze and addressed the camera directly. "No pressure, brother," he said with a grin. It had the glint of a sharp edge.

AT DAWN, GORE was in Tampa, where he held a health policy discussion with a group of graveyard shift nurses before meeting up with Joe Lieberman for a photo op at a Cuban bakery. They both downed shots of café Cubano. In his final speech, Gore noted the time, which was creeping toward 6:30 a.m. on the East Coast. "George W. Bush is still asleep," he said, "and I'm still speaking to people here in Florida!"

At this hour, in the retirement communities of Palm Beach County, the early birds were shuffling out of their condos and heading to their precincts to get in line to vote at 7 a.m. By 7:08, the first complaint call came into a Gore campaign phone bank in West Palm Beach.

There was a problem at the polls.

In Florida, where authority over elections was decentralized, every county had its own voting system. Palm Beach County was enormous, sprawling from the island it was named for all the way inland to the mucky sugarcane-growing communities around Lake Okeechobee, and it used paper punch card ballots, a technology dating to the prehistoric era of computing. The way it worked, voters were handed a paper ballot to insert into a machine, which was really more like a holding device standing on a little folding table. They then used a pointed stylus to poke a hole in the punch card next to the name of the candidate of their choice. Normally, the process was simple, but in 2000 the Palm Beach ballot had an unusual design. It was spread across two pages, which opened like a book, with a row of ovals down the middle.

Bush and Cheney were listed at the top of the first page of the ballot, with Gore and Lieberman just below. Some Palm Beach citizens—many of them liberal Jewish retirees from the Northeast—were marching into the booth, proudly intending to elect Gore and Lieberman, and punching the oval corresponding to line two. But the Democrats were on line three of the ballot.

The second oval, as you could clearly see if you followed the itty-bitty arrow, aligned with the first line on the facing page, which belonged to . . . oh let's see . . . Reform Party candidate Pat Buchanan.

The Brooklyn-accented host of a Palm Beach radio talk show warned her audience to be careful. "I got scared I voted for Pat Buchanan," she said. "I almost said, 'I think I voted for a Nazi.'"

"I just want to say I did the same thing," a caller chimed in. "I'm very worried."

"Wasn't it badly designed? I had to check three times to make sure I didn't vote for a fascist."

AT 8:15 A.M., Rudi Dekkers walked into the break room at his flight school in Venice. "Everybody has to vote, because I can't," said Rudi, a Dutch citizen. "I have to push everybody to vote."

Rudi was a thickset braggart. He lived in Naples, a wealthy vacation community farther down the Gulf Coast, commuted to Venice every day by helicopter, and boasted of his big-time connections. He was in the midst of launching a new commuter airline company, Florida Air—or FLAIR, for short—with support from Jeb Bush and the Republican secretary of state, Katherine Harris.

This morning, though, he had more than the election on his mind. In the break room, he spotted his twenty-two-year-old office manager. He walked up and pinned her against the counter.

"Why do you have to look so good?" Rudi said. "Can I bite into you?"

"No, that's sick," she replied. It was not the first time it had happened. She was keeping a log.

Marwan walked in that morning, ready to practice. He and his roommate, Mohamed, had just passed an FAA test, taking another small step toward earning their commercial pilot licenses. The office manager had heard Rudi trying to convince the pair to apply for jobs at FLAIR, probably figuring he could hire a couple of Middle Eastern pilots on the cheap. But they always rebuffed him, saying they had other plans. Marwan headed out the door leading to the airfield, fired up a small plane, and flew away.

ON THIS CRISP fall morning in New York City, a balding statistician took the subway from the Upper West Side down to the World Trade Center. He walked through the lobby of the North Tower, with its arabesque arched windows, flipped through a turnstile, and took the elevator to the ninety-third floor. No one knew Murray Edelman's name outside his discipline, but every four years, for a few hours, he was the most important person in America. He was the man with the numbers.

The Twin Towers had never been profitable or beloved, but they housed millions of square feet of office space, open trading floors designed for use by financial brokerages. They always had plenty of empty space available to rent for cheap, which was perfect for the temporary needs of the Voter News Service. Tonight, the service would be mounting a massive, labor-intensive data-gathering effort designed to reveal, to Edelman first of all, the identity of the next president.

It had been decades since a presidential election contained any real uncertainty. The night was a choreographed television special, an event that the networks expected to build to a dramatic declaration of victory, like the Super Bowl, or Oscar Night, or the finale of *Survivor*. The TV networks all operated their own "decision desks" that analyzed the results in each state, producing projections and filling out the color-coded graphical maps of the United States as the show built to the clinching number: 270 electoral votes. In 2000, in contrast to previous years, the networks were all using the same color scheme: red for Bush, blue for Gore. This superficial uniformity masked a deeper one. Although the decision desks would compete to be first with their calls, they all relied on the same data from the Voter News Service. Edelman's expensive operation was financed by a consortium of news organizations, including all the TV networks. His numbers made the show.

Edelman had been analyzing elections since 1968, the last time there was a true squeaker. That year, working for CBS, he and his mentor, another statistician, had invented a new prediction method, adapting a market research tool developed for the movie business: the exit poll. Interviewers assigned to sample precincts would pull aside citizens as they left their polling places, asking who had gotten their votes. Since then, the crude tools of electoral prediction had been refined into something resembling a science. In the decade the Voter News Service had existed, covering some seven hundred national, state, and local elections, it had made only one incorrect call.

Edelman's operation was dispersing some forty thousand workers to gather raw numbers from precincts around the United States. In the morning and afternoon, they conducted exit polls. In the evening, they shifted to reporting actual vote totals. The service tabulated all the data at the World Trade Center. Supposedly, the ninety-third floor offered a magnificent view of New York City, but Voter News Service had carved the raw space into a windowless countinghouse, cavernous halls adorned only with the colors of tangled computer cables. Hundreds of data entry clerks sat in groups of six at brown cafeteria-style tables under the eyes of prowling supervisors. The results came in by phone. The clerks answered, took down the numbers, clacked ENTER on their PCs.

All the data was entered into a statistical projection system, which applied an algorithm to the raw numbers to yield a statistical probability of victory. Behind the closed doors of his office, the Decision Room, Edelman spent the day watching numbers flash across the screen of an old computer terminal. His monitors, a reporter later wrote, "looked like something out of the Atari years, ridiculously antique and kludgy, multicolored numbers on dark backgrounds." The prediction system used software designed for archaic mainframe computers and relied on statistical models that were developed in the late 1960s. Still, everyone assumed it was reliable.

If anything, Edelman worried that the decision desks placed too much trust in the system, treating its probabilities like prophecy.

Through the primary season, the networks had been very aggressive, calling races prematurely, drawing false certainty from the numbers before it was safe. Shortly before Election Day, Edelman had circulated a memo reminding his subscribers that vote counting was a messy process, with an inherent margin of error. The memo was ignored.

BY LUNCHTIME, GORE was back in Tennessee, still giddy from his sleepless night. He voted in his hometown of Carthage and headed to the hotel in Nashville that would serve as his Election Night headquarters. In Austin, Bush decided to go for a workout with some friends at a university gym. They all just had to wait . . . wait . . . wait for Murray Edelman's numbers.

In addition to making predictions, the Voter News Service also fed raw exit polling data to its subscribers. (Besides the TV networks, these included many print news organizations.) These exit polls were meant to serve as a rough private forecast, to guide planning for the evening's coverage. The first round of exit polls blasted out of the World Trade Center at 2:09 p.m.

They brought grim tidings to the headquarters of Fox News, a gray modernist slab on Sixth Avenue. Among other surprises, the early polls showed Gore with a 3-point lead over Bush in Florida. Roger Ailes, the Fox News chief executive, had more than just a personal interest in the victory of his 1988 campaign officemate. He knew that the fate of his upstart conservative news network, founded four years before, was intertwined with the fortunes of the Republican Party.

The head of the decision desk at Fox News was a political analyst named John Ellis. He wanted Bush to win even more than Ailes did. He was George W. Bush's first cousin and close friend.

But as Ellis squinted at these early exit polls, he could see, objectively, that they meant serious trouble. The numbers had already made their way to Rove, who had passed the bad news to his boss.

The phone on Ellis's desk rang.

"Ellis," said the tense, twangy voice at the other end of the line. "Bush here."

Throughout the campaign, Ellis had maintained a back channel to his cousin, trading information and chatter. (Dubya truly loved gossip.) Ailes viewed this relationship as a reporting asset, not a conflict of interest. Now the governor, just back from the gym, was calling for an intelligence report.

"Looks tight, huh?" Bush said.

Ellis tried to cushion the blow. "I wouldn't worry about early numbers," he said. "Your dad had bad early numbers in '88, and he wound up winning by seven. So, who knows?"

Bush wasn't fooled. "I got the smell," he would later say—a whiff of unexpected defeat. Back at his mansion in Austin, Bush sat his daughters down and told them to prepare for a hard night.

By a long-standing gentlemen's agreement, the national news organizations did not publish the exit polls, which were intended to be only internal guidance. But they always spread anyway, by word of mouth, serving as a mid-afternoon snack for famished reporters and political operatives before the real results rolled in around dinnertime. And now, thanks to Al Gore, who had invented the internet, no numbers as delicious as these could remain secret for long. Almost instantaneously, a start-up called Inside.com—launched in May 2000 by a bunch of New York media stars with wild expectations of dot-com riches—obtained the exit polls and threw them up on the World Wide Web. News organizations condemned the leak, the public clicked, and Democrats rejoiced.

At around 5 p.m., the Voter News Service sent out a second wave of exit polls. These looked even more favorable for Gore.

When the late-afternoon numbers rolled into Fox News, Ellis ducked out for a cigarette. He used his cell phone to make a furtive call to his cousin at the Governor's Mansion in Austin.

"Is it really this close?" Bush asked. He had believed Rove's predictions of a landslide.

"Yeah," Ellis replied. "It's really close."

Bush wanted to know how Ellis thought the night would go. Ellis said he had no idea, but that was a white lie. After taking a last drag from his cigarette, he rode the elevator back up to Ailes's office. The network head was waiting for a private briefing on the exit polls. Ailes was distrustful of the Voter News Service and what he would later call its "rattletrap computer system."

"What's your gut say?" Ailes asked.

Ellis drew his finger across his throat. He figured that Bush was a dead man.

HERE WAS A number that surely had not escaped Jeb Bush's notice: 59,126. That was how many new Black voters were registered in the drives that followed the protests of his One Florida plan. And now people of color were turning out in Florida on a scale that neither party had anticipated.

In the early evening, around the time everyone in New York was starting to think Gore had it won, a thirty-nine-year-old woman named Janice Kelly was desperately trying to cast her ballot in Jacksonville. There were long lines everywhere. Kelly couldn't find her polling place. Finally, she pulled up to the right site, a church, with a few minutes to spare. Polls closed at 7 p.m.

At the door, she found a line of grumpy people who were being blocked by a gray-haired poll worker. "Polls are closed," said the woman at the church door. "It's seven o'clock."

A woman waiting in the line looked at her watch and showed it to Kelly. It said 6:55.

Kelly thought she knew what was going on. She looked at the people in line. They were Black, like her. She looked at the woman guarding the door. She was white, as were the rest of the poll workers, who had been hired by surrounding Duval County, which was Republican-controlled. She looked inside the polling place. There were white folks inside, and they were still voting. Kelly was outraged.

"I wasn't allowed to vote, and that's it, bottom line," she later testified in a civil rights lawsuit. "I didn't see white people going out the door. All the Blacks were being turned around."

Maybe it was all in her head. Maybe she was just an unlucky victim of America's buggy electoral system, which always failed some voters. And maybe it was just one of those things that in Duval County, more than 20 percent of the votes in majority-Black precincts ended up being invalidated that day because of technical errors; and maybe it was a coincidence that similar things were happening in Black neighborhoods all across Florida. And maybe it was just a mistake that, in Jacksonville, a Democratic congresswoman had to wait more than two hours to vote that morning because of a bureaucratic glitch; and maybe it was yet another mix-up that caused a combat veteran named Willie Steen to be told, when he showed up at his Tampa-area polling place, that he could not vote because he had been purged from the registration rolls as a felon, even though he had never been arrested and had been deployed overseas at the time of his alleged conviction.

Maybe it was just an unavoidable tragedy that one in seven

ballots cast by Black citizens of Florida on Election Day in 2000 would end up being discarded.

Then again, maybe it wasn't entirely an accident.

THAT AFTERNOON, AT Gore's hotel headquarters in Nashville, his campaign manager, Donna Brazile, was looking forward to the end of a stressful year. ("I thought I had experienced every game imaginable in politics," she would later write, "but the Gore campaign set a new low for backbiting and political drama.") Brazile had already made history as the first Black woman to manage a presidential campaign. And the numbers . . . so far, the numbers looked fantastic.

Still, Brazile had a feeling of foreboding. Unsubstantiated rumors were flying around about Black voters in Florida being turned away from the polls. Her sister, down in Orlando, had called her to report that poll workers had demanded three forms of identification from her before she was allowed to vote. Brazile called a friend at the Justice Department to tell him that something fishy was going on. Then she took the elevator to the ninth floor of the hotel to alert Gore.

"They're stealing this election," she told the vice president. "You need to call Janet Reno."

The rest of the Gore campaign leadership was less concerned. These voting problems cropped up every Election Day. The staff had already set up a lectern in Gore's hotel room so he could practice his victory speech. In another room down the hall, aides were picking up the latest technological gadget, a messaging device called a BlackBerry, which Gore was distributing for use during the coming presidential transition. One of his policy advisers had flown in from Washington with a rolling suitcase filled with briefing papers for Gore's first transition meeting.

But the numbers were wrong. The future would be born in error.

ON THE NINETY-THIRD floor of the North Tower, the evening rush was starting, as polls closed in the eastern states and vote totals began to roll in from some 28,000 selected precincts around the country. The Voter News Service was tracking nearly 100 statewide races that evening, including Senate and gubernatorial elections. Its computer system had a screen where it listed all of them, color-coded to indicate the statistical model's level of certainty about the outcome. Light blue meant that a projection was getting close; yellow indicated the system was ready to pick a winner.

When the system reached a high threshold of probability, it posted a status message: *CALL*. Then the actual projections were in the hands of the decision desks at the individual television networks, which all had their own teams of analysts watching terminals linked into the system. Their job was about triage. The blowouts were called early and were usually projected based on exit polls alone. The close races were left for last and were called on the basis of actual vote totals. The ones in the middle could be tricky, and that is where the networks relied heavily on Edelman's predictive model, which weighed a mix of exit polling data and partial precinct results. "Fear of being wrong is the overriding emotion," one decision desk analyst would later recollect.

When the polls closed in Florida, it looked like an easy call. All day, field interviewers had been phoning into the World Trade Center with the results of exit polls from forty-five precincts around the state. They showed Gore with a lead. But no one wanted to be too hasty with a call that consequential. So, the decision desks all waited until the first precinct-level results started to arrive, shortly after the polls closed. If anything, they suggested that Gore was ahead by an even more substantial margin.

At 7:50 p.m., with just 4 percent of Florida's votes counted, the projection system was giving Gore a 99.5 percent chance of winning the state. The screen said it was time to make the call.

NBC News jumped first, declaring Al Gore the winner in Florida.

At Fox News, Ellis took a last look at the numbers from Florida. "Any objections?" he asked his colleagues on the decision desk. No one spoke up, so Ellis shouted out the call to the boss of the network's newsroom. "Okay, Florida goes Gore," he said. Word was passed to the anchor, Brit Hume, who broke the news to his disappointed viewers.

Within moments, Ellis's phone rang. It was Jeb, in Austin, pleading. "Are you sure?" he asked.

"Jeb, I'm sorry," Ellis said. "I'm looking at a screen full of Gore."

"But the polls haven't closed in the Panhandle," Jeb said, reminding Ellis that the most Republican part of the state, along the "Redneck Riviera," was in the Central Time zone.

"It's not going to help," Ellis replied. "I'm sorry."

IN AUSTIN, THE bats took flight at dusk. Hundreds of thousands of them, the world's largest urban bat colony, made their homes in the nooks and crannies under the Congress Avenue Bridge. They emerged each night to hunt for insects among the cypress trees and water willows along the shores of Town Lake, flying in a big black cloud past the floor-to-ceiling windows of the Shoreline Grill, the site of the Bush family's Election Night dinner.

The private party for around sixty family members and friends began with celebratory toasts and false bravado. All the Bushes were nervous, Dubya especially. As the waiters set down plates of Parmesan-crusted chicken, the candidate kept getting up and wandering over to the dining room's only television. It soon brought dire news.

At a little before 7 p.m., Central Time, all the networks—even Fox News!—declared that Al Gore was the winner in Florida. Dubya took the news like a bullet. "Our guests who did not know much about politics continued to babble away," he later wrote in his autobiography. "Those who understood the electoral map recognized I had just lost." His father, eight years removed from his own election defeat, looked stricken. As for Jeb . . .

Jeb may have been thinking about all those times he had said he would never live down the humiliation of losing his state. He crossed the room and wrapped George in a hug. "I'm really sorry, brother," he said, his eyes welling up with tears. (At least that is the way the Bushes told the story afterward, batting back rumors of a brotherly argument.) Jeb then disappeared to make some calls to Florida.

Dubya was stunned, deflated. He pulled his father aside. "I'm not going to stay around," he whispered. "I want to go back to the mansion." He and Laura slipped out of the dinner without taking a bite of the food. The governor was subdued on the short car ride home.

"There isn't much to say when you lose," Bush would later write.

In Nashville, Gore's spokesman took a call from a reporter who told him that Bush had just fled his own victory dinner. "He's in retreat!" the aide gloated. "He's running home!"

AS THE RESULTS started to roll in, Kevin Ingram was at a hotel in East Brunswick, New Jersey, waiting for Jon Corzine to declare victory. Ingram's old boss from Goldman Sachs, a TruMarkets investor, had spent $60 million from his personal fortune to win what was then the most expensive Senate race in American history. Ingram had been dabbling in politics, raising money for the Democratic Senatorial Campaign Committee. His friend Didi was also at the party. Didi was involved in local politics and was very tight with a congressman from Newark who was influential on Africa policy. Didi was working on a new deal involving cell phones in Somalia.

On the television screens, the maps were turning blue, as Gore locked up one important state after another. It was a joyous night for the Democrats, who were on their way to picking up four Senate seats, enough to give them an even fifty and control of the chamber, provided that Vice President Joe Lieberman was there to break the tie. The outcome of the most closely watched Senate race was never much in doubt. Hillary Clinton had crushed her weak Republican opponent. Across the Hudson River, at the Grand Hyatt on Forty-Second Street, she was opening a new chapter in her political saga.

As Senator-elect Clinton sat in her hotel suite, savoring her triumph, President Clinton was doing what made him happiest on Election Day: working the phones, making get-out-the-vote calls to West Coast radio stations, squeezing every single precinct, fighting 'til the last dog died. He paced, beet-faced, in front of a bank of four televisions, cheering and cursing as if he were playing the horses at an OTB. Even now, Clinton was smarting over Gore's standoffish behavior, complaining that his vice president had kept him on the bench down the stretch, refusing to let him campaign in the swing states. He questioned Gore's message, telling the room that it was "consultant populist bullshit." But even Clinton couldn't argue with the result. Gore had won, despite it all.

Downstairs, in the Grand Hyatt's ballroom, the Democratic stalwarts were waiting for Bill and Hillary to take the stage for her victory speech. I was covering Election Night as a newspaper reporter. People at the party were already speculating, no longer so absurdly, about when the First Lady would run for president. But that would have to be eight, or twelve, or sixteen years in the future, after President Gore left office. The world was in a heady state. The centrist consensus ruled, the radicals had been driven to the ends of the earth, and peace and prosperity reigned. Sure, some of these dot-coms seemed a little iffy, and the stock market was wobbling, and children were starving in Sudan, and North Korea was developing nukes, and AIDS was still incurable, and the globe was warming, and the seas were rising. But these were manageable problems, and President Gore would be nothing if not a manager. He had a plan for climate change. He had a plan for everything. His most damaging character flaw was that he sometimes acted a little too smart.

The idyll of the Gore administration would last just a little more than two hours.

FORTY BLOCKS NORTH, at Elaine's, the famed Upper East Side haunt, the air was charged and tinged with cigarette smoke. *Talk* was throwing the evening's most glamorous election party, with editor Tina Brown presiding over the festivities. *Talk*'s co-owner Harvey Weinstein was there, just back from the Gore rally in Miami. Uma Thurman and Ethan Hawke shared a back table. Gwyneth Paltrow and Ben Affleck sat in front of a TV, whispering. Jennifer Lopez picked at a plate of chicken fingers. Russell Simmons and Charlie Rose were cruising around. Weinstein, bearish in his dark brown suit, barked into his cell phone: "How many electoral votes?"

Weinstein reveled in his power—he was more than just some mere movie mogul. It was rumored that the film producer was angling to be the next U.S. ambassador to Israel. He was introducing guests to the party's cosponsor, billionaire Michael Bloomberg, who was talking about running for mayor. The night before, Weinstein had thrown a reporter he considered impertinent out of a party in Tribeca, putting the guy in a headlock and dragging him out onto the street. "You know what?" he'd shouted. "It's good that I'm the fucking sheriff of this fucking lawless piece-of-shit town." Now the Clintons were moving to New York, and the sheriff was organizing the town's welcoming committee. Weinstein was telling everyone at the party that he expected Bill and Hillary to drop by.

All the people who mattered were there, every name you would be likely to see in boldface in the next day's *New York Post*. Well, except for one. Where *was* Donald Trump?

Uncharacteristically, Trump did nothing to draw attention to himself that night, although he was surely in New York. (He was to give a speech to one of his most vital constituencies, New York civil court judges, early the next morning.) If he was keeping to his preferred stay-at-home routine, he was sitting in his rococo condo in Trump Tower eating a takeout burger and watching cable television. It is possible he wanted to stay away from the press. Someone might have asked him about his absurd campaign for president, although most people had already forgotten all about it.

Over on C-SPAN2, Pat Buchanan was speaking to a threadbare Reform Party rally at a Marriott in suburban Washington, conceding his defeat—although that may be too mild a word for the scale of his repudiation. His campaign, with its "America First" message and its scaremongering ads about illegal immigration and Islamist terrorism, had won just four-tenths of a percent of the vote nationwide. (Chuck Harder was not surprised. "I think that the media and the boys in the back rooms have already decided who's won this election," he had predicted months earlier. "And we'll all just sit back and watch it.")

"Folks didn't give us much of a chance," Buchanan told his anemic audience. "Because we had opposition like Mr. Ventura up in Minnesota and that great statesman Donald Trump in New York." At the mention of Trump, the crowd burst out laughing.

"This cause is not going to die," Pitchfork Pat vowed. His microphone cut out, but he forged on. "This party will fight, whether it's the Bush or the Gore administration, any administration, any White House that continues to sell out the national sovereignty of the United States of America to any global institution. On all these issues, my friends, we were not engaged by the other two candidates: our demand that America's borders be controlled; our demand that English be America's language so that we can all come together and be one nation and one people; our demand for trade deals to stop selling out American workers; our insistence that American troops be taken out of places where they don't belong and no longer fight wars that are not America's business. I give you my word, I am with these causes now, right up until the Lord himself calls us home, my friends. And this party and this cause are going to move, and one day, one day . . ."

Just possibly, the man in Trump Tower was listening to the total loser who beat him.

AT THE WORLD Trade Center, at around 9:15 p.m., Edelman learned of a problem in Florida. Something was going glitchy inside the black box of his prediction model. Peering at his computer monitor, he saw an obvious anomaly with the vote from Duval County. It showed Gore winning 98 percent. It would turn out that one of the data entry clerks toiling away for minimal wages had slipped up when typing in Gore's total from precincts in Jacksonville, giving him 43,023 votes instead of 4,302. But for now, the source of the problem was a mystery. At 9:38 p.m., Edelman sent out an urgent, cryptic message about the Florida numbers: "Vote is strange."

Later on, when there was time for a forensic autopsy, multiple failings would be detected in Edelman's prediction system, which had never been tested by such a tight presidential election. The exit polls, which usually leaned a bit toward the Democrats, turned out to have a huge skew—perhaps because conservatives were growing more distrustful of the news media. The service made other mistaken assumptions in selecting precincts to sample and in estimating the number of absentee voters. As actual voting results rolled in, Bush held a steady statewide lead.

By this point, Bush was back at the Governor's Mansion. There, he put on a show of confidence, summoning a group of reporters to his upstairs living room. The press swarmed in, and one photographer knocked over a vase, spilling flowers and water.

The governor ignored the mess, sitting between his wife and his mother with his jacket off, looking comfortable. "I think Americans oughta wait until all the votes are counted," he said. "I don't believe the projections." Back at his hotel, Jeb had been calling around to his people on the ground in heavily contested counties. They reported that the vote tallies looked good for Bush.

"I'm pleased to have carried Tennessee," Bush said, needling Gore one more time for good measure. "That's an interesting development."

At the decision desk for CBS News, which was collaborating for the evening with CNN, an analyst looked up at the television and saw the press conference. "Bush is not conceding Florida," he remarked. Then he called up Edelman to ask what the devil was happening with the prediction system. Once a race was called, it was supposed to go to the bottom of the screen, but on the rare occasions that a reversal might be necessary, the race popped to the top of the list, colored red.

Florida had gone red.

At 9:54 p.m. on the East Coast, CNN and CBS were the first to retract their call for Gore.

"Oh, waiter," CNN analyst Jeff Greenfield exclaimed on-screen. "One order of crow!"

"BACK FROM THE ASHES!"

Jeb came bounding up the back stairs of the Texas Governor's Mansion, taking them a couple at a time, and burst into the up-stairs living room. He pulled out a laptop computer and sat in a corner to monitor the incoming vote in Florida on a state government website.

"Get me figures, little brother," Dubya said.

This is how it remained for a few hours. Bush had 246 electoral votes, and Gore, 267—just an agonizing three short of the presidency. Dubya set himself in an armchair and clicked around with the TV remote. Poppy lay supine on the sofa with his feet propped up, looking more nervous than anyone. Jeb was working the laptop and a couple of cell phones.

On NBC, analyst Tim Russert had been gaming out Electoral College scenarios on a simple dry-erase whiteboard all night. Finally, he reduced it all to three words: *Florida, Florida, Florida.*

Throughout this time, Jeb was frequently comparing notes with John Ellis at Fox News. By around 2 a.m., with 96 percent of the vote counted in Florida, the Voter News Service system showed that Bush had a 29,000-vote lead. There was no longer any need for complex algorithms. Ellis had been doing what he would later describe as "back-of-the-envelope" math, comparing the margin that Gore needed to close the gap against what he was actually getting. The percentage kept climbing as the number of outstanding votes dwindled. Ellis phoned Austin.

"What do you think?" Dubya asked his cousin.

"I think you've got it," Ellis said, briefly going over the numbers.

Then, at 2:08, there was a breakthrough. Bush's statewide margin abruptly widened to more than 51,000 votes. The system estimated that there were only around 179,000 votes left to be counted statewide. Gore would need to win around 63 percent of the remaining votes in order to have a chance. Gore was hitting that number in parts of South Florida, but nowhere else.

Ellis could not see any way for Gore to make up the deficit. He later said that everyone on the decision desk agreed with his math. Another member of the team that night, a Democrat, would remember the moment differently, claiming that Ellis made the call after consulting over the phone one last time with his very knowledgeable sources in Austin and then shouting out across the decision desk: "Jebby says we got it! Jebby says we got it!"

At 2:16, Fox News declared that George W. Bush would be the next president of the United States.

IT'S WORTH PAUSING here for a moment to explain—with the benefit of information no one knew at the time—what exactly was going on inside Murray Edelman's rattletrap computer system at 2:08 in the morning on November 8, 2000. In the cautionary memo Edelman sent out to his service's subscribers the week before, he had warned that, as on every Election Night, there could be anomalies in the vote totals as they were relayed by phone to the temps in the data center on the ninety-third floor. Mistakes happened, and they could screw up the endgame math, especially in a very close race where the total number of ballots cast was still an unknown quantity.

So, the first flaw with Ellis's back-of-the-envelope calculation was that there were not 179,000 uncounted votes left in Florida, as the computer system had estimated. There were around twice that number, including around 90,000 more in Palm Beach County, where Gore was winning by a large margin. The other problem was that at 2:08 a.m., something very odd happened to the vote totals from Volusia County, which includes Daytona Beach. Instead of going up, as they should have as more votes were counted, Gore's countywide total suddenly *decreased* by 10,000.

That night, down at the Volusia County elections headquarters in DeLand, dial-up modems were screeching as memory cards taken from ballot scanners at local precincts and carried in by poll workers were being uploaded into a central vote-tabulation system. The local judge who chaired the county's elections board would later recall noticing the drop in Gore's count. "I said, 'That is strange,' and I went back to work," he said. A little while later, a county employee came up and handed the judge a palm-size piece of plastic. It was a dented memory card from Precinct 216, a community center in DeLand. It looked like it had been dropped on the floor. The judge had the original paper ballots from Precinct 216 recounted. Gore got 193 votes; Bush, 22.

Unfortunately, in the meantime, the damaged memory card had already been uploaded and tabulated. It gave Gore *negative* 16,022 votes in Precinct 216. At the World Trade Center, a supervisor overseeing the results from that part of Florida noticed the sudden deduction, but did not think the anomaly was important enough to escalate to the bosses. There were no TVs in the data center, so hardly anyone on the ninety-third floor realized that the presidency hinged on a minuscule margin in Florida or that even a small fluctuation might be enough to trigger a projection.

Edelman was aware, though, and that was why he was on the phone with the head of the decision desk at NBC in those crucial minutes after 2:08, trying to remind him of his memo's warning about the volatility of close races. Even though the prediction system now showed that Bush had a 99.9 percent chance of winning, Edelman was urging the networks to wait for more votes.

"Gotta go," the NBC executive said, cutting off the conversation at 2:16. "Fox just called it."

Over the next four minutes, NBC and the other networks all did the same, calling Florida and the election for Bush. In the acrimonious months to come, when they would be publicly pilloried and hauled before a congressional committee, the executives who oversaw the decisions denied that they had blindly followed the lead of Fox News. After all, everyone was looking at the same numbers. Nonetheless, two decades later, Edelman would still be wondering what might have transpired if the crucial decision had fallen to someone other than an excited relative of George W. Bush.

"If you want to take Ellis out of this, there's certainly another reality that could have happened," Edelman says. "If Fox had not done it, I think I would have probably sent something out on the wire" warning the other networks not to call Florida. "Then Volusia would have changed, and I would have been a hero instead of being destroyed. It would have been a whole other world."

IN OUR REAL time line, at 2:18 a.m., Dan Rather had just announced the Florida call on CBS. "Let's give a tip of the Stetson to the loser, Vice President Al Gore," said the Texan anchor, "and at the same time, a big tip and a hip, hip, hurrah and a great big Texas howdy to the new president of the United States. Sip it. Savor it. Cup it. Photostat it. Underline it in red. Press it in a book. Put it in an album. Hang it on the wall. George Bush is the next president of the United States."

Sitting in my apartment on the Lower East Side, from which I could see the twinkling office lights of the World Trade Center, I picked up my remote, turned off the television, and crawled into bed.

Al Gore was following the Florida count from the floor of a room at his Nashville hotel, sprawled out in a pair of jeans and flip-flops, his chin propped on his hand, watching the TV. When his staff first heard about the Fox News call, they scoffed—it was just Fox.

Donna Brazile sent Gore a message on his BlackBerry: "Never surrender. It's not over yet."

Then a campaign staffer's phone rang. He told Gore to turn the channel to CBS.

Let's give a tip of the Stetson to the loser . . .

It was on television, so who was going to question it? Certainly not Gore. He was off the floor now, right up against the TV screen, his arms crossed, rocking on his heels as he absorbed the blow. He disappeared to a small room to confer with a couple of close advisers.

"It's over," Gore announced, after a long moment of silent deliberation. "Let's concede."

He returned to the room, where he had been practicing his victory speech, and said he was going back to his family's suite to get ready for his concession. "Let's get this over with," he said.

A smaller man might have allowed himself a moment of grief, might have cycled through the stages of anger, bargaining, and denial. He might even have called for confirmation from his own numbers guy, who was poring over the vote totals from Florida in a boiler room at the campaign's office in Nashville and coming to a much different conclusion than the networks. But Gore's first thought was always for appearances, and he skipped right to acceptance.

Within minutes, Gore placed the obligatory concession call to Bush in Austin.

"You're a formidable opponent and a good man," Bush said.

"We sure gave them a cliffhanger," Gore replied, with forced bonhomie.

Jeb, meanwhile, was still hunched over his laptop computer at the mansion.

"I don't see it," he said quietly. "Where are they getting these numbers?"

"WHY IS IT so fucking close?" Bill Clinton asked aloud.

The president was back up in his hotel suite on the thirty-fourth floor of the Grand Hyatt, watching the Florida endgame in his makeshift war room. If there was one thing Clinton knew how to do, it was count votes, and he could not believe the networks had called the race based on a margin this tiny. To make matters even more confused, there were different sets of numbers floating around. Besides the ones that the networks were using, Florida's secretary of state and the Associated Press each had their own counts, showing Bush with a smaller lead, which was narrowing fast. At 2:02 a.m., Bush's margin in the AP count was 56,486 votes. At 2:16—when the networks made their calls—it was 30,513. Six minutes later, it fell to 15,359, and Florida was still counting.

By 2:48 a.m., the Voter News Service had corrected the Volusia

County error and a smaller mistake in another county, cutting Bush's lead in an instant. It was around this time that one of the operatives sitting with Clinton at the Grand Hyatt placed a call to the insect-infested rental house in Tallahassee that Gore's field staff was using as its Florida headquarters. The field staffer on duty had brought in his mother to help him out with the phones. She politely informed the caller that her son was currently too busy to speak with the president of the United States.

"The numbers are wrong!" the staffer was shouting into another phone, trying to alert Nashville.

But Gore, oblivious, had already made his call to Bush. The TV networks reported that he had conceded and was preparing to speak in Nashville. Clinton could not believe Gore had given up so meekly.

"Should I call Bush?" Clinton asked his chief of staff. "No, should I call Gore?"

"Maybe the Gores don't even want to talk to us," Hillary said.

At this late hour, Harvey Weinstein showed up to visit Clinton's suite with a delegation from the party at Elaine's, including Ben Affleck and Uma Thurman. Hillary gave her friend Harvey a grateful hug. Uma offered condolences to the president, telling him the Gore campaign "made me really miss you." Bill launched into a tirade about the unfairness of the press.

"They set an impossibly high standard, an absurdly high standard, for Gore," Clinton said. "It was disgusting."

On the television, Bush's margin was continuing to dwindle. "This is still not over," the president announced to the partygoers. Gore "can still win it," he said, adding, "He's going to win the popular vote." Indeed, contrary to expectations, Gore would end up beating Bush by more than 500,000 votes nationally. That was just an afterthought, constitutionally speaking, but Clinton was

already looking ahead, to a potential political battle over the legitimacy of the election.

Still, even if Gore did lose, there would always be another race
in the future.

"We have to figure out what we do now," Hillary said to Bill.

"You sound like Robert Redford in *The Candidate*," Bill replied
affectionately.

That's the end of the movie. The Clintons quietly exited their
own party.

ON THE NINTH floor of Gore's hotel, an aide handed him a red folder
containing a brief and generous concession speech. "The people of
the country have spoken, and I accept their judgment," it began.
It closed with a quote from the Bachman-Turner Overdrive: "You
ain't seen nothing yet."

Gore gathered up his sobbing daughters and Tipper and took an
elevator down into the bowels of the hotel, walking through the
kitchen to the loading dock, where the vice-presidential limousine
was waiting to take them to the nearby rally. His motorcade was
unusually long: besides his car, there was a second, decoy limo; an
SUV filled with Secret Service agents; a car for his chief of staff and
the military attaché who carried the nuclear codes; several mini-
vans filled with senior aides and VIPs; another limo for Lieberman;
another decoy; a press van; an ambulance; and numerous police
cars. The night was cold and rainy, giving it the appearance of a
funeral procession.

By the time Gore got in his car, campaign aide Michael Whouley was desperately trying to reach him at the hotel. Whouley, a
tough-talking Boston operative, was Gore's Election Day field
general. He had spent the whole day holed up at the campaign's

Nashville office, coordinating the swing-state turnout operation. He was supposed to be the vote-counting expert.

The campaign's field staffer on the ground in Tallahassee had spotted the discrepancy in the networks' numbers from Volusia County. Once that was corrected, the margin fell into the range that would trigger an automatic recount. And it continued to fall farther. By 2:55 a.m., the Voter News Service had corrected its errors and added a batch of new votes from Palm Beach.

Bush now led by just 9,000 votes. And Florida was still counting.

Whouley was looking for someone who could alert Gore, but right now all the phone circuits in Nashville were jammed. Finally, the field operation managed to get an emergency page to one of the vice president's aides via the White House switchboard, which can always locate anyone.

"Where the fuck are you?" Whouley asked.

"I'm in the motorcade," the aide replied. "Two blocks away."

On the television screens in the field staff's boiler room, the networks were broadcasting the downcast scene outside the War Memorial Auditorium in downtown Nashville, where Gore's drenched supporters were waiting for him to deliver his dignified admission of defeat to the nation.

"You can't go out there!" Whouley shouted into the phone.

Gore was in his limousine, near the front of the procession, and all his campaign operatives were in cars farther back. Everyone was fumbling with their new BlackBerrys and their old flip phones, trying to get the message to Gore. Finally, a staffer managed to intercept him at the base of the stairs leading to the stage, just as he was about to go out and deliver the speech inside his red folder.

Gore was irritated. "I told the governor I was going to do this thing," he snapped. He was ready, the cameras were ready, the nation was ready. Grudgingly, he diverted to a holding room, a small office in the basement of the auditorium, where he was soon joined by a swarm of staffers. They informed Gore that Bush's lead, with an estimated 99.8 percent counted, was now down to just 600 votes.

Gore's mood improved.

The holding room did not have a television, but someone managed to find one, an old clunker with rabbit ear aerials that could pick up only a fuzzy signal from the local NBC affiliate. On the broadcast, Tim Russert and anchor Tom Brokaw were having an awkward conversation.

"There are still some votes that have not been counted," Russert said.

"Because we're at 99.8 . . ." Brokaw stopped midsentence, glanced at a piece of paper, fell silent.

"What if this goes the other way?"

"Well, it's only 3:17," Russert said, as off-camera laughter filled the studio.

"That's entirely possible," Brokaw said, with an incredulous smile.

Gore had thrown his lucky cowboy boots up on a metal desk in the cramped office. The emotional atmosphere was confused; people were giggling and crying at the same time.

At 3:30 a.m., Gore asked his campaign chairman to get Bush on the phone again.

"Circumstances have changed dramatically since I first called you," Gore began. "The state of Florida is too close to call."

"Let me make sure I understand," Bush replied. He had never heard of a candidate unconceding. He would later recall telling Gore that, in Texas, it meant something when a man gave his word.

"Don't get snippy about it," Gore replied.

("I don't know about snippy," Bush would later write, "but I was hot.")

"Let me explain," Gore continued, and then proceeded to coolly lay out a perfectly rational set of conditions under which he would, of course, submit to the will of *all* the voters of Florida.

There were rules that covered recounts. There was a system, and Gore believed they should both wait for that system to complete its work.

"My little brother says it's over," Bush retorted.

"With all due respect to your little brother," Gore replied, before hanging up the phone and flexing his bicep, "he is not the final arbiter of who wins Florida."

That would remain to be seen.

25

Hanging State

It had, in fact, all happened before—back in the nineteenth century, long before the United States became a Great Power and the
outcome of its elections shaped the course of world events. The
most recent disputed presidential election had occurred in 1876,
in the race between Rutherford B. Hayes and Samuel Tilden. That
time, the Electoral College outcome came down to contested results in a handful of states, most notably Florida. The Republicans
were the party of abolition, and Democrats in Florida had worked
to prevent Black citizens from voting with every means at their dis-
posal, from trickery to armed intimidation. Even so, an initial tally
found that Hayes, the Republican, won the state by just 43 votes
out of 45,000 cast. The Democrats cried fraud. Lawyers and party
hacks—"visiting statesmen," the newspapers called them—rushed
down to the southern cotton town of Tallahassee in private railcars
to fight for Florida's electoral votes. After much bickering and
bribery, a state board ended up awarding them to Hayes.

Tilden, who had won the national popular vote, took his dispute
to Washington. The nation's leaders came up with an ungainly
solution: an electoral commission that included ten members of
Congress and five Supreme Court justices. By a single vote, the
commission gave Hayes the presidency. Democrats protested, called

the new president "Rutherfraud." As a concession, Hayes removed federal troops from the South, ending Reconstruction and allowing the former Confederate states to impose a system of white supremacy that endured for nearly a century.

This transaction came to be known to high school students as the Compromise of 1877.

It is reasonable to believe that Jeb Bush was contemplating neither history nor compromise that morning of November 8, as he bounced through the clouds in a small plane, rushing home to Florida at the crack of dawn. He had managed only a snatch of sleep. He had been in the room with his parents and Dick Cheney when his brother left to take an early morning phone call, returning to share the news that Gore had retracted his concession. Dubya then issued an order. "I told Jeb to get up there," he later said, "and find out more about Florida."

Jeb had failed to lock down his state on Election Day. That was not going to happen twice.

The plane descended over the swamps and longleaf pines of the Apalachicola National Forest and came in for a landing at the Tallahassee airport. Jeb looked out his window as the plane taxied to the terminal. Across the tarmac was a DC-9 charter painted with the Gore-Lieberman insignia. A planeload of Democrats—"visiting statesmen," you might say—had just flown in from Nashville. Jeb pulled out his phone and called Karl Rove in Austin.

"We've been invaded," he said.

"BUSH WINS IT," declared the falsely definitive banner headline on the front page of the *Miami Herald*. "BUSH WINS!" blared the big block letters on the cover of the *New York Post*, which started to hit newsstands all over the city in the dark hours of the early morning. Most Americans were still asleep. They had gone to bed thinking the whole thing was over. For about an hour, between 2:30 and 3:30 a.m., George W. Bush had been the president-elect. Bush would retain that presumption of victory as long as he held on to a lead. And at dawn on November 8, he still had one—an edge so infinitesimally tiny that it boggled the imagination.

Bush and Gore were separated by 1,784 votes, out of almost 6 million cast in Florida. Two days later, a statewide machine recount would bring the difference in votes down to 327, a lead of .005 percent—the equivalent of one-fifth of an inch on a football field; one and a half verses in the whole King James Bible; twenty-six minutes in a calendar year, not enough time to finish a broadcast episode of *Friends*.

In an election that close, any factor, no matter how trifling, could be said to have determined the outcome: the huge Cuban turnout in Miami; the 97,488 people in Florida who voted for Ralph Nader; the untold number of Black citizens who never got a chance to vote at all. In his more reflective moments, Gore could intellectualize the madness. People close to him said he saw it as an illustration of chaos theory, a scientific idea popular in the airport bookstores of the time, which held that hidden fractal patterns ran beneath the heartless randomness of the universe. A butterfly flaps its wings in the Amazon, the famous illustration went, and causes a hurricane in Texas. A boy is pulled from the ocean in Florida, and bombs fall on Iraq.

"To him, this is all a fractal," a Gore adviser told the *New York Times*, "the geometric theory that pieces of the whole, regardless of the scale, reflect the universe. He says it all the time."

Gore's campaign operatives were less cosmic. In the early hours of November 8, a group of them gathered at their Nashville headquarters to try to figure out what to do about Florida. Staffers straggled in, soggy from waiting out in the rain for Gore to deliver his concession speech. Someone secured an aircraft, Lieberman's campaign plane, with seats for seventy-two people. Gore's senior advisers convened a meeting to hash out their strategy. They needed a spokesman, someone grave and dignified, so they woke up Warren Christopher, an attorney who had previously served as Clinton's secretary of state. They needed specialists in election law, and luckily, they had three lawyers on hand who had written a self-published forty-three-page booklet entitled *The Recount Primer*.

"Who's gonna deal with voting rights violations?" asked Donna Brazile, the campaign manager. But no one else wanted to have a conversation on race at that time of the morning.

The staff gathered, and a young campaign aide stood on a table. He called out the names of the operatives selected for the Florida airlift. They renamed the plane "Recount One." Sitting up front was attorney Ron Klain. He was a former aide to Janet Reno at the Justice Department and had served as Gore's chief of staff early in the campaign. Klain had lost that job after falling out of favor with Gore, but he had hung around at the margins, as people cast out by Gore tended to do. Now Klain was back, selected by Gore to run the recount effort.

On the flight to Tallahassee, Klain got on the plane's intercom to lay out the plan. He wanted the landing team to get into the field quickly and stealthily, fanning out to determine where the Democrats might find uncounted ballots. One of the authors of *The Recount Primer* offered a basic tutorial. Rule number one: if Gore was behind, extend the game, keep the counting going.

The first rule's corollary was: if you were ahead, sit on the lead and run out the clock. And because Republicans controlled Florida, they would start with an advantage. As Klain got off the plane in Tallahassee, this reality hit him in the face like a gust from a hot jet engine. A small plane was pulling up to the terminal. Governor Jeb Bush got out of it and waved. So much for stealth. Some of the Democrats got off in the capital, and the plane flew onward to Palm Beach.

WHEN RECOUNT ONE departed Nashville, it took all the lawyers and left behind the campaign manager. Brazile had been awake for days, so she went back to her hotel and tried to get some sleep. But early in the morning, the Reverend Jesse Jackson rang, as she knew he would.

Brazile considered Jackson a mentor. She had gotten her start in politics as a staffer on his first campaign for president, in 1984. "We're gonna have to fight," Jackson said. He was in the lobby. Brazile came down and told him that she had already brought up voting rights with the Gore people, but it had been brushed aside. Jackson asked her to get Gore on the phone, but Gore didn't want to talk.

"We ain't gonna lose this battle," the reverend assured Brazile. "I'll take it from here."

THE BUTTERFLY . . . THAT'S what they were calling it.

Technically, among electoral systems experts, it was known as a "facing-page ballot," but sometime during the past twenty-four hours, someone on TV had used the term *butterfly ballot*, and that was the way it would go down in history, fluttering its wings and conjuring the whirlwind.

Theresa LePore, the supervisor of elections in Palm Beach County, had come up with the butterfly design as a solution to a problem created by a new law that had made it easier for small parties to get a place on the ballot in Florida. Besides Bush, Gore, Ralph Nader, and Pat Buchanan, there were six other minor candidates, including three different socialist cranks and a quantum physicist who was running on a platform of Transcendental Meditation. To avoid using tiny print, which would create problems for elderly voters, LePore had opted to spread out all the names on facing pages. "I was trying to make it look nice," she would later explain.

LePore, a soft-spoken forty-five-year-old, had worked in the elections office since she was a teenager. She had awoken at 4 a.m. on Election Day to oversee the difficult task of coordinating the vote in Florida's largest county by area. Later that morning, a group of senior citizens came to the elections office to report to LePore that they might have accidentally voted for Buchanan. The next forty-eight hours went by in a sleepless blur, as improbability compounded improbability. First, the Electoral College fell into place in such a way that the outcome depended on a single state, with a margin so close there that anything could have swung it, and the one thing the whole country seemed to have decided to focus on was *her* design, the one that commentators on TV were now calling "the butterfly ballot"—a term LePore had never used before.

Logic suggested that hundreds of votes had been cast for Buchanan in error. After running as a scorching conservative, Buchanan had won 3,704 votes, 20 percent of his statewide total, in liberal Palm Beach County. Buchanan himself told Larry King that his result there seemed "outsized." Of course, the irony was that Buchanan was supposed to have stolen conservative votes from Bush, and in fact, one of Gore's lawyers in Florida had represented Buchanan in his effort to get on the ballot in the first place. But in the year 2000, right-wing populists shook the world only by accident.

By the morning of November 8, lawyers were barging into Le-Pore's office waving injunctions. Outside, the parties were having dueling press conferences. "This is ground zero," a local Republican congressman told the press. Reporters were knocking on doors at heavily Jewish condo complexes, searching in vain for Buchanan voters. "My precious vote was lost," one eighty-one-year-old *bubbe* wailed to the *Palm Beach Post*. "I lost it on that devil."

Jesse Jackson was also on his way to Palm Beach. He had already announced plans to hold protests in solidarity with the disenfranchised Gore voters.

"Well," Bill O'Reilly grumbled that evening on his top-rated Fox News talk show, "if there's publicity to be had over a divisive situation, who are you going to call? The Reverend Jackson."

"Bill, I think there are people who made a mistake," replied O'Reilly's guest.

"Well, they're morons," O'Reilly retorted.

THE DEMOCRATS BEGAN the recount by airlifting in a plane full of young operatives. The Bushes sent one craggy old Texan. Jim Baker was both superficially similar to Warren Christopher in that he was a respected former secretary of state and totally unlike him because he was also a shrewd political gunslinger. Baker was Poppy's close friend and had managed all his presidential campaigns. He had a more complicated relationship with the junior George Bush, whom he had known since the boy's roughneck days. When Dubya talked about keeping clear of the "people who lost my dad's election," he meant Baker and his crowd. But now his dad's right hand could make himself useful.

Baker had spent Election Night with Donald Rumsfeld and other members of the GOP old guard in Dick Cheney's suite at the Four Seasons in Austin. He was summoned by the Bush family the next morning. Baker canceled a pheasant hunting trip he had planned to take with Poppy and Prince Bandar, the Saudi ambassador, and hopped on a private jet to Tallahassee. Before leaving, he jotted a few notes to himself on a scrap of paper. "Now more of a LEGAL EXERCISE than POLIT. ONE," he scratched. "COUNTRY WON'T TOLERATE PETTY POLITICS."

At the Florida GOP headquarters, a three-story brick building named for George H. W. Bush, Baker found a disorganized group of lawyers. "We need a PR strategy," he barked. "We're getting killed on 'count all the votes.' Who the hell could be against that?"

With that nod to petty politics, the first meeting of the Bush legal team adjourned, and Baker went to see the man he called "Jebby." He and the governor met for ninety minutes at the State Capitol.

Jeb was in an impossible position. Everyone assumed that the governor would have control over the vote-counting process, but that power was in the hands of county boards, which were controlled by Democrats in Florida's most populous areas. They in turn reported to the elected secretary of state, Katherine Harris, a Sarasota citrus heiress and a cochair of the Bush campaign in Florida. No one doubted Harris's loyalties, but her competence was in question. The night before, Jeb had been shocked to learn that she was at home and sound asleep as the vote totals came in. Whatever she did, the Democrats would sue, and legal appeals would likely end up at the Florida Supreme Court, which was full of judges appointed by Jeb's Democratic predecessor and a frequent source of aggravation to him. This problem was not going to be easy to fix.

What's more, Jeb had to be careful. He was up for reelection in two years. He recused himself from the state board that would have to certify the election result, putting a reliable friend in his place. He did not show his face in the lobby of the State Capitol, where the world media was staking out the secretary of state's office, just down the hall from his own. He wanted to work quietly and indirectly, through a political operation that reached into every part of the state.

To steady Harris, Jeb's minions called upon a Tallahassee lobbyist named Mac Stipanovich, one of the governor's former campaign managers and a wily political assassin. ("He's not called 'Mac the Knife' for nothing," one of his Democratic counterparts quipped.) "It was a war," Stipanovich would later say. "Loser leave town." He set up a battle station inside the secretary of state's office, sneaking in through a parking garage, and advised her on how to put a stop to the recount. "My goal," he said, "was to bring it in for a landing with George Bush at the controls."

As for George Bush himself, he mostly delegated the work to the hired help. He had recently purchased a sixteen-hundred-acre spread in Crawford, Texas, using some of the millions he had made from the sale of the Texas Rangers. "I'll be at the ranch," he told his aides, at least according to legend. "Let me know what happens." The land was covered with cedar brush, which was soaking up all the water. Bush put on his headphones and started to clear the brush with a chainsaw.

In truth, he did not need to contribute much to his cause in Florida. "The lawyers are running the show now," a campaign official told the *Times*. And the lawyers were ready.

FOR THE PREVIOUS eight years, the Republicans had been fighting a litigious guerrilla insurgency against the Clinton administration. Whitewater, Paula Jones, Independent Counsel Kenneth Starr's investigation, Lewinsky, impeachment—it was really all just one long, continually mutating court case. The conservative legal establishment was a close-knit network, centering on the Federalist Society, an organization dedicated to challenging what it called the "orthodox liberal ideology" of academia and the judiciary. Its members had watched in dismay as Clinton managed to wriggle out of one jam after another. Now it looked to them that Gore was trying to swipe the presidency—which was rightfully theirs, whatever the popular vote said.

The legal team quickly assembled at the party headquarters in Tallahassee. A Bush staffer called it "Stalag 17," referencing a classic ensemble picture about a breakout from a Nazi prison camp. One of the first to hit the ground was a twenty-nine-year-old member of the campaign policy staff, Ted Cruz. He had played a minor role in Austin, handling issues like the Elián Gonzalez controversy, but he had a Harvard Law degree—as he never tired of reminding exasperated colleagues—and experience as a Supreme Court clerk. After arriving in Tallahassee, Cruz sat down with a top attorney for the Bush campaign, pulled out a yellow legal pad, and began coming up with names.

At the top of his list was John Roberts, an appellate attorney and Federalist Society member who had served in the first Bush administration. "I called John and asked him to come down," Cruz later wrote. "He dropped everything and flew to Florida." So did Brett Kavanaugh, who had worked on the Lewinsky investigation. So did John Bolton, a hawkish foreign policy specialist, who rushed away from a conference in South Korea to help out his old boss, Baker. So did a gaggle of young former Supreme Court clerks: Alex Azar, Noel Francisco, and Amy Coney Barrett, all of whom had clerked for Antonin Scalia; and John Yoo, who had clerked for Clarence Thomas.

The members of the Bush legal team would go on to lives of

note, as cabinet secretaries, elected officeholders, rationalizers of torture, and justices of the Supreme Court. But for the most part, their service in Florida was anonymous. Afterward, it would be a kind of secret handshake among the lawyers. They would all remember what they did in the war.

The most prominent face on the legal team belonged to a reddish-haired Reaganite, Theodore Olson. He was a veteran of the Justice Department and a skilled litigator who had argued thirteen cases before the Supreme Court. He was also one of the founders of the Federalist Society and a leader of the anti-Clinton resistance. Olson served on the board of *The American Spectator*, a magazine that had published sensationalist articles about Bill Clinton's womanizing and supposedly sleazy financial dealings. ("Bill Clinton's worst nightmare," Olson wrote in the *Spectator* in 2000, "is a George W. Bush–appointed attorney general who will have the courage to pry open the secrets that the Clinton administration has kept during its corrupt reign.")

Ted Olson had written of his fervent hope that the American people would choose a Republican in 2000, "to purge the repugnant aftertaste of Clinton and his acolyte Gore." He and Ken Starr, a close friend, watched the returns on Election Night together. A couple of days later, Olson was on a flight from Washington to Los Angeles when he learned that Bush's campaign was looking for him. He accepted his assignment on the seatback phone, stayed on the plane for its return flight to the East Coast, and headed down to Florida. There, he was joined by his wife, Barbara, who was also a well-known attorney.

The Olsons worked in tandem: Ted in the courtroom, Barbara on television. Barbara was a vivacious former professional ballet dancer who had worked in Hollywood before going to law school and becoming a federal prosecutor. She dressed fashionably by

Washington standards, clattering in her signature four-inch heels. She was a new species of public figure: the cable news lawyer. A profile of the Olsons published that year in the *Washingtonian* called Barbara "the best known of all the conservative TV blondes." The Olson home in Virginia, meticulously decorated by Barbara, was a center of conservative social activity. The couple owned a matching pair of Australian shepherd dogs, named Reagan and Maggie (for Margaret Thatcher).

Barbara had just published *Hell to Pay*, a caustic biography of Hillary Clinton, who in turn believed that the Olsons and their crowd exemplified what she memorably described as a "vast right-wing conspiracy." Barbara scoffed at the suggestion. "Rather than the idea that there's this plot, it's just a group of people," she said. "Washington's a small town. . . . It's just friendships."

Now the whole gang was getting together in Florida to fight for the presidency.

When Ted Olson arrived in Tallahassee, he found a madhouse on the third floor of the party headquarters. Bush's lead was down to just around 300 votes, as a result of the first, legally required machine recount. Baker had called on Gore to concede, citing the "rule of law" and democratic norms, but the Democrats were pressing for a second review, by hand, claiming that there were still votes that the scanning machines had missed for technical reasons. Baker countered that machines were "neither consciously or unconsciously biased," unlike the human beings who sat on the county boards. To him, it appeared the Democrats would just keep recounting until they got the result they wanted.

"They're stealing the election," Baker raged to an aide.

The Gore campaign was focusing its recount efforts on a handful of counties that conveniently happened to be Democratic bastions. Some of Bush's lawyers, including Olson, wanted to file a federal lawsuit alleging that recounting only some votes by hand, using subjective human judgment, was a violation of the Fourteenth Amendment's guarantee of equal protection under the law. Other members of Bush's legal team thought the idea was risky. They thought the lawsuit could look ideologically inconsistent. Conservatives supposedly hated trial lawyers and favored states' rights; now they would be asking a federal court to stop the local recounts. Invoking the Equal Protection Clause was audacious. Democrats would accuse Bush of trying to use a mechanism of civil rights to disenfranchise voters.

Bush's legal advisers met in Tallahassee to consider their options. Jeb showed up in casual khakis to offer his expert judgment on Florida politics. They decided they didn't really give a damn if it looked hypocritical. They filed the lawsuit.

Ted Olson argued the case in Miami, and Barbara justified it on the *Today* show. "This is not a way to do a presidential election," she said of the recount, "with these subjective decisions."

"Okay, I've got a deal for you Barbara," replied Alan Dershowitz, a lawyer from the O.J. Simpson case, who had shown up to represent Democratic voters in Palm Beach. "Let's make a determination. Let's find out the facts. And if Gore wins the hand count, that's the end of it."

"There has been no hand count with Mr. Gore ahead," Barbara Olson shot back.

"Because your husband tried to stop it yesterday! And you're trying to stop it today!"

A FEDERAL JUDGE in Miami rejected Olson's argument and dismissed the lawsuit. The Bush team appealed, but the recount could go on—though for how long, no one knew. Katherine Harris gave the counties a tight one-week deadline to submit their official vote tallies. Gore was suing in state court to overturn her decision. But at any moment, a judge could blow the final whistle.

As Jim Baker recognized, the Democrats had a compelling slogan: "Count every vote." But those were just words. Legally, the dispute was more complicated. There was no mechanism to call for a full statewide recount. Everything had to start at the county level. In Palm Beach County, there was a lawsuit over the butterfly ballot, involving Dershowitz, but there was no way to remedy that situation without rerunning the election, which was never going to happen. The Gore legal team figured that case was going nowhere. Some mistakes were just impossible to correct.

"Ask Black people," one top adviser told Gore at a crucial strategy session at the vice president's residence a few days after the election. "They get screwed every day."

So, the Democrats decided to narrow their focus, concentrating on ballots that had not registered a valid vote on Election Day. There were an astounding 175,000 of these statewide, and because of the way they were geographically distributed, it seemed likely they would favor Gore. But the vast majority of these uncounted ballots were "overvotes," on which people had selected two or more candidates for president. How could the lawyers prove that these voters really meant to choose Gore? The Gore team decided to focus on a smaller subset of ballots, the "undervotes"—ones that did not record any presidential choice. There were around 64,000 of these in total. A large percentage were in three counties where Gore won a majority: Palm Beach, Miami-Dade, and Broward, which was home to Fort Lauderdale.

Gore's lawyers speculated that many of these ballots had been invalidated as the result of an equipment failure. All three counties used the same outdated punch card technology. It looked simple enough. Voters were supposed to insert their ballots into a machine and punch out a perforated square next to the name of the candidate of their choice. But if, for some reason, a voter had not punched the hole completely through, a piece of paper measuring one-sixteenth of an inch could remain attached to the ballot, confusing the scanning machine. That little paper square had a technical name. It was called a chad. Chad was now famous.

There were bad chad jokes and dumb chad T-shirts ("Don't Be Had by a Chad"). Newscasters introduced Americans to the chad's many esoteric varieties. A "hanging" chad was detached on three corners. There was also the "swinging door" chad, which was held on at two vertical corners; the "garage door" chad, which swung from the top; and the "moat" chad, which was attached at the bottom. There were "tri-chads," which were punched out only at one corner; and "dimpled," or "pregnant," chads, which were not detached at all.

For the rest of November, the recount moved at an inching pace, as county government employees squinted at punch cards in an attempt to resolve a constitutional crisis. Both parties fixed their attention on the three counties where Gore stood to win the most votes, dispatching teams of partisan lawyers to observe and intervene in the counting process. John Bolton, the walrus-mustached warmonger, was sent to the front lines in Palm Beach County.

"We saw this as the battle for Stalingrad," Bolton later said. "If we lost here, they would just roll over us." At the State Department in the 1990s, he had helped assemble the military coalition that defeated Iraqi dictator Saddam Hussein in the Gulf War. Now Bolton directed his powers of intimidation at the three-member county board that was overseeing the recount.

All along, the nightmare scenario for the Bush team was that some county would turn up enough Gore votes to put him in the lead, even for a moment, inverting the presumption of victory. Both sides agreed that the most likely place for that to happen would be Palm Beach, where Gore had won 62 percent of the vote and where there were some 11,000 undervotes. The Republicans adopted a strategy they called "mudballing." They objected to everything, argued about everything, trying to delay the process until Gore ran out of time.

The county election board was split. In its deliberations, one member voted consistently for Bush, another for Gore. The swing vote was the unfortunate Theresa LePore. She looked ravaged, a picture of despondence: sunken-eyed, sniffling, gaunt. (She would lose twenty-two pounds over the course of the recount.) She had started Election Day with a sinus infection, which then deepened into laryngitis, depriving her of her voice. She was throwing up. She could not sleep or eat. News columnists were calling her "Madame Butterfly." Comedians were ridiculing her. Her name was all over the internet. She was getting death threats.

Every day, it seemed, LePore's world plummeted a little farther into delirium. Dueling mobs of protesters had set themselves up outside the county government building. Elderly Democrats chanted *Gore got more!* Vengeful Cubans waved photos of Elián. Their ranks kept swelling as more out-of-towners arrived, including a rougher crowd that the police referred to as the "WWF/Jerry Springer" contingent. They were Chuck Harder's people. For years, voices on the far right had been warning of a Clinton dictatorship— "a banana republic–type situation," as Harder put it, "where he concocts some kind of national emergency in which he has to stay in power." Now even mainstream Republicans were decrying a "stolen" election. GOP staffers distributed free T-shirts to their protesters that read, "West Palm Beach Banana Republic."

"For the People reports the ballots that Clinton-Gore-Lieberman

report as not having been counted have been counted twice," a Harder fan wrote his local newspaper in Arkansas. "The Clinton-Gore-Lieberman coup d'état must not succeed." Extremists waving Confederate flags joined the more mainstream Rush Limbaugh fans to protest. ("We're fighting for our lives!" Rush was telling his legions of listeners.) One Republican supporter in military fatigues carried a sign that read, in blood-dripping text, "Hey, Tyrants: Bush or Revolution."

There was also a media encampment for the hundreds of reporters covering the event. It was the Elián Show all over again. Donato Dalrymple, the fame-hungry fisherman from the Gonzalez closet, turned up one day wearing a Bush-Cheney sticker. ("Before the election is actually stolen, or someone concedes, I just wanted to come and see," he told reporters.) Cameras were beaming the scene live to the cable news networks. To keep up with the constant developments, the networks came up with an innovation, streaming headlines across the bottom of the screen on a "ticker."

"What we had here was a test of mettle with the prospect of seeing some able political strategy and skullduggery in action, and even some real emotional comeuppance," wrote the *New York* magazine media critic Michael Wolff. "This was theater. Admit it: this was cool."

"It's a wonderful thing for us," said the conservative TV commentator Tucker Carlson, "and a bad thing for the country."

THEN JESSE JACKSON came to town.

He rolled up to the county government center in a chartered bus, and for a moment, the protesters and counterprotesters in front of the building ceased their shouting matches, and county workers came to their windows to listen. Jackson led a group into the building's courtyard. "In Selma, it was about the right to vote," he preached. "Today, it's about making votes count."

An analysis by the *Palm Beach Post* found that in the county's majority-Black precincts, voters were 139 percent more likely than average to see their ballots invalidated. In the poor Black towns near Lake Okeechobee, nearly a quarter of all ballots were tossed out. There was a technical explanation for the disparity. Palm Beach County used two different brands of voting machines, and Black precincts often ended up with the cheaper model. But Jackson mused about a conspiracy. "Something systematic was at work here," he said. "It was large and systematic."

Jackson spent the next few weeks shuttling all over South Florida, holding meetings at Black churches and seeking to make common cause with disenfranchised Jewish retirees. "You are in the middle of a political storm that could define our democracy for years to come," the reverend told a group of senior citizens at a gated community called Century Village.

Jackson announced that he would be staging a protest march through West Palm Beach. "There is a cloud over Florida," he said. "To surrender without a count would be unpatriotic. It would be treasonous." Bush supporters vowed to shut the protest down. The police closed off streets, and schools and businesses shuttered for the day. Jackson, wearing a dark silk shirt, led the marchers north along a palmy waterfront boulevard that looked across an inlet to the marinas and mansions of Palm Beach Island. Police and news helicopters hovered overhead. At the county government center, in front of the stage where Jackson was to speak, an unruly group of counterprotesters was waiting. One heckler, a former grand wizard of the Alabama Ku Klux Klan, held a sign reading, "I Support Sec. Harris and Florida Law."

Go home, Jesse! the Bush supporters shouted.

The chants drowned out the speakers at the rally. The police started to fear a riot. After about ten minutes, officers pulled Jackson from the stage and bundled him into his limousine.

For the Bush recount team, it would go down as a famous triumph. "We ran Jesse Jackson off!" a staffer would reminisce decades later. "We stopped him from speaking and ran him to his car!"

IN WASHINGTON, AL GORE was not happy with the whole distasteful spectacle. He was holed up in his residence at the Naval Observatory in Washington, which his aides took to calling "the bunker." Gore did not want street protests. He was determined to stick to a strategy that was orderly, logical, systems-oriented. Not surprisingly, he was micromanaging it all. He had set up a pair of easels where he diagramed his thoughts on butcher paper. He learned all about voting equipment and the intricacies of Florida's confusing election laws.

"Anger is not . . . what would be the point of feeling that?" Gore told a *60 Minutes* interviewer who asked about his feelings in the midst of the recount. "I'm *concentrating*."

Gore did not want to be perceived as playing the "race card," which at the time was considered—at least by the people who ran Washington and edited newspapers—the most divisive thing a Democrat could do. In mid-November, Gore gave an interview to the popular Black radio host Tom Joyner. "There are a lot of people—I'm serious—who are starting to look at this and see this election about to be stolen," Joyner said.

"I would discourage the use of that word," Gore replied. "However it comes out, we're going to come [together] behind the winner."

Gore was especially reluctant to associate himself with Jackson, a rhetorical bomb-thrower and publicity hound whom many white liberals regarded with snide condescension. He tried to pass word to Jackson, through Donna Brazile, that he wanted him to get out of Florida. "It is time to end all talk of the disenfranchisement of Black voters in Florida," Gore said in an interview with a business publication. "It is time to stop accusing Republicans of racism."

There were some on the Democratic side—most prominently, Bill Clinton—who thought that Gore was making a critical mistake by downplaying allegations of disenfranchisement. The Democrats were not even trying to contest the results in Duval County, which included Jacksonville and its suburbs, where 27,000 ballots had been invalidated, nearly as many as in Miami and Palm Beach. Once again, there was a technical reason: another design flaw. The ballot in Duval had the candidates on two consecutive pages, with Bush and Gore on the first page and minor candidates on the second, causing many people to mistakenly vote twice. Around 9,000 of these overvotes, a third of all the county's spoiled ballots, occurred in just four majority-Black districts. They called this ballot "the caterpillar," but the name never caught on like the butterfly.

The Duval elections supervisor was a white Republican named John Stafford. No one made up sexist nicknames for him. Thousands of Jewish retirees voting for a Nazi apologist? That was a crazy plot twist. Thousands of Black citizens losing their votes? That was just Election Day.

26

Thanksgiving

When he got the first call from Florida, attorney David Boies was in his backyard in Westchester County planting a copper beech tree with the help of a client, a notoriously tyrannical New York real estate developer. ("A billionaire, half-crazed, litigation-minded client is not so bad," Boies had once explained when another lawyer asked how he could stand the guy.) It was Saturday, November 11, four days after the election. The caller on the line was a close friend who had been helping out the Gore campaign in Broward County. "We need you down here," she said.

Boies considered the opportunity to represent Gore in the recount effort and deflected. "Everyone is entitled to a lawyer," Boies liked to say. "But not everyone is entitled to me."

Within the legal profession, Boies was legendary for his prowess in the courtroom. His boutique firm specialized in high-stakes corporate litigation, taking on the most daunting "bet the company" cases. Wealthy and demanding men would come to him, beseeching, with wallets in hand, when their reputations and fortunes were in peril. They saw Boies, a rawboned Californian with tousled hair and a wolfish competitive instinct, as a rare peer—or, rarer still, a friend. He was renowned for his powers of memory and concentration, his quick thinking as a cross-examiner, and the deft, even courtly manner with which he led opposing witnesses into his traps.

Boies did not think that Al Gore required his talents. Boies was a Democrat, but he was not particularly political. Two years before, he had represented the Justice Department in a giant antitrust case against Microsoft, dismantling Bill Gates in an artful deposition, but there was nothing partisan in that. Boies was a litigator, a gun for hire. He knew little about election law. And Gore already had plenty of skilled attorneys: Ron Klain running the traffic, Warren Christopher managing public relations, some seasoned good ol' boys from Tallahassee to handle the Florida courts. For the federal cases, he had Laurence Tribe, a Harvard Law School professor, Supreme Court advocate, and author of the definitive textbook *American Constitutional Law.* That was a lot of talent and ego. Boies wasn't an ensemble player.

Still . . . it *was* the most important case in America, and *that* sounded interesting.

A few days after the first call, Boies was in the middle of a meeting about a copyright infringement case involving Napster, a reckless, young music-sharing software company he represented, when an assistant handed him a message. It was from an old law school classmate who was advising Gore. The Democratic team had just taken a beating in an important state court hearing, and the Republicans were on the verge of shutting down the hand recounts. Klain was looking for the best appellate attorney he could find on short notice to appear before the Florida Supreme Court.

Boies called back his old classmate, who also put Klain on the line.

"Can you get to Florida tonight?"

"Yep," Boies said. He was in.

Boies finished up some business in New York, meeting with his client Calvin Klein and sharing a bottle of white wine with the real estate tyrant, before flying down to Tallahassee on a Learjet that evening. "Welcome to Guatemala," Klain said to him in greeting when he arrived.

IF THERE WAS one point of agreement between the two legal teams, it was that the surreal situation in Florida resembled something out of a corrupt Third World nation. "The person in charge of running the whole thing," Klain said later, "is the fucking candidate's brother." Jeb Bush claimed to be playing a disinterested role, but no one really bought that line, including the Republicans working in his interest. "It was Jeb who, probably, in an indirect way, gave the presidency to his brother," says Mac Stipanovich, the operative dispatched to Katherine Harris's office. "He had people who knew what they were doing, and he put them in place."

Now under steady guidance, Harris was drawing a hard line, continuing to contest the validity of the hand recounts and refusing to accept any tabulations submitted after her one-week deadline. Gore's spokesman had taken to referring to the secretary of state as "Commissar Harris." Comics and commentators were ridiculing her shaky public appearances and heavy makeup regimen. But she was enjoying her newfound importance. The Saturday after Boies arrived, there was a big football game in Tallahassee between the Florida Gators and the Florida State Seminoles, and many of the figures involved in the recount, including Jeb, ended up mingling in the same luxury box. Harris told a group of people there about a dream she had had the night before, in which she took the field on a stallion, carrying a Seminole flag in one hand and a paper in the other: the official certification of Bush's election. So, she was not even pretending to be impartial.

Still, Democrats could mock Harris all they wanted, but unless they convinced a court to overrule her, the recount was over. That was why Gore needed the best lawyer in America. Boies masterfully took over the case, pushing aside Warren Christopher, who had turned out to be a bit too much of an elder statesman. (Watching one of his TV appearances, one of the smart-asses on the Bush team remarked, "Gosh, if Warren Christopher were alive to see this . . .") In contrast to the funereal diplomat, Boies emanated buoyant aggression. "We all hope—we all hope—that what is going to happen here is that the will of the people is going to be heard," Boies said in his first press conference. If Harris would not listen, he promised to beat her in court.

The Bush legal team in Tallahassee would soon be bemoaning the "Cult of Boies." Its converts appeared to include Florida judges, Gore's other lawyers, and Gore himself. Gore had met Boies in person only once, and he wasn't inclined to trust outsiders—or, really, anyone—but he formed a bond with his lawyer, and he would often call Boies from Washington to bounce around ideas. The Cult of Boies found its most fervent following, though, within the media.

Boies knew how to talk to journalists, to cultivate them and make them feel as if he valued their insights. In one of his formative victories, he had defended CBS and *60 Minutes* in a major First Amendment case. He was friends with TV news anchors. He and the talk show host Charlie Rose shared a Paris pied-à-terre. He played in a summer softball game for media muckety-mucks hosted by a magazine and TV entrepreneur. His press clippings were adoring; his idiosyncrasies, charming. Magazine profiles inevitably referenced his fondness for junk food, cheap suits, and casino gambling. He liked to play craps because it offered the best odds of beating the house.

In Tallahassee, Boies could be found most evenings at a sports bar near the capitol, drinking screwdrivers and sharing his thoughts with reporters covering the recount. He kept up a feverish schedule of cable television appearances. A crew from *60 Minutes* appeared and began trailing him around, filming for an upcoming episode. Somehow, amid all this, Boies found time to prepare for court. He kept winning, and that was keeping Gore alive.

On November 20, Boies appeared before the Florida Supreme Court to argue Gore's case for overruling Harris and extending the deadline to complete the hand recounts. So far, the Bush team's delaying tactics had managed to prevent Gore from making up almost any ground in the three counties where he was focused. After the near-riot surrounding Jesse Jackson's protest march, the Palm Beach board had hunkered down, relocating to the county's Emergency Operations Center, a secure bunker next to a strip club near the airport. They had managed to get through only 12 percent of the disputed ballots, and Gore had picked up a grand total of one vote. Progress was similarly slow in Miami. And in Broward County, there was bedlam. Republican observers were howling about fraud, scouring the floor of the recount center for chads that had fallen off ballots and claiming Democrats were deliberately punching out votes. They accused one Democratic observer of eating chads to conceal the evidence.

As Broward County government workers held punch cards in the air, examining chads, a television on the wall was broadcasting live from Tallahassee, where the state supreme court judges were hearing oral arguments. Boies dominated the two-and-a-half-hour hearing, overwhelming the Bush team with his fluid presentation and effortless command of the facts.

"This was amateur hour with the exception of David Boies," Alan Dershowitz said that evening, recapping the day's arguments on MSNBC. "He was the only one thinking on his feet."

"None of this follows the law," Barbara Olson said in rebuttal. "And at some point, I would think, the U.S. Supreme Court will be very, very interested."

The next day, the state supreme court ruled unanimously for Gore, overruling Harris and finding that the state was obligated to determine "the result that reflects the will of the voters, whatever that may be." The court set a new deadline to complete the recounts: Sunday, November 26. It appeared the election would be decided, once and for all, over Thanksgiving weekend.

ON THE SPLENDID isle of Palm Beach, the storm across the water registered only as a distant rumble. Donald Trump was flying down to preside over his annual Thanksgiving banquet for club members at Mar-a-Lago. It was the start of another winter season, and Trump was back to his routines: promoting himself, chiseling contractors, trading in salacious gossip. As always, Palm Beach provided him with a bounty. This year, the billionaire Koch brothers were feuding, and one of them was going through a rancorous divorce from his beautiful young wife. The chairman of Sotheby's was daring to show his face again, just a month after pleading guilty in an auction price-fixing scheme that cheated many of his neighbors. David Boies, as it happened, was representing art collectors in a class action suit against the auction house.

Jeffrey Epstein's pal Prince Andrew was also rumored to be around, as a Palm Beach society columnist reported that the "handsome and uninhibited" royal had come to town "to indulge two of his favorite pastimes," one of which was golf. Speaking of golf, Trump was throwing a grand opening party for his new course in West Palm Beach. Wearing a white collared shirt and baseball cap, the potbellied developer kibitzed with members over breakfast in the clubhouse.

As usual, Trump wanted more. He was pressuring the county to sell him a piece of adjacent public land so he could add another nine holes to the course. Maybe Trump had a little chuckle about this as he drove over the bridge into West Palm Beach that day, heading to the course, just a chip shot away from the county's Emergency Operations Center. The main opponent to his plan was Theresa LePore, who planned to build a new elections department headquarters on the land. "This came out of the blue," she had complained, warning that Trump could "cause some havoc." But as it turned out, LePore was perfectly capable of creating havoc on her own.

THE DAY BEFORE Thanksgiving, Klain and Boies thought they might be on the verge of winning the election. The state supreme court ruling had bought them more time, and then a decision in Broward County brought them hundreds of votes. Gore's team had been lobbying all three counties to loosen their standards for evaluating ballots. Instead of counting votes only when a chad was partially detached, they wanted the boards to consider thousands of "dimpled" ballots, which had shallower indentations. The Democrats claimed the marks were evidence of thwarted attempts to punch the card. Republicans countered that anything could have caused the scratches. But that Wednesday, before heading home to New York for the holiday, Boies flew to Fort Lauderdale on his Learjet to make Gore's case to the Broward board. It decided to opt for the looser standard. This would end up giving Gore another 567 votes.

Bush was picking up new votes, too. Katherine Harris had made one exception to her otherwise uncompromising adherence to deadlines: for the absentee ballots that were trickling in from overseas. These were mostly from members of the armed forces and were expected to favor Bush. Harris decreed that late ballots from overseas would be counted, even though some seemed to have been mailed after the election or even cast fraudulently. These absentee votes—known as the "Thanksgiving stuffing"—would end up padding Bush's lead a bit, offsetting what he lost in Broward County.

It still looked possible, though, that Gore could end the weekend with a lead. Miami-Dade was finally starting its recount, and it had more disputed ballots than any other county. The initial reports suggested that Gore was picking up votes there, fast. Jim Baker was apoplectic.

"This is the whole ballgame," Baker told one of his lawyers in Miami.

It was time for desperate measures. That Wednesday morning, a Winnebago RV pulled up to the drab concrete plaza adjoining the county government center in downtown Miami. It parked amid the TV news trucks and disgorged a group of men in pleated khakis and baseball caps. They were mostly from Washington, Capitol Hill staffers mobilized by word of mouth and mass emails. "Republicans will be needed," read one, "to keep a watchful eye on the highly selective and subjective hunt for phantom Al Gore votes that is set to begin in Miami-Dade County."

The Bush team had airlifted around seven hundred volunteers into the state and was paying for their food and lodging. "We wanted to get down there and stop the fraud so badly," one foot soldier told a newspaper. There was an "air of mystery" about the operation, the *Wall Street Journal* reported. The volunteers would receive orders on slips of paper pushed under their hotel doors at night. "To tell you the truth," one told the *Journal*, "nobody knows who is calling the shots."

A *Time* correspondent on the scene in Miami poked around, though, and reported the name of the man said to be running things inside the RV: "hardball Washington strategist Roger Stone."

Since Donald Trump had quit his presidential race earlier in the year, Stone had returned to his business as a consultant. His rakish personal eccentricities had made him all but unemployable in the Republican Party of George W. Bush, whom Stone disliked. (Stone criticized Dubya's work ethic after the election, telling the *Times*, "The guy thought he was coasting toward a big win.") But Stone had a long relationship with Jim Baker, who had once helped him out with a New Jersey campaign that his candidate ended up winning in a recount. According to Stone, Baker called in the favor in 2000. "I didn't do it for George Bush," Stone says. "I did it for Baker."

Stone first went to Palm Beach, where he and a local Republican official started a front group called the "Committee to Take Back Our Judiciary," which sent out mailings attacking the state supreme court for trying to "hijack the presidential election for Al Gore." But Stone soon got bored. "Too many chiefs and not enough Indians," he says. "There was really nothing for me to do." So, he says, he called Baker, who redirected him down to Miami. This was around November 20, the day Miami-Dade County started its manual recount. "We need demonstrators," Stone says, summarizing the logic. "Get Stone."

Stone knew Miami. He owned a condo in a building on South Beach and his wife, Nydia, was of Cuban descent. The two of them visited the owner of Radio Mambí and enlisted his support. Stone wanted to create a ruckus outside the county government center. He set up phone banks to spread the word, while Nydia went on the radio.

"Baker understood the theater of all this," Stone says. "That the pickets and the rallies and the signs and the crowds and all of that was important in terms of creating the atmospherics. From the very beginning, Baker understands that it's vitally important to declare victory, and then you're fending off a challenge as opposed to saying, 'Well we're not sure who won, let's find out.'

"Warren Christopher and David Boies," Stone says disdainfully; "they thought this is going to be a high-minded debate about democracy and civil society."

By around 8 a.m., when the count was to restart, a mob of demonstrators had materialized. Some of the Republicans in the Winnebago handed out box lunches containing Cuban sandwiches and signs reading, "Sore Loserman." Another contingent of young conservatives marched inside to observe the recount. Gore was starting the morning with a gain of 157 votes in Miami. There was a distinct possibility that, in a few hours, he would overturn Bush's lead.

A Radio Mambí reporter was on the scene, exhorting listeners to come to the plaza. Between segments, he would walk around with a megaphone, leading chants of *Remember Elián!*

The sound of the outdoor commotion floated upward to the nineteenth floor of the government center, where the three members of the county elections board were sitting in a tabulation room, behind a glass window, reviewing ballots. The atmosphere was growing hostile. By law, both parties had the right to observe the proceedings, but the Republican volunteers were not content simply to watch. They started to agitate to get inside the tabulation room. They were suspicious.

The young conservatives had come to fight subjectivism. As

Republicans, they belonged to the party of rules, the one that was supposed to venerate the authority of the system. But as they watched the board notch vote after vote for Gore, their inhibitions loosened. They banged their clipboards, demanding that the board open up the room. They started to shout and chant:

Let us see the ballots!

Voter fraud! Voter fraud!

The fix is in!

Soon, the elevator doors started to open, bringing in more preppily dressed protesters.

Stop the count! Stop the fraud!

Cheaters! Cheaters!

The young conservatives threw fists in the air and chanted an old antiwar slogan:

The whole world is watching!

The county board members, looking rattled, soon announced they were adjourning for a brief break. It was at this time that two Cuban American politicians, veterans of the Elián uprisings, came upstairs with a rowdy Spanish-speaking group. Someone said that a thousand Cubans were ready to storm the building. A local Democratic Party leader who had come upstairs to take care of some innocent business was spotted by the Republicans and accused of trying to steal votes.

"Thief! Thief!" the Republicans shouted as they chased him down the hall.

Outside on the plaza, the atmosphere was even more volatile. Some of the Cubans were talking about burning tires and overturning cars. A Democratic congresswoman, who was Black, was roughed up as she tried to give a television interview. She had to be rescued by police.

The county board disappeared for a few hours. Then, at around 1 p.m., it reconvened and voted to end Miami's recount. The board cited time constraints, but no one believed that.

"They'd been living in Miami during the seven-month siege of Elián Gonzalez," wrote the *Palm Beach Post* columnist Frank Cerabino. "They'd seen how [an] incoherent mob mentality was immune to the rule of law. . . . And the court of last resort became Miami's Spanish-language talk radio stations, which could be counted on to pick the scabs of reason to smithereens. Counting was redefined as fraud."

As the years passed, the role of the local Cuban contingent would be forgotten. The incident would go down in history as the "Brooks Brothers Riot." "They were rigging the system," says Bradley Blakeman, one of the Republican staffers in the Winnebago. "I said, 'Let's do what Democrats do. Let's do civil disobedience.'" It proved to be a key turning point: the moment that the Republicans showed they would do anything to stop Gore from pulling ahead in the count. "We scared the shit out of them," Blakeman says. "We scared the *shit* out of them."

Stone's exact degree of involvement in the unrest remains disputed. The way he tells the story, he was inside the Winnebago, communicating with the volunteers on the nineteenth floor via a walkie-talkie. Blakeman claims *he* was the engineer and that Stone was nowhere to be seen. For his part, Jim Baker has publicly stated that he does not remember enlisting Stone, though he admitted it was possible. Three other Republicans who were involved in the recount effort, however, clearly remember Stone playing an instigating role. "At the time," says Al Cárdenas, a lawyer who helped coordinate the Bush operation as the chairman of the Florida Republican Party, "I thought, 'Who is going to stop Roger Stone from doing something? He's incorrigible.'"

In the moment, Stone's activities in Miami were widely reported, accepted, and even celebrated.

"He is the only living American who actually wears a gold pinky ring in the shape of a horseshoe—I love him," Tucker Carlson said on his CNN talk show, *The Spin Room*, on November 27. "I must say this is so above what I expect of Republicans. I'm really impressed. . . . This is the sort of thing Democrats do pretty well. And I'm surprised the GOP has finally come around with—no surprise—the help of Roger Stone. Amen. Good work, Roger."

The next morning, Carlson received a phone call from Stone, who left a voice mail thanking him for his "warm remarks."

DAVID BOIES WAS in the air, en route to Westchester County, when he received word that Miami was shutting down its recount. When he landed, Gore called and asked him to return to Florida on Thanksgiving. The following afternoon, Boies took a packed turkey supper on his Learjet and flew down to Tallahassee. He brought along a reporter who was writing his biography, to record the moment for posterity. He and Gore discussed their options over the phone during the plane ride. They had appealed to the Florida Supreme Court, asking it to order Miami to restart its recount, but in a one-paragraph opinion, the court had denied them. The Gore legal team had denounced the "riotous and violent mob behavior," but moral outrage did not alter the hard math.

Without Miami, Gore was going to need more votes out of Palm Beach. He wanted Boies to fly to Palm Beach County. It had nearly 7,000 dimpled ballots, a large stash of potential votes for Gore, but thus far, its board had refused to loosen its strict standard.

"So I go down and sprinkle a little fairy dust," Boies said, exasperated, after hanging up the call.

A subsequent analysis by the *Palm Beach Post* would find that had those 7,000 ballots been counted the way the Democrats advocated, Gore would have picked up an additional 784 votes, enough to give him a lead at the deadline. But when the Democrats sued, their cases went before a county judge who was the former head of Palm Beach's Cuban American Republican Club. Boies thought the Palm Beach case was a loser. He was a gambler, not a magician.

Gore was like a cardplayer who kept drawing to an inside straight. *Palm Beach, Palm Beach . . . come on Palm Beach.* Boies believed his client was hurting himself by passing up other options. For instance, there were a number of lawsuits brought by private parties that were seeking to throw out thousands of Republican absentee ballots based on technical mistakes. Gore didn't want to back those cases because it would compromise his call to count every vote. He had also ruled out making any effort to overturn the result in the Electoral College by attempting to woo a few "faithless electors," even though Gore, as the undisputed winner of the popular vote, could reasonably claim he had a democratic mandate.

"If this were simply up to me as a lawyer," Boies said, "I wouldn't give up anything." But Gore was always reassessing, wondering how far to press his case. He wanted to be president. "He was not, however, prepared to sacrifice principle to win," Boies later wrote; "there were simply certain means that the end of winning the presidency did not, in his mind, justify."

Gore felt that he was a victim of a grave injustice. He was mounting a personal investigation of the shutdown in Miami, working with a team of Democratic researchers to confirm that many of the rioters worked for Republican congressmen. But he was extremely sensitive to the criticism that he was playing the spoiler, attempting to undermine the legitimacy of the president. Jim Baker was calling his refusal to concede "a black mark on our democracy." Although there was never much evidence that rank-and-file Gore voters felt the same way—they just wanted to win—some Democratic leaders in Washington had been undermining his case in the press, anonymously suggesting that it was time to give up. The *New York Times*, the nation's fountainhead of conventional wisdom, had even tried to give Gore a deadline. "Another week and no more," Washington correspondent R. W. Apple declared in the lead sentence to a front-page article five days after the election.

Over Thanksgiving weekend, the Republicans sent protesters to rally outside the vice president's mansion, chanting, *Get out of Cheney's house!* One visitor to the residence anonymously told the press that Gore seemed like "a lost soul."

"When does it end?" Tipper asked a dinner guest that weekend. "When do we end it?"

The Republicans never asked themselves such questions. On Thanksgiving, the Brooks Brothers rioters celebrated with a Vegas-style banquet at a hotel in Fort Lauderdale; Wayne Newton sang a rendition of "Danke Schoen." From his ranch in Crawford, Bush called in to congratulate them. So did Cheney, from his sickbed. (In the midst of all the other chaos that Wednesday, he had suffered a mild heart attack.) Meanwhile, at the Governor's Mansion in Tallahassee, Jeb was passing his wife's chipotle stuffing to his general counsel, whom he had detailed to work on the recount effort. That day, the governor had called the leader of the state senate to discuss a backup plan: calling a special session of the state legislature to directly appoint Bush electors. Some Republican hard-liners were pushing the idea.

Jeb was uneasy about the legislative option, a view shared by some of his brother's advisers. ("It didn't sound like . . . a comfortable place for the country to land," a Bush campaign official later said, to "throw out everybody's vote and let the president's brother decide.") Bush still had another line of defense. Decrying the "circus" in Florida, his legal team had just filed an emergency appeal of their federal lawsuit to the U.S. Supreme Court. But no one on either side seriously thought that the justices would intervene in the state dispute at this juncture.

"The U.S. Supreme Court is irrelevant," Boies told his biographer on the plane. "Nobody is worried about that." To him, the immediate threat was the deadline set by the state supreme court to finish the recounts, which would pass at the end of the weekend. George W. Bush was likely to still be ahead, which meant that Katherine Harris could finally certify Bush as the winner. Then Gore would have to decide whether to concede or to continue his struggle.

After Boies landed, he hurried to a strategy session to consider Gore's final option: filing a lawsuit in state court to contest the result. It would be an unprecedented move: suing to overturn the declared outcome of a presidential election. The nation was veering into the unimaginable.

If Boies had happened to cast a glance around the airfield in his rush, he might have seen a little two-seat Cessna carrying a pilot and a passenger. At 3:57 p.m., Mohamed Atta and Marwan al-Shehhi paid thirty-three dollars for a tank of gas and continued on their path south, back to Venice.

27

Fort Lauderdale

On the morning of Thursday, November 9, two days after the election, an ominous cloud appeared over the town of Venice, Florida. Hundreds of people witnessed it, and someone took a photograph and alerted the local paper, the *Gondolier*. The cloud was black at the rim, with two white semicircular forms in the middle, punctured by a dark oval. It looked like a giant eye to some, the paper wrote; to others, "a sign of pending doom." A reporter called up a TV weatherman, who said the most likely cause of the strange puncture mark was "an airplane."

Ziad Jarrah took off that morning from the municipal airport, flying a single-engine Piper Cherokee. He was becoming more confident at the controls. He had learned the art of pilotage, navigating by dead reckoning and visual reference to landmarks. He was thinking about airspeed, heading, track, drift angle, charting the crosswind component. He knew the factors used to plot his direction: true heading, variation, magnetic heading, deviation, compass heading. The technical terms, flight instructors sometimes told students, could be recalled by using a salty mnemonic: True Virgins Make Dull Companions. So, now Jarrah knew where he was headed.

The men from Hamburg had reached the last stage of their

commercial pilot training program. They were now skilled enough to fly by themselves on longer trips, and they spent that November crisscrossing the peninsula of Florida, passing serenely over the turmoil of the recount. The FAA required students to complete a number of these "cross-country" trips, defined as flights of more than fifty nautical miles, in order to earn their commercial licenses. Jarrah and his classmates were flying almost every day now, venturing farther, enjoying their time aloft. One weekend, he and a couple of roommates took a jaunt to the Bahamas in a school plane.

In October, Jarrah had spent almost three weeks in Europe, and some fellow students thought he might be dropping out. But then he had returned to Florida with an aura of purpose. He was now staying in an apartment right next to the airfield, with a coed group of young Germans. He was a quiet roommate, decent and courteous, but the others sometimes overheard him fighting on the phone with his girlfriend back in Germany. Once again, Aysel felt he was pulling away.

"I'm angry that you don't think about me," she wrote in a plaintive missive to Ziad after their trip to Paris. "I wait for a message here and have to think about you all the time. Can you think about me once and try to pretend to be me? You're taking so many risks and I know a lot even though you don't tell it. It's no surprise that I'm afraid for you, right? I love you."

"I'm sorry," Ziad replied in an email. "I did get your letter and I found it super sweet. And full of understanding and compassion. It's not about trust. I love you, Aysel, and don't worry."

Aysel thought he was cheating on her, and in a way, she was right. Jarrah's roommates found him to be secretive, always guarded about his activities. At one point, he rented himself another apartment, but he never fully moved into it, instead crashing on the couch at his old place. One roommate would later theorize that perhaps this other apartment was a meeting place. But none of Jarrah's behaviors raised serious suspicion. He expressed some casual negativity about the United States, but so did many other foreign students. The only complaint classmates voiced was about Jarrah's flying. Some of them thought he was too intense, didn't share the controls.

The planes operation was progressing well, as if it really were blessed. For a while, it seemed as if Ramzi bin al-Shibh's inability to get approval for a U.S. visa would be a major setback. But in mid-2000, a Saudi named Hani Hanjour showed up at an Al Qaeda training camp in Afghanistan. Hanjour put down on an intake form that he had trained as a pilot in the United States. He was quickly pulled aside and recruited into the planes operation. By early December, the fourth pilot was on the West Coast, where he linked up with one of the Saudis who had arrived in California earlier in the year. He went to Arizona to freshen up his skills at his old flight school.

Jarrah, meanwhile, was learning how to navigate a small plane over long distances solely by its instruments, rather than by sight. This could be done using a system of high-frequency ground transmitters called VORs. (The acronym stood for "very-high-frequency omnidirectional range.") The radio transmitters basically created invisible roads in the sky. To navigate, Jarrah would set his plane's navigational radio to a specific VOR station on his flight map. Then he would fly his plane toward the signal, making sure to watch the deviation needle, to correct his direction when the wind pushed him off course. Once he reached the station, Jarrah would program in the next VOR on his route, repeating the process until he reached his destination. Once he mastered the system, he could guide a plane anywhere.

On November 19, Jarrah set out on a two-day training flight

with an instructor from his school. Their blue-and-yellow propeller plane flew to Tallahassee, where the lawyers were arguing; and then headed east, passing over White Springs, where Chuck Harder was broadcasting; and Jacksonville, where no one was counting votes. They landed in St. Augustine, the oldest city in the United States, and spent the night at a motel. The next afternoon, they flew down the Atlantic coast, flying blind through the clouds, the windshield picking up fine droplets of mist—what pilots call "baby rain." He came in to land at Palm Beach International Airport.

At major airports, private planes do not use the passenger terminals but, rather, smaller facilities known as fixed-based operators, or FBOs. In Palm Beach, the FBO was positioned on a major road at the airport's southern edge. The spot was easy to recognize on the weekends in the colder months because there would usually be a Boeing 727 parked there with the name "TRUMP" on its fuselage. Across the street stood the county's Emergency Operations Center, where, at that moment, protesters and the media were massed and where poor Theresa LePore was peering at ballots under watchful eyes. Jarrah gassed up and flew on to his next stop, Fort Lauderdale.

THE DAY AFTER Thanksgiving, Mike Malik talked to his arms suppliers down in West Palm Beach and let them know he had returned from his business trip to London and Hong Kong. He said he was on his own now, working independently from his partner R. G. Abbas, who was still bogged down in his endless negotiations with the Pakistani military. These new "private" buyers were ready to move on a deal for the "sugar" and the "water stuff," by which Malik meant Stinger missiles and heavy water. He had assured the buyers that Randy Glass and Ray Spears were "trustworthy." The last obstacle, Malik said, was getting the money to Florida. U.S. law enforcement watched for suspicious wire transfers from abroad, and the buyers were sending a huge sum: $32 million. Dick Stoltz, the undercover agent posing as Spears, asked Malik if his buyers in Dubai really had that kind of money. Malik laughed.

After almost two years, it appeared that Operation Sphinx had finally landed a serious customer.

On December 8, Malik flew down to Fort Lauderdale, bringing a bottle of Tanqueray gin as a present for Ray Spears. The undercover agent had set up a sham company to process the transaction. He and Malik opened a joint corporate bank account. They went over the complicated logistics of the deal. First, Spears would fill a shipping container with an initial load of Stingers and night-vision goggles. Once the $32 million reached the joint account in Florida, the cargo would be put onto a ship, and after it left port, Malik would authorize the transfer of $2 million to Spears to complete the first sale. The rest of the money would be held for subsequent purchases of weapons and heavy water. Malik said that wealthy Saudis were providing the financing and that the first weapons shipment was bound for Kashmir.

The buyers were paying a $200,000 bribe to a bank official in Dubai to handle the wire transfer at its origin, Malik said, and they were dispatching a representative to finalize the sale. The money-man would be coming to Fort Lauderdale in a few weeks.

THE DOT-COM BOOM reached its apex on March 10, 2000. The day before, a Thursday, the NASDAQ stock index had crossed the 5,000-point threshold for the first time; and that Friday, it set another record, closing at 5,048.64. Then the market collapsed. During one week in April, the NASDAQ plunged by 25 percent, causing a brief panic. While the rest of the stock market soon stabilized, the tech sector was devastated. Dot-coms started to die off like creatures caught in an extinction event. Over Memorial Day weekend, an anonymous programmer created a website, a spoof of the breathless business publication *Fast Company*, called FuckedCompany.com. The site offered crowdsourced "happy fun slander" on all the latest dot-com casualties.

"DOT'S ALL, FOLKS," read a headline on the cover of *New York* magazine. "The dot-com gold rush is over," wrote Jim Cramer, a financier and the founder of TheStreet.com. "It was just this moment, this crazy wild moment where the glee of the individual investor, the love of the Net . . . and the democratization of Wall Street all coalesced into eighteen months of capitalism sans rigor." Start-ups that did not generate profits would not be able to survive for long. "The crash you heard," Cramer wrote, "was all the doors slamming shut on any more financing."

Kevin Ingram was on the wrong side of the doors. By the end of 2000, his internet start-up, TruMarkets, had burned through roughly $30 million in venture capital. He had plowed his savings into the company. Now it was running out of money. TruMarkets had convinced some major financial firms to use its bond-trading platform, but the technology was still buggy. Its launch date, originally scheduled for July, was pushed back to the fall and then to early 2001.

Ingram was convinced that TruMarkets still had a sound concept, but the dot-com crash made it impossible to raise any more venture capital. As the company failed, its investors replaced Ingram with a new chief executive, who began negotiating to sell the start-up to a competitor financed by a consortium of investment banks. Ingram thought they were trying to buy his technology so they could smother it in the cradle. "We were at the brink of making it a reality," he says. "That was basically the Death Star for Wall Street." TruMarkets had many competitors, but whoever managed to make it through the crash alive would have the bond market to themselves. (In fact, one of TruMarkets's rivals would later grow into a company worth many billions of dollars.)

Ingram says he was desperate to save TruMarkets. But that would take money, and he was broke.

"I was reaching for straws," he says. "One of those straws ended up being in Florida."

A FEW WEEKS after his trip to Fort Lauderdale, Mike Malik returned, as promised, with his "key guy." The visitor said his name was "Abdul."

Dick Stoltz introduced himself as Ray Spears.

Abdul was Pakistani. He had a gaunt face, a mustache, and hooded eyes. "This guy was scary-looking," Stoltz recalls. "He kind of had a Count Dracula look to him. Very serious. I could tell this guy was the real deal." From the airport, Stoltz drove the Pakistanis to a restaurant to have Sunday brunch. Abdul spoke little, but Malik was more talkative. He stressed that Abdul was not representing any government and disclosed that his group intended to sell the weapons on the black market to militant Islamists in various countries, including India, Russia, and Somalia. Stoltz took the two men to the Doubletree Hotel, where they were staying. They went up to the room to discuss the deal. Stoltz assured Abdul that he had come to the right place—that no one else could procure Stingers. Malik told him that Abdul was also "the heavy water guy."

Over the next week, there was a series of meetings and phone calls, all of which were monitored by a law enforcement surveillance team that had set up in an adjoining hotel room and included

386 | THE YEAR THAT BROKE AMERICA

a Punjabi interpreter. At an early point in the discussions, Abdul made a call on his cell phone and, in Punjabi, told an unknown party to come to Florida. Malik said that two other men were on their way down from New York to assist in the transaction.

The feds had another surveillance team staking out the Fort Lauderdale airport. Agents watched as a pair of South Asian males got off a flight from Newark and rented a large van. That night, a surveillance team observed Abdul slipping away from the Double-tree Hotel for a furtive meeting with the two unidentified men in the rental van. The federal agents speculated that instead of shipping the Stingers by sea, the buyers now planned to take them someplace by road.

They were all just waiting for the money. Abdul placed another call and told the person on the other end of the line that his men were in place and that he was ready to take possession of the merchandise. A U.S. intelligence agency, which was watching the financial wires, confirmed that a $32 million transfer had been initiated in Dubai.

A bank transaction that large would take some time to clear. But the next day came, and the $32 million still had not arrived at the bank in Boca Raton. It seemed there was some kind of problem with the wire transfer. "We know it's not bullshit," recalls another ATF agent who worked the case, "because when they're on the cell phone they're yelling [in Punjabi] to someone else, saying, 'Hey, where's the frickin' money?'" This went on for days, with the Pakistanis remaining holed up in their hotel room, expressing exasperation in various languages.

The federal investigators determined that whoever was wiring the money from Dubai was making a deliberate error, a technique that black marketeers sometimes used to allow them to call back a payment in the event that they were double-crossed. Stoltz was frustrated. Without a completed sale, all federal prosecutors would have was a lot of conspiratorial talk, not an arms deal. "I get it— they were looking at the criminal case," Stoltz says. "You know how it is: everyone wants the guns and the drugs and the cash on a big table for a press conference."

What they needed was someone who could move money. Of course, Glass and Stoltz already knew one such person: Kevin Ingram. But Stoltz was hesitant to call him. Based on Ingram's previous caution, the ATF agent thought he would never get involved with the Pakistanis. So, the back-and-forth continued. Abdul flew all the way back to the Middle East to try to sort out the wire transfer and then returned to Fort Lauderdale. This time, he said that the money was coming through a different channel, Deutsche Bank. But once again, the payment never arrived.

Stoltz was upset, wondering why his superiors did not just round up the whole group right then. "This is the thing that bothers me, and haunts me," he said much later. "Set aside the criminal case— find out who the hell these people are and why they are in South Florida."

But there was no rush. It would be another six months before Kevin Ingram, grasping at straws, picked up the call that drew him back to Florida. By then, it was the summer of 2001.

28

Bush v. Gore

John Paul Stevens, the eldest justice on the U.S. Supreme Court, owned a condo down in Fort Lauderdale, and he saw no reason to stick around Washington for Thanksgiving. George W. Bush could appeal all he wanted, but the Constitution seemed to speak clearly: it was up to the states to decide how to select their electors, and that meant there was no role for the federal courts in Florida. Stevens was a Republican, but as the Court had moved rightward during his tenure, he had become part of a four-member liberal minority. Time and again, he had watched the more conservative justices argue for the principles of federalism and deference to state law.

What's more, Stevens knew that, despite their ideological differences, his colleagues all shared a reverence for the institutional authority of the Supreme Court. It "seemed implausible," Stevens later reflected, "that the Court would wager the vast amounts of its hard-earned institutional capital to wade into a bitter partisan dispute over the identity of the next president." But over Thanksgiving weekend, one of the justice's clerks reached him by phone as he was playing a round of golf. The clerk said the conservatives on the Court were circulating a memo arguing for immediate action on Bush's appeal. They were ready to plunge into Florida.

The following Friday, the fight for the presidency reached the highest court in the land, a grandiose columned chamber topped by marble friezes depicting great lawgivers from history and scripture. "Oyez! Oyez! Oyez!" the grand marshal shouted, uttering the ritual incantation. The gallery sprang to its feet. There stood the top advisers to Bush and Gore. There stood Senators John Kerry and John Edwards, the Democrats who would run the next time. There stood TV talkers Ted Koppel and George Will. There stood the four Gore children. There stood Senator Ted Kennedy, right next to conservative commentator Barbara Olson.

On the other side of a brass railing, Olson's husband, Ted, took in the tableau and thought to himself, "This is never going to happen like this again." In fact, this would be only round one.

Chief Justice William Rehnquist took a seat at the center of the curved mahogany bench and glowered through his clunky square glasses. "We'll hear argument this morning in number 00-836," he said, brusquely. "George W. Bush v. the Palm Beach County Canvassing Board."

Olson started to make his case. Bush's side claimed that the Democrat-aligned state supreme court had overstepped its authority, arbitrarily reinterpreting the laws governing the recount and stretching its deadlines after the election had been held. Effectively, Olson argued, the referee was changing the rules of the game after the final buzzer. The state court was aggravating the "controversy, dispute and chaos that's been taking place in Florida," Olson said. He called for the justices to restore order. As was their custom, they almost immediately interrupted him.

"I suppose we normally would leave it alone, where the state supreme court found it," said Justice Sandra Day O'Connor, a Reagan appointee who had a moderate voting record.

"We are looking for a federal issue," said Justice Anthony Kennedy, the other swing vote.

The three other members of the conservative majority were less reserved.

When Olson finished, Professor Laurence Tribe rose to speak for Gore. Tribe was an eminent legal figure: a liberal scholar-advocate who was arguing his thirtieth case before the Court. He had a prodigious, almost empathic understanding of the Constitution, which he saw as an ever-evolving document. He was an intellectual archenemy of Justice Antonin Scalia, an originalist who believed the Constitution had to be interpreted in accordance with the intent of the long-dead men who wrote it.

Scalia and Rehnquist immediately tried to knock Tribe off stride, posing skeptical questions that reached back to an obscure nineteenth-century decision for precedent. Scalia suggested that the Florida court had grounded its decision on the right to vote. "That is a real problem, it seems to me," he said, because according to Article II of the U.S. Constitution, it was the state *legislature* that had final say over the awarding of electors. "In fact, there is no right of suffrage under Article Two," Scalia said. The Constitution did not require a state to appoint its electors based on the popular vote, and in the early days of the republic, it was common for state legislatures to appoint electors. It had been generations since that had happened, but Scalia appeared to be opening the door for the Florida legislature to overrule the results of the recount.

In fact, Republicans in Florida were already moving legislation to directly appoint a slate of Bush electors. Jeb Bush ultimately overcame his reservations and endorsed the move. "I can't recuse myself from my constitutional duties as governor of the state, and I can't recuse myself, frankly, of being my brother's brother, either," he told reporters. "I know the Gore campaign would love for me to basically disown my family, but I'm going to do what's right."

Tribe tried to speak to the other justices, saying that it was most important to interpret the recount rules "in the light not only of the literal language but of the fact that they are dealing with something very important, the franchise, that disenfranchising people, which is what this is all about, disenfranchising people isn't very nice."

Justice Stevens looked on, worried that the argument was heading in the wrong direction. He could count five votes for Bush.

OUTSIDE THE BUILDING, the argument over the right to vote took a more visceral form. The Reverend Jesse Jackson and leaders of the Congressional Black Caucus were marching from the Justice Department's headquarters to the Supreme Court to draw attention to allegations of voter suppression. Jackson locked arms with the Georgia congressman John Lewis, a fellow veteran of the civil rights movement. Protesters chanted, *G-W-B. How many votes did you steal from me?*

Gore's objections be damned, Jackson was continuing to travel all over Florida, leveling allegations of systemic racial bias. He was focused on Jacksonville and was preparing to file a lawsuit over the election in Duval County. The morning of the Supreme Court argument, he had an unpublicized "drop by" meeting with Janet Reno and some of her deputies at Main Justice, where he demanded a voting rights investigation.

The attorney general had tried mightily to avoid becoming entangled in the electoral controversy in her home state. As the rest of Washington sat riveted on Election Night, Reno had gone to bed early, learning the outcome only when she awoke, as usual, at around 5 a.m. "I want to be very careful that we don't do anything that politicizes what is a very important moment in American history," she told the press corps when allegations of voting rights violations first arose, saying, "I get damned if I do and damned if I don't." But as the days passed, Reno appears to have grown more seriously concerned. The day after Jackson's visit, she traveled to Jacksonville to speak to a group of law students. She said nothing publicly about the election, telling the students she was looking forward to leaving office in a few weeks, so she could "sit on my front porch, watch the peacocks go by, just take off my shoes and wiggle a little bit."

After her public appearance, Reno paid an unannounced visit to the FBI field office in Jacksonville, where she met with agents and prosecutors. Within days, the Justice Department disclosed that its Civil Rights Division had opened an inquiry into the election in Florida.

"WELCOME BACK TO *Crossfire*," said Jake Tapper, the young Washington correspondent for the website Salon.com, who was sitting in as host the night of the Supreme Court argument. "In the Governor's Mansion in Austin right now, Governor George W. Bush is hosting a Christmas party, enjoying a delicious meal of arugula and fennel salad and Gulf Coast blue crab cakes with jalapeño tartar sauce. But here in Washington, we're chewing over today's Supreme Court case with Bush supporter and former assistant U.S. attorney Barbara Olson . . ."

Olson had returned from Tallahassee to see the argument and reinforce the case on television.

"Let me tell you something," Tapper said. "Something that you and Mr. Olson have been talking about, you're active in a group called the Federalist Society, and it is states' rights this and states' rights that. . . . Now the Florida Supreme Court makes a decision that you guys don't like, and all of a sudden, 'States' rights? Forget about states' rights.' What happened?"

"No, I think the argument today was perfectly consistent," Barbara Olson replied, smoothly denying the contradiction. The Supreme Court was simply stepping in, she said, to stop Al Gore and the out-of-control Florida courts from throwing out the verdict of the valid ballots. "They have been counted," Olson said.

"They haven't been hand-counted," Tapper replied.

"They have not been hand-counted, they have not been foot-counted," Olson shot back sarcastically. "They have been *counted*, and they have been objectively counted."

MEANWHILE, KATHERINE HARRIS had made her less-than-objective final tally. As soon as the recount deadline passed, at 5 p.m. on November 26, she certified that George W. Bush was the winner in Florida, setting the official margin: 537 votes. Her reckoning left out all the votes from Miami's suspended recount and another 192 that the county board in Palm Beach had awarded to Gore. Theresa LePore and company had missed the deadline to complete the recount, submitting their count a few hours late, and Harris had declared that the rules were the rules. Her tabulation was complete. Later on, when Democrats got low and dispirited, calculating how America had veered off course, they would keep coming up with that number: 537.

As Washington waited to see how the Supreme Court would rule, Gore's lawyers in Florida were continuing to fight in state court, suing to overturn the official certification. "Ignoring votes means ignoring democracy itself," Gore said in a televised speech from his residence, blaming "organized intimidation" of the county boards for their failure to complete the recount. By federal law, Florida's electoral slate needed to be sent to Washington by December 12, meaning that this second phase of the legal battle would have to be completed within just two weeks.

The first step would be a trial in Tallahassee. LePore had her employees pack 166 gray metal boxes containing 462,644 ballots into a rented Ryder truck and said good riddance to the election. "Whatever the court wants, they can have," she said as the yellow truck pulled away. With that, LePore's catastrophic Election Day finally came to an end, and the ballots were moved into evidence. For the trip up the Florida Turnpike, the rental truck was surrounded by a squadron of media vehicles and tracked from above by four TV news helicopters. Inevitably, the scene brought to mind the O.J. Simpson chase, although O.J. himself rejected the comparison. "This is boring!" the Miami resident told the Associated Press as he followed the procession on TV. Watching at his ranch, though, Governor Bush was riveted. If some Democrat judge decided to start looking at all those ballots with a lenient eye, he told his lawyers, there was going to be hell to pay.

It turned out that Bush didn't need to worry. The state court case was assigned by lottery to a judge who was certain to be friendly to the Republicans. (When his name was pulled, one of Gore's local lawyers muttered to the others, "Redneck.") The Gore lawyers convened for a session with David Boies, wondering how he was going to try to pull off the impossible at trial.

"My strategy is to lose quickly," Boies said.

He succeeded. After a two-day trial, held over the weekend of December 2, the judge issued a decision that sided with Bush on every point.

"They won. We lost. We're appealing," Boies told the press outside the courtroom.

The same day, the U.S. Supreme Court handed down a unanimous decision in the case it had heard the week before. It deferred judgment, asking the Florida Supreme Court for clarification about the legal grounds for its decision to allow the recounts. But the whole constitutional argument would end up being moot, anyway, if Boies could not get the trial verdict overturned. He had just two days to prepare for the appeal to the Florida Supreme Court. He planned to make a simple case. The trial judge had gone to the trouble of trucking all the disputed ballots up to Tallahassee—a second shipment had come from Miami, too—and then he had not even bothered to examine them. The ballots were evidence, Boies told the state supreme court. Why not look and see what they said?

At the oral argument, some of the Florida judges pressed Boies to specify exactly how many potential votes were in dispute. Why was Gore asking the courts to look only at Miami and Palm Beach and not at all the roughly 64,000 "undervote" ballots statewide? The next day, by a vote of 4 to 3, the court ordered a manual recount of all the undervotes in Florida. The majority opinion found that the law "expressly recognized the will of the people of Florida as the guiding principle." It directed that the recount would begin the next day, across the entire state, with officials to count any ballot that bore a "clear indication of the intent of the voter."

Once again, Florida was counting.

In Washington, Al Gore was euphoric. It was a Friday, so he asked the Liebermans to come and celebrate Shabbat dinner. Donna Brazile and some of the campaign staff were invited, too. There was a roaring fire, and they sat around a big table in the dining room, which Gore had been using as his command center. Brazile said a prayer from the Book of Psalms that the Reverend Jackson had given to her. "Weeping may endure for a night," she said, "but joy cometh in the morning."

Across town at Main Justice, Janet Reno was having her annual office holiday party. When the decision came down, the Democrats in the building erupted in cheers. An aide ran up to Reno at the buffet table to tell her Gore might win. She popped a grape in her mouth and said nothing.

AT THE GOP headquarters in Tallahassee, the ruling came as a stunning setback. "I felt like those Russian sailors on the *Kursk* must have felt," said John Bolton, referring to a submarine disaster earlier that year. "All you could do is stand by and feel your air run out."

Dubya had been certain the court would seal his victory, and he told Karl Rove that the decision felt like a punch to the solar plexus. He sent Jim Baker out to make a statement. "It is sad for Florida," Baker said. "It is sad for the nation. And it is sad for our democracy." But by this point Bush had dropped any pretense of delegation, becoming "fully engaged," as he described it, in the political combat. ("I've got a lot of Lyndon Johnson in me, I guess," he said afterward.) He signaled to his brother and his allies in the Florida legislature that it was time to press forward with their failsafe option, directly appointing a slate of electors. If Florida sent two competing slates to Washington, the dispute over its electoral votes would be thrown to the U.S. House of Representatives, where Republicans held a majority. "This judicial aggression must not stand," declared Tom DeLay, the most powerful Republican in the House.

Bush also directed Ted Olson to return to the U.S. Supreme Court. Olson filed an appeal, along with an emergency petition for a stay of enforcement, a legal action that would freeze the implementation of the state court's order to begin a statewide recount. To win a stay, Bush would have to prove that conducting the recount while he waited for a U.S. Supreme Court hearing threatened him "irreparable harm." Olson's brief argued that the harm to Bush was that he might fall behind, an outcome that would be "incurable in the public consciousness."

The new federal case would carry a straightforward legal caption: *Bush v. Gore.*

ON THE MORNING of Saturday, December 9, inside a public library in Tallahassee, a group of eight state judges gathered to review 9,000 disputed ballots from precincts in Miami. The judges, working in groups of two, overseen by party observers who were forbidden from speaking, started to open envelopes filled with ballots. They would look at them, confer, and drop them in boxes: one for Bush, one for Gore, and another for ballots the counters couldn't agree on, which the top judge would review.

Working without interruption and legal objections at last, the counters were able to plow through the disputed ballots at a pace of about 1,000 an hour.

Similar scenes were unfolding in most of the sixty-seven counties in Florida. After thirty-two days of litigation and delay, they were making quick work, finding a vote here for Bush, a couple of votes there for Gore—a hail of pebbles, not a landslide. Nonetheless, Ron Klain was allowing himself to think that Gore might become president after all. Sitting in the law office in Tallahassee that had served as the Gore team's headquarters, he was hearing preliminary counts from across the state. By mid-afternoon, Klain guesstimated that Gore had gained around 58 votes.

A little before 3 p.m., Klain was on the phone with Gore, sharing the positive reports, when a call came in on another line. It was bad news: the U.S. Supreme Court had agreed to hear the case of

Bush v. Gore. Even more dire, by a 5-to-4 vote, it had granted the emergency stay.

By the order of the nation's highest court, Florida was no longer counting.

David Boies was eating a burger and fries at the sports bar with a big-shot investigative reporter from *Newsweek* when the news flash appeared on the bar's TV screen.

"There's no irreparable harm!" Boies shouted in disbelief. He would soon learn that in a rare move, Scalia had gone so far as to write an opinion explaining the order to halt the recount. It said that Bush had a "substantial probability of success" in his appeal and that, therefore, the recount could damage him "by casting a cloud upon what he claims to be the legitimacy of his election."

Bush received word of the Supreme Court's intervention while driving around his ranch with a reporter and an editor from *Time*. "That's great news," he said into his cell phone. Simultaneously, all over Florida, the process was grinding to a halt, and the Republicans staked out at the county offices where ballots were being counted were breaking into celebrations. John Bolton barged into the counting room at the public library where the Miami ballots were being reviewed. The judges were almost halfway done.

"I'm with the Bush-Cheney team," Bolton bellowed, "and I'm here to stop the count!"

That afternoon, Gore was supposed to be trimming his Christmas tree with his family for the benefit of news cameras, but he abruptly canceled the photo opportunity. He tried to remain hopeful. He could not believe that five conservatives were really going to ignore the doctrine of state sovereignty to overrule Florida's courts and override its voters. His advisers were less optimistic. "Forget it," one of them said. "Five Republicans. We're going right in the tank."

Gore picked up his favorite new technological gizmo, the Black-

Berry, which he used to send out emails under a pseudonym, "Robert Stone." The vice president tapped out a message to staffers: "Please make sure that no one trashes the Supreme Court."

AS MUCH AS outsiders might try to divine the entrails of the Supreme Court's thinking, parsing the signals it sent via asides and footnotes, few really had much sense of its opaque inner workings. The first argument had been inconclusive, and Gore thought he might still be able to persuade one of the moderate justices. In truth, he never stood much of a chance.

No one knew it at the time, but Justice O'Connor was preoccupied with her husband's health. He had recently been given an Alzheimer's diagnosis, and she spent part of Election Day talking to his doctor. O'Connor wanted to retire, and as a loyal Republican, she did not want to be replaced by a Democrat. There were rumors around Washington—soon to be reported in *Newsweek*—that at an Election Night party, when the networks called Florida for Gore, she had exclaimed, "This is terrible!" Now she just wanted it finished. She was aghast at the legal chaos. She was determined to stop Gore and was only groping for a justification.

Scalia, Rehnquist, and Thomas were prepared to deliver summary justice, deciding the case without even a hearing. This left one hope for Gore: Justice Kennedy. He occasionally voted with the four liberals. He liked it that he was seen as an independent thinker. He could be self-important, was apt to agonize and ruminate. The Court's law clerks had nicknamed him "Flipper."

Larry Tribe, the Harvard constitutional scholar, knew the Court and the justices' minds about as well as any outsider, and he had a long history and a strong intellectual rapport with Kennedy. Tribe believed he had a shot to flip him. But Gore had decided to make a change. The Harvard professor was off the case. He wanted Boies, his Florida man, to make the final argument.

The following morning, Boies woke up early to appear on four Sunday television talk shows from his home study in New York, offering the opposing lawyers a helpful preview. Then he headed to the local airport, carrying legal briefs and a duffel bag containing one of his signature cheap blue suits, a blue pinstriped shirt, a blue knit tie, and a box of sourdough pretzels. A little before 10:30, Boies boarded his jet, accompanied by his biographer, for the flight to Washington.

"Well, I have twenty-four hours," he said as the plane prepared for takeoff.

"To do what?" his biographer asked.

"To learn the constitutional law," he replied.

When Boies arrived, he went straight to the Watergate complex. Tribe had set up there in a hotel suite to ready himself for the argument, but the evening before, an emissary had come to deliver the news that Gore had opted for Boies. The professor gave the trial lawyer a constitutional crash course. Tribe was particularly concerned with Bush's argument that the recount violated the Equal Protection Clause. Bush had made this claim in his first federal lawsuit, and it had been rejected by lower courts, but Tribe thought it might prove to be important to Kennedy. Boies absorbed the information quickly and, after a few hours, went back to his hotel to rest up for the next morning, when the crew from *60 Minutes* would be meeting him before court.

"OYEZ! OYEZ! OYEZ!"

Ted Olson was up first. He began by reiterating the argument that Scalia had seized on the first time, saying the legislature, not the state courts, had the authority over selecting presidential electors.

But Kennedy interrupted: "Oh, and I thought your point," the swing justice said, "was that the process is being conducted in violation of the Equal Protection Clause and it is standardless."

"And the Due Process Clause . . ." Olson agreed, picking up the signal.

The Fourteenth Amendment said that no state could take away rights "without due process of law" or "deny to any person within its jurisdiction the equal protection of the laws." At Olson's urging, Bush's side had argued from the beginning that the recounts violated these principles, because if each ballot were evaluated by individuals according to their subjective eyesight, there was no way they would all get equal treatment. By ordering all sixty-seven counties in Florida to stage recounts and by setting only a fuzzy standard— "the intent of the voter"—the state court had aggravated the problem. And now Kennedy was expressing constitutional concerns.

Unbeknown to anyone outside the Court, Kennedy had been aggressively urging his colleagues to step in to resolve the election. He thought the Supreme Court needed to act as the final arbiter. But he also seemed to think the Court needed to make a sweeping gesture. It mattered little that his logic led to a perverse conclusion: throwing out votes in the name of equality.

"Do you think," Kennedy asked Boies when it was his turn to argue, "there must be a uniform standard for counting the ballots?"

"I do, Your Honor," Boies replied. "I think there is a uniform standard. The question is whether that standard is too general or not. The standard is whether or not the intent of the voter is reflected by the ballot. That is the uniform standard throughout the state of Florida."

"That's very general," Kennedy replied bluntly. "And you would say that from the standpoint of the Equal Protection Clause, could each county give their own interpretation?"

"I think . . ." Boies began.

"Could that vary from county to county?" Kennedy asked.

"I think it can vary from individual to individual," Boies replied.

Justice Stevens was watching with growing dismay. He was certain that if Larry Tribe had been up there, the constitutional scholar would have made the obvious counterargument: that there was no equal protection problem unless the varying standards uniformly favored one party.

Justice Ruth Bader Ginsburg was equally frustrated. She would have pointed out that if anyone had an equal protection complaint, it was the many thousands of Black voters whose ballots had been disproportionately discarded because they had voted on crappy machines.

Justice David Souter still had a faint hope that he might be able to convince Kennedy to merely kick the case back to the Florida Supreme Court again, with instructions to set a uniform statewide standard. "I think we would have a responsibility to tell the Florida courts what to do about it," Souter said to Boies. "On that assumption, what would you tell them to do about it?"

"Well," Boies replied, and went silent for a long moment. "I think that's a very hard question."

"You would tell them to count every vote!" Scalia interjected.

"I would tell them to count every vote," Boies cheerfully agreed.

The courtroom gallery broke into peals of laughter. What a funny joke.

GORE STILL REFUSED to believe he was going to lose. After the argument, Boies went over to the vice president's residence and finally met with his client in person. They listened to a tape of the arguments. Gore heard what he wanted to hear. "You really nailed their questions," he congratulated Boies. Afterward, in an act of blind faith, Gore got to work on an opinion column for the *New York Times*, which he intended to publish once the Court had ruled in his favor. He closed it by quoting Lincoln's First Inaugural Address: "Why should there not be a patient confidence in the ultimate justice of the people? Is there any better or equal hope in the world?"

Boies knew it was all over. The next day, as the Supreme Court deliberated, the lawyer flew back to New York, where he went out to dinner at Chin Chin, an expensive Chinese restaurant, with some family and friends. He ordered Mai Tais and salt-and-pepper shrimp, and his wife, Mary, told a story about how Bill Cosby, the beloved entertainer and Gore campaigner, had just cold-called their house on behalf of his agent, who wanted Boies to write a memoir.

Down in Great Falls, Virginia, the Olsons were waiting nervously at home. "It was very hard to keep Barbara from climbing the walls," Ted Olson later told an oral historian. "She was going completely nuts." Olson took his wife out to Neiman Marcus, but not even shopping could calm her down. They went to a gourmet grocery store and bought a huge quantity of steaks, caviar, and other delicacies; invited over Ken Starr and his wife; and opened up a fine wine from the cellar.

At 9:54 p.m., MSNBC anchor Brian Williams put his hand to his earpiece. "We're having this baby tonight," he announced. Within about fifteen minutes, the decision was issued.

"Here comes our runner," the MSNBC reporter outside the Court said excitedly. All around him, under the klieg lights, his competitors were grabbing the decision and rifling through its sixty-five pages. "Hang on," the reporter said. "Looking for the summary."

George W. Bush was watching on TV, in his pajamas, in his bed in Austin. The correspondents were reading passages live on the air, looking for a clear statement of what had been decided. No one could find one. Bush got on the phone with Karl Rove, who assured him he had won (again).

"I'm calling Baker," Bush said.

Down in Tallahassee, a fax machine was spitting out pages of the decision.

"What does it say?" Baker asked.

The decision in *Bush v. Gore* was the product of the kind of lobbying and outright bargaining seldom seen in the decorous Supreme Court. "That day!" Ginsburg would later recall. "That was some day, when a lot of people tried to influence other people." Normally, the nine justices spent months crafting decisions and issued them from the bench. This time, they dashed off six discordant opinions and slinked out through the parking garage in the dark. The majority opinion was such a shambles that the primary authors, Kennedy and O'Connor, did not put their names on it, taking the unusual step of writing it "per curiam"; and they specified that it was "limited to the present circumstances," so as not to set any unfortunate precedent. The opinion found that the recount violated the Equal Protection Clause. And by a vote of 5 to 4, the justices had decided that because federal law said the deadline for certifying electors was December 12, that very day, the state courts had run out of time to sort out the mess in Florida.

Ted Cruz located the key passage. "It says it's over," he announced. "We won."

The phone rang. It was the governor, calling from Austin to get Baker's analysis.

"Good evening, Mr. President-elect," Baker said.

Gore's lawyers were reaching the same conclusion. The majority opinion was muddled, but the fiery dissents from the liberals spoke clearly. Justice Breyer decried a "self-inflicted wound" that "runs the risk of undermining the public's confidence in the Court itself." Ginsburg's dissent questioned how the Court could fault Florida for missing the deadline after it had stopped the recount. (In an earlier draft, she had also brought up racial disparities, but she had ultimately bowed to a request from Scalia, a personal friend, to tone down the "Al Sharpton tactics.")

Stevens was most eloquent. "Although we may never know with complete certainty the identity of the winner of this year's Presidential election, the identity of the loser is perfectly clear," he wrote. "It is the Nation's confidence in the judge as an impartial guardian of the rule of law."

On a conference call, Gore went over the opinions page by page with his attorneys. They looked for options and saw none. "It may have been wrong to shoot us," Boies said, "but we're still dead." Ron Klain wanted to fight on. He spent the rest of that night drawing up legal papers in the hope that Florida might establish a uniform standard, thus satisfying the equal protection problem. Early the next morning, Gore convened his legal team for another call.

"Then proceeded the most fascinating kind of historic thing that I have ever been witness to," recalls Tom Goldstein, an appellate attorney who assisted Boies in the *Bush v. Gore* argument. "It was the debate and discussion about whether to adhere to the Court's decision, which was really, really, really interesting. There was a debate back-and-forth between the people on the call about whether to fight notwithstanding the Supreme Court and insist that the Court had effectively tinkered with democracy. It was a real conversation that lasted twenty minutes."

Finally, Gore shut his lawyers down. "It was Gore," Goldstein says, "who just said, 'No. This is America. We're done. We're not going to fight anymore.'"

That evening, Gore delivered the most moving speech of his life. "I do believe," he said, quoting from his father, "that no matter how hard the loss, defeat may serve as well as victory to shake the soul and let the glory out." With that, he conceded the election to the next President Bush.

29

Gasparilla

On December 11, 2000, the day *Bush v. Gore* was argued before the Supreme Court, Jeb Bush paid an awkward visit to the White House. The occasion, scheduled long before, was the ceremonial signing of a bipartisan bill to save the Everglades. The $7.8 billion program, a product of years of negotiation, was meant to clean up and preserve what was left of the Reno family's beloved sawgrass wilderness, much of which had been poisoned, drained, and driven into retreat over decades of merciless human expansion. Though Al Gore had championed the legislation, he did not attend the ceremony. But Governor Bush of Florida, a belated convert, came to town to celebrate the bill's passage. An aide to President Clinton quipped that it was like "a scene from a Fellini movie."

Jeb appeared before the White House press pool, deflecting questions about his brother. "We're here to talk about something that is going to be long-lasting," he said, "way past counting votes. This is the restoration of a treasure for our country."

Bill Clinton watched the scene unfold, fully aware of what was at stake in the case of *Bush v. Gore*: "If we don't do something about climate change," the president told one of the Floridians at the White House that afternoon, "your Everglades is going to be underwater."

That November, as the recount controversy raged in Florida, world leaders were supposed to be working out the implementation of a treaty to limit carbon emissions at a summit in The Hague. But the summit collapsed without an agreement. It appeared that the rest of the world would have to wait for the United States, the nation that spewed out the most carbon dioxide, to determine its next president. Over the next eight years, with Bush as president, the world would dither, emissions would increase, and climate change would take on unstoppable momentum.

At the time, though, it didn't really seem like the end of the world. It was amazing how quickly Washington reverted to normal after *Bush v. Gore*. As the oft-repeated adage went, the center had held. After Gore conceded, Bush gave a reassuring speech. "I know America wants reconciliation and unity," he said, stressing the "common ground" that the parties shared. "During the fall campaign, we differed about the details," the president-elect said, "but there was remarkable consensus about the important issues before us: excellent schools, retirement and health security, tax relief, a strong military, a more civil society."

It was a reassuringly modest agenda. He had no big plans. "George W. Bush may be forgotten soon enough," the journalist David Kaplan concluded in a book published soon after the 2000 election. "His presidency is accidental and the tranquil times don't cry out for great leadership."

On January 6, 2001, in his capacity as vice president, Gore performed his constitutional duty and presided over the U.S. Senate as it went through the formality of counting the electoral votes, formalizing his own defeat. Gore pursued the task with superficial good humor, pumping his fist in mock celebration when it came time to count his haul from California. When Florida's turn came, a group of Democrats from the House of Representatives, most of them Black, arose to object, calling the result "illegitimate," making accusations of fraud and voting rights violations.

"Votes in Florida were not counted," said Representative Jesse Jackson Jr. of Illinois, the son of the reverend. Gore gaveled the Democrats silent, ruling that their objections were out of order.

When the ceremonial task was complete, Gore ratified that George W. Bush of Texas had been elected president of the United States. Then he went to the White House. A white tent had been erected on the South Lawn. Bill and Hillary Clinton were having a farewell party.

AFTER THE COUNTING, there were other reckonings. Gore requested a private meeting with Clinton. They met in the Oval Office, alone. Only they know exactly what was said.

Fragmentary accounts of the conversation would later emerge. Gore entered the Oval Office angry and ready to unburden himself. He knew that Clinton had been calling around, complaining that Gore had shown no fighting spirit. In Clinton's view, he had behaved as if the recount were some kind of pious exercise, instead of the continuation of a partisan war. He fumed to confidants that Gore got more votes, both nationally and in Florida. "He's being screwed," Clinton would say. "The fix is in." Why not take the battle to the streets, why not unleash Jesse Jackson, why not attack the bastards on the Supreme Court? He likened *Bush v. Gore* to the Court's infamous decisions upholding slavery and segregation.

When Clinton and Gore met for their first serious conversation in many months, it was Gore who started off on the offensive. He told Clinton that it was his fault, that his irresponsible affair had destroyed Gore's opportunity to win the White House. ("In 1992, I provided the moral energy for Clinton to win," Gore had told his advisers at one campaign strategy session. "This year, he's sapping the moral energy of my campaign.") Clinton was taken aback by Gore's criticism. He vented his own pent-up frustration, saying that he had given his vice president an ideal set of circumstances to run for a third Clinton-Gore term, and yet, time and again, Gore had ignored his advice and repudiated Clinton's economic record. Clinton told Gore he had blown it.

The argument was shaped, as always, by Clinton's personal calculations. He was only fifty-four years old and was not ready to retire from politics. His loyalists were fighting with Gore's for control of the Democratic National Committee and, with it, the party's future. It was presumed that Gore would want a rematch with Bush in 2004—"He's like a shadow president," one of Gore's aides said after his concession—but already, other Democrats were angling to run. "Gee whiz, I wouldn't begrudge the guy for wanting to try again," one of them, Senator Joseph Biden of Delaware, told the *Times*. "Ironically, the closeness of the election has put a sheen back on him that I'm not sure can be sustained for four years. It will be an uphill battle for him to get the nomination again."

Perhaps the most formidable potential contender, though, would be Senator Hillary Clinton. Bill dismissed rumors of her interest as "worse than idle speculation." This was not a convincing lie.

THE BUSHES ALL needed a rest. Dubya had been nervously chainsawing brush at the ranch. Jeb had been through his ordeal in Tallahassee. Poppy may have been the most stressed. He would regularly call Jeb and Jim Baker to agonize. He "was a living wreck," Jeb later said. "It was horrible."

In the midst of the recount, a reporter caught up with Poppy at a bonefishing tournament in the Florida Keys. "We'll survive this," Poppy assured him, in his usual choppy syntax. "The country will do just fine. Sooner not later. You know, you hear talk of healing, but the country isn't in need of healing. . . . The country is strong. Has been. Will be. And the Bushes will be fine."

Over dinner with a group of anglers, Poppy started to choke up as he told his story about Election Night, when Jeb hugged George and apologized about Florida. "It's hard," he said. "Harder than *anything* that ever happened to me. The press beat me up pretty bad—ratings up after Desert Storm, ratings down. Up, down. Beat me up bad. But that's ok. Goes with the territory.

"But when it's your boys . . . it's hard. This is my *family*. Of course most of the attention is on George, but Jeb, too, he's getting hit, and for me, their dad, this is tough."

The day after Christmas, around sixty members of the Bush clan gathered for a family vacation on Gasparilla Island, a resort named for an imaginary Gulf Coast pirate. (In true Florida fashion, the pirate had been invented by a twentieth-century newspaper editor to give colorless Tampa a bit of buccaneering history.) The Bushes stayed in little cottages, took fishing charters out to catch some snook. "He should be grateful to Florida, absolutely," Jeb told a reporter from the *Los Angeles Times* who managed to catch him out for a stroll. It was the first time the brothers had seen each other since Election Night. But Dubya was already moving on, working on his delayed presidential transition. He spent most of the vacation with a cell phone at his ear.

On December 26, as various Bushes and their courtiers were jetting into the small airport nearest to the resort, in the town of Venice, Mohamed Atta and Marwan al-Shehhi were flying out. A few days before, the pair had passed an FAA test to obtain their commercial pilot rating and were now licensed to fly light commercial aircraft. On this day, though, they rented one of their school's small planes for one last, unexplained trip across Florida.

The plane took off and headed south, likely flying over Charlotte Harbor and the gathering Bushes on Gasparilla Island, before banking east, into Florida's sparsely populated inlands. The pilots passed over the dirt-poor town of Immokalee, where Mexican migrant workers were harvesting winter tomatoes. They continued on above the Big Cypress Swamp and the marshy green grasslands of the endangered Everglades. At nature's edges, as always, there were yellow diggers and bulldozers at work. Finally, the pilots came in to land at Miami International Airport.

That evening, at dinnertime, the chief instructor at the flight school in Venice received an angry phone call from Atta, who complained that his rented plane's engine had quit. "He said they were at Miami International," the instructor later testified. "And my first thought is 'Why?'" Soon the instructor received a second call, this one from the Miami air traffic control tower, demanding to know why a single-engine aircraft registered to the school had been abandoned at the edge of a taxiway, amid the traffic of a busy holiday travel day.

"We have had students do some incredibly questionable things—run out of gas, land at the wrong airports—but to go into an international airport, at night, on a holiday, is highly unusual," the instructor later testified. It was "a really strange environment at a really strange time of the year." A pilot at Atta's level was not skilled enough to fly into an international airport. "It is the equivalent of letting a kid who just got his driver's license drive in a NASCAR race," the flight school's owner later wrote. The stunt was likely to attract the attention of the authorities. The Miami tower told the flight school to expect a call from the FAA. But the agency never investigated.

Up to this point, Atta had been extremely careful, doing little to draw unwanted scrutiny. What was so important to him that he had taken such a reckless risk? It is impossible to say for certain, but it seems that he and al-Shehhi urgently needed to meet someone in Miami. As it happened, Ziad Jarrah had just booked a last-minute flight home to Beirut. He was due to depart from Miami International Airport in the early afternoon. Back in those days, before security was tightened, anyone could enter an airport terminal, even without a ticket to fly. You could walk right up and meet a friend at the gate. No one had to take off their shoes.

Jarrah had been in Miami for the previous two weeks, training on commercial jet simulators at an advanced flight academy. Now, suddenly, he was leaving, returning to Lebanon to attend his sister's wedding. Jarrah's family had been worried about his disappearance the year before, and suspected his jihadist sympathies. His father had long been pressuring him to come home. The men who had enlisted in the planes operation were not supposed to maintain contact with their families. But Jarrah had ignored the rules.

Later, the only surviving core member of the Hamburg group, Ramzi bin al-Shibh, would tell interrogators that there was conflict within Jarrah. He was always bickering with Atta about his domineering attitude and wavering in his commitment to the mission. Maybe that was why Atta rushed to Miami that day: to reel him back. Then again, maybe the airport just seemed like an inconspicuous place to confer. Whatever happened, Jarrah went on his trip, and Atta got into his plane, only to have it stall as he awaited clearance to take off for his return flight to Venice.

Atta and al-Shehhi reappeared at their flight school the next day, settled their outstanding bills, and never returned. But Jarrah soon returned to Venice, this time accompanied by a guest: a pretty young woman named Aysel. He introduced her as his girlfriend to everyone at the Florida Flight Training Center. "Ziad looked happy and was proud when I complimented him on his great 'catch,'" the owner of the school, Arne Kruithof, later wrote. The couple flew one of the school's planes down to the Florida Keys for a romantic getaway. Aysel brought her camera. She took a snapshot of her lover in midflight, wearing a headset, sunglasses, and a giant goofy grin.

Ziad also took Aysel on a trip to Miami, where he showed her the academy where he had been training on a flight simulator. He had signed up for ten hours of classes. No one learned how to fly passenger jets by taking them up in the air—they were too expensive—but the simulator replicated the experience. It was an enclosed metal cabin that contained an exact replica of a Boeing cockpit, with all its many gauges, switches, and dials. It sat on top of hydraulic legs that could move it around, to create the feeling of turbulence. The simulator allowed pilots to test themselves against extreme conditions. Plus, you could crash and then go have lunch.

An instructor walked Jarrah through the basics. Taking off and landing required advanced expertise, but for most of the flight, you had to know only how to work a relatively simple system called the mode control panel. If you could figure out the panel, you could fly a 757. Aysel watched as Jarrah took his final two-hour lesson. She snapped a photo of him sitting in the captain's chair, his hand on the throttle. She was making plans for them to settle down near her parents, in Stuttgart. Ziad told her he wanted to have children.

While Ziad and Aysel were enjoying their holiday, Atta was in Berlin to meet Ramzi bin al-Shibh, who had moved into a coordinating role in the operation, given that his plans to participate had been foiled by his inability to obtain a U.S. visa. Atta told him that he, al-Shehhi, and Jarrah had now taken courses on commercial jet simulators. They had learned what they needed to know. Their training was complete. After the meeting, Ramzi flew to Tehran and traveled overland to Afghanistan. He met the Sheikh to brief him on the operation's progress.

Osama bin Laden felt that God was smiling on him. He was delighted by the election of another George Bush. The father had brought the crusaders to the Arabian Peninsula to fight Saddam Hussein in the Gulf War. Now bin Laden could strike a blow against the son. Ramzi told the Sheikh that the pilots had finished the first phase of the mission. It was time to send the soldiers.

THAT SAME DECEMBER, the newly elected president paid a visit to Washington, for separate meetings with Clinton and Gore, a traditional ritual in the transition of power. Gore was merely obliging, but Clinton wanted to talk with Bush about foreign policy and national security issues. He warned his successor that he would find terrorism to be the most dangerous threat he faced. He said that one of his greatest regrets was not capturing or killing bin Laden before leaving office.

Some of Clinton's advisers continued to press him to attack bin Laden's camps in retaliation for the *Cole* attack, but the president seemed content to leave the decision to Bush. During the transition, CIA analysts drew up what became known as the "Blue Sky memo," which outlined covert and diplomatic actions that the United States could use to neutralize Al Qaeda. It was "not some narrow, little terrorist issue," Clinton's counterterrorism chief wrote to Bush's incoming national security advisor, Condoleezza Rice, in a transition memo, describing the group as an "active, organized major force that is using a distorted version of Islam as its vehicle."

Bush had other priorities. He was assembling an administration full of experienced hands in the mold of Dick Cheney: Colin Powell to the State Department, Donald Rumsfeld to Defense. A horde of hawkish "neoconservatives" was filling in the middle tiers of the foreign policy bureaucracy. At the Justice Department, Janet Reno was to be replaced by John Ashcroft, a former senator from Missouri. Ashcroft was a moralistic evangelical Christian who was so unpopular that he had just managed to lose his seat to a Democratic opponent who had died in a plane crash before the election. But the appointment was a gesture to Bush's core conservative supporters. The new attorney general showed little interest in terrorism or Al Qaeda. During the summer of 2001, Ashcroft would tell the acting FBI director that he was tired of briefings on the subject.

The lawyers who volunteered to fight the recount in Florida were rewarded with important jobs at the Justice Department or inside the White House. Bush nominated Ted Olson to be solicitor general, acting as the administration's advocate before the Supreme Court. The Democrats, still unforgiving about *Bush v. Gore*, tried to block his nomination, but Olson received assistance from an unlikely party: David Boies. His former adversary called up Democratic senators to lobby for Olson. After he was finally confirmed, Boies attended the swearing-in ceremony and a celebratory Washington cocktail party thrown by Barbara Olson.

Before *Bush v. Gore*, Boies was an attorney; afterward, he was a celebrity. "No lawyer in memory has ever won so much by losing," *Time* wrote in its "Person of the Year" issue in December 2000, which named Boies as a runner-up to Bush. The public exposure from his performance in Florida attracted new clients: investment banks, tech billionaires, tobacco companies. His boutique litigation practice expanded into a large and immensely profitable corporate law firm, Boies Schiller Flexner. Although the firm employed hundreds of lawyers, its value to its clientele came from the power of one name. "When these folks wanted someone to scare the other side," says a former associate at the firm. "They said, 'I have David Boies.'"

In January 2001, Boies went out to lunch with Tina Brown, the editor of *Talk*. He had decided to take up Bill Cosby's suggestion about writing a memoir. Brown was launching a new *Talk* publishing imprint, and Boies was, in Brown's lexicon, "v. hot." Brown brought along her financial backers, the film producers Bob and Harvey Weinstein. They offered Boies a substantial advance for his memoir. Before long, they had also hired him to act as their company's legal counsel. "That's how Harvey pursued things," says another attorney who worked for Weinstein. "Give him a book deal, and then he'd have a relationship with the greatest fucking lawyer there is."

With others, Weinstein may have acted like a crass bully, but he treated Boies with great deference, calling on him for matters large and small. When the Weinstein brothers wanted to extricate their production company from an unhappy marriage with Disney, Boies acted as their divorce attorney, threatening a $400 million lawsuit. (It worked.) When the filmmaker Michael Moore was fighting with the Bush administration over a reporting trip to Cuba for the documentary *Sicko*, Boies and Weinstein staged a bellicose press conference with Moore, resulting in a bunch of beneficial headlines. Boies recognized that many legal battles were won outside the courtroom, and he knew how to use his name and reputation to generate publicity.

Sometimes, though, Weinstein wanted problems to disappear quietly. There were issues with women. Everyone in New York had heard the whispers, although Boies would later claim he thought Weinstein was merely a philanderer. Boies was a friend of the press, and he knew how to apply pressure in the right places. He lobbied editors, oversaw confidential legal settlements, defended his client's privacy and public reputation, ensuring that the silence would continue. And it did, for many years. He was a very good lawyer.

JESSE JACKSON WANTED to keep fighting. "There is something afoot in Florida that does not pass the smell test," the reverend said after filing a lawsuit over racial disparities in the rates that votes were thrown out in Jacksonville. The day after *Bush v. Gore* was decided, Jackson led a small march through the streets of Tallahassee and called for "disciplined, massive, nonviolent demonstrations around our nation." Even after Gore conceded, Jackson forged onward.

"None of this was an accident," he told a reporter from the *Palm Beach Post* one day in late 2000 as he rode around Florida in the backseat of a limousine, working several cell phones.

The *Post* had recently published a series of stories about the state's purge of felons from its voter rolls. No one seemed to know exactly how many registered voters had been removed, and it was impossible to say whether those people would have voted for Gore. But one thing was clear: a disproportionate number of them were Black. To Jackson, it was part of a generations-long pattern. "It is a loss of our franchise," he told the reporter. "You had intimidation of African Americans at or near the polls by the police, thousands of ballots left uncounted, obsolete voting machines placed in targeted precincts. Where was equal protection? And for the entire month since the election, Jeb Bush took a hike. He did not recuse himself. He *reclused* himself."

The *Post* reporter was skeptical. Was Jackson really trying to say that there was a conspiracy, that Republicans had thought this all out, devising a plan to distribute faulty voting machines in Democratic precincts, designing ballots that were deliberately confusing, somehow knowing far ahead of time that a few thousand miscast votes would change the result in Florida?

"We may never know what was said at some meeting, but I believe there was a meeting, or meetings took place," Jackson replied. "This many votes, this quantity, in numbers and geography, is not accidental. It is part of a scheme to suppress votes. It is not a gut feeling. We will have the data." The NAACP was preparing to file a class action lawsuit. The U.S. Commission on Civil Rights was holding investigative hearings. On Inauguration Day, Jackson was going to appear at a rally in Tallahassee to publicize his allegations of voter suppression.

Even if nothing could stop George W. Bush from becoming president, Jackson vowed to unearth the real story of his election. "History," he said, "will answer the questions."

The week of the inauguration, the Drudge Report started to drop hints that Jackson was hiding his own secret. Soon, the latest issue of the *National Enquirer* hit the supermarket checkout aisles. "JESSE JACKSON'S LOVE CHILD," read its front page, trumpeting its "world exclusive." The tabloid reported that, even as Jackson guided Clinton through the Lewinsky scandal, he had been conducting his own affair with an academic who had written a biography of him. Jackson had given her a job and paternity payments and had even taken her to visit Clinton in the Oval Office at the time she was pregnant. On January 17, Jackson released a statement to the press, acknowledging that the story was true and announcing that he was retiring from public life.

His enemies, in both parties, were overjoyed. "Jesse Jackson's long reign of terror in the Democratic Party may be finally over," gloated Mary McGrory, the voice of the liberal establishment, in her Sunday column in the *Washington Post*. Jackson skipped the inauguration rally, staying secluded in his house in Chicago. He soon announced a comeback, but he would never again occupy the same place in the political firmament. Eight years later, Jackson would witness the election of the next Democrat, a "post-racial" Chicago progressive who took care to keep the reverend and his polarizing persona at a chilly distance. Jackson would be there in Grant Park on Election Night, joyful tears streaming down his face, but he was "on the wrong side of the rope line," a journalist observed—far from the first Black president.

JANET RENO WAS finished with Washington. After eight arduous years, she was looking forward to returning home to Miami. She said she wanted to kayak in the Everglades. She had just bought a red pickup truck. She was telling people she planned to take it on a solitary road trip, like in *Thelma and Louise*, she joked, with "no Louise."

At around 11 a.m. on Inauguration Day, shortly before the new president was sworn in, Reno departed her private office at Main Justice for the final time. She walked out to Pennsylvania Avenue, where an aide was waiting for her in a chauffeured government vehicle. She closed her eyes and exhaled. "I no longer have to worry about the bombs," she said. "I no longer have to worry about the terrorists." The car took her to Andrews Air Force Base, where Bill Clinton—now *former* President Clinton—was to receive a formal send-off from his staff and cabinet.

"It's been a great adventure," Reno told a reporter from the *New York Times* as she sat on a folding chair inside a hangar, waiting for Clinton's motorcade, which now had to stop for red lights just like anyone else. "I'm going to go home and sit on my front porch."

Reno had one last act to perform. Without breathing a word, she and a small entourage of aides and security personnel slipped out of Washington and flew up to New York City. Reno went to Rockefeller Center, the home of NBC Studios, and took an elevator to a studio on the eighth floor, where she was met by a whiff of illicit pot smoke.

And now from the home of the attorney general of the United States, it's time for the final episode of Janet Reno's Dance Party . . .

As the *SNL* announcer intoned his introduction, Will Ferrell, dressed in a shapeless blue dress and white pearls, grooved to a techno beat amid moshing young dancers.

"Well, here it is," Ferrell said, in his deep Janet Reno voice. "My last day as attorney general."

"Awwwwww," the dancers said.

"Zip it! Just zip it!"

Ferrell introduced a montage of some of the long-running skit's finest moments: the barbell-pumping workout routine, the time fake Reno punched the real Rudy Giuliani in the gut.

"We sure had some fun times," Ferrell said. "I guess the dance party is finally over."

Then Janet Reno herself came crashing through a fake brick wall, wearing an identical blue outfit.

"It's Reno time!" she bellowed, trembling a little.

And then, for the amusement of the nation, Janet Reno did the Twist.

30

The Sting

The brides were on their way. All through that spring and summer of 2001, they would arrive in Dubai in groups of two or three, meeting up with facilitators, who worked under the cover of a computer store. The facilitators would tell them to wait for word from the man they knew as Abdul Rahman. He called in periodically, asking after the facilitator's sister, talking as if he was making plans for an arranged marriage. "Pay for her ticket," he would say, "and send her to the USA." This was coded language; the "sisters" were the killers.

Then Mohamed Atta would name a destination city, usually in Florida. The facilitators who worked for Mukhtar—or Khalid Sheikh Mohammed, as he was known to the CIA—would get the operatives prepared, buying them traveler's checks, driving them to one of Dubai's enormous malls to shop for appropriate clothing, and when necessary, instructing them to get U.S. visas. Some of them looked surprised when they were told of their destination. They had volunteered to be martyrs, but until that moment, they didn't know they were going to die in America.

They were later referred to as the "muscle," but they were really not much to look at as physical specimens. Most of them were Saudis, chosen by Osama bin Laden based on tribal loyalties and the ease with which they could obtain visas, owing to their oil-rich nation's alliance with the United States. Despite this advantage, Mukhtar and his men were worried about the Saudis. They were unworldly and spoke little English. One of them was rejected by a U.S. Customs officer at the airport in Orlando as Atta waited outside to fetch him. Mukhtar later dismissed the thwarted operative as a "Bedouin."

Mukhtar, as the operation's self-proclaimed brain, was growing annoyed with bin Laden. It wasn't just his selection of the hijacking personnel. The Sheikh was terrible at management, the sort of boss who was always meddling with settled plans and contributing unrealistic ideas. For instance, the Sheikh wanted to destroy the White House—it would be great for the brand—but Atta believed it to be an impossibly small target. In the middle of 2000, when the operation was already well under way, the manager of Al Qaeda's guesthouse in Kandahar, a French Moroccan named Zacarias Moussaoui, came to the Sheikh and told him he'd had a dream in which he was dressed in a pilot's uniform and had opened a map of Washington with a big *X* on it over the White House. (At least that's the way Moussaoui later told the story.) Over the objections of Mukhtar, who thought Moussaoui an idiot, bin Laden dispatched the potential fifth pilot to an Oklahoma flight school. His instructors there found him completely hopeless.

Based on a dream, bin Laden had upset months of disciplined preparation. Worse, the Sheikh couldn't stop blabbing about the operation. He kept appearing at his camps, speaking to the recruits, dropping hints about a large number of brothers who had recently "departed . . . seeking death where it is found for the pleasure of Allah." Gossip about a big attack started to spread. When a group of inquisitive young jihadis from Buffalo asked the Sheikh about the attack rumors, he offered coy confirmation. "Just know that there's brothers that are willing to carry their souls in their hands," he said. Mukhtar was concerned about the chatter in the camps. He pleaded with bin Laden to keep his mouth shut. The operation was at a vulnerable juncture.

After months of quiet training, Atta was now surfacing, coordinating a growing number of subordinates. The first two newcomers arrived in Florida in late April. Five more came in May, and four in June. Atta set them up in apartments, helped them to join gyms, and got them local bank accounts to use as they went about their daily lives in Florida. One of the Saudis used his bank card at a Sports Authority to purchase a Mountain Dew, a piece of Bazooka gum, and a T-shirt that said "Fast Times." Another spent hundreds of dollars on porn videos and sex toys.

The operatives divided into four teams, each headed by a pilot. They started to take cross-country reconnaissance flights on commercial airlines. To manage all the movement, Atta signed up for a Travelocity account, using the email address mohamedatta @hotmail.com.

There was no need to hide because no one was looking. On June 11, 2001, Atta and Marwan al-Shehhi checked into a fleabag motel near Fort Lauderdale called the Deluxe Inn. Three newly arrived Saudis piled out of a rented Oldsmobile. They got the nicest room, a suite with a kitchen. But after two nights, the manager told them someone else had reserved it, and he moved them to a smaller room next door. This caused a loud argument with Atta. He checked out in a huff.

On the morning of June 12, five miles up the road from the Deluxe Inn and its conspicuously rude guests, a pair of federal agents were driving to a hotel and preparing to break up a criminal conspiracy. "Time is, uh, approximately eight forty-five," ATF agent Steve Barborini announced as he started a surveillance tape. "With, uh, wearing the wires, Richard Stoltz."

In the background, a cell phone rang. "It's Randy," Barborini said aloud, before picking up the call. The ATF's very excited confidential informant, Randy Glass, was demanding an update.

"I really can't talk now; I'm on a surveillance," Barborini said as Glass kept chattering away.

"Oh, after it, I will call you," the ATF agent assured his informant. "Believe me, I will."

This was the big event. They were finally making the sting.

"ARRIVING EMBASSY SUITES," Dick Stoltz said into his hidden microphone.

The undercover ATF agent, dressed in a sharp suit, was in character as Ray Spears. He walked into the hotel lobby, a twelve-story skylit atrium with an enormous grotto-like fountain surrounded by tropical plants and café tables. Glassed-in elevators were zipping up and down.

"How are you doing, man?" Kevin Ingram said in greeting to the person he knew as Spears.

"Do you want a cup of coffee?" Spears said casually.

The month before, the federal agents and prosecutors involved in Operation Sphinx had made the decision to wrap up their investigation. In more than two years of undercover work, the phony arms dealers had never managed to make a sale. The foreign customers who had come to Florida to buy Stinger missiles never did deliver the $32 million. "Abdul," whoever he was, had flown back to Pakistan and vanished. R. G. Abbas was still in Islamabad, stuck in his negotiations with the military. Mike Malik, from his shop in

Jersey City, was now talking about sales leads in West Africa. Didi Mohsen had more or less given up on trying to deal with Randy Glass and was concentrating on his potential telecommunications business in Somalia.

Enough talk, the investigators decided. It was time to round up anyone they could charge.

By this point, it had been many months since Ingram was involved with Spears and Glass. In that time, he had lost millions of dollars, including most of his personal wealth, in his dot-com debacle. That March, TruMarkets filed for bankruptcy, listing $14 million in outstanding liabilities. There was a deal in place to sell off its assets—mainly, its trading technology. And it was at that moment, just as Ingram's hopes were about to be liquidated, that Spears reached out again.

Based on the two earlier transactions, the ATF already had grounds to arrest Ingram, but the money-laundering case was far from solid. Because the cash wasn't really dirty—it was all provided by the government as part of the sting—prosecutors would need to prove that Ingram believed he was handling illegal sales proceeds. And Ingram had always been kept away from the discussions of weapons. The only person who claimed to have spoken directly to him about arms dealing was Glass, in their meeting at Ingram's office at the World Trade Center. Prosecutors were not thrilled about putting a convicted con artist on the stand as their star witness.

So, "Ray Spears" had to rope Ingram into one more deal. In late May 2001, Stoltz called up Didi and told him he had sold a load of surplus weapons from Vietnam and had $1 million to launder. Didi was enthusiastic about helping, but he said he was no longer talking to Ingram. He told the undercover agent that his former friend had fallen on hard times, had sold his Ferrari, and was behaving erratically. He complained that Ingram had "screwed him out of money" after he tried to bring him in on his Somali cell phone business. But Didi agreed to leave a message on Ingram's voice mail, telling him to call Spears.

The undercover agent knew Ingram would be wary. He had been so nervous the first time around. But now Ingram was desperate and thinking, irrationally, about ways to rescue his business. He remembered how Didi had claimed that Spears and company had a connection to billionaire Wayne Huizenga. Maybe he and Spears could get him to Huizenga. He called Spears back.

Spears said he was going to need someone to move "one large unit" a month for several months. Ingram replied that he would prefer to talk about "long-range plans" involving offshore investment. They had a preliminary meeting at the marina. According to the ATF's account, Spears told Ingram he was expecting to bring in around $16 million from arms sales over the next year or so. Ingram allegedly said he didn't want to hear anything about arms dealing and asked Spears if he was wearing a wire. Spears tried to reassure him, pointing out that they had done deals before. Ingram asked in reply how he knew his organization had not been infiltrated by law enforcement.

Spears told Ingram that it sounded like he wasn't interested. Ingram allegedly said he was just being careful, adding that while he had a reputation to think about, he didn't mind making money.

Ingram said he knew someone who could take the cash to Europe by private jet. A few minutes after Spears left, Ingram paged him to say he would do it. This time, his fee would be 25 percent, including the cost of transportation.

The first installment was now to be $2.2 million. They agreed to make the handoff at the Embassy Suites. Ingram brought along the man with the plane, a golfing acquaintance named Walter

Kapij. A Learjet, parked at the nearby private airport, was waiting to fly them to Europe.

"It was a long, long night," Spears said as they waited for coffee. "I have the stuff coming in."

Ingram introduced his friend Walter, and they all sat down at a table in the atrium.

"We are all set," Ingram said.

Spears handed him an envelope containing a piece of paper on which he had written the name and address of the Royal Lancaster Hotel in London, along with a photo of a man, their contact.

"We are going to do it like I said," Ingram told Spears.

"I've done this . . . a few times," Walter added. "So, you don't have to worry." He paused. He wanted to know more about the man they were supposed to meet in London. "This gentleman," he said, "have you known him for quite a long time?"

"Oh yeah," Spears replied. "This is our guy. I mean . . . you know what I do."

"No, actually, I don't know a lot about what you do at all," Walter said. "I have no idea."

"Kevin," Spears said gingerly, "I want to, you know . . ."

"Right," Ingram said.

"You need to know, okay. I mean, this, this, this, this money is, is, you know . . ."

"Important," Ingram said.

"It's important," Spears said. "It's coming in from . . ."

"Yeah," Ingram said.

"This . . . it's coming in from arms shipments."

"Um-hum," Ingram replied.

"And I need you to protect that," Spears said.

"Okay," Ingram said.

"This money has to be protected," Spears said. "It has to be done in a way where no one, you know—you can't just go through customs or anything else."

"It won't go through customs," Walter said. "Quite frankly, I've handled quite a bit more."

Spears made a call to his driver. "I'm not going to be driving around with two-point-two million without a guy," he explained.

"There are just two regular-size suitcases, right?" Ingram said.

"Absolutely," Spears said.

As they waited for the driver to bring in the bags, Ingram made small talk.

"How is everything else going?" he asked.

"I mean, it's just waiting for these guys to come in, you're on pins and needles," Spears said. He mentioned that he and his partner Randy Glass were planning to go golfing.

"He is a scratch golfer," Ingram said.

"Oh shit. Then I ain't playing," Spears replied.

"It's a great game, but it's a tough game," Kapij said. "How long have you been doing this?"

"I've been doing this twenty-two years," Spears said. "But like I was telling Kevin, I was always the guy that went out and located the arms, materials, and that kind of stuff. . . . Now I'm kind of doing it on my own." Spears spotted his driver, Steve. "Oh, there is our guy. There he is, right there."

Steve was carrying two bags. He handed them to Ingram.

"We'll see you," Ingram said.

"Take care," Spears replied.

"God bless you," Walter added.

There was a pause as Ray Spears walked away and Special Agent Dick Stoltz reassumed his identity. Stoltz muttered into his microphone.

"Let's go baby," he said. "Both. Do both."

Federal agents surrounded the targets, flashed their badges, and took Ingram and his associate into custody. "I don't think Ingram was surprised," Stoltz said. After all, he understood risk.

"BIZ BIG BUSTED IN ARMS SALE RING," screamed the headline in the *New York Post*. "A Wall Street hotshot and three other men have been busted in a spy-novel tale of arms smuggling and money laundering," the tabloid reported, "aimed at putting high-tech Stinger missiles in terrorists' hands." Didi and Mike Malik had been arrested separately on the same day, after being lured to the warehouse to check out the supposed new shipment. Prosecutors would never present any evidence that Ingram knew anything about Stinger missiles or terrorists. But this distinction was lost in the media coverage, which focused on his spectacular fall from grace. *Talk* published a long, juicy profile headlined "WALL STREET'S SOLDIER OF FORTUNE."

Sparkle was pregnant when Kevin was arrested. She rushed down to West Palm Beach to see him in jail. "On my way to Florida is when I saw his face and Didi's face on CNN," she says, recalling her thoughts: "'Like, this is real, right now. What have you gotten yourself into?'"

Many of Ingram's Wall Street colleagues were similarly astonished. "I literally spat my coffee across the table," one of them told the *New York Observer*. Senator Jon Corzine, a TruMarkets investor, lamented the squandered potential of the former Goldman Sachs phenom. "The tragedy is that this guy is a role model for what could be," he said. Some of Ingram's Black peers were furious with him, believing that his arrest reinforced the racist stereotypes.

"We'll all have to crawl out of the rubble," one anonymously told *Talk*. Other friends of Ingram's were less shocked. "It seemed to me that Kevin was set up," says an acquaintance from the hip-hop world. "For an African American to be doing what he was doing at that time, he was already a target."

Ingram's arrest was not huge news, though. The *Post* was delighted to learn of his connection to Jesse Jackson—"JESSE'S $20M CHAT," read the headline of a follow-up article, likely exaggerating Ingram's payout from Deutsche Bank—but that was more or less where the story ended. It was just another bizarre little tabloid morsel in a summer of delectable scandals.

Important aspects of the case—including the nuclear trafficking and the possible involvement of Pakistan's intelligence service— were kept secret. According to an internal ATF report dated two days after the sting, the most serious potential charges against Malik and Mohsen, involving the sale of deadly explosives, were never presented to a grand jury at the direction of "Main DOJ," for fear that "information about the intent of the end user of the arms in Pakistan" would "potentially become public knowledge." No reference was to be made to the nationality of the would-be buyers in court papers. Indictments against individuals in Pakistan were to be delayed, the report said, "so as not to interfere with current sensitive ongoing State Dept meetings." The Bush administration was pressuring Pakistan to de-escalate nuclear tensions, and Pervez Musharraf was about to travel to India for a peace summit. Arms trafficking was a lesser priority.

As promised, President George W. Bush was interested mainly in a domestic policy agenda. The first six months of the administration were devoted to advancing a huge tax cut, which passed along party lines, and an education reform bill, which won support from prominent Democrats, including Senator Hillary Clinton. From their Georgian mansion off Embassy Row, Hillary and Bill had solidified their position as the leaders of the Democratic government-in-exile.

Janet Reno was back in Miami, trying to heal the emotional rift that had opened up between her and her beloved hometown. The Cuban community viewed her as a traitor and would never forgive her for how she handled the fate of Elián Gonzalez. Reno confronted her ostracism in a surprising way. That summer, she invited the press to the porch of her mother's old house to make an announcement: she was running for governor against Jeb Bush. The national media covered the event in predictable fashion. (In his lead paragraph, a male *Newsweek* reporter noted Reno's "dowdy, below-the-knee summer dress" and her "spinster-prim schoolmarm persona.") But Reno got in her red pickup truck and started to drive around the state, campaigning as a populist.

At home in Cuba, Elián seemed happy. He celebrated his seventh birthday during the recount. Fidel Castro attended a party at the boy's grade school. Elián would grow up to be a fervent Communist.

On the broader issue of immigration, Bush and the Democrats appeared to have reached a consensus. Both parties favored legislation that would offer legal status to millions of undocumented immigrants. Comprehensive immigration reform appeared possible that fall. Bush had won around a third of Latino voters nationally and often spoke to their concerns in his charmingly clumsy Spanish. He banished talk of "illegals." Everyone in Washington seemed to accept the warming trend, with a few lonely exceptions. Pat Buchanan retreated to the basement of his home in McLean, Virginia, to write a new anti-immigration screed entitled *The Death of the West*. That September, he returned to CNN to renew his call for fortifications to halt "the greatest invasion in American history across our southern border."

But Buchanan no longer had much of a voice. After his miserable performance in 2000, the Reform Party shrank into irrelevance. Jesse Ventura would soon decline to run for reelection as governor of Minnesota. (He would later go on to host a TV show called *Conspiracy Theory*.) Chuck Harder kept talking, doing his show every day from his wheelchair in his studio in White Springs. But his syndicated network went defunct, and *For the People* was gradually pushed off the airwaves. He would move from the AM band to other platforms: shortwave, satellite radio, the internet, and finally podcasts. He continued to write columns on chuckharder .com, warning of encroaching globalism, and he self-published a memoir, *Will We Ever Learn?*

Although Harder urged listeners to rally against the "coup" in Florida, he soon decided that Bush was a quisling. "Globalists cannot contain themselves," Harder wrote on his website. "Is it not enough that we have given continuous aid and comfort to our enemies, provided food to sustain the very people who have conspired to defeat us and still continue to allow our borders to be the laughingstock of the world?"

As for Donald Trump, he was still sitting in his Fifth Avenue tower and watching TV, looking for some way to remain relevant. The *Post* reported that Trump was unsuccessfully shopping around a TV competition called *Billionaire*, the "latest of a slew of reality shows" seeking to mimic the success of *Survivor*, which was coming off a highly rated second season set in the Australian outback. The creator of *Survivor*, Mark Burnett, was busily setting up future seasons—such as *Survivor: Arabia*, which was to begin shooting in the Jordanian desert in the fall of 2001—and concocting new reality show concepts. He had announced a series called *Destination*

Mir, in which contestants would compete for a trip to a Russian-built space station.

Burnett also had a germ of an idea for a reality show set in the "urban jungle," about the cutthroat competition of the business world. His working title was "The Sorcerer's Apprentice."

That show needed a star.

SHORTLY AFTER BUSH was inaugurated, Al Gore started to teach a class at Columbia Journalism School. He enjoyed being an instructor. Privately, he was uncertain about running for president again. He did not have Bill Clinton's compulsions. This was the year that Gore grew a beard and got fat. He and Tipper bummed around Europe for six weeks. She encouraged him to pull out and update the old slide show presentation he used to give about global warming, which he would eventually turn into an Oscar-winning documentary, *An Inconvenient Truth*. He would become a climate sage. He would win the Nobel Peace Prize. People would love this version of Gore.

"You know the old saying," Gore would joke over and over again in his speeches. "You win some, you lose some—and then there's that little-known third category."

But, really, who *did* win? It no longer made a difference to the outcome, but over the course of 2001, news organizations conducted their own unofficial recounts. (The paper ballots were open to inspection as public records.) These forensic analyses judged the ballots by various standards of evaluation. They found that if the statewide recount had not been halted by the Supreme Court, Gore almost certainly would have lost anyway—although, in one unlikely scenario, he won by just three votes. But if you just started over and took a fresh look at all the invalid ballots, Gore might have prevailed. This was because, besides the 65,000 "undervote" ballots that were at issue in the lawsuits, there were another 111,000 ballots rejected because the scanners detected votes for two or more candidates. A tiny percentage of the "overvotes" *did* show clear evidence of intent to vote for Gore, enough to give him a victory by, at most, 332 votes, if you used a loose evaluation standard. But despite his public call to "count every vote," Gore had never petitioned a court for such a complete statewide recount.

When you considered everything—the undervotes and the overvotes, the caterpillar and the butterfly—there could be little serious doubt that, in a world of flawless humans and perfectly functioning machines, Gore would have won a healthy majority of the ballots cast in Florida and thus the presidency. But it turned out to be impossible to turn the presumed intention to vote for Gore into actual Gore votes. His narrowly focused strategy would be endlessly second-guessed. Why didn't Gore press for a full statewide recount from the beginning? Why did he waste all that precious time fighting over pinpricks in front of county election boards instead of going straight to the more sympathetic Florida Supreme Court? Gore could have mobilized mass protests; he could have claimed the election was being stolen. After all, if you forgot Florida and discarded the antidemocratic anachronism of the Electoral College, Gore won 543,895 more votes nationwide, just as the Democrat would win the popular vote in four of the next five elections.

But there were rules, there was a system, and Gore was a man who believed in systems.

"I could have handled the whole thing differently," he told reporter Liza Mundy of the *Washington Post* in 2002, "and instead of making a concession speech, launched a four-year rear guard guerrilla campaign to undermine the legitimacy of the Bush presidency, and to mobilize for a rematch. And there was no shortage of advice to do that." But in the end, Gore said he decided that the legitimacy of the institution of the presidency was too important to call into question.

"I just didn't feel like it was in the best interest of the United States, or that it was a responsible course of action," Gore said. "I don't think I made the wrong decision, but I could certainly—if somebody hired me to write a brief for the other side, I wouldn't have any trouble doing it."

Later on, one choice more than any other ate at the conscience of some of Gore's advisers: the strategic decision to downplay claims of racial suppression. A federal civil rights commission held investigative hearings in 2001. It issued a report finding a "strong basis for concluding" that voting rights violations had occurred in Florida, but determining that there was no proof that "the highest officials of the state conspired to disenfranchise voters." The problem was systemic, the commission decided, not a product of conscious racism. The Republicans on the commission dissented from its report, placing the blame on voters. "We know that some Americans today, regrettably, find it extremely difficult to understand even the simplest written instructions," the Republicans wrote. "And, unfortunately, this group is disproportionately black."

The federal commission's report did not put an end to the suspicion that Florida's failures were the product of deliberate design. In the coming years, many Republican-controlled southern states conducted registration purges and enacted laws that effectively curtailed Democratic representation and participation. "You can trace it all back to Florida," says John Lantigua, a journalist who investigated the 2000 election for *The Nation*. But the mainstream press showed diminishing interest in the story. Bush was now president. It was time to leave Florida behind.

The recount would instead become a fixation of conspiracy theorists, who spun real evidence of dysfunction and injustice in Florida into a nefarious heist plot. "What would we say . . ." a much-forwarded mass email asked, if this happened in another country, and the guy was the son of a president, and that president previously was in charge of the intelligence service, and his other son governed the state where the disputed vote happened, and so forth. Michael Moore, the left-wing filmmaker, delved into Florida conspiracy theories in the opening scenes of *Fahrenheit 9/11*, the highest-grossing documentary of all time. Roger Stone, the right-wing agent provocateur, relocated to South Florida and wrote a scurrilous book called *The Bush Crime Family*, in which he described his own (disputed) role in Miami. "It is an action I would regret," he concluded.

A muckraking leftist journalist would write a book on the 2000 election, *The Best Democracy Money Can Buy*, attacking the "docile sheep" of the American media and the "shepherds of the New World Order" who employed them for ignoring the "theft of the presidential race."

A copy of the book would be found in Osama bin Laden's library at his compound in Abbottabad.

IN JULY 2001, Mohamed Atta left the United States one last time to meet with Ramzi bin al-Shibh in Spain. The fourth member of the Hamburg cell had been shuttling between Europe and Afghanistan, serving as a link between Al Qaeda's leadership and the operatives who were supposed to carry out the mission. Atta told him that the preparations were almost complete. Nineteen men were in place. They had been taking test flights, finding they had no trouble bringing box cutters through security checkpoints in their carry-on bags. They had been casing the routines of the pilots and flight attendants, determining that the best opportunity to seize the craft would come around fifteen minutes into the flight. They had settled on four targets.

Ramzi told Atta that he had recently visited bin Laden in Afghanistan. He said the Sheikh had instructed him to convey an urgent message. Bin Laden wanted Atta to know that he still preferred hitting the White House to the U.S. Capitol. He urged Atta to strike as soon as possible, as he was concerned about having so many operatives in the field. Atta said he would take that under advisement, but he still thought the Capitol made a better target. Ultimately, he would delay the operation until after Labor Day, so he could strike while Congress was in session.

Atta said he was struggling to coordinate the complex mission. He complained that some of the Saudis were being undisciplined, asking to bid farewell to their families before they martyred themselves—a violation of his rules. His most vexing headache, though, involved Ziad Jarrah.

Jarrah continued to be defiant of Atta's authority as the emir of the planes operation. It seemed as if he might be on the verge of quitting the operation entirely. Soon after Atta returned from Spain, Jarrah left the United States, flying from Miami to Dusseldorf on a ticket purchased by Aysel. It was a one-way.

In coded communications, Mukhtar told Ramzi to mediate between Atta and Jarrah, calling them an "unhappy couple." He said that if Jarrah wanted "a divorce," it would "cost a lot of money."

In the same conversations, Mukhtar told Ramzi to contact Zacarias Moussaoui, the hapless fifth pilot, who had been sitting idle in Oklahoma after failing to learn how to fly a Cessna. After a flurry of phone calls, Ramzi sent $14,000 to Moussaoui via wire.

Moussaoui drove to another flight school, in Minnesota. Some investigators would later theorize that Moussaoui was activated in order to serve as a backup to Jarrah. If so, it was a potentially disastrous miscalculation.

The school in Minnesota offered training on Boeing jet simulators, mainly to commercial airline pilots. Moussaoui had none of the necessary training, but the school took his $8,300 in cash. He told his simulator instructor that he was in the "import-export business" and wanted to feel the thrill of flying a jumbo jet. This was odd, but the instructor figured that maybe he was like one of those middle-aged men who paid a fortune to go to fantasy baseball camps. During the lesson, the instructor got a weird feeling. Moussaoui mentioned something about the Hajj pilgrimage, and the instructor asked if he was Muslim. Moussaoui snapped, "I am nothing."

The flight instructor thought it over and went to see his supervisor at the school.

"Should we be doing this?" the instructor asked.

"He paid the money," the supervisor said. "We don't care."

"We'll care when there's a hijacking," the instructor said, "and all the lawsuits start coming in."

The supervisor told the instructor that if he really cared that much, he could call the head office in Miami. He did, and the school's administrators belatedly contacted the FBI. Moussaoui was arrested on an immigration violation. But there was a bitter argument between the FBI field agents in Minnesota and their superiors at headquarters over whether to investigate further while he awaited deportation. (One of the Washington group, the head of the Bureau's Radical Fundamentalist Unit, was the same FBI supervisor who had allegedly told the ATF it was "chasing ghosts" with Randy Glass.) The agents had seized Moussaoui's laptop and a cell phone, but they lacked probable cause for a criminal search warrant. The FBI considered whether to pursue the case as an intelligence matter, which would have allowed them to perform a search, but this move was rejected at headquarters because there was no evidence that Moussaoui was acting as an agent of a "foreign power," as required by the Foreign Intelligence Surveillance Act. As attorney general, Janet Reno had set up guidelines for the use of surveillance, which had taken on a life of their own within the bureaucracies of the Justice Department and the FBI. Government lawyers interpreted the guidelines more strictly than Reno had intended, turning the "wall" between intelligence and law enforcement into an almost insurmountable obstacle. There were rules, and they broke the system.

AFTER HIS CHANGE of heart, Ziad Jarrah went to stay with Aysel at her apartment. It was not a romantic reunion. Aysel was feeling very sick, suffering from what turned out to be tonsillitis. Ziad was withdrawn. She thought he seemed depressed. He didn't even want to get out of bed.

Jarrah met up with Ramzi bin al-Shibh, his closest friend among the plotters. They had a deep conversation. As Ramzi later retold it, perhaps embellishing, he asked Jarrah how he was feeling about the plan. The man who had taken the battlefield name "Abu Tareq," for the warrior who burned his boats behind him, said he thought the operation would succeed. Ramzi, reassured, asked his friend to pray for him and forgive him and his brothers, for they were "at an hour of strife" on "a battlefield." He asked Jarrah to offer his greetings to the Prophet in the afterlife. Jarrah replied, "Inshallah!"

The other plotters had no idea that Moussaoui had been captured. But it no longer mattered. Jarrah returned to Florida. The fourth pilot had accepted his mission to destroy the U.S. Capitol.

IT SURVIVED UNSCATHED, at least for another twenty years.

On Inauguration Day in the year 2021, a silver-haired Al Gore appeared on NBC News. He did not attend the swearing-in ceremony of his former colleague and frenemy Joe Biden, but spoke via satellite, with that famous photo of Earth as viewed from the moon over his left shoulder.

"What are your thoughts as you see this ritual of democracy?" Savannah Guthrie asked.

"It means our republic lives, the center has held, democracy will return," Gore said. On the other side of the split screen, masked dignitaries, including George W. Bush and Bill and Hillary Clinton, were solemnly filing through the Rotunda of the traumatized U.S. Capitol.

"I know this is not your favorite subject, but we would be remiss if we didn't ask you," Guthrie said, "what was that like for you in those moments, what was going through your mind?"

"Well, thank you for asking, Savannah," Gore replied, "and the answer is pretty simple." He sighed deeply, threw up his hands. "Because of the importance of the United States of America in all of human history, in Lincoln's phrase, we still are the last best hope of humankind. And the choice between one's own disappointment in your personal career and upholding the noble traditions of America's democracy is a pretty easy choice when it comes down to it."

Gore would never really answer the question. He did not want to revisit Florida.

But the argument about what happened there two decades before had never really been settled. In the eyes of many Democrats, Bush never gained legitimacy, even after he won reelection in 2004. That time around, the conspiracy theorists focused on a new decisive state, Ohio, probing flaws in its electronic voting machines. Four years after that, when the Democrat won clearly, conspiracy theorists on the losing side claimed he was never eligible to run at all, propagating a racist lie that he had not been born in the United States. The loudest proponent of that conspiracy theory became the next president. His opponents immediately set out to prove that *his* election was rigged by a hostile foreign power. When he lost his reelection bid, he refused to concede, decrying imaginary "voter fraud," demanding recounts, trying to overturn the result in court in a depraved reenactment of *Bush v. Gore*. Egged on by the president and his henchman Roger Stone, crazed conspiracy theorists stormed the Capitol, chanting, *Stop the steal!*

America's democratic institutions were left battered and debased. It seemed the system might never produce another president whose legitimacy was accepted by all Americans. After Florida and 2000, the paranoid strain had infected the whole body politic. The nation split into two camps, known as the Red and the Blue, names taken from the shading of the maps the TV newscasts used on that impossibly close Election Night. "Red America and Blue America as we now know them were born on November 7, 2000," a historian writes, "the product of an entire nation torn perfectly in half." After Florida, the citizens of these rival Americas would inhabit separate realities, consuming different news and different conspiracy theories, believing different truths, united only in their assumption that the other side was wrong, wicked, and voracious for power.

Maybe the most consequential victim of Florida was not Gore, but the concept of objective truth. Afterward, it was popular to say the winner was impossible to determine. "The problem was," the epistemologist George W. Bush concluded, "that we were dealing in a standardless world."

"Look, the other guy was sworn in," Al Gore said in 2002. "End of story."

Not quite.

Out of Time

It's Tuesday. Kevin Ingram wakes up in the bedroom of his soon-to-be vacated triplex apartment in Jersey City with an electronic monitoring bracelet clamped tightly around his ankle. He is waiting to go to prison. There is nothing to do about it. He is just living in the present.

Ingram's lawyer, a prominent Palm Beach criminal defender, has negotiated him a good deal. Randy Glass has been talking to the Florida newspapers, hinting that the sting operation has "far greater ramifications than have so far been revealed." But federal prosecutors want to dispose of the case without risking a messy trial. All four of the men arrested in June will be offered plea bargains. The most severe sentence, thirty-three months, goes to Ingram's unfortunate golfing buddy, the man with the plane, who only stumbled into the sting at the last moment.

Ingram pleaded guilty to a single charge of money laundering at a hearing in August. He will end up receiving the lightest sentence, eighteen months and a $185,000 fine. Still, you can't say he is lucky. As a bail condition, he has turned over the titles to his real estate, his boat, and his 1996 platinum Porsche. His wife—who stood behind him, wearing a designer suit and sunglasses, when he faced a judge in West Palm Beach—will eventually divorce him.

It is a little before 9 a.m. The markets are about to open. The traders are at their desks. But his old life and his career on Wall Street are over.

At the hearing two weeks before, Ingram told the judge he was suffering from depression, attributing some of his disastrous decisions to his mental condition. But honestly, he does not view his way of thinking as an illness. This morning, he is in a contemplative state, just sitting and staring out his bedroom window. Across the Hudson River, the skyline of lower Manhattan is a forest of steel and glass, glinting against the eastern sun. The great gray trunks of the Twin Towers loom ponderously over the waterfront. The weather is perfect, crisp and cloudless.

The plane comes south down the Hudson, flying at around 460 miles an hour—so fast that Ingram's mind has no time to process what his eyes are seeing before the plane disappears, instantly swallowed up by the North Tower. From the building's core, there is a fiery burst of orange, what another witness will describe as a "great gassy flower." Ingram is more perplexed than terrified.

"Witnessing it was a surreal experience, and it wasn't one where I was able to create an understanding of the event, even though I was looking at it, because it was so illogical," he will later recall. "I was thinking that I was just not seeing something right."

AMERICAN AIRLINES FLIGHT 11, piloted by Mohamed Atta, collided with the face of the North Tower at 8:46 a.m. Eastern Time. As he went in, Atta banked the plane so that the upper tip of the right wing cut through the ninety-ninth floor. The left side hit the ninety-third floor, obliterating the space once occupied by the headquarters of the Voter News Service, where Election Night went awry.

David Boies is in his chauffeured car preparing for a court

hearing as he heads down the highway along the East River. He is back to his regular business, representing a billionaire client in a big commercial dispute. Boies starts to hear police sirens: one, two, then a symphony. As the car approaches the Brooklyn Bridge, Boies looks up and sees that the top of the North Tower is engulfed in inky black smoke.

Up in Windows on the World, waiters and diners are choking. The stairwells are severed. Everyone above the ninety-second floor, 1,344 people, will perish.

As Boies watches this horror, he sees another plane fly into the South Tower. It impacts just below the eighty-fifth floor, where Kevin Ingram once met Randy Glass. Fire and debris explode from the building's face. It takes some time for Boies's mind to grasp what he has seen, and what it means. He continues to the courthouse, still imagining that the judge might hold the hearing. Inside, he compares notes with other witnesses. Some say the planes were passenger jets. But Boies swears he saw a small private aircraft. The hearing is soon canceled.

Boies gets back in his car and tells the driver to head north, to his law firm's office in Midtown Manhattan. There is a roar behind them as the South Tower collapses in a cloud of dust and ash.

BOIES'S OPPONENT IN the case of *Bush v. Gore*, Ted Olson, is in Washington, sitting in his office at Main Justice, watching as the events in New York play out on live television. CNN is rebroadcasting an unbelievable image captured by a news chopper, of the North Tower in flames and the dark silhouette of United Airlines Flight 175 crossing the screen. "*Another* passenger plane hitting the World Trade Center," the anchor says. "These pictures are frightening indeed."

One plane might be an accident. Two planes mean a monstrous crime. Across the street, at FBI headquarters, agents are rushing into position inside the Bureau's crisis command enter.

Someone is trying to place a collect call to the solicitor general through the office switchboard. After several aborted tries, Barbara Olson manages to connect to her husband's secretary.

"Can you tell Ted . . ."

The secretary cuts her short and patches her through to her husband.

Ted knows Barbara is on a plane from Washington to Los Angeles, where she is scheduled to appear on the nighttime chat show *Politically Incorrect*. She booked a morning flight so she could wake up at home. Today, September 11, is Ted's birthday. Barbara was scheduled to take off after 8 a.m., and Ted is feeling relieved, having done the math in his head. There is no way a flight from Washington could have made it to New York in that time. He picks up his phone.

"Hijacked!" his secretary hears him say.

Barbara is frantic. She tells Ted that men carrying knives and box cutters have taken over the plane and have herded her and the rest of the first-class passengers to the back of the cabin.

The call lasts about a minute before the connection drops. Ted Olson alerts the authorities to another hijacking. After a short time, a second call comes through. Barbara is calmer. She asks Ted what she should tell the captain; she seems to indicate he is still alive. Ted feels he must inform Barbara that two hijacked planes have already crashed into the World Trade Center. She absorbs this news. She looks out the window. She says the plane is flying low. She can see houses.

Ted tells Barbara that he knows it will all be okay—although, by this time, he thinks otherwise.

The line goes dead. A few minutes later, the TV reports the news of a crash at the Pentagon.

JANET RENO, ON her way to a Miami-area synagogue to give a campaign speech to a group of Jewish women, is listening to the developing reports on the car radio. Distraught, she asks her driver to pull over to the side of a busy road and wonders what to do next.

Reno decides to go on to the synagogue. She stands up on the bimah, facing an audience of around fifty older women. They are not the type of people who carry cell phones, and most of them arrived earlier than Reno, so the room has only a vague awareness of what is transpiring. Reno tells them the Pentagon has also been hit and says her heart is heavy. Then she delivers her stump speech, talking about the environment and the Everglades, crime and child welfare.

Her aide's phone starts ringing. It is the White House, calling to confirm that Reno is safe.

Reno finishes her speech quickly, and she and the aide ride back to the house Reno's mother built. They sit out on the long porch, facing the overgrown backyard, and watch the rest on TV. Reno says little. "*Taciturn* is the word that comes to mind," the aide will later remember of the former attorney general.

But Reno knows who did it.

SO DOES AL GORE. When he hears about the attack, he is in a hotel suite in Vienna, nerding out with a group of technologists. It is mid-afternoon in Europe, and Gore is attending a conference where he is scheduled to give a talk about the future of the internet.

CNN International is passively playing in the background on

the room's TV. After it broadcasts the report of the first crash at the World Trade Center, the former chairman of the White House Commission on Aviation Safety and Security starts to pay close attention. When he watches the second plane hit the South Tower, Gore announces to the room, "Osama bin Laden."

THE SHEIKH IS already on the move. Shortly before the attack, he evacuated his camp outside Kandahar, traveling in a caravan up into the forbidding mountains. The fourth vehicle in his convoy, a beige minivan, serves as a mobile media center. The van contains a computer, video cameras, a VCR, television sets, and a satellite dish. Bin Laden settles down inside a cave and tells his Yemeni media man to set up the TV. He says it is very important that they watch the news this evening. But the satellite receiver can't pick up a signal.

Bin Laden is frustrated. They move the dish this way and that, but nothing works. As the world watches the attack unfold on television, the Sheikh listens on a shortwave radio.

The joyous tidings arrive in Kandahar around sundown. Although the Taliban have banned TVs, word spreads quickly. People spill out into the alleyways, whooping and cheering.

Mukhtar is in Karachi, watching TV with some of his facilitators, including Ramzi bin al-Shibh, who has just arrived from Germany. They get treats from a nearby Dunkin' Donuts and celebrate the endless TV replays of the direct hit on the South Tower, chanting, *Aim! Aim! Aim!*

Even Mukhtar is shocked by the scale of his success. Supposedly, he will later tell interrogators that as the towers fell, he came to a startled realization: "Shit, I think we bit off more than we could chew."

"SHALL WE FINISH it off?" Ziad Jarrah asks.

"No, not yet."

It is precisely 10 a.m. Inside the cockpit of United Flight 93, Jarrah and another hijacker are conversing in Arabic. A murdered woman lies on the cockpit floor. They are flying over rural Pennsylvania. They can hear the passengers in the cabin fighting for their lives.

"When they all come, we finish it off."

I AM STANDING on the Brooklyn side of the Manhattan Bridge, wearing a press badge and holding a notebook as evacuating office workers pass in a dusty, hollow-eyed procession.

"I saw the building drop in front of me," a woman says.

"I was at the fifty-ninth floor," says a lawyer. "There were body parts all over the plaza."

"What I'm wondering," says another man, "is what America is going to do about it?"

A young man wearing a gold medallion comes across the bridge and shouts in my direction, "I'm going to go home and clean my guns and I'm going to take out every *A*-rab I see!"

AFTERWARD, THE AUTHORITIES will scour the world for the masterminds, seeking answers and vengeance. But the truth is, the men most responsible annihilated themselves with the planes.

They leave only jagged fragments. Fleeing from his lower Manhattan office, a young tech entrepreneur sees a jet engine resting in the middle of Church Street. "Very odd," he thinks to himself. Soon, he joins a long line for a pay phone, scrounging up some quarters from friendly bystanders so he can call to his loved ones long-distance, to let them know he is alive.

The circuits are all jammed up, as everyone is trying to phone everyone at once.

In Chicago, Reverend Jesse Jackson is trying to locate his son, the congressman, who has just published a book and is scheduled to do an event at the World Trade Center. It turns out that Jesse Jackson Jr. has been diverted.

As she rushes to the Capitol, Senator Hillary Clinton calls her husband, who is visiting Australia, traveling and delivering speeches for millions of dollars. He is at a seaside resort, having just finished an enjoyable day of snorkeling, when Hillary reaches him.

Inside the Capitol, the Pakistani general who runs the ISI is lecturing a group of American lawmakers, including Senator Bob Graham of Florida, telling them that they cannot grasp the mind-set of fundamentalist zealots. "The Taliban and Al Qaeda are different," he says. "For them, only the future of paradise after death matters." The meeting is interrupted by an alert about the ongoing attack. Soon, the entire Capitol will be evacuated. Yet another plane is on the way.

The ISI chief receives a call from his nation's ruler. "Don't *argue* with them," General Pervez Musharraf says. "Offer *condolences*. They need to hear they have our *unqualified* support."

A red message—"EVACUATE"—is flashing on the computer terminals at the CIA's headquarters in Langley, Virginia. Members of the team focused on Al Qaeda refuse to leave their desks. "We're going to war," their leader announces. "Use your imagination."

Not far away, a former top official in the Justice Department's intelligence office is trying to get through to John O'Neill, the FBI agent who ran the millennium crisis response. He is now the head of security at the World Trade Center. She leaves a voice mail, and he sends back a page: "I'm OK." Then he closes his flip phone and walks across the plaza from the collapsed South Tower to the still-burning North Tower, entering a stairwell where he will die.

Uptown, at the Grand Hyatt on Forty-Second Street, members of the Chicago White Sox, resting up to face Yankees ace Roger Clemens that evening, are awakened by calls from worried families. Jose Canseco, who has just hit the next-to-last home run of his career, retreats from the lobby to his hotel room to consider plans of escape. "I thought it was a dream," he later tells a reporter.

David Boies is back at his office a few blocks from the Grand Hyatt. A fuller comprehension is beginning to hit him. Both towers have fallen. That afternoon, he meets his biographer at a favorite haunt, Sparks Steak House, to share the enormity of the experience.

"We need a good lawyer," the maître d' says to Boies.

"We need a good army," Boies replies.

AYSEL SENGÜN IS watching the television set in her hospital room in Hattingen, Germany, where she is recovering from a tonsillectomy. She is not worried about Ziad. She knows that America is a large country and that he is in Florida, a long distance from New York. She has just spoken to him. It was a perfectly normal conversation, although Aysel was distracted by a nurse who came in and impatiently asked her to place a meal order. Aysel told Ziad she would have to call him back. Before she hung up, Ziad told her he loved her three times.

The next day, Aysel will try to phone Ziad but will get only his voice mail. After she checks out of the hospital, she will come home to find a message on her answering machine from Arne Kruithof, the man who runs the Florida Flight Training Center. She returns the call.

"Ziad is suspected to have helped to conduct the attacks here in America," Kruithof tells Aysel. "Until we know where he is, or if he's alive, he will continue to be a suspect."

"I have tried to get ahold of him myself, but I can't reach him," Aysel replies.

"It is very important," Arne says, "if he does end up contacting you, that we know right away."

"So, do you have a message?" Aysel asks, still believing that Ziad might call.

"The only message that we have is that he isn't alive anymore."

Aysel breaks down in hysterics.

Later, she will receive a letter from Ziad dated September 11. It addresses her as *habibi*, or "my darling," and tells her that she should be "very proud" of what he has done. "I am what you wish for," the letter says. "I did not escape from you, but I did what I was supposed to do." The letter tells Aysel that they will meet in the afterlife, where they will live in "castles of gold and silver." This time, Ziad promises to stay with her forever.

The terrorist signed off, "See you again!"

THE DOOMSAYERS PREDICTED that the millennium would end with a grand unifying cataclysm. It turns out they weren't all wrong. At the headquarters of Fox News, Roger Ailes dusts off a tool some of the networks employed to keep up with constant developments during the Florida recount, a "ticker" that streams headlines across the bottom of the screen: DAY OF TERROR IN THE UNITED STATES . . . WTC TOWERS COLLAPSED . . . MANHATTAN IS SEALED OFF . . . The ticker will never stop.

A local TV station reaches Donald Trump, who is watching from his tower on Fifth Avenue.

"Donald, you have one of the landmark buildings down in the Financial District, Forty Wall Street," says the interviewer. "What's happened down there?"

"Well, it was an amazing phone call I made," Trump replies. "Forty Wall Street actually was the second-tallest building in downtown Manhattan, and it was actually before the World Trade Center, was the tallest. And then when they built the World Trade Center it became known as the second tallest. And now it's the tallest. And I just spoke to my people, and they said it's the most unbelievable sight."

"In the year 2000, Donald," the interviewer asks, "you considered running for president. If you had done that, if you had been successful, what do you think you'd be doing right now?"

"Well," Trump replies, "I'd be taking a very, very tough line."

DOWN IN WHITE SPRINGS, Chuck Harder swells with vindication. He writes out a monologue to read on the air, a manifesto entitled "America in Terror: What Went Wrong? What to Do?"

"While our national liberal press wallows in the concepts of 'diversity, tolerance and multiculturalism,' you must be aware that our enemy wants none of that," Harder's manifesto says. "You don't have to be a 'rocket scientist' to realize that the terrorists all fit a common profile. Detain those suspects, strap them to a gurney and treat them abundantly with 'truth serum,' then interrogate them and record it all." To Harder, this Islamist menace is merely another manifestation of the grand globalist conspiracy. "Wherever this religion has taken hold," he says, "you see an end to modernity. They will not stop. This is an ongoing war of cultures that has invaded U.S. shores due to our incompetent people in Washington. Worse, new potential terrorists get off planes landing here each day. We are fools."

SHORTLY BEFORE DAWN at the true edge of the new millennium, President George W. Bush rises in Florida. He is on a campaign-style swing to promote his education reform initiative, and he is staying on the island of Longboat Key, at the same beach resort Al Gore used as a retreat when he came to prepare for the first debate. The night before, he had a private dinner with Jeb and some allies from the recount. Now, in the morning, after a brisk run, he heads to Emma E. Booker Elementary in Sarasota. These school events are easy for Bush. In Jacksonville the day before, a local reporter was charmed as he watched the president make funny faces with children in the front row.

As Bush walks into the school building, Karl Rove says something to him about a plane crashing into the World Trade Center. "That sounded strange," Bush will later write. But he goes on with his plan to sit in on a reading lesson. The president takes a seat, legs crossed, in front of around a dozen second-graders, mostly children of color. Out of the camera shot, against the white tile wall, reporters and staffers are murmuring into their cell phones. After a few minutes, Bush's chief of staff walks up to him at the front of the room and whispers the news of a second crash. A dumbstruck look passes over Bush's face. Eyes darting, he grinds his jaw for six long minutes as the children read aloud from a story called "The Pet Goat." In a nearby holding room, Bush's aides are scrambling to set up a TV.

"Hoo!" Bush says when the story is done. "These are great readers!"

Then he is rushed into the holding room, where he picks up

one of the secure phones that always travel with the president and starts to jot down notes on a legal pad. He swivels around to look as the television shows a replay of the second impact. Bush gathers himself to make some hurried remarks in the school auditorium. "Terrorism against our nation will not stand," he vows.

Then the president is back in his motorcade, heading up the Tamiami Trail at breakneck speed. Air Force One is waiting on the tarmac at the Sarasota airport. Bush dashes up the stairs to the plane. He says he wants to fly back to Washington immediately, but no one knows if its airspace is secure. As his aides discuss the president's next moves, Bush places a call to Dick Cheney, who has been taken to a bunker beneath the White House.

"We're at war," Bush says. "Somebody's going to pay."

Across the tarmac, at Jones Aviation, instructor Kendall Coleman has been watching the TV with the rest of the staff. He has no idea that his former students Mohamed Atta and Marwan al-Shehhi were involved, but given the flight school's proximity to the president this morning, he figures that someone from law enforcement may soon come to check around the building. He realizes he needs his driver's license, and heads outside to retrieve it. So, Atta's instructor is watching from the ground as Air Force One roars off.

Normally, the president flies in comfortable fashion, but today the Secret Service is worried about the possibility that terrorists with Stinger missiles might be waiting to ambush Air Force One. The colonel at the controls lifts off fast, with so much force that the plane tears up the runway's concrete, and ascends at a sickening vertical angle. The president's course is still undecided. The plan is simply to get in the sky, to an altitude of forty-five thousand feet, high above any conceivable danger.

The plane climbs up, up, up in the air, its destination unknown, out of Florida and into the future.

NOTES ON SOURCES
AND ACKNOWLEDGMENTS

This book started out as journalism and turned into a work of history. I first covered some of its events and major characters as a reporter at the *New York Observer*. Over the ensuing years, I often found myself in Florida, writing articles about real estate, corruption, or politics, before those subjects all came together in the person of Donald Trump. Portions of this book grew out of my coverage of Trump for *New York*, as well as profiles of the attorneys Laurence Tribe and David Boies. I sincerely thank my editors at the magazine, Genevieve Smith and David Haskell.

I conducted many interviews for this book. Quotes from these present-day conversations are generally placed in the present tense—so "she says," or "he remembers"—and are attributed to the source in the text or the endnotes. However, after twenty years, memories grow dull. As much as possible, I tried to assemble this narrative from archival records and contemporaneous accounts.

Practical constraints do not permit me to credit every person who shared recollections and every reporter who covered these events in real time. I relied particularly heavily on the excellent work of two newspapers. The *Miami Herald* published more than a thousand stories on the Elián Gonzalez controversy, and its staff shared a Pulitzer Prize for its efforts. And both the *Herald* and the *Palm Beach Post* provided comprehensive coverage of the 2000 election and recount.

My account of the 2000 campaign is based primarily on news coverage, supplemented by interviews with former aides to Al Gore and George W. Bush. Bush has recorded his version of events in a memoir, as have Bill Clinton and many other principal characters. Oral histories of both presidencies compiled by the Miller Center at the University of Virginia were a rich source of anecdotal material. University of Florida professor Julian Pleasants conducted oral history interviews with many players in the recount. Gore has never discussed his 2000 presidential campaign at length. "Forty-nine per cent of the people are still not ready to hear what I have to say about it," Gore told *The New Yorker* in 2004. "At the right time, I'll have a lot to say about it. I myself need more perspective on it." Unfortunately for historians, the right time has not yet arrived. Gore declined to be interviewed for this book.

Janet Reno died in 2016. Her sister, Maggy Hurchalla, was a helpful guide as I explored her life and the Reno family's colorful lore. Reno left behind many devoted admirers. Retired FBI agent Todd Rowley, a former member of Reno's security detail, offered particularly rich recollections and shared useful records, including many of her daily schedules. The staff of the special collections department of the University of Miami library provided me with access to Reno's papers over several days of research. Miami artist Norman Silva, who designed floats for the 1999 Orange Bowl Parade, offered photos, recollections, and a guided tour of its route.

Donald Trump turned down an interview request, but many reporters followed the Trump 2000 campaign at a time when he was unguarded and glad to grant access. It was not so easy to unearth the history of the ideology he later made his own. I first learned about Chuck Harder from a podcast called *Surviving Y2K*. I tracked down a former producer of his talk show, Keith Alan, who introduced me to Harder's daughter, Darlene Stewart, who gave me several large boxes containing cassette tapes of *For the People* shows from 1999 and 2000. I thank both of them for their assistance.

The September 11 attacks are one of the most exhaustively

documented criminal acts in history, but relatively little is publicly known about the activities of the plotters during their many months in the United States. The 9/11 Commission received some cooperation from the FBI in preparing its 2004 report, and a relative handful of the Bureau's investigative records are available for review in the commission's files at the National Archives. But as of this writing, much remains classified or closed from view. Bob Graham, a former senator from Florida who chaired a congressional 9/11 inquiry, provided helpful research advice. Surprisingly, the military commission at Guantanamo Bay proved to be an important source of materials, including summaries of the FBI's interrogations of some imprisoned 9/11 plotters and the never-broadcast martyrdom video of Ziad Jarrah. I thank Evan Kohlmann, Marc Sageman, Karen Greenberg, Stanley Cohen, and several former law enforcement and government officials for guiding me through the labyrinth of investigative material. Nelly Lahoud, whose forthcoming book *The Bin Laden Papers* reveals much about Al Qaeda's internal workings, also offered generous insights.

Much of my account of Ziad Jarrah's journey is based on Terry McDermott's book *Perfect Soldiers*. McDermott was also kind enough to share records of the 9/11 investigation conducted by German law enforcement. Susanne Schweitzer provided crucial research assistance to me in reviewing and translating the German documents. Portions of the description of the pilots' flight training are based on evidence introduced at the 2006 trial of Zacarias Moussaoui. Erik Rigler, a retired FBI agent and private investigator on Moussaoui's defense team, offered useful perspective, as did former flight instructors Kendall Coleman and Franck Martin. I especially thank Martin for taking me on a thrilling flight over Venice. My brother-in-law John Saba, a licensed pilot, provided valuable feedback.

My interest in Kevin Ingram dates back to 2001, when a colleague of mine at the *Observer*, Landon Thomas Jr., wrote a series of articles about his case. Nearly two decades later, I contacted Ingram, and he warily embarked on a conversation. Over time, Ingram introduced me to friends and family members, including his twin sister, two of his sons, and his former wife, Deann Prince, all of whom added pieces to the story. Meanwhile, via the Freedom of Information Act, I managed to obtain more than 1,500 pages of internal ATF investigative records. Former ATF spokesman Bradley Engelbert offered much appreciated help to me in this long process. Retired agents Dick Stoltz, Steve Barborini, and Dale Armstrong also proved to be voluble storytellers. Mark Hibbs shared his expertise on the black-market nuclear trade. Richard Greenberg, the executive editor of investigations at NBC News and the producer of the original *Dateline NBC* episodes about the ATF sting operation, offered advice, reporting assistance, and help with accessing archival materials. I extend him my most profound gratitude.

Many other journalists offered a collegial hand with various parts of this book. Special thanks to Frank Cerabino, Dan Christensen, Karen Donovan, John Lantigua, Jim McGee, Bob Mudge, Frank Rich, Nicholas Schmidle, Philip Shenon, and Ben Taub. I have benefited from the advice and assistance of friends and colleagues, including Anne Barnard, Josh Benson, Chris Buck, Gabriel Debenedetti, Matt DeBord, Felix Gillette, Andrew Goldman, Joe Hagan, Garth Hallberg, Ted Hart, Alexandra Jacobs, Sheelah Kolhatkar, Steve Kornacki, Jonathan Mahler, Sridhar Pappu, Gravelle Pierre, Joe Pompeo, Maria Russo, Gabe Sherman, Vera Titunik, Ben Wallace, Reeves Wiedeman, and Howard Yoon. Manolis Priniotakis and Amy Rofman offered me their guest room in Washington, and Ben and Kate Brashares served up much-needed drinks around the firepit.

My agent, PJ Mark, enthusiastically encouraged my work on this project and offered sage counsel at every step of the process. My editor, Sara Nelson, gravitated to the concept of the book from the moment we first discussed the proposal and skillfully ushered it into print. I thank my talented fact-checker, Will Peischel, for keeping me out of trouble, so far.

I returned home from a trip to Florida on March 8, 2020, expecting to sequester myself in my attic as I prepared to write this manuscript. Little did I know that the rest of the world would lock down, too. The pandemic created research challenges, but it also focused my mind on what was most important in this book, and also in my own story. I send my love to my parents, Tom and Diane, and most especially to my wife, Jennifer, and my son, Eddie, to whom this book is jointly dedicated. We make a lovely pod.

NOTES

Abbreviations

Media
AP: Associated Press
FTP: Chuck Harder, *For the People* radio broadcast
MH: *Miami Herald*
NYT: *New York Times*
PBP: *Palm Beach Post*
WP: *Washington Post*

Reports
9/11 Commission Report: National Commission on Terrorist Attacks Upon the United States, *The 9/11 Commission Report: Final Report of the National Commission on Terrorist Attacks Upon the United States*, Government Printing Office, 2004, Washington, DC.
USCCR Report: U.S. Commission on Civil Rights, *Voting Irregularities in Florida During the 2000 Presidential Election*, Government Printing Office, June 2001, Washington, DC.

Archival Collections
9/11 Commission Files: Declassified files of the National Commission on Terrorist Attacks Upon the United States, National Archives, Washington DC.
Clinton Library: Digital collection of the William J. Clinton Presidential Library and Museum, Little Rock, AR.
Miller Center: Presidential Oral History Project, Miller Center, University of Virginia, Charlottesville.
National Security Archive: The Central Intelligence Agency's 9/11 File, National Security Archive, George Washington University, declassified document collection. Posted June 19, 2012.
Reno Papers: Janet Reno Papers, University of Miami Library Special Collections.
UF Election Project: Florida Election Project Oral History Collection, Samuel Proctor Oral History Program, University of Florida Digital Collections.

Criminal Investigations and Legal Proceedings
ATF Report: Report of Investigation, Bureau of Alcohol, Tobacco, and Firearms, Case No. 764055 99 0015 (Title of Investigation: Diaa Mohsen).
BKA Files: Files of the Bundeskriminalamt (BKA), the German federal law enforcement agency.
FBI Timeline: FBI, "Hijackers Timeline (Redacted)," FBI Records: The Vault, vault.fbi.gov.
NAACP v. Harris: *National Association for the Advancement of Colored People et al. v. Katherine Harris et al.*, U.S. District Court for the Southern District of Florida, 2001.
USA v. al-Bahlul: *USA v. Ali Hamza Ahmad Suliman al-Bahlul*, U.S. Military Commission at Guantanamo Bay, Cuba. Case tried in 2008.
USA v. Ingram: *USA v. Kevin Ingram, Walter Kapij and Diaa Mohsen*, Case No. 01-cr-8090, U.S. District Court for the Southern District of Florida, 2001.

USA v. KSM: *USA v. Khalid Sheikh Mohammed et al.*, U.S. Military Commission at
Guantanamo Bay, Cuba. Case filed in 2008.

USA v. Moussaoui: *USA v. Zacarias Moussaoui*, Case No. 01-cr-455, U.S. District Court for
the Eastern District of Virginia. Case filed in 2001, tried in 2006.

Prologue: Inauguration Day

1   It is Inauguration Day: C-SPAN, "President George W. Bush Inaugural
Ceremony," C-SPAN.org, Jan. 20, 2001.

2   "The underlying vibe": Hank Stuever, "Under a Shroud of Gray, Muffled Cheers
and Jeers," *WP*, Jan. 21, 2001.

2   *Hail to the thief*: *NYT*, Jan. 21, 2001.

2   "We can only wonder": *NYT*, Jan. 21, 2001.

4   knew Gore was in trouble: Karl Rove, oral history, interviewed by Russell Riley et
al., Miller Center (hereafter "Rove, Miller Center oral history").

4   He has promised: Nicholas Lemann, "All Together Now?," *The New Yorker*,
Nov. 26, 2000.

4   calling his boy "Quincy": Frank Bruni, *Ambling into History* (New York:
HarperCollins, 2002), p. 220.

4   Dubya has been reading up: George W. Bush, *Decision Points* (New York: Crown,
2010), p. 86.

5   "shockingly good": Hendrik Hertzberg, "Comment: The Word from W," *The New
Yorker*, Feb. 5, 2001.

5   "My fellow citizens": George W. Bush, "President George W. Bush's Inaugural
Address," Jan. 20, 2001.

5   *The Onion* sums it all up: "Bush: 'Our Long National Nightmare of Peace and
Prosperity Is Finally Over,'" *The Onion*, Jan. 17, 2001.

6   "I left the White House": "Text: Former President Clinton's Farewell," *WP*,
Jan. 20, 2001.

6   back at the White House by 11:37: Bruni, *Ambling into History*, p. 223.

6   a wistful Darrell Hammond: *Saturday Night Live*, Episode 495, Jan. 20, 2001,
NBC.

1: Zero Zero

7   That day, in Germany: Passenger manifest, Turkish Airlines Flight 1662, Nov. 25,
1999, BKA Files.

7   Ziad Jarrah had spent: This account of Jarrah's preparations for his trip to
Afghanistan was compiled from various primary and secondary sources, including
9/11 Commission Report, July 22, 2004; witness interviews with Aysel Sengün and
others, BKA Files; Terry McDermott, *Perfect Soldiers* (New York: HarperCollins,
2005); Mary Anne Weaver, "The Indecisive Terrorist," *London Review of Books*,
Sept. 8, 2011.

8   "The morning will come": McDermott, *Perfect Soldiers*, p. 88.

9   In the still hours: This description of the boat voyage primarily drawn from: Ann
Louise Bardach, "Elián's Boat: The Untold Story," *George*, May 2000; Elaine De Valle,
"The Deadly Voyage: How It Happened," *MH*, Dec. 13, 1999.

11 but when he awoke: Elián Gonzalez, interview in the documentary *Elián*, dir. Tim
Golden and Ross McDonnell (Five Point Films/Jigsaw Productions, 2017).

11 Janet Reno spent the weekend: Janet Reno, Schedules for Nov. 20–27, 1999.
Reno's schedules for 1999–2000 provided by Todd Rowley.

11   Reno picked up the *Herald*: Janet Reno, oral history, interviewed by Russell Riley et al., Miller Center (hereafter "Reno, Miller Center oral history").

12   "The ocean is a dangerous": *MH*, Nov. 26, 1999.

12   "Little Rafter Leaves Hospital": *MH*, Nov. 27, 1999.

13   "toilet paper will be totally computerized": Conan O'Brien, *In the Year 2000 . . .* (New York: Riverhead Books, 1999), p. 12.

13   the tiny Pacific nation of Kiribati: Colin Woodard, "South Pacific Battles for Y2K Bragging Rights," *Christian Science Monitor*, Dec. 1, 1999.

14   A Manhattan hotelier: *PBP*, Nov. 28, 1999.

14   For the cost of $40,000: "Planning for the Eve of 2000," CBSNews.com, April 1, 1999.

14   In the words of one scholar: Author interview, Chip Berlet.

14   "Something's coming": *FTP*, July 26, 1999.

14   Harder called himself: Charles Harder, *Will We Ever Learn? The Man Who Sees Tomorrow* (Bloomington, IN: AuthorHouse, 2009).

14   "They say Soviet-built nuke plants": *FTP*, Dec. 16, 1999.

15   "The Day the World Crashes": *Newsweek*, June 1, 1997.

15   a whole apocalyptic belief system: Dan Taberski (host), *Headlong: Surviving Y2K* (podcast series), 2018.

15   "You may be tired of Y2K": *FTP*, Oct. 25, 1999.

16   "'Stone-Age' conditions": "Y2K packages by Chuck Harder," chuckharder.com, 1999, archive.org.

16   "coming dark times": Chuck Harder, "BLACKOUT! Preparing for the Coming Dark Times. An Introductory Primer," chuckharder.com, archive.org.

16   Harder's own home: Author visit, 2020.

16   "Ladies and gentlemen": *FTP*, Dec. 13, 1999.

16   "Don't Be Y2Krazy": *MH*, Dec. 28, 1999.

17   "He *did* invent": Elaine Kamarck, oral history, interviewed by Russell Riley et al., Miller Center (hereafter "Kamarck, Miller Center oral history").

18   had sized Gore up: Tucker Carlson, "Devil May Care," *Talk*, September 1999.

18   "He's not a dunce": Author interview, Martin Peretz.

18   "The times just don't call": Dana Milbank, *Smashmouth: Two Years in the Gutter with Al Gore and George W. Bush* (New York: Basic Books, 2001), p. 30.

19   Clinton's limousine passed: *Orlando Sentinel*, Dec. 12, 1999.

19   "You may have noticed": Bill Clinton, Remarks to the Florida State Democratic Convention in Orlando, Florida, Dec. 11, 1999.

20   He prowled the stage: *Orlando Sentinel*, Dec. 12, 1999.

21   Gore took a typically nuanced position: *PBP*, Dec. 12, 1999.

21   Elián was also coming to Disney World: De Valle, "The Deadly Voyage."

21   Bill Clinton could see political peril: *MH*, Dec. 12, 1999.

22   a briefing from the CIA: 9/11 Commission Staff, "Chronology of Key Events," background binder for President Clinton and Vice President Gore's interviews, 9/11 Commission Files.

22   a high-level briefing memo: CIA, "Bin Ladin to Exploit Looser Security During Holidays," Senior Executive Intelligence Brief, Dec. 11, 1999, National Security Archive.

22   "unique opportunities": CIA, "Millennium Threat Briefing for DCI," Dec. 17, 1999, National Security Archive.

22   between five and fifteen attacks: Steve Coll, *Ghost Wars* (New York: Penguin, 2004), p. 485.

22   On December 14: Ahmed Ressam, witness testimony, *USA v. Haouari*, July 3,

2001. See also *9/11 Commission Report*, pp. 176–80; Richard A. Clarke, *Against All Enemies* (New York: Free Press, 2004), pp. 205–26; Garrett M. Graff, *The Threat Matrix: The FBI at War in the Age of Global Terror* (New York: Little, Brown, 2011), pp. 248–52; Lawrence Wright, *The Looming Tower* (New York: Alfred A. Knopf, 2006), pp. 296–99.

23 an editorial cartoon: Jeff MacNelly, "Freeze!," *Chicago Tribune*, republished in the *PBP*, Dec. 31, 1999.

23 "the biggest asses-to-elbow": George Tenet, deposition given to 9/11 Commission, 9/11 Commission Files.

23 Reno slept on a couch: 9/11 Commission Staff, interview of Frances Fragos Townsend, 9/11 Commission Files.

23 "Christmas is cancelled": Graff, *The Threat Matrix*, p. 251.

24 "I wouldn't be anywhere else": *PBP*, Dec. 29, 1999.

24 the island's foremost party planner: Author interview, Bruce Sutka.

24 thirty-pound mound of caviar: Laurence Leamer, *Mar-a-Lago* (New York: Flatiron Books, 2019), p. 138.

24 "That's Stephanie Seymour": Shannon Donnelly, "Midnight Madness," *Palm Beach Daily News*, Jan. 2, 2000.

24 His teenage daughter, Ivanka: Thom Smith, "Singer, Top Chef Help Trumps Greet 2000," *PBP*, Jan. 4, 2000.

25 The first humans to reach midnight: "Straddling Two Years: One Sub," CBSNews.com, Dec. 31, 1999. Other details of celebrations from coverage in AP, *NYT*, and *MH*, Jan. 1, 2000.

26 an Al Qaeda operative was sitting: *9/11 Commission Report*, pp. 158–59; FBI, "Encore Investigation Update, Review and Analysis," April 4, 2016, declassified Sept. 2021.

26 "We're taking your calls": *FTP*, Dec. 31, 1999.

27 That night, Kevin Ingram: This account of the New Year's Eve party is compiled from interviews with people who attended, including Ingram, his wife at the time, Deann, and Ingram's former colleague Jerry McMillan.

27 what another guest later described: Author interview, Jerry McMillan.

28 Sean "Puffy" Combs took the stage: "MTV 2 Large: New Year's Eve 2000," MTV, Dec. 31, 1999, video accessed via YouTube.

29 the Artist then known as: Prince, *Rave Un2 the Year 2000*, dir. Geoff Wonfor (2000), DVD, released in 2019 as part of the Prince box set *Ultimate Rave*.

29 he told CNN's Larry King: Larry King interview with Prince, *Larry King Live*, CNN, Dec. 10, 1999, interview transcript accessed on prince.org.

30 enjoyed a quiet dinner: "Bands Deliver Standards, Surprises on New Year's Eve," MTV.com, Jan. 3, 2000.

30 was watching Times Square: Clarke, *Against All Enemies*, p. 214.

30 a "super-duper command post": Reno, Miller Center oral history.

30 Reno and the leadership of the FBI: Louis Freeh, *My FBI* (New York: St. Martin's Press, 2005), pp. 295–97.

30 bored technicians relaxed: *PBP*, Jan. 1, 2000.

30 His guests included: Josh Gerstein, "Millennial Capital," ABCNews.com, Dec. 31, 1999.

31 Muhammad Ali gave Reno a kiss: Author interview, Maggy Hurchalla.

31 "The moral arc of the universe is long": Marshall Frady, *Jesse: The Life and Pilgrimage of Jesse Jackson* (New York: Simon and Schuster Paperbacks, 1996), p. 48.

31 "The change of centuries": Bill Clinton, Remarks at the "America's Millennium" Celebration, Dec. 31, 1999.

31 "I think we dodged the bullet": Clarke, *Against All Enemies*, p. 214.

32 It was a balmy night: Descriptions of South Florida millennium festivities compiled from reports in the *Miami Herald*, *South Florida Sun Sentinel*, *Palm Beach Post*, and *Palm Beach Daily News*, Jan. 1, 2000.

32 proceeded to noodle through: Phish set list, Dec. 31, 1999, Big Cypress Indian Reservation, audio file at www.phishtracks.com.

32 paramedics responded: *Palm Beach Daily News*, Jan. 5, 2000.

32 Thousands gathered on the parade route: "Orange Bowl Parade Still a Family Tradition," *MH*, Jan. 1, 2000.

32 The Orange Bowl Parade was famed: Author interview, Norman Silva.

33 "It will welcome the United States": "Magic City Millennium," Orange Bowl Committee, 1999, p. 12. The parade program and float sketches are archived in Orange Bowl Parade Collection, Smithsonian National Museum of American History, Washington, DC.

33 The float sputtered: "Orange Bowl Parade Still a Family Tradition."

2: Strange Land

34 stroke of midnight: *MH*, Jan. 2, 2000.

34 packed in so tightly: *MH*, July 23, 2000.

35 "Two things play against Haitians": *MH*, Jan. 6, 2000.

36 the inspiration for the minstrel tune: T. D. Allman, *Finding Florida* (New York: Atlantic Monthly Press, 2003), pp. 340–45.

36 "Hello, everybody": *FTP*, Jan. 4, 2000.

36 "maybe 3,000 people": Marc Cooper, "The Paranoid Style," *The Nation*, April 10, 1995.

37 "enslave us all": Chuck Harder, "The Gray Bomb," chuckharder.com, 2000, archive.org.

37 an exemplar of an emerging phenomenon: Michael Kelly, "The Road to Paranoia," *The New Yorker*, June 11, 1995.

37 "These things came from the global elite": *FTP*, July 29, 1999.

37 "the first globalist president": Joe Klein, "Eight Years," *The New Yorker*, Oct. 8, 2000.

38 "the central reality of our time": Bill Clinton, State of the Union Address, Jan. 27, 2000.

38 he continued to shuffle: *FTP*, Jan. 4, 2000.

39 "Kid is with relative": John Pogash to Arthur Strathern, email, Nov. 30, 1999, Reno Papers.

39 The caseworker scrawled: Adria Martinez, "Unaccompanied Minor Statement of Suitability Determination," Dec. 1, 1999, Reno Papers.

40 "I want my son back": Janelle Jones to Philip Busch, email, Jan. 27, 2000, Reno Papers.

41 Fidel excused himself: *MH*, April 13, 2000.

41 an honored guest: *MH*, Jan. 10, 2000.

41 Polls showed: AP, Dec. 15, 1999.

41 "Where Does He Belong?": *Time*, Jan. 17, 2000.

42 "another aspect of cultural life": *NYT*, Jan. 29, 1996.

43 "you don't conform": Richard Blow, "Janet Reno Stands Tall," *George*, September 1999.

43 "dumb, dull and flat": Jane Wood Reno, *The Hell with Politics* (Atlanta: Peachtree Publishers, 1994), p. 33.

43 "I saw the hurricane": Paul Anderson, *Janet Reno: Doing the Right Thing* (Hoboken, NJ: John Wiley and Sons, 1994), p. 15.

43 "She could storm and rage": "Oral History of Janet Reno," interviewed by Hilarie Bass, five interviews held over June 25, 2005, to Jan. 31, 2008, Women Trailblazers Project, American Bar Association.

44 "as far west as they could go": Anderson, *Janet Reno*, p. 22.

44 "What they would do": Author interview, Ann McDade.

45 "When the world gets old": Reno, *The Hell with Politics*, p. 114.

46 "Janet saw the end of the movie": Author interview, former Justice Department official.

3: Kandahar

47 Kandahar smelled like shit: The smell of Kandahar and the configuration of its plumbing are intricately described by Osama bin Laden's son Omar in his memoir, *Growing Up Bin Laden*, a book he cowrote with his mother, Najwa bin Laden, and Jean Sasson ([New York: St. Martin's Griffin, 2009], p. 209). Other jihadi perspectives include *Nine Lives*, by Aimen Dean (London: Oneworld, 2018); and Nasser al-Bahri (aka Abu Jandal) with Georges Malbrunot, trans. Susan de Muth, *Guarding Bin Laden: My Life in Al Qaeda* (London: Thin Man Press, 2013). Other scenic elements compiled from contemporary photographs and travelogues, including William Vollmann, "Across the Divide," *The New Yorker*, May 7, 2000.

47 rehearses for a propaganda video: Video introduced into evidence in proceedings of *USA v. al-Bahlul*.

48 retrace every step of his journey: See McDermott, *Perfect Soldiers*; Anthony Summers and Robbyn Swan, *The Eleventh Day: The Full Story of 9/11 and Osama bin Laden* (New York: Ballantine Books, 2011); Staff of *Der Spiegel*, *Inside 9-11: What Really Happened* (New York: St. Martin's Press, 2001); Peter Finn, "Hamburg's Cauldron of Terror," *WP*, Sept. 11, 2002.

48 a red Mercedes: Weaver, "The Indecisive Terrorist."

49 a paranoid library: "Atta's Army," *Der Spiegel*, July 9, 2006.

49 ten thousand to twenty thousand: Wright, *The Looming Tower*, p. 301.

49 Jarrah traveled: Weaver, "The Indecisive Terrorist."

50 "the Sheikh's group": Zacarias Moussaoui, testimony, *USA v. Moussaoui*; deposition of Saajid Badat, *USA v. Adis Medunjanin*, 2012.

50 "forget their pasts": Bin Laden, *Growing Up Bin Laden*, p. 198.

50 Men who arrived: CIA, "Afghanistan Camps Central to 11 September Plot: Can Al Qaeda Train on the Run?," June 20, 2003, p. 2; Dean, *Nine Lives*, p. 58.

50 Jarrah took the *kunya*: Yosri Fouda and Nick Fielding, *Masterminds of Terror* (New York: Arcade Publishing, 2003), p. 112.

50 the brothers would put Hollywood movies: Wright, *The Looming Tower*, p. 303.

50 It is likely that Jarrah: Khalid Sheikh Mohammed, in a written deposition submitted into evidence as part of the trial of Zacarias Moussaoui, claimed that the four men from Hamburg "expressed a desire to fight the Northern Alliance in Afghanistan, but Bin Laden insisted that they instead proceed as soon as possible to the US."

51 handbooks published by American survivalists: Reuel Marc Gerecht, "Blueprint for Terror," *Talk*, October 2000.

51 One mad bomb maker: Dean, *Nine Lives*, pp. 98–106; Bin Laden, *Growing Up Bin Laden*, pp. 229–30.

51 a more isolated guesthouse: Ali Soufan, testimony, *USA v. al-Bahlul*.

51 former government farm: A detailed description of the camp's layout can be found in Coll, *Ghost Wars*, p. 391. See also Wright, *The Looming Tower*, p. 248; Bin Laden, *Growing Up Bin Laden*, p. 208; Dean, *Nine Lives*, p. 93.

51 it was known as al-Matar: Badat deposition.

52 his lieutenants knew him to be: Cathy Scott-Clark and Adrian Levy, *The Exile* (New York: Bloomsbury, 2017), p. 5.

52 "Who had a good dream?": Al-Bahri, *Guarding Bin Laden*.

52 often went hungry: Bin Laden, *Growing Up Bin Laden*, p. 223.

52 sermons in which he boasted: McDermott, *Perfect Soldiers*, p. 173.

53 "poorly educated peasants": Gerecht, "Blueprint for Terror."

53 "They seemed wily": Al-Bahri, *Guarding Bin Laden*.

53 "I came to you": McDermott, *Perfect Soldiers*, p. 88.

53 "Talk yourselves into martyrdom": As-Sahab Media Foundation, *Knowledge Is for Acting Upon*, 2006. English translation of this Al Qaeda propaganda video provided by Evan Kohlmann.

54 "He had the beady gaze": Dean, *Nine Lives*, pp. 94–95.

54 whirlwind of meetings: CIA, "11 September: The Plot and the Plotters," 2003, National Security Archive; "The Confession," *Der Spiegel*, November 2003.

54 claim they protested: Scott-Clark and Levy, *The Exile*, p. 4.

54 Only Jarrah and Atta: Author interview, Nelly Lahoud.

54 an Indian airliner landed: Yudhijit Bhattacharjee, "The Terrorist Who Got Away," *New York Times Magazine*, March 22, 2020.

55 the leadership of Al Qaeda celebrated Eid al-Fitr: This event was videotaped by Al Qaeda propagandist Ali al-Bahlul. The U.S. government later recovered raw footage and identified many Al Qaeda members who attended, including Jarrah. The footage was entered into evidence during al-Bahlul's military commission trial. The translations of bin Laden's sermon are likewise from the evidence presented at that proceeding.

4: The Wall Street Project

57 "You get out of the limo": American Express advertisement, *New York*, Dec. 20, 1999, p. 137.

57 On a winter day in 1999: C-SPAN, "Wall Street Project," Jan. 14, 1999, C-SPAN .org.

58 Arrayed before the stage: Rainbow/PUSH Coalition, 2nd Annual Wall Street Project conference agenda, archive.org.

58 Jackson described the Wall Street Project: George Packer, "Trickle Down Civil Rights," *New York Times Magazine*, Dec. 12, 1999; David Whitford, "Jesse Shakes the Money Tree," *Fortune*, June 21, 1999; Peter Boyer, "Man of Faith," *The New Yorker*, Oct. 22, 2001; Karin Stanford, "Reverend Jesse Jackson and the Rainbow PUSH Coalition: Institutionalizing Economic Opportunity," in Stanford and Ollie Johnson III, eds., *Black Organizations in the Post-Civil Rights Era* (New Brunswick, NJ: Rutgers University Press, 2002).

59 "If you want to carve out": David Garrow, *Bearing the Cross* (New York: Vintage, 1988), p. 616.

59 "Jesse, I want you to come": Frady, *Jesse*, p. 227.

61 "We will go from discussing Monica": Amy Feldman, "Clinton Bringing Cash to Jackson Confab," *New York Daily News*, Jan. 15, 2000.

61 on the cover of *Forbes*: *Forbes*, March 1999.

62 "Kevin was more or less": Author interview, Jerry McMillan.

62 Ingram was at the stock exchange gala: Author interview, Deann Prince.

62 "Everybody was treating him": Author interview, friend of Sparkle's from the modeling world.

63 "the Black version of Gordon Gekko": Author interview, Philmore Anderson.

63 Ingram came from Philadelphia: Author interview, Kevin Ingram.

63 A brilliant but troubled man: Author interview, Karen Ingram.

63 Kevin would hint to friends: Leah Nathans Spiro, "Wall Street's Soldier of Fortune," *Talk*, November 2001.

63 determined to be suicide: Germaine Ingram, letter to Judge Donald Middlebrooks regarding Kevin Ingram's sentencing, Nov. 19, 2001. Ingram's older sister told the judge that although she had heard that he had "attributed our father's death to a gun battle, and that he had even claimed to be an orphan," there was "never any serious doubt about the fact that the cause of death was suicide."

64 The real excitement was in bonds: This account of the development of the mortgage bond market in the 1980s and '90s is indebted to Michael Lewis's personal history of his time on the Salomon Brothers trading floor, *Liar's Poker* (New York: W.W. Norton, 1989), and its post-2008 sequel, *The Big Short* (New York: W.W. Norton, 2010). Two other books that inform this account are Mark Zandi, *Financial Shock* (Upper Saddle River, NJ: FT Press, 2009), and Howard Hill, *Finance Monsters* (self-published, 2014).

66 "They were minting money": Author interview, Howard Altarescu.

66 "He was as analytical": Author interview, former Wall Street investment bank executive.

66 one of only six Black bond traders: Spiro, "Wall Street's Soldier of Fortune."

66 "People tend to think of this": "On the Edge with CMOs," *Black Enterprise*, October 1992, p. 72.

66 A friend later quipped: Spiro, "Wall Street's Soldier of Fortune."

67 "Kevin walks in": Author interview, Howard Altarescu.

67 Ingram was married: Demetra Ingram, letter to court regarding Kevin Ingram's sentencing, June 14, 2005.

67 "When I started at Goldman": Author interview, former Goldman Sachs investment bank executive. It should be noted that some other contemporaries of Ingram's remember no such culture of modesty at Goldman Sachs.

68 "difficult to manage": Jon Corzine, quoted in Spiro, "Wall Street's Soldier of Fortune."

68 he was told to wait: William Cohan, *Money and Power: How Goldman Sachs Came to Rule the World* (New York: Doubleday, 2011), pp. 423–24.

68 "I guess I'm not the chosen one": Landon Thomas Jr., "Ex-Goldman Trader Stung in Arms Plot, Shocks Colleagues," *New York Observer*, July 2, 2001.

68 sometimes disappeared: Author interviews, former Goldman Sachs colleagues; Spiro, "Wall Street's Soldier of Fortune."

69 back at the World Trade Center: Affidavit of ATF agent Stephen Barborini, *USA v. Ingram*, Doc. No. 25, filed June 29, 2001; ATF Report No. 39, June 22, 1999.

69 related to Egypt's deposed royal family: Author interview, Diaa Mohsen.

69 a high-stakes table: "Link Diagram #1," ATF, Intelligence Division, Intelligence Summary, updated March 15, 1999; author interview, Benjamin Seaman.

69   "a certain amount of cash": Affidavit of ATF agent Stephen Barborini.

70   "My offices are at Two World Trade": Recorded telephone call between Kevin
      Ingram and Randy Glass, June 15, 1999.

70   the details of which are in dispute: In a contemporaneous internal report, ATF
      agents running the sting operation record that the confidential informant (CI), Glass,
      "told Ingram that the money was from illegal arms deals and he wanted [the] money
      laundered. The CI even showed pictures of the CI holding various arms (ATF props)"
      (ATF Report No. 39, June 22, 1999). In his sworn affidavit, ATF agent Stephen
      Barborini alleges that after Glass told him the money was from arms deals, Ingram asked
      him to "retract that statement" before proceeding with the $100,000 transaction. Mohsen
      alleged in an interview with ATF agents after his arrest that he and Glass had disclosed
      in their initial talks that the money was coming from arms deals, and Ingram replied,
      "I don't want to know." To this day, Ingram denies ever being told anything about arms
      deals. Todd Petrie, a former undercover federal agent who posed as an accountant for the
      arms syndicate, told the author that he never explicitly discussed the origin of the funds
      with Ingram in their subsequent conversations about moving funds. "The representations
      were made through the informant [Glass] that we moved munitions illegally," Petrie
      said. "So I really didn't have to reinforce that when I met him." Although ATF records
      disclosed via FOIA indicate Glass secretly recorded the initial World Trade Center
      meeting, no tape or transcript of it has been made publicly available.

70   He told Glass he was forming offshore shell companies: Recorded phone calls
      between Ingram and Glass, June–August 1999.

70   "IAM Global Money Fund": Spiro, "Wall Street's Soldier of Fortune." Ingram
      claims he has no recollection of proposing to create any such entity and says it would be
      outside his realm of financial expertise.

70   "He explained to me": Recorded phone call between Ingram and Glass, June 26,
      1999.

71   "It's going to be": Recorded phone call between Ingram and Glass, July 13, 1999.

5: Baseball Man

72   "It's King Kong": *Big League Challenge*, ESPN, 2000. TV special accessed via
      YouTube, Oct. 5, 2016.

73   Canseco was Mr. Miami: Jose Canseco, *Juiced: Wild Times, Rampant 'Roids,
      Smash Hits, and How Baseball Got Big* (New York: ReganBooks, 2005); Jose Canseco,
      Vindicated: Big Names, Big Liars, and the Battle to Save Baseball (New York: Simon
      Spotlight Entertainment, 2008). Although Canseco's credibility was challenged
      when his memoirs were published, much of what he claimed about the prevalence of
      performance-enhancing drugs was confirmed by subsequent investigations, including
      George Mitchell's official *Report to the Commissioner of Baseball* on steroid use (New
      York: MLB, 2007).

73   financed by his hometown's cocaine cowboys: Tim Elfrink and Gus Garcia-
      Roberts, *Blood Sport* (New York: Dutton, 2014), p. 7.

73   called him "the Chemist": Howard Bryant, *Juicing the Game* (New York: Viking,
      2005), p. 190.

73   added twenty-five pounds of muscle: Canseco, *Juiced*, p. 50.

74   "Look at his arms": Jerome Holtzman, "'Look at His Arms' . . . Scouts Go Ga-Ga
      over Rookie Slugger Canseco," *Chicago Tribune*, April 3, 1986.

74   He was a steroid user, too: Mark McGwire refused to answer questions about
      allegations of steroid usage when he testified under oath before a congressional

committee in 2005. In 2010, he admitted that he had used performance-enhancing drugs during an injury-marred period in the early 1990s (*NYT*, Jan. 11, 2010). McGwire has continued to deny Canseco's claim that he used steroids as a young player for the A's.

74 Canseco would later claim: Canseco, *Juiced*, p. 74.

74 he looked like a wholesome white boy: Canseco, *Juiced*, pp. 76–80.

75 "What the hell have you been doing?": Canseco, *Juiced*, p. 215. Other accounts of this locker room conversation, with slight variations in wording, appear in Bryant, *Juicing the Game*, and Mark Fainaru-Wada and Lance Williams, *Game of Shadows* (New York: Gotham Books, 2006).

75 "I told him everything I knew": Canseco, *Vindicated*, p. 36; Fainaru-Wadu and Williams, *Game of Shadows*, reports that Bonds started to experiment with steroids well before the locker room encounter in 2000. In 2011, a jury found Bonds guilty of obstruction of justice in a case connected to an investigation of his alleged steroid use. The conviction was later overturned.

75 his teammates would discreetly seek out his expertise: Canseco, *Juiced*, p. 263.

75 he believed that, if used properly: Canseco, *Juiced*, p. 3.

76 "Bombastic Bushkin": Lois Romano and George Lardner Jr., "Bush's Life-Changing Year," *WP*, July 25, 1999. This article was the first in a seven-part series, "The Making of George W. Bush."

76 "I never dreamed of being president": Carlson, "Devil May Care."

77 champagne unit: Jean Edward Smith, *Bush* (New York: Simon and Schuster, 2016), p. 17.

77 "chased a lot of pussy": Mark Updegrove, *The Last Republicans* (New York: HarperCollins, 2017), p. 13.

77 Lee Atwater was a liquor-drinking: John Brady, *Bad Boy: The Life and Politics of Lee Atwater* (New York: Addison-Wesley, 1997).

77 working for a rival Republican: Roger Stone and another partner in the firm were consultants to Jack Kemp, a former NFL quarterback and congressman.

77 "I said, 'How can we trust you?'": Evan Smith, "George, Washington," *Texas Monthly*, June 1999.

77 "If someone throws a grenade at our dad": Bush, *Decision Points*, p. 43.

78 "If I'm disloyal": Romano and Lardner, "The Making of George W. Bush," *WP*, July 31, 1999.

78 "He was itching to go": Romano and Lardner, "The Making of George W. Bush," *WP*, July 25, 1999.

78 an office in between Atwater and Roger Ailes: Smith, *Bush*, pp. 48–49.

78 Dubya would spend his days: Nicholas Lemann, "The Redemption," *The New Yorker*, Jan. 31, 2000.

78 Bush was Atwater's "alter ego": Smith, *Bush*, p. 53.

78 A furious Dubya called up: Evan Smith, "George, Washington."

79 Atwater later claimed that he realized the effectiveness: Brady, *Bad Boy*, p. 181.

79 "make Willie Horton his running mate": *NYT*, Jan. 13, 1991.

79 At a rally in California: Brady, *Bad Boy*, p. 189.

79 Atwater had once cracked: Evan Smith, "George, Washington."

79 "George went up as Sonny Corleone": Updegrove, *The Last Republicans*, p. 196.

80 "anchors him clearly as a Texas businessman": Romano and Lardner, "The Making of George W. Bush." *WP*, July 31, 1999.

80 The Rangers were a miserable franchise: Joe Nick Patoski, "Team Player," *Texas Monthly*, June 1999.

80 personally contributed just $600,000: Smith, *Bush*, p. 60.

81 One time, late in an extra-inning game: Milbank, *Smashmouth*, p. 320.
81 "A blockbuster": T. R. Sullivan, "Get Ready for Another Star in Town," *Fort Worth Star-Telegram*, Sept. 2, 1992.
81 tired of the never-ending chaos: Bryant, *Juicing the Game*, pp. 107–9.
81 Shortly after he joined the team: Canseco, *Juiced*, p. 133–36. In his book, Canseco names three players on the Rangers he claimed to have instructed: Rafael Palmeiro, outfielder Juan Gonzalez, and catcher Ivan Rodriguez. At a congressional hearing held in the wake of the publication of Canseco's book, Palmeiro wagged his finger and declared under oath, "I have never used steroids. Period." Five months later, he was suspended after testing positive for steroids. Juan Gonzalez also denied using steroids. But as described in the Mitchell Report, in 2001, Canadian border patrol officers would find steroids and syringes in a search of a duffel bag belonging to Gonzalez. Gonzalez has continued to maintain he never used steroids. Rodriguez, who went on to become a Hall of Fame catcher, declared in his autobiography, "I never took steroids." No evidence beyond Canseco's account has ever surfaced against him.
82 "Before long," Canseco later wrote: Canseco, *Juiced*, p. 136. Elfrink and Garcia-Roberts would later describe the Rangers as "Team Zero" for the epidemic of steroid use in baseball during the 1990s (*Blood Sport*, p. 62).
82 Who knows what Bush observed: In *Juiced*, Canseco notes that Bush and the team management would have seen his teammates "getting bigger before their eyes, starting within weeks after I joined the team" (pp. 133–34). Bush has always denied he was aware of any steroid use by Rangers players during his tenure as team owner.
82 Its centerpiece was his personal collection: Milbank, *Smashmouth*, p. 315.
82 he replied: "Nolan Ryan": Carlson, "Devil May Care."
82 "I have always been underestimated": Roger Simon, *Divided We Stand* (New York: Crown, 2001), p. 98.
83 "Nobody needs to tell me": Carlson, "Devil May Care."
83 "I know who I am": Paul Burka, "The Man Who Isn't There," *Texas Monthly*, February 2004.
83 "The man dyes his hair": Bruni, *Ambling into History*, p. 30.
83 "you can't win": Bush, *Decision Points*, p. 53.
83 "family values don't stop at the Rio Grande": Smith, *Bush*, p. 104.
84 more than one hundred fifty convicts to the death chamber: "Executions by State," Death Penalty Information Center, deathpenaltyinfo.org.
84 "'How bad can I be?'": Updegrove, *The Last Republicans*, p. 280.
84 "I'm coming to learn": Allison Adato, "Anchor Astray," *George*, May 2000.
84 "Bush brought both of his hands": Seth Mnookin, "The Charm Offensive," *Brill's Content*, September 2000.
85 "the second-handsomest man": Lemann, "The Redemption."
85 "He came, he said, he accomplished": Lemann, "The Redemption."
85 "I'm not interested in the people": Evan Smith, "George, Washington."
85 For every stop in this campaign: Joshua Bolten, oral history, interviewed by Russell Riley et al., Miller Center (hereafter "Bolten, Miller Center oral history").
85 "I'm amazed": Frank Bruni, "The Bushes Talk of History and How It Favors Their Son," *NYT*, July 8, 2000.
86 Poppy started arranging for his geopolitical education: Smith, *Bush*, pp. 98–99.
86 "In the big boys' game": Bob Woodward, *State of Denial* (New York: Simon and Schuster, 2006), p. 5.
86 who surprised him with a pop quiz: Terry Neal, "Bush Falters in Foreign Policy Quiz," *WP*, Nov. 5, 1999.

6: The Magic City

87   awoke to a front-page article: Bill Carter, "Television's New Voyeurism Pictures Real-Life Intimacy," *NYT*, Jan. 30, 2000.

87   called it "Camp Elián": *MH*, April 7, 2000.

88   One day, a newspaper writer: *MH*, Jan. 12, 2000.

88   the cultural critic Frank Rich: Frank Rich, "The Age of the Mediathon," *New York Times Magazine*, Oct. 29, 2000.

88   the second-biggest celebrity story: *MH*, April 20, 2000.

88   He was locally renowned: *MH*, Jan. 12, 2000.

89   "the monster that tyrannizes": *MH*, Jan. 8, 2000.

89   "He is surrounded": *PBP*, Jan. 10, 2000.

89   "Elián said to me": *MH*, Jan. 9, 2000.

89   "the highest levels": Rebecca Sanchez-Roig to numerous recipients, email, Dec. 17, 1999, Reno Papers.

90   one of only sixteen women: Anderson, *Janet Reno*, p. 37.

90   She warned Janny: Reno, *The Hell with Politics*, p. 175.

91   "Whoever you are": Anderson, *Janet Reno*, p. 68.

91   Reno watched the smoke rise: "Oral History of Janet Reno."

92   The Reverend Jesse Jackson flew down: Anderson, *Janet Reno*, p. 81.

92   Reno would sometimes sing: Tom Junod, "Janet Reno Is Innocent," *Esquire*, October 2000.

92   Joan Didion wrote: Joan Didion, *Miami* (New York: Simon and Schuster, 1987).

93   The militants had aged: T. D. Allman, *Miami: City of the Future* (Gainesville: University Press of Florida, 1987), p. 270.

93   "He has a father": *MH*, Jan. 7, 2000.

94   "What we want": *PBP*, Jan. 6, 2000.

94   As a plane flew overhead: *MH*, Jan. 13, 2000.

94   That evening, Juan Miguel appeared: *MH*, Jan. 14, 2000.

95   "What I want is to go: *MH*, Jan. 15, 2000.

96   "Janet Reno Is a Man": *MH*, Jan. 9, 2000.

96   "an old maid who prefers men": Anderson, *Janet Reno*, p. 153.

96   "At a certain point": Liza Mundy, "Punch Lines: What Is It About Janet Reno that So Fascinates and Confounds and Even Terrifies America," *WP*, Jan. 25, 1998.

97   referred to her as "the Martian": Jane Mayer, "Janet Reno, Alone," *The New Yorker*, Dec. 1, 1997.

97   also had a hideaway apartment: Author visit, 2019.

98   "Far beyond the moon and stars": Rosemary Wells, *Voyage to the Bunny Planet* (New York: Viking Books for Young Readers, 1992).

99   "The things that went on": Author interview, Lula Rodriguez.

99   On a Saturday afternoon: *MH*, Jan. 23, 2000.

99   "They flew to Washington": *MH*, Jan. 23, 2000.

100 That Monday: *MH*, Jan. 25, 2000.

100 CBS announced: *MH*, Jan. 26, 2000.

101 "Well," Elián informed them: *MH*, Feb. 8, 2000.

102 As the family arrived: *MH*, Jan. 27, 2000.

102 Elián called in to Radio Mambí: *MH*, Jan. 27, 2000.

102 "My grandson is different": *MH*, Jan. 28, 2000.

102 The grandmothers flew home: *MH*, Jan. 31, 2000.

102 "mystery of bonding": *MH*, Jan. 29, 2000.

102 She was troubled: Jeanne O'Laughlin, "Why I Changed My Mind About Elian," *NYT*, Feb. 1, 2000.

103 "I was shocked": *MH*, March 31, 2000.

103 a new sign appeared: *MH*, March 31, 2000.

7: *For the People*

104 After my first article was published: *New York Observer*, March 6, 2000.

105 nowhere near as rich: In 2000, Trump claimed he was worth $5 billion, while Forbes estimated his net worth at $1.6 billion. But a skeptical *Wall Street Journal* article suggested his fortune fell "far short" of either figure, pointing out a pattern of exaggerations in Trump's estimates of the value of his assets (*WSJ*, Jan. 19, 2000). Five years later, journalist Tim O'Brien, author of the biography *TrumpNation*, would report that sources familiar with Trump's finances estimated his true net worth to be in the range of $150 million to $250 million. Trump filed a libel lawsuit against O'Brien. In a deposition, Trump admitted that his estimate of his net worth "fluctuates, and it goes up and down with markets and with attitudes and with feelings, even my own feelings." The suit was dismissed in 2009.

105 a story in the *National Enquirer*: "Get Ready for President Trump? Poll Shocker," *National Enquirer*, Aug. 3, 1999.

106 "Everywhere you look": Matt Labash, "Body Slam," *Weekly Standard*, Aug. 9, 1999.

107 "If it rains": Matt Labash, "Roger Stone, Political Animal," *Weekly Standard*, Nov. 5, 2007.

107 the *National Enquirer* revealed: Jeffrey Toobin, "The Dirty Trickster," *The New Yorker*, June 2, 2008.

107 Stone was also helping: Andrea Bernstein and Ilya Marritz, "A Front Group, a Lawsuit and a Private Investigator: How Trump Rigged the System to Delay Gambling in New York," WNYC.org, Oct. 20, 2016.

107 calling him "butt boy": Author interview, former consultant to Trump.

108 "Our way of life is ending": *FTP*, Nov. 30, 1999.

108 "beach ball with legs": Author interview, Keith Alan.

108 Since the summer: "Chuck Harder update, July/August 2000," chuckharder.com, archive.org.

109 he began broadcasting: Neely Tucker, "Shooting from the Lip," *Fort Myers News-Press*, Oct. 18, 1987.

109 "Naturally, the elite media": Harder, *Will We Ever Learn?*

109 aired on hundreds of stations: Bob Davis, "Bashing Big Business Becomes Business for Talk-Show Host," *Wall Street Journal*, May 16, 1996.

109 "He is the king": Morris Dees with James Corcoran, *Gathering Storm* (New York: HarperCollins, 1996), p. 114.

109 in White Springs: Monica Davey, "A Big Voice," *Tampa Bay Times*, June 9, 1996.

110 "workingman's PBS": Cooper, "The Paranoid Style."

110 *For the People* club: William Freivogel, "Talking Tough," *St. Louis Post-Dispatch*, May 10, 1995.

111 "The wackiest people": Author interview, former Reform Party official.

111 "Why should his legacy": Maureen Dowd, "Trump L'Oeil Tease," *NYT*, Sept. 19, 1999.

112 obliged the would-be president: Adam Nagourney, "President? Why Not? Says a Man at the Top," *NYT*, Sept. 25, 1999.

112 "This is what this country": Ian Goldstein, "Five of David Letterman's Best Late Night Donald Trump Takedowns," *Vulture*, March 28, 2017.

112 One Sunday morning: Tim Russert interview with Jack Gargan, *Meet the Press*, NBC, Oct. 10, 1999.

113 "favor is a positive thing": James Bennet, "The Cable Guys," *New York Times Magazine*, Oct. 24, 1999.

113 "the greatest architect": Lisa Birnbach, "Mi Casa Es Su Casa," *New York*, Feb. 12, 1996.

113 homespun party leaders: Brian Crowley, "Trump Woos Reform Leaders with Soiree at Mar-a-Lago," *PBP*, Jan. 15, 2000.

114 "It was hilarious": Author interview, former Reform Party official.

8: The Life

115 At around eleven o'clock: ATF Report No. 45, Aug. 6, 1999.

115 Ingram called from the road: Recorded telephone call between Kevin Ingram and Randy Glass, Aug. 4, 1999.

115 bringing their tennis gear: Recorded telephone call between Kevin Ingram and Randy Glass, Aug. 3, 1999.

115 That was how they first connected: Author interview, Kevin Ingram.

116 Glass owned a jewelry store: Indictment, *USA v. Randy Glass*, U.S. District Court for the Southern District of Florida, filed June 19, 1998.

116 Didi had come to Glass: ATF Report No. 108, June 26, 2001.

116 maybe stolen a few of the diamonds: ATF Report No. 109, Oct. 2, 2001.

116 passing off phony Picassos: ATF Report No. 40, July 1, 1999.

116 truckload of stolen Minolta copiers: ATF Report Nos. 45–49, Aug. 6–31, 1999.

116 plundered Egyptian antiquities: Dale Armstrong, "Case Study: Operation Sphinx," *Firearms Trafficking: A Guide for Criminal Investigations* (Augusta, GA: Prudens Group Consulting, 2018), p. 326.

116 lived a charmed life: Author interview, Benjamin Seaman.

116 pulled up in the Ferrari: ATF Report No. 45, Aug. 6, 1999.

116 He had flown in from the West Coast: Author interview, Dick Stoltz.

116 "I'm a financial engineer": Landon Thomas Jr., "Kevin Ingram Pal Questioned About Bin Laden," *New York Observer*, Oct. 1, 2001.

116 He diagrammed on the whiteboard: Spiro, "Wall Street's Soldier of Fortune."

117 Glass presented $250,000: ATF Report No. 45, Aug. 6, 1999.

117 gave Ingram a bank account number: Affidavit of ATF agent Stephen Barborini.

117 Ingram and Didi drove back: Affidavit of ATF agent Stephen Barborini.

117 went out to a strip club: Thomas, "Kevin Ingram Pal Questioned About Bin Laden."

117 Glass had promised: Author interview, Dick Stoltz; ATF Report No. 52, Oct. 12, 1999.

117 finalize the settlement: Stipulation and order of dismissal, *Deutsche Bank v. Ingram*, U.S. District Court for the Southern District of New York, case closed Aug. 5, 1999.

117 "I wasn't particularly shocked": Author interview, former Goldman Sachs executive.

118 "He was a golden boy": Author interview, Yves Jadot.

118 Ingram first glimpsed her: Author interviews, Kevin Ingram and Deann Prince.

Sparkle also describes her first encounter with Kevin in thinly veiled fashion in a romance novel (D. A. Prince, *Disastrously Fabulous* [self-published, 2016]).

118 "If you like what you see": Author interview, Deann Prince.

118 "He was a little arrogant": Author interview, friend of Sparkle's from the modeling world.

119 The first use of *google* as a verb: Virginia Heffernan, "Just Google It: A Short History of a Newfound Verb," *Wired*, Nov. 15, 2017.

119 a swashbuckling megalomaniac: David Enrich, *Dark Towers: Deutsche Bank, Donald Trump, and an Epic Tale of Destruction* (New York: Custom House, 2020), pp. 44–48.

119 "Let's kick Goldman's ass": Enrich, *Dark Towers*, p. 72.

119 "It was a totally cowboy mentality": Author interview, former Deutsche Bank colleague of Ingram's.

120 an unexplored niche: Author interview, Mike Offit; Enrich, *Dark Towers*, pp. 72–73.

120 multimillion-dollar bonus: Spiro, "Wall Street's Soldier of Fortune."

120 "Kevin's life was a gamble": Author interview, friend of Sparkle's from the modeling world.

121 a silent investment: Author interview, Frank Cilione.

121 "a ghetto fabulous place": Author interview, Jay Norris.

121 big weekend nights: This description is based in part on a review of archival issues of *Tastemakers*, a nightlife magazine published by Jay Norris.

121 Simmons's beach wedding: Nancy Jo Sales, "The Mix Master," *New York*, May 10, 1999.

121 "We would always kick their ass": Author interview, former Wall Street investment bank executive.

122 "Russell knows the market": Sales, "The Mix Master."

122 discovered on the shore: Ronald Kessler, *The Season* (New York: HarperCollins, 1999), p. 191.

122 "ignorant of Black culture": "Meet the First Babes," *George*, February/March 2000.

122 Ingram had recruited: Enrich, *Dark Towers*, pp. 73–77.

123 commemorated the transaction: Enrich, *Dark Towers*, pp. 76–77.

124 "at about a hundred twenty miles per hour": Author interview, Philmore Anderson.

124 "Instead of having a couple of cups": Author interview, Frank Cilione.

124 "Sometimes you're too smart": Author interview, Jerry McMillan.

125 a diagnosis of bipolar disorder: Dr. Amar Das, "Psychiatric Evaluation and Treatment Summary," Nov. 23, 2001, filed in a probation violation proceeding in U.S. District Court for the Eastern District of New York, 2004 (Docket No. 04-261).

126 raised some eyebrows: Author interview, Karen Ingram.

126 Ingram's department lost: Christopher O'Leary, "From ARMs to Arms," *Investment Dealers' Digest*, June 25, 2001.

126 he would have to fire him: Thomas, "Ex-Goldman Trader Stung in Arms Plot."

127 a $10 billion merger: Enrich, *Dark Towers*, pp. 65–66.

127 a rumor ripped across: Author interviews, Mike Offit and Jerry McMillan.

127 "challenging the finance culture": Whitford, "Jesse Shakes the Money Tree."

127 Jackson later told a journalist: Kenneth Timmerman, *Shakedown: Exposing the Real Jesse Jackson* (Washington, DC: Regnery, 2002), p. 327.

127 Ingram sobbed: Spiro, "Wall Street's Soldier of Fortune."

127 Deutsche Bank alleged: Leslie Wayne, "From Riches to Relative Rags," *NYT*, Oct. 27, 2001.

128 He wanted to reopen: Kevin Ingram, affidavit, *Zoran Chanin v. Kevin Ingram*, New York State Supreme Court, filed May 18, 2001.

128 ignoring his lawyer's bills: Complaint, *Broach & Stulberg LLP v. Kevin Ingram*, New York State Supreme Court, filed Nov. 19, 1999.

128 "Kevin became a pretty damn good": Author interview, Jerry McMillan.

129 "I am the main man": Author interview, Diaa Mohsen.

129 a construction company called BIA: Thomas, "Kevin Ingram Pal Questioned About Bin Laden."

130 represented Egypt in the Olympics: "Defendant's Objections to Pre-Sentence Investigation Report," *USA v. Diaa Mohsen*, U.S. District Court for Southern District of Florida, Document No. 94, filed Jan. 30, 2002.

130 brother was a retired army general: ATF Report No. 107, June 19, 2001.

130 on a trip to Egypt: ATF Report No. 50, Sept. 22, 1999; ATF Report No. 108, June 26, 2001; ATF Report No. 110, Oct. 9, 2001.

130 "Hi . . . from Africa": Email from Kevin Ingram to Zoran Chanin, Sept. 7, 1999, filed as an exhibit in *Chanin v. Ingram*.

130 connected to a Florida billionaire: Author interview, Kevin Ingram.

130 as large as $300 million: ATF Report No. 52, Oct. 12, 1999.

131 Didi told Glass that Ingram was "shaking": ATF Report No. 49, Aug. 31, 1999.

131 "You know when you get a horse": Recorded telephone call between Diaa Mohsen and Randy Glass, July 26, 1999.

131 Ingram received around $6 million: Timmerman, *Shakedown*, p. 327.

132 "Let me ask you a question": Recorded telephone call between Diaa Mohsen and Randy Glass, Aug. 5, 1999.

132 Glass later claimed that in their initial meeting: ATF Report No. 39, June 22, 1999. See detailed discussion in notes to chapter 4, "The Wall Street Project."

132 "don't mix the two things": Recorded telephone call between Diaa Mohsen and Randy Glass, Aug. 16, 1999.

133 "Remember the guy": Recorded telephone call between Diaa Mohsen and Randy Glass, July 8, 1999.

9: The Force of Things

134 "This is a good place": Raw video and a translation of Jarrah's martyrdom statement was introduced into evidence in proceedings of *USA v. al-Bahlul*. The footage was never incorporated into a propaganda video.

136 "Joy kills the heart": McDermott, *Perfect Soldiers*, p. 61.

136 *la force des choses*: Marc Sageman, *Turning to Political Violence: The Emergence of Terrorism* (Philadelphia: University of Pennsylvania Press, 2017), p. 5.

136 But there was another force in Jarrah's life: Aysel Sengün was extensively questioned by the Bundeskriminalamt (BKA), the German federal law enforcement agency, and those interrogations form the basis of what is publicly known about the process of his radicalization.

137 By the time he called: Terry McDermott and Josh Meyer, *The Hunt for KSM* (New York: Back Bay Books/Little, Brown, 2012), p. 139.

137 "While they use their muscles": Written testimony of Khalid Sheikh Mohammed, *USA v. Hage et al.*, proceedings against defendant Sulaiman Abu Ghaith, filed April 2, 2014, p. 7.

137 later told interrogators: FBI, summary of interrogation of Abdul Aziz Ali, *USA v. KSM*, filed Nov. 27, 2017.

137 He hatched plots: Khalid Sheikh Mohammed, statement to military commission at Guantanamo Bay, March 10, 2007.

137 He had first pitched the concept: *9/11 Commission Report*, p. 154.

138 Egyptian pilot: Author interview, Nelly Lahoud.

138 a one-legged Yemeni jihadi: Ali Soufan, *The Black Banners* (New York: W.W. Norton, 2011), p. 255.

138 "cover language": Zacarias Moussaoui, testimony, *USA v. Moussaoui.*

138 "faculty of architecture": CIA, "11 September: The Plot and the Plotters," 2003, National Security Archive.

138 Mukhtar was under the impression: Khalid Sheikh Mohammed, written testimony, *USA v. Moussaoui.*

139 he was pulled aside by Emirati security officials: McDermott, *Perfect Soldiers*, pp. 186–87.

140 "Without trying to judge": Aysel Sengün, statement, BKA Files.

140 "He wanted to make": Sengün, statement, BKA Files.

141 "I couldn't sleep last night: McDermott, *Perfect Soldiers*, p. 81.

141 a quiet wedding: McDermott, *Perfect Soldiers*, p. 78. The marriage was never officially registered, and Sengün appears to have considered it unofficial.

141 Aysel referred to it as his "rebellious" phase: Sengün, statement, BKA Files.

141 "We came here to Germany": Carol Williams, "Friends of Terror Suspect Say Allegation Made No Sense," *Los Angeles Times*, Oct. 23, 2001.

142 He doodled pictures: McDermott, *Perfect Soldiers*, p. 188.

142 At night, lying beside him: McDermott, *Perfect Soldiers*, p. 187.

142 "The hearts of freemen": "The Al Qaeda Manual," 9/11 Commission Files. This book, also referred to by the title *Military Studies in the Jihad Against Tyrants*, was recovered by British police in the search of an Al Qaeda member's home in the 1990s.

142 Atta composed an email: Email contained in BKA Files.

143 in a trade magazine called *Aerokurier*: Pascal Schreier, testimony, *USA v. Moussaoui.*

143 Jarrah struck the recruiter: Author interview, Pascal Schreier.

143 This sparked another fight: McDermott, *Perfect Soldiers*, p. 188.

10: Oscar Night

145 a chance encounter with inspiration: Russ Spencer, "Where You Find It," *Salon*, March 25, 2000; Alex Koenig, "Anything but Ordinary: American Beauty Screenwriter Alan Ball on the Film's 15th Anniversary," *Huffington Post*, Sept. 3, 2014.

145 "An amazing film": Brian Raftery, *Best. Movie. Year. Ever.: How 1999 Blew Up the Big Screen* (New York: Simon and Schuster, 2019). The films featured in the 2000 Oscar ceremony were all released during the previous year. This account is indebted to Raftery's excellent retrospective of the movies of 1999.

146 "I hope you'll put me to work for you": *PBP*, Feb. 7, 2000.

146 publicly mulling: Peter Biskind, "He Stars, She Stars," *Vanity Fair*, February 2000. Beatty told Biskind that Roger Stone urged him to run before turning to Trump.

146 "If you had your choice": Warren Beatty, Irving G. Thalberg Award acceptance speech, March 26, 2000.

147 "that plastic bag": Alan Ball, Academy Award acceptance speech, March 26, 2000.

148 The thirteen-minute film: *Untitled Al Gore Documentary*, directed by Spike Jonze, Democratic National Committee, 2000, accessed via YouTube.

149 "One suspects that": Louis Menand, "After Elvis," *The New Yorker*, Oct. 26, 1998.

149 a book called: Katherine Boo, "The Drama of the Gifted Vice President," *WP*, Nov. 28, 1993.

149 He had been groomed: This account of Al Gore's early life and career is based primarily on the excellent biography *The Prince of Tennessee*, by David Maraniss and Ellen Y. Nakashima (New York: Simon and Schuster, 2000).

149 Family legend had it: Maraniss and Nakashima, *The Prince of Tennessee*, p. 41.

149 "I pointed out": Al Gore, *The Assault on Reason* (New York: Penguin, 2007), p. 9.

150 "I'm going to run": Maraniss and Nakashima, *The Prince of Tennessee*, p. 165.

150 He held the first congressional hearing: Al Gore, *Earth in the Balance* (New York: Houghton Mifflin, 1992), pp. 4–6.

151 "Gore comes off to me": Richard Berke, "Campaign C.E.O.: Gore Dots the i's that Bush Leaves to Others," *NYT*, June 9, 2000.

151 "You hear folks": Frady, *Jesse*, p. 43.

151 Jackson brought down the house: Maraniss and Nakashima, *The Prince of Tennessee*, p. 214.

152 "hustler from Chicago": AP, April 6, 1988.

152 "We're not choosing a preacher": Frady, *Jesse*, p. 398.

152 Gore would privately call Jackson: Maraniss and Nakashima, *The Prince of Tennessee*, p. 236

153 "Y'all know who my *real* hero is?": Frady, *Jesse*, pp. 502–3.

153 "I began to doubt": Gore, *Earth in the Balance*, p. 8.

154 map of the world: Roy Neel, oral history, interviewed by Russell Riley et al., Miller Center (hereafter "Neel, Miller Center oral history").

154 Gore would later recall looking down: Melinda Henneberger, "Writing and Healing; Career in the Balance, Gore Focused His Energy on a Book," *NYT*, Sept. 3, 2000.

154 He got rid of his ghostwriter: Neel, Miller Center oral history.

155 "we concentrate on form": Gore, *Earth in the Balance*, p. 168.

155 "I have become very impatient": Gore, *Earth in the Balance*, p. 15.

155 Today he was in New Hampshire: Ceci Connolly, "Gore Paints Himself as No Beltway Baby," *WP*, Dec. 1, 1999.

156 McGlynn's Media Literary class: Description of the *Love Canal* episode primarily drawn from: Sarah Vowell, "Eliminate the Middleman," *This American Life*, NPR, Episode 151, Jan. 28, 2000; Mike Pride, "Just One Word," *Brill's Content*, March 2000.

157 they were hyper-attuned: Evgenia Peretz, "Going After Gore," *Vanity Fair*, October 2007.

157 "I was the one who started it all": Connolly, "Gore Paints Himself as No Beltway Baby"; Katherine Seelye, "Gore Borrows Clinton's Shadow Back to Share a Bow," *NYT*, Dec. 1, 1999.

158 3,383 toxic waste sites: Mark Raabe, letter to the editor, *WP*, Dec. 25, 1999.

158 tried to defend Gore: *Boston Globe*, Dec. 26, 1999.

158 "mad scientist": Rove, Miller Center oral history.

158 "It's not just the information": Bolten, Miller Center oral history.

158 guys who led the "oppo" team: Bolten, Miller Center oral history.

158 constantly hangry: Kamarck, Miller Center oral history.

158 campaign staff was a mess: See Donna Brazile, *Cooking with Grease* (New York:

Simon and Schuster, 2004); Robert Shrum, *No Excuses* (New York: Simon and Schuster, 2007); Carl Cannon, "Rotten at the Gore," *George*, November 1999.

159 Karenna, who was twenty-six: Claire Shipman, "Searching for Al," *George*, December 1999.

159 It was Karenna's idea: Kamarck, Miller Center oral history; Shipman, "Searching for Al."

159 Wolf convinced Gore of her insight: Michael Duffy and Karen Tumulty, "Gore's Secret Guru," *Time*, Nov. 1, 1999.

159 "full-blown tizzy": Melinda Henneberger, "Naomi Wolf, Feminist Consultant to Gore, Clarifies Her Campaign Role," *NYT*, Nov. 5, 1999.

159 "The heart of the storyline": Shrum, *No Excuses*, p. 313.

159 advisers would place the blame: Richard Berke, "Gore's Campaign Struggling to Regain Primary Energy," *NYT*, May 15, 2000. In their memoirs, both Brazile (p. 234) and Shrum (pp. 330–31) repeat this analysis.

160 "It is no longer possible": Gore, *The Assault on Reason*, p. 3.

160 A *Saturday Night Live* skit: *Saturday Night Live*, Episode 475, Jan. 15, 2000.

160 Reno appealed for calm: *MH*, March 31, 2000.

160 "Elian should never have been forced": *PBP*, March 31, 2000.

161 "Shame on Gore": *Los Angeles Times*, March 31, 2000.

161 "Just when we needed Solomon": Mary McGrory, "How Low Can Al Go," *WP*, April 2, 2000.

161 With tears streaming down her cheeks: *MH*, April 4, 2000.

161 Paramedics wheeled her out: *MH*, April 5, 2000.

11: The Siege

162 107th straight month of economic expansion: Gregg Fields, "Economic Nirvana Sets Record, Growth Expected to Continue," *MH*, Feb. 1, 2000.

163 "Every time that Jeff Bezos sells": *FTP*, Dec. 27, 1999.

163 Another day, he ranted: *FTP*, Jan. 11, 2000.

163 A study published by the Federal Reserve: Kimberly Blanton, "U.S. Families Richer, Deeper in Debt," *Boston Globe*, Jan. 19, 2000.

163 "Is your job better": *FTP*, Dec. 22, 1999.

164 "The *biggest* merger to date": *FTP*, Jan. 11, 2000.

164 "She lives Waco": *Newsweek*, April 24, 2000.

165 she lay awake at night: FBI, summary of interview with Attorney General Janet Reno, Aug. 2, 1993, Reno Papers.

165 "carnal wives": John Danforth, "Interim Report to the Deputy Attorney General Concerning the 1993 Confrontation at the Mount Carmel Complex, Waco, Texas," July 21, 2000.

165 "She found out on live TV": Author interview, Richard Scruggs.

165 "I made the decisions": Anderson, *Janet Reno*, p. 195.

166 "The United States government": *FTP*, July 28, 1999.

166 a Chuck Harder fan: Freivogel, "Talking Tough."

166 alternative explanations: Harder and an Oklahoma reporter would later coauthor a book entitled *Deathtrap Oklahoma City: Were Innocent Victims Used as Bait?*

166 "'Ooooh, we have to take those guns'": *FTP*, Sept. 23, 1999.

167 "overwhelming evidence exonerating": Danforth, "Interim Report to the Deputy Attorney General."

167 she gave a deposition: Janet Reno, deposition taken March 28, 2000, *Andrade et al. v. Chojnacki et al.*, U.S. District Court for the Southern District of Texas, 1996.

167 she kept a picture: "Oral History of Janet Reno."
167 "Elián is afraid": *MH*, April 1, 2000.
167 she was enraged: *MH*, March 29, 2000.
167 "That old bitch hag": *MH*, April 16, 2000.
168 A vision of the Virgin Mary: *MH*, March 26, 2000.
168 "We are the only people": *PBP*, March 31, 2000.
168 "We are Elián's true family": *MH*, April 7, 2000.
168 "The boy lives in Florida": *MH*, April 12, 2000.
169 "Janet Reno cannot make up her mind": *The Bulletin's Frontrunner*, April 14, 2000.

12: One Florida

170 "He is God's child": Email from Anne Sanborn to Jeb Bush, Jan. 6, 2000, Bush email archive, Florida Center for Investigative Reporting, St. Petersburg, FL.
171 "Maybe when you inherit a name": Unless otherwise noted, descriptions of the One Florida rally from *MH* and *PBP*, March 8, 2000.
171 "Maybe this isn't the way": Gerald Ensley, "It Was About Commitment—and Being Heard," *Tallahassee Democrat*, March 8, 2000.
172 what he called BHAGs: Dexter Filkins, "Swamped," *The New Yorker*, Jan. 4, 2016.
173 for sprinting up the stairs: Steve Bousquet, "For Jeb Bush, A Wild Ride in Year One," *MH*, Jan. 3, 2000.
173 a family system called "the rankings": Updegrove, *The Last Republicans*, p. 94.
173 "As far as I'm concerned": Richard Berke, "Feeling the Burden of a Name, One Bush Focuses on Florida," *NYT*, July 14, 2000.
173 "the Senator from Yale": Smith, *Bush*, p. 13.
173 Jeb spoke fluent Spanish: Joel Achenbach, "The Family's Business," *Tropic, MH*, June 1, 1986. For a critical perspective on Jeb Bush's early political career and tenure as governor, see S. V. Dáte, *Jeb: America's Next Bush* (New York: Jeremy Tarcher/Pengiun, 2007).
173 at rallies in a guayabera: Dáte, *Jeb: America's Next Bush*, p. 339.
174 "He is probably the most serious": Achenbach, "The Family's Business."
174 "I want to be able to look my father": Tom Fiedler, "Bush and Sons," *MH*, Sept. 25, 1994.
174 "My father saw politics as service": Dáte, *Jeb: America's Next Bush*, p. 1.
174 "Jeb will always seem more thoughtful": Fiedler, "Bush and Sons."
174 "It turns it into a *People* magazine story": Maureen Dowd, *Bushworld* (New York: Putnam, 2004), p. 43.
174 "Jeb's my little brother": Updegrove, *The Last Republicans*, p. 260.
175 "Can you believe *this?*": Marjorie Williams, "Brothers in Arms," *Talk*, September 2000.
175 "The joy is in Texas": Smith, *Bush*, p. 79.
175 "But, Dad," he said: Updegrove, *The Last Republicans*, p. 264.
175 The morning after the election: Jeb Bush and Brian Yablonski, *Profiles in Character* (Tallahassee, FL: Foundation for Florida's Future, 1995), pp. 74–75.
175 "Bush governs like a man": Bousquet, "For Jeb Bush, a Wild Ride in Year One."
176 "We had a blind dumb faith": Rove, Miller Center oral history.
176 Jeb spent the holiday: *MH*, Jan. 16, 2000.
176 Two Black state legislators: This account of the One Florida sit-in is based on the extensive contemporaneous press coverage in the *MH* and the *PBP*, Jan. 19–20, 2000.

177 "all of Jeb's weaknesses": Dáte, *Jeb: America's Next Bush*, p. 188.

178 "white men can't jump": *PBP*, Feb. 12, 2000.

178 someone from his campaign called: *PBP*, Jan. 21, 2000.

179 "Rove had the charts": Karen Hughes, quoted in Simon, *Divided We Stand*, p. 96.

179 Bush called his staff "crybabies": Judd Gregg, oral history, interviewed by Mike Nelson et al., Miller Center (hereafter "Gregg, Miller Center oral history").

179 "I'm looking forward to going down South": *Journeys with George*, dir. Alexandra Pelosi (HBO Films, 2002).

179 "People are seeing": Helen Thorpe, "How Bush Became a Brawler," *George*, May 2000.

180 "the jungles of Africa": "Blacks Still Not Wanted at Many Christian Colleges," *Journal of Blacks in Higher Education* 17 (1997): 79–82.

180 Jeb personally attended: *MH*, Feb. 4, 2000.

180 "This is an attempt": *PBP*, Feb. 4, 2000.

180 "What I concluded": Berke, "Feeling the Burden of a Name."

180 "It is wrong to discriminate": Steve Bousquet, "Bush Says Hearings Will Not Alter Plan," *MH*, Feb. 1, 2000.

181 "Remember in November": Jake Tapper, *Down and Dirty: The Plot to Steal the Presidency* (New York: Little, Brown, 2001), p. 10.

181 "I am for affirmative action": *MH*, Feb. 9, 2000.

181 Vote suppression was not a by-product: Erika Wood, *Florida: An Outlier in Denying Voting Rights*, Brennan Center for Justice, 2016.

182 initiated a massive purge: This account is based on thousands of pages of documents and depositions filed in *NAACP v. Harris*. See also John Lantigua, "How the GOP Gamed the System in Florida," *The Nation*, April 12, 2001.

182 Republican Party loyalist: Dara Kam and John Lantigua, "New Law Is GOP Lawyer's Encore," *PBP*, Oct. 28, 2012.

182 "dirtbags of the nation": Lantigua, "How the GOP Gamed the System in Florida."

182 "cast a wide net": "The Reality of List Maintenance," USCCR Report, chap. 5.

182 a new version: *NAACP v. Harris*, Doc. No. 306, p. 73.

182 65,776 alleged felons: USCCR Report.

183 coworkers and family members: Deposition of John Stafford, *NAACP v. Harris*, Doc. No. 406.

183 misdemeanors in Texas: Deposition of Marlene Thorogood, *NAACP v. Harris*, Doc. No. 409.

183 20,000 other voters: Expert report of David Klausner, *NAACP v. Harris*, Doc. No. 412.

183 Black voters accounted for 10 percent: Expert report of David Klausner, p. 171.

183 "This was a first": Deposition of Pam Iorio, *NAACP v. Harris*, Doc. No. 410.

183 One Black man in Tampa: USCCR Report.

184 one newspaper analysis: Scott Hiaasen, Gary Kane, and Eliot Jaspin, "Felon Purge Sacrificed Innocent Voters," *PBP*, May 27, 2001. The *Post* analysis was based on a list of 42,389 possible felons identified by the state's contractor. Roughly 20,000 of them were purged, and more than 5,000 filed appeals. Around half of those appeals resulted in exoneration. The *Post* found that at least 108 "law abiding" voters were unable to restore their rights before the 2000 election. Nearly 1,000 more were incorrectly disqualified even though they had received clemency. Katherine Harris, who oversaw the process as Florida's secretary of state, later cited the *Post*'s figure of roughly a thousand "innocent" voters to call claims of mass disenfranchisement an "egregious and unfounded attack" made by "politicians interested in wielding the sword of racial division" (Harris, *Center*

of the Storm [Nashville: WND Books, 2002], pp. 176–80). But the *Post* analysis accounts only for voters who took the time to appeal or who had clear-cut clemency cases. Even if the rest were *all* ex-felons, many would have been eligible to vote in other states, and often they had been doing so in Florida until they were disenfranchised by the renewed enforcement of a nineteenth-century law designed to prevent Black citizens from participating in elections. The largest source of disenfranchisement was not the errors; it was the Florida constitution.

184 a short article on the "glitch": *PBP*, June 22, 2000.
184 "You're about to hear from my older": Williams, "Brothers in Arms."

13: Palm Beach

185 "Sometimes you play dirty": *Palm Beach Daily News*, March 4, 2001.
185 He had bought the place: Leamer, *Mar-a-Lago*, pp. 25–31.
185 hung an oil painting of himself: Les Standiford, *Palm Beach, Mar-a-Lago, and the Rise of America's Xanadu* (New York: Atlantic Monthly Press, 2019), pp. 244–45.
185 it was in Palm Beach: Frank Cerabino, "Trump's War with Palm Beach," Politico, Sept. 5, 2015.
186 "It's an entertainment club": Loretta Grantham, "Private Clubs of Palm Beach Very Hush Hush—Then Came Mar-a-Lago," *Palm Beach Daily News*, June 5, 1999.
186 "a kind of real-life *Love Boat*": Christopher Byron, "Behind Trump's Political Fling," *George*, February/March 2000.
187 guys like Bernie Madoff: Erin Arvedlund, *Too Good to Be True* (New York: Portfolio, 2009), p. 231.
187 some crazed financial analyst: Harry Markopolis, *No One Would Listen* (New York: Wiley, 2010).
187 Trump performed: Kessler, *The Season*, pp. 177–202.
187 Out late with a reporter: Paul Reid, "Quasi-Candidate Loves to Serve but Hates to Lose," *PBP*, Feb. 13, 2000.
187 "On takeoff": Robin Givhan, "On a Different Plane," *WP*, Dec. 23, 1999.
188 interrupted by the intrusion: Byron, "Behind Trump's Political Fling."
188 Dan Rather came: *60 Minutes II*, CBS News, Jan. 11, 2000.
189 "You control": Kermit Pattison, "Pinning Jesse Down," *George*, March 1999.
189 "Jesse Ventura, in my mind": *FTP*, Sept. 20, 1999.
189 whom he had first met: David Freedlander, "An Oral History of Donald Trump's Almost-Run for President in 2000," *New York*, Oct. 11, 2018.
190 "It's almost the late empire": Bennet, "The Cable Guys."
190 "impure thoughts": Timothy Stanley, *The Crusader* (New York: St. Martin's Press, 2012), p. 323.
190 "I think they should remember": *FTP*, July 29, 1999.
191 "drain this swamp": Stanley, *The Crusader*, p. 342.
191 He called the Confederate flag: AP, Jan. 19, 2000.
191 support of white nationalists: The cochairman of Buchanan's 1996 campaign quit after it was revealed he had spoken to a group of neo-Nazis. His 2000 campaign received support from the Sons of Confederate Veterans and from David Duke, the former KKK leader, who endorsed Buchanan and joined the Reform Party.
191 "I believe, and I hope": Stanley, *The Crusader*, p. 351.
191 In another speech: AP, Jan. 19, 2000.
191 "Let me say": *WP*, Oct. 26, 1999.
191 recently given an interview to *Playboy*: AP, Oct. 1, 1999.

192 combed the book for objectionable passages: Francis X. Clines, "Buchanan's Views on Hitler Create a Reform Party Stir," *NYT*, Sept. 21, 1999.

192 Harder welcomed Buchanan: *FTP*, Sept. 20, 1999.

192 He fired off: Steve Kornacki, *The Red and the Blue* (New York: Ecco, 2018), p. 410.

193 a *Wall Street Journal* column: Donald Trump, "America Needs a President Like Me," *Wall Street Journal*, Sept. 30, 1999.

193 called him a "Hitler lover:" Kornacki, *The Red and the Blue*, p. 412.

193 "Does being captured": *60 Minutes II*, CBS News, Jan. 11, 2000.

193 bylined essay in the *National Enquirer*: Donald Trump, "Why I Should Be President," *National Enquirer*, Nov. 9, 1999.

193 MSNBC host Chris Matthews gave Trump: Chris Matthews interview with Trump, *Hardball with Chris Matthews*, MSNBC, Nov. 18, 1999.

14: Sugar

195 a small, shabby warehouse: Author visit, 2019.

195 One Tuesday morning: ATF Report No. 47, Aug. 18, 1999.

195 connections to the Pakistani military and the ISI: ATF, Significant Activity Report, June 25, 2002.

195 "They're the central intelligence": Recorded telephone call between Diaa Mohsen and Randy Glass, July 9, 1999.

196 When they arrived: Author interview, Dick Stoltz; ATF Report No. 47, Aug. 18, 1999.

197 The tubby Pakistani: Photo appended to arrest warrant for Rajaa Ghulam Abbas, issued June 25, 2002.

197 Abbas called Glass: ATF Report No. 48, Aug. 24, 1999.

197 could probably do one hundred: ATF Report No. 49, Aug. 31, 1999.

197 In February 2000: ATF Report No. 64, Feb. 10, 2000.

197 "private people": ATF Report No. 60, Dec. 29, 1999.

197 in the "north": ATF Report No. 69, March 28, 2000.

197 conceal the arms as farm equipment: Author interview, Todd Petrie.

197 via a roundabout route: ATF Report No. 73, April 24, 2000.

197 a simple code: ATF Report No. 67, March 15, 2000, and No. 68, March 16, 2000.

198 had first approached Didi: ATF Report No. 1, Dec. 7, 1998.

198 come across a supplier: ATF Report No. 2, Dec. 8, 1998.

198 "always fucking boiling": Recorded telephone call between Diaa Mohsen and Randy Glass, Dec. 23, 1998.

198 "overseas.com": ATF Report No. 49, Aug. 31, 1999.

198 tried to peddle: Armstrong, "Case Study: Operation Sphinx," pp. 326–31.

198 looked like a striving immigrant: "Trail of Terror," *Dateline NBC*, reported by Chris Hansen, produced by Richard Greenberg, NBC, aired Aug. 2, 2002.

198 went out to dinner: ATF Report No. 44, Aug. 4, 1999; Randy Glass interview for "Trail of Terror." For unclear reasons, Glass was not accompanied by an undercover law enforcement agent at this meeting and instead was "wired up" and sent in alone (9/11 Commission Staff, interview of Richard Stoltz, April 12, 2004). The tape recording proved to be unintelligible. In debriefings immediately afterward, Glass claimed that Malik and Abbas boasted of connections to Osama bin Laden at the dinner. Glass elaborated on this story after the September 11 attacks, claiming that Abbas told him, "Americans are the enemy," and pointed to the World Trade Center as they walked out of the restaurant, saying, "The Towers are coming down" (9/11 Commission Staff,

interview of Randy Glass, May 4, 2004). Dick Stoltz told the commission that Glass never mentioned this exchange before September 11, calling him a "con man who was misleading family members" of the victims for personal gain.

198 "Who exactly am I dealing": Recorded telephone call between Diaa Mohsen and Randy Glass, Aug. 5, 1999.

199 traced back to a single imperative: ATF Report No. 64, Feb. 10, 2000.

199 could no longer buy: ATF, Significant Activity Report, June 25, 2002.

199 "Now we have our own": ATF Report No. 52, Oct. 12, 1999.

199 "evident personal enthusiasm": Steve Coll, *Directorate S: The CIA and America's Secret Wars in Afghanistan and Pakistan, 2001–2016* (New York: Penguin Press, 2018), p. 47.

199 ISI operatives facilitated: Al-Bahri, *Guarding Bin Laden.*

200 a secret budget: ATF, Significant Activity Report, June 25, 2002.

200 once it "clicks": ATF Report No. 65, Feb. 24, 2000.

200 a temporary obstacle: ATF Report No. 67, March 15, 2000.

200 an unusual summit: Coll, *Ghost Wars*, pp. 511–13.

200 Ziad Jarrah took his trip: "Contact Report," created by Pascal Schreier for FFTC, exhibit, *USA v. Moussaoui.*

200 "We want to do business": Faxed letter from "Ray Spears" to Mohammed Malik, sent March 27, 2000, referenced in ATF Report No. 68, March 28, 2000.

201 a four-page handwritten reply: Faxed letter from R. G. Abbas to "Ray Spears," sent April 14, 2000, referenced in ATF Report No. 72, April 20, 2000.

201 "You must understand": Faxed letter from "Ray Spears" to R. G. Abbas, sent April 17, 2000, referenced in ATF Report No. 72, April 20, 2000.

201 many generals had to approve: ATF Report No. 74, May 3, 2000.

201 a retired general: Author interview, Dick Stoltz; ATF Report No. 76, May 8, 2000.

201 officer named Farid: ATF Report No. 77, May 12, 2000.

202 "way off": ATF Report No. 52, Oct. 12, 1999.

202 patch things up: ATF Report No. 51, Sept. 27, 1999.

202 "Of all the targets": Author interview, Dick Stoltz.

203 approved the purchase: ATF Report No. 78, May 22, 2000.

15: Go Time

204 When her medication: Mundy, "Punch Lines."

204 She would clasp her hands: Roger Parloff, "Fort Reno," *American Lawyer*, March 4, 2000.

205 "I'm just going to go": Author interview, Myron Marlin.

205 In her shaky hand: Janet Reno, meeting notes, Reno Papers.

205 Elián would barge into the dining room: *MH*, April 16, 2000.

206 Reno came out of the meeting: Author interview, Todd Rowley.

206 Lázaro gave a threatening statement: *MH*, April 16, 2000.

206 a forty-second statement: *MH*, April 14, 2000.

206 "You know, I've never felt important": Michael Leahy, "A Fisherman and His 15 Minutes," *WP*, April 27, 2000.

207 An FBI official: *MH*, April 14, 2000.

207 "I have done everything": *MH*, April 14, 2000.

207 his aides said they were "fed up": *NYT*, April 21, 2000.

207 "A lot of us think": *MH*, April 30, 2000.

207 "The resolution of the Elián case": Maureen Dowd, "Never on Sunday, Monday or . . ." *NYT*, April 19, 2000.

208 "We have come to rededicate": Janet Reno, Remarks at the Oklahoma City Bombing Memorial Dedication, April 19, 2000.

208 tense forty-five-minute conversation: *WP*, April 21, 2000.

208 "Operation Reunion": Reconnaissance reports and planning documents, Reno Papers.

209 "You think we just have cameras": *MH*, April 23, 2000.

209 Juan Miguel faxed a letter: *NYT*, April 26, 2000.

210 "It's a go": Carol Florman, interview in documentary *Elián*.

210 It was all over very quickly: This account of the raid was synthesized from news articles, including dozens of stories published by the staff of the *Miami Herald*, which won a Pulitzer Prize for Breaking News Reporting for its coverage.

210 "They're here!": *AP*, first person account of photographer Alan Diaz, April 23, 2000.

211 "God, how could you": *NYT*, April 23, 2000.

211 "She lied to this country": AP, April 23, 2000.

211 "One of the beauties of television": *NYT*, April 23, 2000.

211 Reno went back to her apartment: "Oral History of Janet Reno."

212 She read her favorite book: *MH*, April 25, 2000.

212 "I was confident": Bill Clinton, *My Life* (New York: Alfred A. Knopf, 2004), p. 906.

16: Earth Day

213 framed poster: Bob Graham, *Intelligence Matters* (New York: Random House, 2004), p. 118.

213 "I remember the fierce criticism": Al Gore, Earth Day 2000 speech, April 21, 2000.

214 a $125 billion package of proposals: *NYT*, June 28, 2000.

214 "While hammering Mr. Bush": Katherine Seelye, "Gore's Campaign, Confident on the Issues, Still Struggles with His Image," *NYT*, April 22, 2000.

214 read the headline: *Detroit Free Press*, April 22, 2000.

215 a swift and bipartisan backlash: Reaction to the Gonzalez raid in Florida, including all quotes, compiled from *MH*, April 23–24, 2000.

215 Six players on Miami's team: *MH*, April 26, 2000.

216 still held strategy sessions: Richard Berke, "Running for Office? The President Has Some Ideas," *NYT*, May 7, 2000.

216 From mid-May to mid-October: Melinda Henneberger and Don van Natta Jr., "Once Close to Clinton, Gore Keeps a Distance," *NYT*, Oct. 20, 2000.

216 never as compatible: Marjorie Williams, "Scenes from a Marriage," *Vanity Fair*, July 2001.

216 "correct, but not warm": Clinton, *My Life*, p. 414.

216 "Gore was much more linear": Kamarck, Miller Center oral history.

217 "There was a sandbox intensity": Klein, "Eight Years."

217 "the bill is coming due": Maraniss and Nakashima, *The Prince of Tennessee*, p. 291.

217 "Is the cigar story really in there?": Kamarck, Miller Center oral history.

217 "The women in the White House": Kamarck, Miller Center oral history.

218 Hillary appeared on the cover: Lucinda Franks, "The Intimate Hillary," *Talk*, September 1999.

218 "Bill and I were talking again": Sally Bedell Smith, "White House Civil War," *Vanity Fair*, November 2007.

219 She attended the Inner Circle Dinner: Gail Sheehy, "Cheer and Loathing in New York," *Vanity Fair*, June 2000.

219 "I hope that": Lynne Duke, "Roast of the Town: Hillary and Rudy Do Dinner," *WP*, March 13, 2000.

219 "you're really beautiful": Christine Nguyen and Cait Munro, "Once Upon a Time, Rudy Giuliani and Donald Trump Starred in the Most Bizarre Comedy Sketch Ever," *New York*, April 8, 2016.

219 The audience groaned: Duke, "Roast of the Town."

220 "aider and abettor": Barbara Olson, *Hell to Pay* (Washington, DC: Regnery Publishing, 1999), p. 5.

220 "You're the best": *New York Post*, May 18, 2000.

221 the president called up the reporter: Richard Berke, "Clinton Admits to Concerns as Gore Campaign Stumbles," *NYT*, May 14, 1999.

221 "She felt that would kill": Author interview, former Gore campaign adviser.

221 was shocked to learn: In an interview, a former campaign official who discussed the issue with Clinton recalled him saying something to the effect of "Please don't tell me that a twenty-six-year-old is the one who is preventing me from participating in the campaign."

221 "stand on the doorstep": Clinton, *My Life*, p. 873.

222 "beyond imagination": *WP*, May 22, 1994.

222 "He always felt very strongly": Author interview, former Gore campaign official.

222 "Al is not a person who likes conflict": Author interview, Martin Peretz.

222 "Once I focus on politics": Shipman, "Searching for Al."

222 the *Times* released a poll: *NYT*, May 16, 2000.

223 he obsessed over it with his speechwriters: Shrum, *No Excuses*, pp. 336–43.

224 "I think it's a way": Scene described in John Harris, *The Survivor* (New York: Random House, 2005), p. 390.

224 "self-righteous, sanctimonious": Jake Tapper, "Joe Lieberman's Blank Slate," *Talk*, November 2001.

17: The Breakup

225 The writer would later say: Freedlander, "An Oral History of Donald Trump's Almost-Run for President in 2000."

225 "What office has a receptionist": Author interview, Abraham Wallach.

225 Trump's campaign manifesto: Donald Trump and Dave Shiflett, *The America We Deserve* (New York: Renaissance Books, 2000).

225 a signing event: *New York Post*, Jan. 6, 2000.

226 "America's greatest living comedian": Walter Kirn, "Donald Trump: The Funniest Man in America," *New York*, Jan. 17, 2000.

226 After following around Al Gore: Michael Wolff, "How I Got Over My Al-Gore-a-phobia," *New York*, Feb. 21, 2000.

226 "I think it would be wrong": Michael Wolff, "Citizen Wolff," *New York*, Oct. 11, 1999.

226 "I think it's barbaric": Stone Phillips interview with Trump, *Later Today*, NBC News, Oct. 6, 1999.

226 Melania told an interviewer: Matt Labash, "A Chump on the Stump: Donald Trump Pretends to Run for President," *Weekly Standard*, Dec. 20, 1999.

226 For his first event: Newspaper reports from Nov. 16, 1999, including: Brian Crowley, "Trump Tests His Presidential Act on Cuban Americans," *PBP*; Carolyn Barta, "Trump on the Stump," *Dallas Morning News*; Ana Acle, "Flirting with Election Bid, Trump Does Miami," *MH*.

227 This was a lie: Kurt Eichenwald, "How Donald Trump's Company Violated the United States Embargo Against Cuba," *Newsweek*, Sept. 29, 2016.

227 "Let me ask you": Dave Barry, "He Doesn't Want to Hold Your Hand," *MH*, Nov. 16, 1999.

227 "Evaluating Donald's riches": Tim O'Brien, *TrumpNation* (New York: Open Road, 2005).

227 According to a Gallup poll: Jerry Useem, "What Does Donald Trump Really Want?," *Fortune*, April 3, 2000.

228 In another poll: "Trump for President?," CBSNews.com, Jan. 11, 2000.

228 He bragged about his friendships: *New York Post*, Oct. 15, 1999.

228 Simmons immediately demanded: *New York Post*, Oct. 16, 1999.

229 "It was strange": Author interview, Trump 2000 campaign adviser.

229 "She is actually naked": *The Howard Stern Show*, Nov. 9, 1999.

229 "Her primary function": Barry, "He Doesn't Want to Hold Your Hand."

229 a two-page photo spread: *Talk*, February 2000, pp. 76–77.

229 "I'm the only one": Byron, "Behind Trump's Political Fling."

230 "She's a *real* celebrity": Labash, "A Chump on the Stump."

230 "Hey, Donald": Labash, "A Chump on the Stump."

230 When the cameras rolled: *The Tonight Show with Jay Leno*, Dec. 7, 1999.

230 Walking through: Milbank, *Smashmouth*, pp. 215–16; Nathaniel Meyersohn, "Donald Trump's Trip to the Holocaust Museum," *BuzzFeed*, Oct. 21, 2016.

231 "Get even": *60 Minutes II*, CBS News, Jan. 11, 2000.

231 "I'm building a ninety-story building next to it": Labash, "A Chump on the Stump." Trump World Tower is actually seventy-two stories tall.

232 "I certainly like what Donald Trump is saying": *FTP*, Dec. 27, 1999.

233 "man-hating misandry": Kenneth Turan, "A Psycho Carves Path from Novel to Screen," *Los Angeles Times*, April 14, 2000.

233 In March of that year: "Bill Cosby Threatens to Sue National Enquirer," *Tallahassee Democrat*, March 8, 2000

234 "I mean, terrible choice": Nagourney, "President? Why Not?"

234 a first-person essay: Donald Trump, "The Big Issue," *Gear*, March 2000.

234 remembers the article's composition: Author interview, Bob Guccione Jr.

235 "duty as an American citizen": AP, Oct. 20, 1999.

235 "Bachelor Ball": Leamer, *Mar-a-Lago*, pp. 88–92.

235 "It's a fantasy": Dowd, "Trump L'Oeil Tease."

235 One weekend in 2000: Michael Corcoran, "18 with the Trumpster!," *Maximum Golf*, August 2000.

236 "They seemed to be awfully chummy": Author interview, Abraham Wallach.

236 "Terrific guy": Landon Thomas Jr., "Jeffrey Epstein: International Moneyman of Mystery," *New York*, Oct. 28, 2002.

236 "like first-rate pussy": In the original text of Corcoran's article, this quote is rendered as "There is nothing in the world like first-class talent." In 2017, Corcoran revealed that Trump actually used the word *pussy*, and the quote was altered by an editor in deference to Trump, an account confirmed by a second editor at the magazine (Brandy Zadrozny, "Trump Bragged: Nothing in the World Like First-Rate P**sy," *Daily Beast*, Nov. 30, 2017).

236 Chuck Harder had news: *FTP*, Jan. 11, 2000.

237 Melania arrived at Trump Tower: *New York Post*, Jan. 27, 2000.

237 "Rather than being upset": Author interview, Trump campaign source.

237 "He seemed like": Author interview, Jerry Useem.

237 at another Reform Party rally: Useem, "What Does Trump Really Want?"; Vincent Morris, "Trump: 'Bush Is a Dim Bulb,'" *New York Post*, Jan. 8, 2000.

238 "surgically enhanced beauties": Jose Lambiet, "The Donald Looks Like a Politico—in More Ways than One," *Fort Lauderdale Sun-Sentinel*, Jan. 19, 2000.

238 "She meant a lot to me": *New York Post*, Jan. 12, 2000.

238 "She's a great girl": *New York Post*, Jan. 11, 2000.

238 "She's a one-man woman": *New York Post* gossip item reprinted in *MH*, Jan. 14, 2000.

238 "Donald already has spent": *New York Daily News*, Jan. 11, 2000.

238 "I will have to follow": "Meet the First Babes."

239 He took Melania to a candlelit dinner: *New York Post*, Jan. 27, 2000.

239 He gave Reform Party leaders the impression: Author interview, Russell Verney.

239 he took out the mortgage: *PBP*, June 2, 2000.

240 "So, waddya think": Reid, "Quasi-Candidate Loves to Serve but Hates to Lose."

240 "ashamed of this party!": Ryan Lizza, "Earful," *The New Republic*, Feb. 28, 2000.

240 "exploiters such as Donald Trump": Adam Nagourney, "Reform Bid Said to Be a No-Go For Trump," *NYT*, Feb. 14, 2000.

240 Ventura appeared at a press conference: *MH*, Feb. 12, 2000.

240 Mar-a-Lago held a pro-am tennis tournament: Michael Strauss, "Trump-Ilie Take Pro-Am Tennis Title," *Palm Beach Daily News*, Feb. 15, 2000.

241 snapped a picture with Jeffrey Epstein: "Pictured: Prince Andrew, Donald and Melania Trump at a party with billionaire paedophile Jeffrey Epstein at the President's Florida Mar-a-Lago Club in 2000," *Daily Mail*, Aug. 30, 2019.

241 "Doesn't that sound": *New York Post*, Feb. 17, 2000.

241 Trump issued a statement: "Statement of Donald J. Trump," Feb. 14, 2000.

241 decrying the "fringe element": Donald Trump, "What I Saw at the Revolution," *NYT*, Feb. 19, 2000.

241 sat down on *Today*: Matt Lauer interview with Trump, *Today*, NBC, Feb. 14, 2000.

18: Circus Town

242 "Contrary to popular belief": Daniel Boorstin, *The Image: A Guide to Pseudo-Events in America* (New York: Vintage Books, 1992), p. 209.

242 off-season headquarters: "When the Circus Was in Town," *Venice*, Feb. 9, 2015.

243 The Miami relatives were praying: *MH*, June 29, 2000.

243 Janet Reno learned of the decision: Janet Reno, Schedule for June 28, 2000.

243 "I hope everyone will accept": Account of Elián's departure compiled from *NYT*, June 29, 2000.

244 He had passed through U.S. border controls: FBI Timeline, p. 70.

245 "I'm trying to demystify it": Author interview, Franck Martin.

245 The flying Dutchmen: Arne Kruithof, *Unbelievable!* (self-published, 2011); Rudi Dekkers, *Guilty by Association* (Sydney: Brio Press, 2011); Daniel Hopsicker, *Welcome to Terrorland: Mohamed Atta and the 9/11 Cover-up in Florida* (Mad Cow Press, 2004).

245 left behind a huge tax-evasion case: Dekkers, *Guilty by Association*, pp. 72–73.

He writes that he was convicted but that his one-year sentence was later overturned on appeal.

245 He would later be imprisoned: Susan Carroll, "Flight Trainer of 9/11 Terrorists Faces Federal Drug Charges," *Houston Chronicle*, Dec. 13, 2012. Dekkers pleaded guilty to one count of conspiracy to possess with intent to distribute cocaine in 2013 and was sentenced to fifty-seven months in federal prison.

245 Kruithof shot a video: "FFTC and Arne Kruithof," undated promotional video, accessed via YouTube.

246 "It's newlyweds and nearly deads": *Venice Gondolier*, March 22, 2000.

246 were still in New York: FBI Timeline, p. 70.

246 He kept around $100,000: FBI, summary of interrogation of Abdul Aziz Ali, *USA v. KSM.*

246 who picked up the money: FBI Timeline, p. 71.

247 He smiled broadly behind his sunglasses: Fouda and Fielding, *Masterminds of Terror*, p. 131.

247 "I sensed pretty quickly": Kruithof, *Unbelievable!*, p. 111.

247 Kruithof would often: Author interview, Franck Martin.

247 Jarrah told the one: Rachel Davis, testimony, *USA v. Moussaoui.*

247 *Saus und Braus*: Aysel Sengün, statement, BKA Files.

248 a country Davis had never even heard of: Rachel Davis, testimony, *USA v. Moussaoui.*

248 Jarrah spent the sticky Florida summer: FBI, Investigative Summary, PENTTBOM, United Airlines Flight 93, 9/11 Commission Files, p. 3216.

248 he drove to school: The retail geography of Venice is reconstructed from the archives of the *Venice Gondolier*, including a yearly supplement entitled "Venice Profile," and from a tour of the town given by *Gondolier* reporter Bob Mudge.

248 where kids lined up at midnight: Fran Valencic, "Harry Potter Casts a Spell on Venice," *Venice Gondolier*, July 19, 2000.

248 flapping from the hands of a mannequin: Ed Scott, "Mannequin Adds Wrinkle to Sign Rule," *Venice Gondolier*, July 12, 2000.

248 "collision avoidance": "Record of Stage Check Private Pilot—Stage 1, July 13, 2000," exhibit, *USA v. Moussaoui.*

248 From above, he could take in: Aerial view observed by author during training flight, March 2020.

249 The waters off Venice: Caity Whiteaker, "Sharks Make Presence Known," *Venice Gondolier*, June 21, 2000.

19: TruMarkets

250 creation of a con artist: This portrait of Randy Glass, who died in 2008, is compiled from court records, news coverage, and interviews with former ATF agents. Glass's son, Benjamin Seaman, also contributed his recollections.

250 cocaine possession: John Mintz, "U.S. Reopens Arms Case in Probe for Taliban Role," *WP*, Aug. 2, 2002.

250 some gullible marks: John Pacenti, "Taliban Showed Interest in Boca Snitch," *PBP*, Sept. 29, 2001.

250 described his philosophy: *Dateline NBC*, "Trail of Terror."

250 Glass got pinched: Indictment, *USA v. Randy Glass.*

251 "between me and you": Recorded conversation between Randy Glass and Diaa Mohsen, Dec. 7, 1998, referenced in ATF Report No. 2, Dec. 8, 1998.

251 brought up Osama bin Laden: ATF Report No. 2, Dec. 8, 1998.

251 "You don't know": Recorded conversation between Glass and Mohsen, Dec. 7, 1998.

251 "thought it was bullshit": Author interview, Steve Barborini.

251 "Randy was a wild man": Author interview, Dick Stoltz.

251 secretly dubbed copies: Author interview, Benjamin Seaman.

251 "I was a rogue": John Pacenti, "Con Man Revels in Redemption as Terror Fighter," *PBP*, Aug. 3, 2002.

252 "force of nature": Armstrong, "Case Study: Operation Sphinx," p. 328.

252 out of his own pocket: Defendant Mohsen's Notice Under Seal of Intent to Present the Defense of Public Authority, *USA v. Diaa Mohsen*.

252 alias "Robert Blake": "Trail of Terror."

252 talked up Ingram's influence: ATF Report No. 37, May 25, 1999.

252 "They set him up": Author interview, Diaa Mohsen.

253 "one of the most prolific": Pacenti, "Taliban Showed Interest in Boca Snitch."

253 "There is a pattern": Author interview, Neil Karadbil.

253 "What we have": Pacenti, "Taliban Showed Interest in Boca Snitch."

253 "a cavalcade of negotiations": Armstrong, "Case Study: Operation Sphinx," p. 328.

254 "'What's the hottest thing'": "40 Under 40," *Crain's New York Business*, 1997.

255 homeowners would owe: Louis Uchitelle, "Equity Shrivels as Homeowners Borrow and Buy," *NYT*, Jan. 19, 2001.

255 Ingram had experimented: Joshua Brockman, "Deutsche Bank Adds Mortgage Securities to On-line Trading System," *American Banker*, Dec. 29, 1997.

255 dashed off a memo: Gary Morgenthaler, "Investment Memorandum," Jan. 23, 2000.

256 an initial $6.2 million: Morgenthaler Ventures, "Confidential Term Sheet," Dec. 28, 1999. Corzine's contribution reported in *NYT*, October 27, 2001.

256 "pie-in-the-sky guy": Author interview, Michael Herskovitz.

257 Ingram paid a visit: Affidavits of Charles Smart and Kevin Ingram, *TruMarkets Inc. v. Charles Smart and Visible Markets Inc.*, New York State Supreme Court, 2000.

257 "Kevin was really brilliant": Author interview, Michael Herskovitz.

257 "You never knew": Author interview, Charles Smart.

258 a sales proposal: ATF, Significant Activity Report, June 25, 2002.

258 twenty-four-page sales brochure: ATF Report No. 85, Aug. 25, 2000.

258 army chief of staff: ATF Report No. 84, Aug. 24, 2000.

258 really did appear to have ties: Author interviews, Dick Stoltz, Steve Barborini, and Dale Armstrong.

258 thought it was "crazy": ATF Report No. 78, May 22, 2000.

259 suspected he was a double agent: ATF Report No. 106, June 15, 2001.

259 Malik told the undercover ATF agents: ATF, Significant Activity Report, June 25, 2002.

259 dealers in Dubai: ATF Report No. 86, Sept. 21, 2000.

259 a fifteen-page weapons wish list: ATF Report No. 84, Aug. 24, 2000.

259 "I'm scared to death": Recorded conversation between Glass and Mohsen, Dec. 7, 1998.

259 nuclear materials could be procured: ATF, Significant Activity Report, June 25, 2002.

20: Remote Control

260 which he shared with the world: Teresa Wiltz and Paul Fahri, "Death Follows Ugly Scene Played Out on 'Springer,'" *WP*, June 27, 2000.

260 a local belly dancer: "Murder Scandal Could Kill Jerry Springer Show," *National Enquirer*, Aug. 15, 2000.

260 highest-rated syndicated programs: Greg Braxton, "Them's Fighting Words," *Los Angeles Times*, April 5, 1998.

260 This sounded good to Nan: Amended complaint for wrongful death, *Jeffrey J. Campbell v. Jerry Springer et al.*, filed in Circuit Court for Sarasota County, Florida, July 17, 2002.

260 The episode was to be titled: Julian Borger and Merope Mills, "A View to a Kill," *Guardian*, July 28, 2000.

261 paid for by the show's producers: Amended complaint, *Campbell v. Springer*.

261 It was an ambush: In his defense in the wrongful death litigation, Springer's attorneys produced a variety of legal waivers signed in advance by Ralf and Eleanor Panitz, including one entitled "Secrets Supplemental Consent and Release," which stated they understood that they might "learn allegations or information of which I was not previously aware" on the show and that "each SECRET may be private or personal and may be distressing to me if and when revealed to me." The wrongful death case was ultimately settled out of court.

261 "redheaded bitch from hell": Amended complaint, *Campbell v. Springer*. Other passages of dialogue from the *Springer* episode taken from above-cited articles in the *WP* and the *Guardian* and from Rochelle Steinhaus, "Florida v. Panitz: Talk Show Murder Trial," *Court TV*, March 1, 2002; archived article retrieved from CNN.com.

262 Nan appeared before a Sarasota County judge: Steinhaus, "Florida v. Panitz," March 1, 2002.

262 Ralf got drunk: Jennifer Sullivan, "Wife Takes Stand in Panitz Trial," *Sarasota Herald-Tribune*, March 16, 2002.

262 "To Jerry Springer": Transcript of sentencing hearing before Judge Nancy Donnellan, *Florida v. Panitz*, Circuit Court for Sarasota County, Florida, May 24, 2002, p. 20.

262 Based on a Swedish series: Patrick Radden Keefe, "Winning," *The New Yorker*, Jan. 7, 2019.

263 had pitched his concept: Mark Burnett, *Jump In!* (New York: Ballantine, 2005), p. 85.

263 "Outright lying is absolutely essential": "Old and New Bonds," Season 1, Episode 9, *Survivor*, created by Mark Burnett, first aired July 26, 2000. This account of *Survivor*'s first season is indebted to a series of episode recaps published in 2020 by Andy Dehnart on his blog *Reality Blurred*.

264 putting *Survivor* on its cover: *Newsweek*, Aug. 28, 2000.

264 "Machiavellian politics": Mark Burnett, *Survivor: The Ultimate Game* (New York: TV Books, 2000), p. 12

264 *dramality*: Burnett, *Jump In!*, p. 93.

264 "It's quite a mean game": Keefe, "Winning."

265 "Vote Hillary Off the Island": Tish Durkin, "In GOP's Big Tent, the Hillary-Haters Obey the Gag Order," *New York Observer*, Aug. 7, 2000.

265 *George* threw a bash: Amy Wallace, "Hollywood Turns Out in Force for Party in Its Backyard," *Los Angeles Times*, Aug. 18, 2000.

265 Chelsea Clinton showed up: Michael Wolff, "L.A. Nonstory," *New York*, Aug. 28, 2000.

265 Bill and Hillary kicked off their week: Unless otherwise noted, all descriptions of the DNC are based on reporting by Tish Durkin, Josh Benson, and staff of the *New York Observer*, Aug. 21, 2000. Some online news items accessed via archive.org.

265 state legislator named Barack Obama: David Axelrod, "Episode 108: President Barack Obama," *The Axe Files*, Dec. 26, 2016, transcript from CNN.com.

266 wanted to go out like Babe Ruth: Maureen Dowd, "Prudes and Playboys," *NYT*, Aug. 13, 2000.

266 kept his plan secret: Simon, *Divided We Stand*, p. 198.

266 entering the arena: "Video Recording of President William Jefferson Clinton Speaking at the 2000 Democratic National Convention," Aug. 14, 2000, accessed via YouTube.

266 Gore picked up 5 points: Simon, *Divided We Stand*, p. 199.

267 "If it means we have to hold our noses": *NYT*, Aug. 15, 2000.

267 toiling over his own convention speech: Shrum, *No Excuses*, pp. 348–49.

268 "I stand here tonight": Al Gore, DNC acceptance speech, Aug. 17, 2000.

268 "gained more in forty-five minutes": Author interview, Robert Shrum.

268 between 16 and 22 points: Shrum, *No Excuses*, p. 351.

268 "He's a rock star": Kevin Sack, "Gore and Company Making a Serious Play for Florida," *NYT*, Aug. 24, 2000.

268 "There's Al Gore": *PBP*, Sept. 1, 2000.

269 a champagne-colored Mercedes: Keefe, "Winning."

269 "Maintaining a thumb": Jan Tuckwood, "It's a Game, and It's Still Playing Us," *PBP*, Aug. 25, 2000.

269 "How do you stay true": Caryn James, "Critic's Notebook; Machiavelli, on a Desert Isle, Meets TV's Reality. Unreal," *NYT*, Aug. 24, 2000.

270 Bill Clinton was sitting: Michael Paterniti, "The Last Will and Testament of William Jefferson Clinton," *Esquire*, December 2000.

270 the first test: CIA, "DCI Report: The Rise of UBL and Al-Qa'ida and the Intelligence Community Response," March 19, 2000, National Security Archive, pp. 60–63; Coll, *Ghost Wars*, pp. 526–36.

270 "proof of concept": *9/11 Commission Report*, p. 189.

271 "live and prolonged coverage": Samuel Berger, "Memorandum for the President: Improving Intelligence Collection Against Usama bin Ladin," Aug. 20, 2000, Clinton Library.

271 "truly astonishing": *9/11 Commission Report*, p. 190; See also: Scott Swanson, "War Is No Video Game—Not Even Remotely," *Breaking Defense*, Nov. 18, 2014.

272 administration's secret councils: An authoritative description of the internal Clinton administration debate over the plans to kidnap or kill Osama bin Laden can be found in Coll, *Ghost Wars*, pp. 421–30 and 534–36.

272 "Is it stupid?": Frances Fragos Townsend, oral history, interviewed by Russell Riley et al., Miller Center (hereafter "Townsend, Miller Center oral history").

272 "a bunch of black ninjas": *9/11 Commission Report*, p. 189.

272 "We all wanted him dead": George Tenet, deposition given to 9/11 Commission, 9/11 Commission Files.

273 only if an Al Qaeda attack were "imminent": Coll, *Ghost Wars*, p. 426.

273 chances of success at 30 percent: *9/11 Commission Report*, p. 113.

273 "I was concerned": Janet Reno, deposition given to 9/11 Commission, 9/11 Commission Files.

274 haunted, in particular: Coll, *Ghost Wars*, p. 536.

274 nuclear submarines: Samuel Berger, "The 1993–2000 Record on Counterterrorism," confidential memo dated June 17, 2002, Reno papers.

274 sometimes play volleyball: Al-Bahri, *Guarding bin Laden*.

274 "the O.J. thing": Coll, *Ghost Wars*, p. 532.
274 "see it/shoot it" option: CIA, "Strategy for Eliminating the Threat from Jihadist Networks of al-Qida [*sic*]: Status and Prospect," memo sent to White House adviser Richard Clarke, Dec. 29, 2000, Clinton Library.
275 made an entry in his diary: Anthony Graziano, testimony, *USA v. al-Bahlul*, trial transcript p. 418.
275 "In October, an event may occur": Diary, Ali al-Bahlul, original and English translation introduced into evidence in *USA v. al-Bahlul*.
275 bearing the face of Bill Clinton: Dean, *Nine Lives*, p. 186.

21: Black September

276 "Eight months after": *FTP*, Aug. 5, 1999.
277 "This cannot be episodic": Email from Richard Clarke to Mona Sutphen, "FOR SANDY [SECRET]," Jan. 11, 2000, Clinton Library.
277 "worldwide political conspiracy": Clarke, *Against All Enemies*, pp. 216–18.
277 "one mosque to another": Janet Reno, deposition given to 9/11 Commission, 9/11 Commission Files.
278 The FBI catches bank robbers: Ned Zeman, David Wise, David Rose, and Bryan Burrough, "The Path to 9/11: Lost Warnings and Fatal Errors," *Vanity Fair*, November 2004.
278 one of at least eleven opportunities: Amy Zegart, *Spying Blind: The CIA, the FBI, and the Origins of 9/11* (Princeton, NJ: Princeton University Press, 2007), p. 102.
279 "a very serious man on the telephone": FBI, summary of interrogation of Mustafa Ahmed Adam al-Hawsawi, *USA v. KSM*.
279 an Arab prince: Dekkers, *Guilty by Association*, p. 148.
279 "asshole first class": Interview with Dekkers, Oct. 21, 2001, Australian Broadcasting Corporation.
280 "a collective sigh": Daniel Pursell, testimony, *USA v. Zacarias Moussaoui*.
280 "the little terrorist": Susan Hall, testimony, *USA v. Zacarias Moussaoui*.
280 "enemy's excitement trap": "The Al Qaeda Manual," 9/11 Commission Files.
281 showing him political websites: FBI report on interview with flight school classmate of Atta and al-Shehhi (name redacted), Sept. 15, 2001.
281 an odd Web page: FBI report on interview with Nicole Antini, Sept. 13, 2001.
281 believed that Monica Lewinsky: Wright, *The Looming Tower*, p. 306.
281 wired $70,000 in cash: FBI, summary of interrogation of Abdul Aziz Ali, *USA v. KSM*.
281 "They brought a roll": Author interview, Kendall Coleman.
282 received another visitor: The Bush and Gore rallies at the Sarasota airport were covered by the national and local media, including the *MH*, *AP*, and *Bradenton Herald*, as well as *The Catalyst*, a student publication of the New College of Florida, Sarasota.
282 a "Bush blitz": *MH*, Sept. 23, 2000.
283 "almost reclusive": Berke, "Feeling the Burden of a Name, One Bush Focuses on Florida."
283 his "Black September": James Moore and Wayne Slater, *Bush's Brain* (New York: Wiley, 2003), p. 273.
284 "I beat his brains in": Gregg, Miller Center oral history.
284 training camp: Stuart Stevens, *The Big Enchilada* (New York: The Free Press, 2001), pp. 156–61 and 194–97.

284 "We're doomed": Stuart Stevens, interviewed by Patrick Healy, "Debacle: What Al Gore's First Debate Against George W. Bush Can Teach Hillary Clinton," *NYT*, Sept. 25, 2016.

284 Inside was a videotape: DOJ, "Former Employee of Media Consultant to Bush Campaign Charged in Leak of Debate Preparation Materials to Gore Associate," press release, March 6, 2001.

284 popped the tape: Sam Stein, "The Crazy Inside Story of Al Gore's 'Trump Tower Moment,'" *Daily Beast*, Aug. 31, 2018.

284 was dressed casually: Author interview, Stuart Stevens.

285 a cover story: James Fallows, "An Acquired Taste: How Al Gore Learned to Love the Jugular," *Atlantic Monthly*, July 2000.

285 "We felt the first debate": Tad Devine, interviewed in Healy, "Debacle."

285 For extra luck: Chris Anderson, "Al Gore Slept Here," *Sarasota Herald Tribune*, Sept. 25, 2016.

286 plane rolled up: *The Catalyst*, Oct. 4, 2000.

286 at a dead sprint: Luke Frazza, AFP wire photo, Sept. 30, 2000. Gore's routine of running from his aircraft to greet waiting crowds is memorably described in Nicholas Lemann, "Gore Without a Script," *The New Yorker*, July 31, 2000.

286 "I'm not planning": Richard Berke and Katharine Seelye, "Gore Says He Will Focus on Substance, Nicely, in Debate," *NYT*, Oct. 2, 2000.

287 read the father's note: Shrum, *No Excuses*, p. 355.

288 Coleman flunked them: *9/11 Commission Report*, p. 224.

288 fought with him: FBI report on interview with Ivan Chirivella, Sept. 15, 2001.

22: Hurricane Season

289 "I love Florida": Harold Evans, "Bill Clinton's Fighting Farewell," *Talk*, December 2000/January 2001.

290 Clinton rambled off: Ellen Nakashima, "For One Gore Fan, Debate Was Near-Washout," *WP*, Oct. 5, 2000.

291 "important to resist": All debate quotations from transcripts archived on the Commission on Presidential Debates website, www.debates.org.

291 Jackson was there: Simon, *Divided We Stand*, pp. 237–39.

292 "world's preeminent debater": Simon, *Divided We Stand*, p. 233.

292 "steroid-crazed football player": Stevens, *The Big Enchilada*, p. 158.

292 "raw, unbridled contempt": Paul Begala, interviewed in Healy, "Debacle."

292 his Harvard thesis: Lemann, "Gore Without a Script."

292 final moments before: Simon, *Divided We Stand*, p. 239; Shrum, *No Excuses*, p. 355; Brazile, *Cooking with Grease*, p. 265.

294 Hit that harder: Shrum, *No Excuses*, p. 354.

294 blowing the whole election: Bruni, *Ambling into History*, p. 187.

295 "I bet that's a lie": Stevens, *The Big Enchilada*, p. 240.

295 "We're going to ram": Stevens, *The Big Enchilada*, p. 241.

296 "cannot do that": Simon, *Divided We Stand*, p. 240.

296 "The missing desk": Daniel Kennedy, "Note to Gore: Sarasota High Is Not a Sob Story," *Wall Street Journal*, Oct. 6, 2000.

296 "the pumpkin-headed sigh master": Bruni, *Ambling into History*, p. 187.

296 debate parody sketch: *Saturday Night Live*, Episode 486, Oct. 7, 2000.

296 came the deluge: "South Florida a Disaster Area," *MH*, Oct. 5, 2000.

297 a secret meeting: Jim Defede, "Collision Course," *Miami New Times*, Nov. 23, 2000.

298 "From crisis comes": Michael Grunwald, *The Swamp* (New York: Simon and Schuster, 2006), pp. 347–48.

298 General Motors introduced: Keith Bradsher, "G.M. Has High Hopes for Vehicle Truly Meant for Road Warriors," *NYT*, Aug. 6, 2000.

298 the opposite effect: Shrum, *No Excuses*, p. 358.

299 roused from his sleep: Brazile, *Cooking with Grease*, p. 266.

299 a navy destroyer: *9/11 Commission Report*, p. 190.

299 the first time: Henneberger and van Natta, "Once Close to Clinton, Gore Keeps a Distance."

300 he told Janet Reno: Reno, Miller Center oral history.

300 an emotional eulogy: *NYT*, Oct. 19, 2000.

300 most effective recruitment film: Ali Soufan, testimony, *USA v. al-Bahlul*, trial transcript p. 534.

300 slaughtering sheep and camels: *9/11 Commission Report*, p. 236.

23: Chasing Ghosts

301 least prepared for: Janet Reno, deposition given to 9/11 Commission, 9/11 Commission Files. See also Jim McGee and Brian Duffy, *Main Justice* (New York: Touchstone, 1996), pp. 303–65.

302 two or three a day on average: Junod, "Janet Reno Is Innocent."

302 "Bureau of Intelligence": "Oral History of Janet Reno."

302 "My job was to balance": Reno, 9/11 Commission deposition.

303 Freeh had not spoken: Zegart, *Spying Blind*, p. 143. In *My Life*, Bill Clinton contends that Freeh had decided to "sell me down the river" to win political support from Republicans in Congress after a "whole series of missteps" at the FBI under his watch (pp. 763–64). Freeh declined to be interviewed for this book.

303 only about 6 percent: 9/11 Commission, "Staff Statement No. 9," 9/11 Commission Files.

303 "real men don't type": Zegart, *Spying Blind*, p. 4.

303 "the joke of Washington": Zegart, *Spying Blind*, p. 137.

303 Freeh didn't even have: Zegart, *Spying Blind*, p. 4.

303 ordering Freeh to: Janet Reno, memorandum for FBI director Louis Freeh, "Threats to U.S. National Security Interests," May 2, 2000, Reno Papers.

304 "feel that the FBI": Reno, 9/11 Commission deposition.

304 the aftermath of the *Cole* attack: See Soufan, *The Black Banners*, pp. 149–270; Wright, *The Looming Tower*, pp. 365–72.

304 "criminal investigations of terrorism": Email from Richard Clarke to Roger Cressey, "Considerations," Oct. 25, 2000, Clinton Library.

305 "support" from Al Qaeda: CIA, DCI Counterterrorist Center, "Attack on the USS Cole: Preliminary Findings," Nov. 10, 2000, National Security Archive.

305 "History is written": Samuel Berger, Public Hearing Statement to the 9/11 Commission, March 24, 2004.

305 "didn't really want to know": *9/11 Commission Report*, pp. 195–96.

305 "Who the shit": Clarke, *Against All Enemies*, p. 224.

305 a jarring outburst: Dekkers, *Guilty by Association*, p. 147.

306 Jarrah was in Germany: FBI Timeline pp. 94–99.

306 had their picture taken: Summers and Swan, *The Eleventh Day*, p. 298.

306 picked him up: Thorsten Biermann, statement, BKA Files.
307 familiar with the phenomenon: Author interview, former CIA officer.
307 "chasing ghosts": Author interview, Dale Armstrong.
307 was curiously inaudible: 9/11 Commission Staff, interview of Richard Stoltz, 9/11 Commission Files.
307 controlled by Freemasons: Author interview, Diaa Mohsen.
307 refused to designate: Mintz, "U.S. Reopens Arms Case in Probe for Taliban Role."
307 all the "three-letter agencies": Author interviews, Dick Stoltz and other former ATF agents.
308 "This was not bullshit": Author interview, Steve Barborini.
308 "These were ISI agents": Author interview, Dale Armstrong.
308 interest in obtaining "sweet water": The ongoing efforts to obtain nuclear material were first reported by *Dateline NBC* (Chris Hansen and Richard Greenberg, "The Most Dangerous Man in the World?," NBC, Jan. 14, 2005) and are described most fully in ATF, Significant Activity Report, June 25, 2002.
308 dropped the name: Author interview, Dick Stoltz. Detail first reported by Hansen and Greenberg in "The Most Dangerous Man in the World?"
308 Khan also had a side business: William Langewiesche wrote a definitive two-part profile of A. Q. Khan in the *Atlantic* after the exposure of Khan's network ("The Wrath of Khan," November 2005; "The Point of No Return," January/February 2006).
309 mentioned intercepted shipments: ATF Report No. 47, Aug. 18, 1999, and No. 48, Aug. 24, 1999.
309 a $32 million order: ATF Report No. 90, Nov. 28, 2000.
309 "very smooth": ATF Report No. 87, Oct. 30, 2000.
310 "It looked like I was kissing": Simon, *Divided We Stand*, p. 256.
310 Dick Stoltz called: ATF Report No. 88, Nov. 13, 2000. In an interview, Stoltz described his procedure for handling tapes of his undercover phone calls.

24: The Numbers

311 Al Gore's motorcade: Simon, *Divided We Stand*, p. 13.
311 *Let us in!*: MH, Nov. 7, 2000.
311 There was Jesse Jackson: Simon, *Divided We Stand*, p. 19.
311 It was Harvey Weinstein: AP, Nov. 7, 2000.
312 assembled on a stage: "USA: MIAMI: PRESIDENTIAL ELECTION: AL GORE," AP video, accessed via YouTube.
312 "the future is being born": AP, Nov. 7, 2000.
312 in Little Havana: Tapper, *Down and Dirty*, p. 13.
312 "punish the enemy": Jeffrey Toobin, *Too Close to Call: The Thirty-Six-Day Battle to Decide the 2000 Election* (New York: Random House Trade Paperbacks, 2002), p. 146.
313 "going pretty wild": Correspondents of the *New York Times*, *36 Days: The Complete Chronicle of the 2000 Presidential Election Crisis* (New York: Times Books, 2001), pp. 57–58 (hereafter *36 Days*).
313 "New Jersey": Lou Dubose, *Boy Genius* (New York: Public Affairs, 2003).
313 craftier motive: Simon, *Divided We Stand*, p. 13.
313 his final day: Bruni, *Ambling into History*, pp. 198–200.
313 Jeb's people: Author interviews, Jeb Bush advisers.

314 "never live it down": AP, Oct. 11, 2000.

314 "I don't want to live": *PBP*, Aug. 3, 2000.

314 Leno ribbed Dubya: AP, Aug. 31, 2000; video accessed via YouTube.

314 Gore was in Tampa: Tapper, *Down and Dirty*, pp. 3–4.

314 first complaint call: Frank Cerabino, "How Al Gore Lost the Presidency," *PBP*, Dec. 17, 2000.

315 "I got scared": Cerabino, "How Al Gore Lost the Presidency."

316 "Everybody has to vote": Scene and dialogue reconstructed from contemporaneous notes, dated Nov. 7, 2000, taken by Nicole Antini, a twenty-two-year-old female employee of Huffman Aviation who filed a sexual harassment claim against Dekkers in 2001. Dekkers and his company settled the claim for $15,000, without any admission of wrongdoing. He could not be reached for comment.

316 Marwan walked in: Huffman Aviation, "General History," Marwan al-Shehhi, *USA v. Moussaoui*.

316 just passed an FAA test: FBI Timeline p. 101.

316 manager had heard: FBI report on interview with Nicole Antini, Sept. 13, 2001.

316 a balding statistician: Author interview, Murray Edelman. Other elements of this account of Election Day at the Voter News Service can be found in David Moore, *How to Steal an Election* (New York: Nation Books, 2006); Alicia Shepard, "How They Blew It," *American Journalism Review*, January/February 2001; Seth Mnookin, "It Happened One Night," *Brill's Content*, Dec. 18, 2000; Warren Mitofsky and Murray Edelman, "Election Night Estimation," *Journal of Official Statistics* 18, No. 2 (2002): 165–79; Warren Mitofsky, "Voter News Service After the Fall," *Public Opinion Quarterly* 67 (2003): 45–58; Neal Ungerleider, "Voter News Service, World Trade Center, 2000," medium.com, Sept. 16, 2016; Leon Neyfakh, "Real Numbers," Episode 2, *Fiasco: Bush v. Gore* (Luminary Media, May 30, 2019).

317 all using the same color scheme: Kornacki, *The Red and the Blue*, pp. 4–5.

318 "out of the Atari years": The Political Staff of the *Washington Post, Deadlock: The Inside Story of America's Closest Election* (New York: PublicAffairs, 2001), p. 31 (hereafter *Deadlock*).

319 first round of exit polls: *Deadlock*, p. 31.

320 as Ellis squinted: John Ellis, "A Hard Day's Night: John Ellis' Firsthand Account of Election Night," Inside.com, November–December 2000.

320 "I got the smell": *Deadlock*, p. 255.

320 a start-up called Inside.com: Patricia Jacobus, "Web Sites Run with Early Election Results," CNET, Nov. 7, 2000.

321 Ellis ducked out: Ellis, "A Hard Day's Night."

321 "rattletrap computer system": Roger Ailes, testimony, "Election Night Coverage by the Networks," House Committee on Energy and Commerce, Feb. 14, 2001.

321 "What's your gut": Gabriel Sherman, *The Loudest Voice in the Room* (New York: Random House, 2014), p. 245.

321 59,126: Martin Merzer and the staff of the *Miami Herald, Democracy Held Hostage: The Complete Investigation of the 2000 Presidential Election, Including Results of the Independent Recount* (New York: St. Martin's Press, 2001), p. 122 (hereafter *Democracy Held Hostage*).

321 trying to cast her ballot: Deposition of Janice Kelly, Doc. No. 409, *NAACP v. Harris*, pp. 82–90.

322 more than 20 percent: *36 Days*, p. 92.

322 a Democratic congresswoman: David Margolick, Evgenia Peretz, and Michael Schnayerson, "The Path to Florida," *Vanity Fair*, October 2004.

323 ballots cast by Black citizens: USCCR Report, p. 22.

323 "a new low": Brazile, *Cooking with Grease*, p. 232.

323 "They're stealing this election": Brazile, *Cooking with Grease*, p. 277.

323 latest technological gadget: Shrum, *No Excuses*, pp. 371–72.

324 a rolling suitcase: Kamarck, Miller Center oral history.

324 "Fear of being wrong": Mitofsky and Edelman, "Election Night Estimation."

325 "Any objections?": Ellis, "A Hard Day's Night."

325 Election Night dinner: T. Trent Gegax, "The Inside Story," *Newsweek*, Nov. 19, 2000.

326 "Our guests who": Bush, *Decision Points*, p. 77.

326 "I'm really sorry, brother": Gegax, "The Inside Story."

326 rumors of a brotherly argument: Bruni, *Ambling into History*, p. 202.

326 "I'm not going to stay": *Deadlock*, p. 33.

326 "There isn't much to say": Bush, *Decision Points*, p. 77.

326 "He's in retreat": Tapper, *Down and Dirty*, p. 23.

327 the most expensive Senate race: *NYT*, Nov. 8, 2000.

327 cell phones in Somalia: ATF Report No. 104, May 29, 2001, and No. 108, June 26, 2001.

327 Clinton was doing: Gegax, "The Inside Story."

327 "consultant populist bullshit": Tapper, *Down and Dirty*, pp. 24–25.

328 Grand Hyatt's ballroom: "She Wins," *New York Observer*, Nov. 13, 2000.

328 at Elaine's: Frank DiGiacomo, "Glitzocracy Awaits Hillary at Elaine's on Triumphal Night," *New York Observer*, Nov. 13, 2000. See also Lloyd Grove, "The Reliable Source," *WP*, Nov. 9, 2000; Mitchell Fink, George Rush, and Dave Goldiner, "Bill Jumps at Role as Cheerleader," *New York Daily News*, Nov. 9, 2000; Liz Smith, "People She Knew at Elaine's," *Newsday*, Nov. 9, 2000.

329 "You know what": Author interview, Andrew Goldman.

329 He was to give a speech: "New York Commercial Division Celebrates Fifth Anniversary," Metropolitan Corporate Counsel, January 2001.

329 stay-at-home routine: Author interview, Roger Stone.

330 "media and the boys": *FTP*, July 26, 1999.

330 "Folks didn't give us": Federal News Service, "Remarks by Patrick Buchanan, Reform Party Presidential Candidate," Nov. 7, 2000.

331 43,023 votes instead of 4,302: Shepard, "How They Blew It."

331 "Vote is strange": Moore, *How to Steal an Election*, p. 36.

331 a forensic autopsy: Mitofsky, "Voter News Service After the Fall."

331 a show of confidence: Tapper, *Down and Dirty*, pp. 27–29.

331 "Bush is not conceding": Moore, *How to Steal an Election*, p. 36.

332 colored red: Mitofsky and Edelman, "Election Night Estimation."

332 "Back from the ashes!": Karen Hughes, *Ten Minutes from Normal* (New York: Viking, 2004).

332 "Get me figures": Gegax, "The Inside Story."

332 *Florida, Florida, Florida*: Scott Stump, "My Strongest Memory Is Chaos: A Look Back at Election Night 2000," today.com, Oct. 5, 2020.

332 frequently comparing notes: Ellis, "A Hard Day's Night."

333 at 2:08, there was a breakthrough: Mitofsky and Edelman, "Election Night Estimation."

333 "Jebby says we got it!": Moore, *How to Steal an Election*, p. 59. The witness, an analyst named Cynthia Talkov, repeated the story to Gabriel Sherman in an interview for *The Loudest Voice in the Room*. Ellis has denied her version of events, contending that

he was too busy with his calculations to consult with Jeb on the call and pointing out that all his colleagues, including Talkov, a Democrat, signed off on the decision.

334 twice that number: Mitofsky and Edelman, "Election Night Estimation."

334 dial-up modems were screeching: Michael McDermott, oral history, interviewed by Julian Pleasants, UF Election Project.

334 did not think the anomaly: Mitofsky and Edelman, "Election Night Estimation."

335 "Gotta go": Moore, *How to Steal an Election*, p. 72.

335 "Let's give a tip": Shepard, "How They Blew It."

336 Al Gore was following: Shrum, *No Excuses*, p. 373.

336 "Never surrender": *36 Days*, p. 4.

336 "It's over": Simon, *Divided We Stand*, p. 31; author interviews, Gore advisers William Daley and Carter Eskew.

336 "Let's get this over with": Shrum, *No Excuses*, p. 373.

337 "You're a formidable opponent": Dialogue taken from *Decision Points* (p. 78) and from Bush's contemporaneous notes, which his former spokeswoman Karen Hughes reprints in her memoir, *Ten Minutes from Normal*.

337 "I don't see it": Hughes, *Ten Minutes from Normal*.

337 "Why is it so fucking close?": David Kaplan, *The Accidental President* (New York: William Morrow, 2001), p. 29.

338 placed a call: Kaplan, *The Accidental President*, pp. 30–31.

338 "Should I call Bush?": Kaplan, *The Accidental President*, p. 13.

338 Weinstein showed up: Grove, "The Reliable Source."

338 "still not over": Fink, Rush, and Goldiner, "Bill Jumps at Role as Cheerleader."

339 "We have to figure out": Grove, "The Reliable Source."

339 handed him a red folder: Simon, *Divided We Stand*, p. 35.

339 "The people of the country": Kaplan, *The Accidental President*, p. 22.

339 motorcade was unusually long: Simon, *Divided We Stand*, p. 36.

340 By 2:55 a.m.: Linda Mason et al., "CBS News Coverage of Election Night 2000: Investigation, Analysis, Recommendations," CBS News, January 2001, p. 22.

340 "Where the fuck": Conversation recounted with slightly varying wording in Toobin, *Too Close to Call* (p. 23), Kaplan, *The Accidental President* (p. 18), and Simon, *Divided We Stand* (p. 38).

340 "I told the governor": Kaplan, *The Accidental President*, p. 21.

341 "There are still some votes": Stump, "My Strongest Memory Is Chaos."

341 "Circumstances have changed": *Deadlock*, p. 49.

342 "I was hot": Bush, *Decision Points*, p. 78.

25: Hanging State

343 most notably Florida: Allman, *Finding Florida*, pp. 282–86.

344 snatch of sleep: David Margolick, "Brother Dearest," *Vanity Fair*, July 2001.

344 "I told Jeb": *Deadlock*, p. 257.

344 "We've been invaded": Karl Rove, *Courage and Consequence* (New York: Threshold Editions, 2010), p. 202.

345 illustration of chaos theory: *36 Days*, p. 325.

346 "Who's gonna deal": Brazile, *Cooking with Grease*, p. 283.

346 stood on a table: Tapper, *Down and Dirty*, p. 43; author interview, Donnie Fowler.

346 On the flight to Tallahassee: *Deadlock*, pp. 51–53; Toobin, *Too Close to Call*, pp. 31–32.

347 Jesse Jackson rang: Brazile, *Cooking with Grease*, pp. 283–84.

347 "facing-page ballot": Tapper, *Down and Dirty*, p. 6.

347 Theresa LePore, the supervisor of elections: Cerabino, "How Al Gore Lost the Presidency"; author interview, Theresa LePore.

348 "I was trying": Cerabino, "How Al Gore Lost the Presidency."

348 one of Gore's lawyers: Mark Herron, oral history, interviewed by Julian Pleasants, UF Election Project.

349 "This is ground zero": *PBP*, Nov. 9, 2000.

349 "My precious vote": *PBP*, Nov. 9, 2000.

349 Bill O'Reilly grumbled: *The O'Reilly Factor*, host Bill O'Reilly, with guest Juan Williams, Fox News, Nov. 8, 2000.

350 "more of a LEGAL EXERCISE": Peter Baker and Susan Glasser, *The Man Who Ran Washington: The Life and Times of James A. Baker III* (New York: Doubleday, 2020), p. 533.

350 "We need a PR strategy": Toobin, *Too Close to Call*, p. 46.

350 met for ninety minutes: *Deadlock*, p. 73.

351 "He's not called": Bob Poe, oral history, interviewed by Julian Pleasants, UF Election Project.

351 "It was a war": Mac Stipanovich, oral history, interviewed by Julian Pleasants, UF Election Project.

351 "I'll be at the ranch": Updegrove, *The Last Republicans*, p. 288.

351 "The lawyers are running": *36 Days*, p. 40.

352 played a minor role: Matt Flegenheimer, "Before Rise as Outsider, Ted Cruz Played Inside Role in 2000 Recount," *NYT*, Jan. 25, 2016.

352 Cruz sat down: Ted Cruz, *One Vote Away* (Washington, DC: Regnery, 2020), pp. 167–68. In interviews, other members of the Bush legal team recalled Cruz playing a more junior role than he suggests.

353 "Bill Clinton's worst nightmare": Theodore Olson, "The Most Political Justice Department Ever: A Survey," *The American Spectator*, September 2000.

353 "to purge the repugnant": Theodore Olson, "Father Confessor to the President's Men," *American Spectator*, September 1999.

353 watched the returns: Theodore Olson, oral history, interviewed by Barbara Perry et al., Miller Center (hereafter "Olson, Miller Center oral history").

353 worked in tandem: Kim Eisler, "Look Out Liberals, It's the Olsons!," *Washingtonian*, April 2000.

354 "just a group": Mary Jacoby, "Couple at Center of 'Conspiracy' Theory," *St. Petersburg Times*, Dec. 11, 2000.

354 "neither consciously": *36 Days*, p. 40.

354 "They're stealing the election": Robert Zelnick, *Winning Florida: How the Bush Team Fought the Battle* (Washington, DC: Hoover Institution Press, 2001), p. 12.

355 "This is not a way": Barbara Olson and Alan Dershowitz, interviewed by Matt Lauer, *Today*, NBC, Nov. 14, 2000.

356 "Ask Black people": Gore campaign chairman, William Daley, quoted in *Deadlock*, p. 93.

356 an astounding 175,000: "Examining the Vote: The Overview," *NYT*, Nov. 12, 2001.

356 There were around 64,000: *Democracy Held Hostage*, p. 9.

357 "battle for Stalingrad": Zelnick, *Winning Florida*, p. 71.

358 called "mudballing": Author interviews, Reeve Bright and Mary McCarty.

358 lose twenty-two pounds: *Democracy Held Hostage*, p. 7.
358 a rougher crowd: Paul Lomartire, "GOP Sent T-shirt Team of Dedicated Infiltrators," *PBP*, Dec. 1, 2000.
358 "a banana republic–type situation": *FTP*, Aug. 12, 1999.
359 "*For the People* reports": Letter to the Editor, *Baxter Bulletin*, Dec. 12, 2000.
359 "We're fighting for our lives!": David Brock, "Fire on the Right," *Talk*, February 2001.
359 "Bush or Revolution": *PBP*, Nov. 22, 2000; and *PBP*, Nov. 26, 2000.
359 fame-hungry fisherman: *PBP*, Nov. 20, 2000.
359 on a "ticker": Kaplan, *Accidental President*, p. 84.
359 "a test of mettle": Michael Wolff, "A Duel in the Sun," *New York*, Nov. 27, 2000.
359 "a wonderful thing": Howard Kurtz, "On the Airwaves, Election Aftermath Is All Talk, All the Time," *WP*, Nov. 12, 2000.
359 He rolled up: *PBP*, Nov. 10, 2000.
360 139 percent more likely: *PBP*, Nov. 13, 2000.
360 poor Black towns: William Cooper and Alexandra Clifton, "Glades Blacks' Ballots Tossed More," *PBP*, Nov. 18, 2000.
360 ended up with the cheaper: Joel Engelhardt, "Black Voters Angered by Election Day Hurdles," *PBP*, Dec. 10, 2000.
360 "Something systematic": *PBP*, Nov. 13, 2000.
360 "a political storm": *PBP*, Nov. 12, 2000.
360 led the marchers: *PBP*, Nov. 14, 2000.
360 former grand wizard: Tapper, *Down and Dirty*, p. 161.
361 "We ran Jesse Jackson off!": Author interview, Bradley Blakeman.
361 "Anger is not": *36 Days*, p. 232.
361 radio host Tom Joyner: Radio show interview clip replayed on *Hannity and Colmes*, Fox News, Nov. 16, 2000.
362 He tried to pass word to Jackson: Tapper, *Down and Dirty*, p. 83.
362 "It is time to end": Brazile, *Cooking with Grease*, p. 288.
362 making a critical mistake: Toobin, *Too Close to Call*, p. 194.
362 9,000 of these overvotes: Shannon Colavecchio, "Lost Votes Sting Blacks in Jacksonville," *PBP*, Dec. 17, 2000.

26: Thanksgiving

363 When he got the first call: David Boies, *Courting Justice* (New York: Miramax Books, 2004), p. 358.
363 Boies was legendary: Portions of this chapter are drawn from Andrew Rice, "The Bad, Good Lawyer," *New York*, Sept. 30, 2018.
364 Boies was in the middle: Karen Donovan, *v. Goliath: The Trials of David Boies* (New York: Vintage Books, 2007), p. 263.
364 "Can you get to Florida": Toobin, *Too Close to Call*, p. 107.
365 sharing a bottle: Donovan, *v. Goliath*, p. 266.
365 "Welcome to Guatemala": Boies, *Courting Justice*, p. 364.
365 "The person in charge": Ron Klain, oral history interview, "The Bush-Gore Recount Is An Omen for 2020," *Atlantic*, Oct. 17, 2020.
365 a big football game: Toobin, *Too Close to Call*, p. 129.
366 "Gosh, if Warren Christopher": Bolten, Miller Center oral history.
366 "We all hope": Donovan, *v. Goliath*, p. 268.

366 Charlie Rose shared: Donovan, *v. Goliath*, p. 229.

367 bar near the Capitol: Donovan, *v. Goliath*, p. 271.

367 a grand total of 1 vote: *PBP*, Nov. 21, 2000.

367 there was bedlam: *PBP*, Nov. 19, 2000; *36 Days*, pp. 104–6.

367 a television on the wall: Staff photo, *South Florida Sun-Sentinel*, Nov. 21, 2000.

367 "This was amateur hour": Dershowitz and Olson, interviewed by Chris Matthews, *Hardball with Chris Matthews*, MSNBC, Nov. 20, 2000.

368 "the result that reflects": Supreme Court of Florida, per curiam opinion, Nov. 21, 2000.

368 flying down to preside: *Palm Beach Daily News*, Nov. 26, 2000.

368 "handsome and uninhibited" royal: Shannon Donnelly, "Is He Here? Duke of York May Distract Us from Ballot Snafu," *Palm Beach Daily News*, Nov. 12, 2000.

369 the potbellied developer: "A Downpour for the Donald," *Palm Beach Daily News*, Nov. 26, 2000.

369 "This came out of the blue": *PBP*, Jan. 11, 2000.

369 flew to Fort Lauderdale: Donovan, *v. Goliath*, pp. 283–88.

370 "the whole ballgame": Zelnick, *Winning Florida*, p. 67.

370 a Winnebago RV: *PBP*, Nov. 23, 2000.

370 "Republicans will be needed": Tapper, *Down and Dirty*, p. 259.

370 "air of mystery": Nicholas Kulish and Jim VandeHei, "GOP Protest in Miami-Dade Is a Well-Organized Effort," *Wall Street Journal*, Nov. 27, 2000.

371 A *Time* correspondent: Tim Padgett, "Mob Scene in Miami," *Time*, Nov. 26, 2000.

371 Stone criticized Dubya's: *36 Days*, p. 56.

371 "Committee to Take Back Our Judiciary": *WP*, July 11, 2003. The local Republican official, Mary McCarty, was later fined $2,000 for election law violations. "That's Roger Stone," she said. "He's a provocateur."

373 their inhibitions loosened: Coverage in the *MH* and *PBP* and *Wall Street Journal*, Nov. 24, 2000; *Deadlock*, pp. 138–41; Tapper, *Down and Dirty*, pp. 260–66. See also *537 Votes*, dir. Billy Corben (HBO Films, 2020).

373 "Thief! Thief!": Joe Geller, oral history, interviewed by Julian Pleasants, UF Election Project.

374 "They'd been living": Frank Cerabino, "Ready for Quick Fix? Turn Mess Over to Cuban-Americans!," *PBP*, Nov. 25, 2000.

374 Baker has publicly stated: Toobin, "The Dirty Trickster."

374 Three other Republicans: Author interviews, Al Cárdenas, Mac Stipanovich, and Mary McCarty. See also *Get Me Roger Stone*, dir. Dylan Bank, Daniel DiMauro, and Morgan Pehme (Netflix, 2017).

375 "He is the only living American": *The Spin Room*, hosted by Tucker Carlson and Bill Press, CNN, Nov. 27, 2000.

375 Carlson received a phone call: Tucker Carlson, "Unscripted: Diary of a Talking Head," *Talk*, February 2001.

375 David Boies was in the air: Boies, *Courting Justice*, p. 402.

375 "So I go down": Donovan, *v. Goliath*, pp. 290–91.

376 an additional 784 votes: Toobin, *Too Close to Call*, p. 86.

376 "up to me as a lawyer": Margaret Carlson, "Backstreet Boies," *Time*, Dec. 4, 2000.

376 "He was not": Boies, *Courting Justice*, p. 411.

376 "a black mark": *36 Days*, p. 53.

377 "Another week": R. W. Apple, "The Limits of Patience," *NYT*, Nov. 12, 2000.

377 "a lost soul": AP, Nov. 29, 2000.
377 "When does it end?": Kaplan, *The Accidental President*, pp. 193–94.
377 a Vegas-style banquet: Toobin, *Too Close to Call*, pp. 158–59.
377 his wife's chipotle stuffing: Lisa Getter, "Jeb Bush's Recount Role Examined," *Los Angeles Times*, July 14, 2001.
377 a backup plan: *PBP*, Nov. 28, 2000.
377 "a comfortable place": Bolten, Miller Center oral history.
378 "The U.S. Supreme Court": Donovan, *v. Goliath*, p. 291.
378 At 3:57 p.m.: FBI Timeline p. 106.

27: Fort Lauderdale

379 an ominous cloud: "Strange Phenomenon," *Venice Gondolier*, Nov. 11, 2000.
379 Ziad Jarrah took off that morning: FFTC, "General History," Ziad Jarrah, exhibit, *USA v. Moussaoui*.
380 a quiet roommate: Statements from flight school classmates, BKA Files.
380 "I'm angry": McDermott, *Perfect Soldiers*, pp. 197–98.
381 He expressed some casual negativity: Kruithof, *Unbelievable!*, p. 123.
381 Saudi named Hani Hanjour: *9/11 Commission Report*, p. 226.
381 two-day training flight: Ziad Jarrah, navigation and weather logs, Nov. 19–20, 2000, exhibits, *USA v. Moussaoui*.
382 The day after Thanksgiving: ATF Report No. 90, Nov. 28, 2000.
383 a bottle of Tanqueray: ATF, Property Inventory, Item No. 454: "One bottle of Tanqueray gin," Dec. 8, 2000.
383 wealthy Saudis were providing: ATF, Significant Activity Report, June 25, 2002.
383 a $200,000 bribe: ATF, Significant Activity Report, June 25, 2002.
384 "Dot's All, Folks": James Cramer, "Bubble Trouble," *New York*, May 1, 2000.
384 roughly $30 million: Spiro, "Wall Street's Soldier of Fortune."
385 one of TruMarkets's rivals: In 2021, investor Gary Morgenthaler pointed out that a company called MarketAxess had "built a $16.7 billion market capitalization using the same idea, technology and business model" and "was 2nd only to Netflix in its percentage share price appreciation during the last decade."
385 "key guy": ATF, Significant Activity Report, June 25, 2002. This account of the January 2001 meeting is additionally derived from interviews with investigators and the subsequent indictment in the case *USA v. Rajaa Abbas and Abdul Malik, aka Sajaad Malik, aka Rahi Nazar Malik*. There is some mystery surrounding the true identity of the visitor. Federal investigators referred to him as "Abdul Malik," but a former intelligence officer familiar with the region said that this was likely only a partial name. The defendants were never apprehended, and as of 2002, they were believed to be residing in Pakistan.
385 intended to sell: ATF, Significant Activity Report, June 25, 2002.
386 U.S. intelligence agency: Author interview, Dick Stoltz.
386 "We know it's not bullshit": Author interview, Steve Barborini.
387 Abdul flew all the way: ATF Report No. 100, Feb. 26, 2001.

28: *Bush v. Gore*

388 "seemed implausible": John Paul Stevens, *The Making of a Justice* (New York: Little, Brown, 2019), p. 360.
388 a round of golf: Margolick, Peretz, and Schnayerson, "The Path to Florida."
389 "This is never going": Kaplan, *The Accidental President*, p. 202.

389 "We'll hear argument": Oral argument, *Bush v. Palm Beach County Canvassing Board*, U.S. Supreme Court, Dec. 1, 2000, accessed via oyez.org.

390 eminent legal figure: Andrew Rice, "Et tu, Tribe," *New York*, July 28, 2015.

390 "I can't recuse myself": AP, Dec. 1, 2000.

391 He could count: In Margolick, Peretz, and Schnayerson, "The Path to Florida," Margolick reports that Stevens and the other liberals, presuming the five conservatives would rule for Bush, "began drafting a dissent even before the case was argued in court."

391 Jackson locked arms: *36 Days*, p. 209.

391 "drop by" meeting: Janet Reno, Schedule for Friday, Dec. 1, 2000.

391 "I want to be very careful": DOJ, "Weekly Media Briefing with U.S. Attorney General Janet Reno," Nov. 9, 2000.

392 traveled to Jacksonville: *PBP*, Dec. 3, 2000.

392 FBI field office in Jacksonville: FBI, "Visit of the Attorney General Janet Reno to Jacksonville, Florida," memo dated Nov. 30, 2000.

392 opened an inquiry: *PBP*, Dec. 4, 2000.

392 "Welcome back": *Crossfire*, hosted by Jake Tapper and Robert Novak, CNN, Dec. 1, 2000.

393 "Ignoring votes means": *36 Days*, p. 178.

394 "Whatever the court wants": *PBP*, Dec. 1, 2000.

394 "This is boring": AP, Dec. 1, 2000.

394 he told his lawyers: Author interview, Bush legal team member.

394 "Redneck": Toobin, *Too Close to Call*, p. 203.

394 "My strategy is": Author interview, Ron Klain.

394 "They won": Donovan, *v. Goliath*, p. 299.

395 majority opinion found: Supreme Court of Florida, per curiam opinion, Dec. 8, 2000.

395 Shabbat dinner: Brazile, *Cooking with Grease*, pp. 289–90.

396 Across town at Main Justice: Eric Lichtblau and Ronald Ostrow, "Cussed at, Fussed at, Reno Shrugs, Survives," *Los Angeles Times*, Jan. 19, 2001.

396 "those Russian sailors": Zelnick, *Winning Florida*, p. 138.

396 "It is sad for Florida": *NYT*, Dec. 9, 2000.

396 "fully engaged": *Deadlock*, p. 261.

396 "This judicial aggression": *36 Days*, p. 268.

397 "incurable in the public consciousness": Kaplan, *The Accidental President*, p. 238.

397 working in groups of two: *MH*, Dec. 10, 2000.

397 Klain was allowing himself: Toobin, *Too Close to Call*, p. 247.

397 around 58 votes: Tapper, *Down and Dirty*, p. 439.

398 eating a burger: Donovan, *v. Goliath*, p. 308.

398 "That's great news": Tapper, *Down and Dirty*, p. 438.

398 "I'm with the Bush-Cheney team": *MH*, Dec. 10, 2000.

398 "Forget it": *Deadlock*, p. 213.

399 tapped out a message: Toobin, *Too Close to Call*, p. 252.

399 Alzheimer's diagnosis: O'Connor's perspective conveyed in: Evan Thomas, *First: Sandra Day O'Connor* (New York: Random House, 2019), pp. 323–34.

399 nicknamed him "Flipper": Jeffrey Rosen, "Supreme Leader," *The New Republic*, June 16, 2007.

400 woke up early: Donovan, *v. Goliath*, pp. 3–4.

400 crew from *60 Minutes*: Donovan, *v. Goliath*, p. 315.
401 "Oh, and I thought your point": Oral argument, *Bush v. Gore*, U.S. Supreme Court, Dec. 11, 2000, accessed via oyez.org.
401 aggressively urging: Margolick, Peretz, and Schnayerson, "The Path to Florida."
402 the obvious counterargument: Stevens, *The Making of a Justice*, p. 367.
402 She would have pointed out: Toobin, *Too Close to Call*, p. 266.
403 "You really nailed": Boies, *Courting Justice*, p. 447.
403 dinner at Chin Chin: Donovan, *v. Goliath*, p. 320.
403 "It was very hard": Olson, Miller Center oral history.
403 "We're having this baby": *New York Daily News*, Dec. 13, 2000.
403 "Here comes our runner": *NYT*, Dec. 13, 2000.
404 "I'm calling Baker": Rove, *Courage and Consequence*, p. 216.
404 "What does it say?": Cruz, *One Vote Away*, p. 180.
404 "That day!": Thomas, *First*, p. 331.
405 dissents from the liberals: Stevens, *The Making of a Justice*, pp. 370–73.
405 "Al Sharpton tactics": Toobin, *Too Close to Call*, pp. 266–67.
405 "wrong to shoot us": Boies, *Courting Justice*, p. 451.
406 "I do believe": "Al Gore Concedes Presidential Election of 2000," CNN, Dec. 13, 2000.

29: Gasparilla

407 an awkward visit: Grunwald, *The Swamp*, pp. 350–53.
407 "a scene from a Fellini movie": Bob Deans, "Clinton Inks $7.8 Billion Everglades Cleanup Bill," *PBP*, Dec. 12, 2000.
407 "If we don't do something": Grunwald, *The Swamp*, p. 352.
408 "I know America": "Text of Bush's Speech," *NYT*, Dec. 13, 2000.
408 "George W. Bush may be forgotten": Kaplan, *The Accidental President*, p. 301.
409 "Votes in Florida": "USA: Formal Certification of George W. Bush Victory Wrap," AP video, Jan. 6, 2001, accessed via YouTube.
409 a farewell party: Williams, "Scenes from a Marriage."
409 Fragmentary accounts: John Harris, "Clinton and Gore Clashed Over Blame for Election," *WP*, Feb. 7, 2000.
409 "He's being screwed": Toobin, *Too Close to Call*, p. 194.
409 likened *Bush v. Gore*: Tapper, *Down and Dirty*, p. 458.
409 Gore who started off: Harris, *The Survivor*, p. 426.
409 "I provided the moral energy": Harris, *The Survivor*, p. 385.
410 "Gee whiz": Richard Berke, "Many Democrats Appear Skeptical of Gore's Future," *NYT*, Dec. 17, 2000.
410 "worse than idle speculation": Smith, "White House Civil War."
410 "was a living wreck": Updegrove, *The Last Republicans*, p. 289.
411 "We'll survive this": Paul Reid, "Father Knows Best: All Will 'Be Fine,'" *PBP*, Nov. 30, 2000.
411 pirate had been invented: Allman, *Finding Florida*, p. 318.
411 "He should be grateful": Mike Clary, "Bush Does Winter Break in Florida," *Los Angeles Times*, Dec. 27, 2000.
411 were flying out: FBI Timeline p. 114.
412 an angry phone call: Daniel Pursell, testimony, *USA v. Zacarias Moussaoui*.

412 amid the traffic: "9/11 Commission Briefing: Flight Training," Jan. 13, 2004, 9/11 Commission Files; incident first reported in *NYT*, Oct. 17, 2001.
412 "It is the equivalent": Dekkers, *Guilty by Association*, p. 119.
413 due to depart: Flight records of Ziad Jarrah, BKA Files.
413 commercial jet simulators: Receipts, Aeroservice Aviation Center, exhibits, *USA v. Zacarias Moussaoui*.
413 sister's wedding: Aysel Sengün, statement, BKA Files.
413 conflict within Jarrah: Weaver, "The Indecisive Terrorist."
414 "Ziad looked happy": Kruithof, *Unbelievable!*, p. 117.
414 a romantic getaway: FBI report on interview with Aysel Sengün, Sept. 18, 2001.
414 She snapped a photo: BKA Files.
414 Atta told him: *9/11 Commission Report*, p. 226.
414 flew to Tehran: "The Confession," *Der Spiegel*, November 2003.
415 delighted by the election: Scott-Clark and Levy, *The Exile*, p. 45.
415 He warned his successor: *9/11 Commission Report*, p. 199.
415 "not some narrow": Richard Clarke, "Presidential Policy Initiative/Review—The Al Qida Network," memo to Condoleezza Rice, Jan. 25, 2001, Clinton Library.
416 tired of briefings: Dan Eggen and Walter Pincus, "Ashcroft's Efforts on Terrorism Criticized," *WP*, April 14, 2004. Ashcroft denied the former acting FBI director's claim in testimony before the 9/11 Commission.
416 Olson received assistance: Jo Becker, *Forcing the Spring* (New York: Penguin, 2014), pp. 41–42. As Becker's book describes, Boies and Olson later took on a fight together, advocating to overturn the ban on gay marriage.
416 Boies attended: Donovan, *v. Goliath*, p. 260.
416 "No lawyer in memory": Daniel Okrent, "Get Me Boies!," *Time*, Dec. 25, 2000.
416 "When these folks": Rice, "The Bad, Good Lawyer."
417 Bill Cosby's suggestion: Boies, *Courting Justice*, p. 488.
417 "v. hot": Author interview, former *Talk* editor.
418 "afoot in Florida": Paul Reid, "Problems with Vote No Accident, Jackson Says," *PBP*, Dec. 17, 2000.
418 a series of stories: Robert King, "Hunt for Fraudulent Voters Triggered Confusion, Anger," *PBP*, Dec. 11, 2000.
419 "JESSE JACKSON'S LOVE CHILD": *National Enquirer*, Jan. 30, 2001.
419 "Jackson's long reign": Mary McGrory, "Scandalous Symmetry," *WP*, Jan. 21, 2000.
420 "wrong side of the rope line": Jonathan Alter, *The Promise: President Obama, Year One* (New York: Simon and Schuster, 2010), p. 41.
420 like in *Thelma and Louise*: Lichtblau and Ostrow, "Cussed at, Fussed at, Reno Shrugs, Survives."
420 "worry about the bombs": Author interview, Myron Marlin.
420 "a great adventure": *NYT*, Jan. 21, 2001.
421 *And now*: *Saturday Night Live*, Episode 495, Jan. 20, 2001.

30: The Sting

422 arrive in Dubai: FBI, summaries of interrogations of Abdul Aziz Ali and Mustafa al-Hawsawi, *USA v. KSM*.
423 as a "Bedouin.": Khalid Sheikh Mohammed, written testimony, *USA v. Moussaoui*.
423 destroy the White House: *9/11 Commission Report*, pp. 243–44; McDermott and Meyer, *The Hunt for KSM*, p. 142.

423 came to the Sheikh: Zacarias Moussaoui, testimony, *USA v. Moussaoui.* Moussaoui was an unreliable witness, but his account of how he came to volunteer seems to fit with other available evidence.

423 completely hopeless: At the Moussaoui trial, the admissions director of the Oklahoma flight school testified that while it normally required around fifteen hours of training to get a student ready for a solo flight, Moussaoui took fifty-seven hours of instruction without attaining the necessary proficiency.

423 "departed . . . seeking death": As-Sahab Media Foundation, *Knowledge Is for Acting Upon.*

423 inquisitive young jihadis: Sahim Alwan, testimony, *USA v. al-Bahlul.*

424 arrived in Florida: FBI, Investigative Summary, PENTTBOM, April 19, 2002, 9/11 Commission Files.

424 porn videos and sex toys: FBI, investigative summary, PENTTBOM, pp. 3306–11.

424 mohamedatta@hotmail.com: FBI Timeline p. 164.

424 fleabag motel: FBI, Investigative Summary, PENTTBOM, pp. 3313–14; FBI Timeline, pp. 155–59.

424 On the morning of June 12: The arrest of Kevin Ingram is described in ATF Report No. 106, June 15, 2001. Dialogue is taken from the transcript of an ATF undercover recording made by Agent Dick Stoltz on June 12, 2001, and entered into evidence in connection with the sentencing of Walter Kapij (*USA v. Ingram*, filed Jan. 11, 2002).

425 made the decision to wrap up: ATF, Significant Activity Report, June 25, 2002.

426 sales leads in West Africa: ATF Report No. 101, March 27, 2001.

426 weapons from Vietnam: ATF Report No. 105, May 30, 2001.

427 He complained that Ingram: ATF Report No. 104, May 29, 2001, and No. 108, June 26, 2001.

427 He remembered how: Author interview, Kevin Ingram.

427 "one large unit": ATF Report No. 104, May 29, 2001.

427 Spears told Ingram: ATF Report No. 106, June 15, 2001.

428 "long, long night": All dialogue taken from ATF undercover recording, June 12, 2001.

430 "BIZ BIG BUSTED": *New York Post*, June 15, 2001.

430 "I literally spat": Thomas, "Ex-Goldman Trader Stung in Arms Plot, Shocks Colleagues."

430 "The tragedy is": Spiro, "Wall Street's Soldier of Fortune."

431 "It seemed to me": Author interview, Jay Norris.

431 his connection to Jesse Jackson: *New York Post*, June 27, 2001.

431 an internal ATF report: ATF, Significant Activity Report, June 14, 2001.

432 "dowdy, below-the-knee": Joseph Contreras, "Janet Versus Jeb," *Newsweek*, Sept. 5, 2001.

432 celebrated his seventh birthday: AP, Dec. 7, 2000.

432 retreated to the basement: Stanley, *The Crusader*, p. 354.

432 renew his call: Interview with Pat Buchanan, *Late Edition with Wolf Blitzer*, CNN, Sept. 9, 2001.

433 "Globalists cannot contain": Chuck Harder, "Nation Building . . . Here We Go Again!," chuckharder.com, April 5, 2002.

433 unsuccessfully shopping around: Don Kaplan, "Trump Holding Cards for New 'Billionaire' Game Show," *New York Post*, Feb. 9, 2001.

434 the "urban jungle": Burnett, *Jump In!*, pp. 186–93.

434 old slide show presentation: Patrick Healy, "The End of the Line," *NYT*, Aug. 25, 2012.
434 "You know the old saying": David Remnick, "The Wilderness Campaign," *The New Yorker*, Sept. 5, 2004.
434 their own unofficial recounts: See *NYT*, "Examining the Vote"; *Democracy Held Hostage*. The *Herald*'s subsequent analysis of the overvotes was published on the website www.overvote.net, which can still be accessed via archive.org.
434 just 3 votes: *Democracy Held Hostage*, p. 9.
435 *did* show clear evidence: The *Herald* study found that 97 percent of the overvotes were legally irretrievable because it would be impossible to prove which candidate the voter intended to select. But 3,146 ballots did show clear intent, generally "when voters chose a candidate and then cast a write-in vote for that same candidate." Counting these double votes produced a theoretical net gain of 682 votes for Gore.
435 543,895 more votes: "2000 Presidential Popular Vote Summary," Federal Election Commission, fec.gov. Other sources report slightly different totals.
435 "I could have handled": Liza Mundy, "Mr. Resident," *WP*, Nov. 17, 2002.
436 "strong basis": USCCR Report, executive summary.
436 "simplest written instructions": USCCR Report, appendix, p. 86.
437 delved into Florida: *Fahrenheit 9/11*, dir. Michael Moore (Dog Eat Dog Films, 2004).
437 "It is an action": Roger Stone and Saint John Hunt, *The Bush Crime Family* (New York: Skyhorse Publishing, 2016).
437 A muckraking leftist journalist: Greg Palast, *The Best Democracy Money Can Buy* (London: Pluto Press, 2002), pdf retrieved from "November 2017 Release of Abbottabad Compound Material," www.cia.gov/library/abbottabad-compound.
437 Atta left the United States: *9/11 Commission Report*, pp. 244–45.
438 so he could strike: Coll, *Ghost Wars*, p. 571.
438 Jarrah continued to be defiant: *9/11 Commission Report*, p. 246.
438 an "unhappy couple": Weaver, "The Indecisive Terrorist."
439 The school in Minnesota: Clancy Prevost, testimony, *USA v. Zacarias Moussaoui*, transcript pp. 716–90.
439 a bitter argument: DOJ, Office of Inspector General, "A Review of the FBI's Handling of Intelligence Information Related to the September 11 Attacks," November 2004.
439 the same FBI supervisor: The DOJ inspector general's report concluded that there were "significant problems" in the FBI's handling of Moussaoui's case, but that they were attributable to systemic issues rather than "intentional misconduct." The supervisor, David Frasca, declined interview requests. "He did nothing wrong," said an attorney who represented Frasca in the proceeding. "He got blamed for it. It wasn't him."
440 feeling very sick: Aysel Sengün, statement, BKA Files.
440 As Ramzi later retold it: "Translation of Ramzi Binalshibah Audio Tape—22 September 2002," 9/11 Commission Files.
441 a silver-haired Al Gore: "The Inauguration of Joseph R. Biden Jr.," NBC News, Jan. 20, 2021.
441 would never really answer: Gore declined interview requests for this book.
442 "Red America and Blue America": Kornacki, *The Red and the Blue*, p. 5.
443 "The problem was": *Deadlock*, p. 260.
443 "Look, the other guy": Mundy, "Mr. Resident."

Epilogue: Out of Time

444 Ingram wakes up: Author interview, Kevin Ingram.

444 "far greater ramifications": Jon Burstein, "Ex-Jeweler a Major Link in Arms Case," *South Florida Sun-Sentinel*, Aug. 7, 2001.

444 stood behind him: Spiro, "Wall Street's Soldier of Fortune."

445 "great gassy flower": Summers and Swan, *The Eleventh Day*, p. 19.

445 his chauffeured car: Author interview, David Boies.

446 Everyone above the ninety-second: Summers and Swan, *The Eleventh Day*, p. 20.

446 sitting in his office: Theodore Olson, interview by Larry King, "Encore Presentation: Barbara Olson Remembered," transcript, *Larry King Weekend*, CNN, Jan. 6, 2002; FBI reports on interviews with Olson and DOJ staff members Helen Voss, Allen Ferber, and Lori Lynn Keyton, Sept. 11, 2001, 9/11 Commission Files.

446 *"Another* passenger plane": "9/11, Second Plane Hits South Tower," Sept. 11, 2001, archival video accessed via CNN.com.

448 Reno tells them: Dana Canedy, "Changed Political Climate May Aid Jeb Bush," *NYT*, Sept. 28, 2001.

448 *"Taciturn* is the word": Author interview, Julie Simon.

448 hotel suite in Vienna: Mundy, "Mr. Resident."

449 The Sheikh is already: Scott-Clark and Levy, *The Exile*, p. 1.

449 The van contains: Former NCIS agent (name redacted), testimony, *USA v. al-Bahlul*, transcript pp. 648–49.

449 in Karachi: Scott-Clark and Levy, *The Exile*, p. 14.

450 "Shall we finish it": Cockpit voice recording transcript, United Flight 93; *9/11 Commission Report*, p. 15.

450 A murdered woman: Summers and Swan, *The Eleventh Day*, p. 50.

450 "I saw the building": Author's notes, Sept. 11, 2001.

450 "Very odd": Author interview, Jonathan Carson.

451 Jesse Jackson is trying: "Rev. Jesse Jackson Reflects on 9/11 and Its Impact on His Lifelong Mission," *Eight Forty-Eight*, WBEZ (Chicago), radio interview, wbez.org.

451 seaside resort: AP, Sept. 12, 2001.

451 lecturing a group: Graham, *Intelligence Matters*, pp. x–xi.

451 "Don't *argue*": Scott-Clark and Levy, *The Exile*, p. 12.

451 "We're going to war": Coll, *Directorate S*, p. 35.

452 leaves a voice mail: Townsend, Miller Center oral history.

452 Jose Canseco: Rick Gano, "White Sox Escape New York on Bus," AP, Sept. 13, 2001.

452 "I thought it was": Chris De Luca, "White Sox Consider Forfeits, Hope to Get Out of N.Y.," *Chicago Sun-Times*, Sept. 12, 2001.

452 "We need a good lawyer": Author interview, Karen Donovan.

452 Aysel Sengün: FBI report on interview conducted by German authorities with Sengün, Sept. 18, 2001.

453 "Ziad is suspected": Transcript of call between Arne Kruithof and Aysel Sengün, BKA Files.

453 letter from Ziad: McDermott, *Perfect Soldiers*, pp. 230–31.

453 Ailes dusts off: Sherman, *The Loudest Voice in the Room*, pp. 260–61.

454 reaches Donald Trump: "Donald Trump Call into WWOR/UPN 9 News on 9/11," Sept. 11, 2000, accessed via YouTube.

454 a manifesto: Chuck Harder, "America in Terror: What Went Wrong? What to Do?," chuckharder.com, 2001, retrieved via archive.org.

455 George W. Bush rises: Bush, *Decision Points*, pp. 126–30; Rove, *Courage and Consequence*, pp. 249–55; *9/11 Commission Report*, pp. 38–40.

455 dinner with Jeb: Robert Plunket, "The President in Sarasota: September 11, 2001," *Sarasota Magazine*, Sept. 7, 2016.

455 Out of the camera shot: "September 11, 2001," photo gallery, retrieved from the online collection of the George W. Bush Presidential Library and Museum.

455 "Hoo!" Bush says: Summers and Swan, *The Eleventh Day*, p. 39.

456 He swivels around: "September 11, 2001" photo gallery, Bush Library.

456 "Terrorism against our nation": Bush, *Decision Points*, p. 128.

456 "We're at war": *9/11 Commission Report*, p. 39.

456 instructor Kendall Coleman: Author interview, Kendall Coleman.

456 tears up the runway's concrete: Summers and Swan, *The Eleventh Day*, p. 47.

456 of forty-five thousand feet: Bush, *Decision Points*, p. 129.

INDEX

ABOUT THE AUTHOR

Andrew Rice is a contributing editor at *New York* magazine and the author of *The Teeth May Smile but the Heart Does Not Forget: Murder and Memory in Uganda* (Metropolitan). He is a former staff writer at *The Hill* and the *New York Observer* and was a cub reporter in the year 2000.